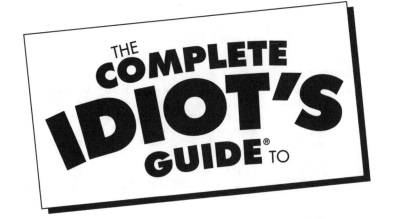

THE COMPLETE **IDIOT'S** GUIDE® TO

Buying and Selling a Home

Fourth Edition

by Shelley O'Hara and Nancy D. Lewis

ALPHA

A member of Penguin Group (USA) Inc.

To Darlene J. Ball

Copyright © 2003 by Shelley O'Hara

THE COMPLETE IDIOT'S GUIDE TO and Design are registered trademarks of Penguin Group (USA) Inc.

International Standard Book Number: 1-59257-120-4
Library of Congress Catalog Card Number: 2003106938

05 04 03   8 7 6 5 4 3 2 1

Interpretation of the printing code: The rightmost number of the first series of numbers is the year of the book's printing; the rightmost number of the second series of numbers is the number of the book's printing. For example, a printing code of 03-1 shows that the first printing occurred in 2003.

Printed in the United States of America

Note: This publication contains the opinions and ideas of its authors. It is intended to provide helpful and informative material on the subject matter covered. It is sold with the understanding that the authors and publisher are not engaged in rendering professional services in the book. If the reader requires personal assistance or advice, a competent professional should be consulted.

Most Alpha books are available at special quantity discounts for bulk purchases for sales promotions, premiums, fund-raising, or educational use. Special books, or book excerpts, can also be created to fit specific needs.

For details, write: Special Markets, Alpha Books, 375 Hudson Street, New York, NY 10014.

Publisher: *Marie Butler-Knight*
Product Manager: *Phil Kitchel*
Senior Managing Editor: *Jennifer Chisholm*
Senior Acquisitions Editor: *Renee Wilmeth*
Development Editor: *Jennifer Moore*
Production Editor: *Billy Fields*
Copy Editor: *Christina Smith*
Illustrator: *Chris Eliopoulos*
Cover/Book Designer: *Trina Wurst*
Indexer: *Angie Bess*
Layout/Proofreading: *Mary Hunt, Ayanna Lacey, Donna Martin*

Contents at a Glance

Part 1:   **Getting Started**   1

   1   The Dream of Owning a Home   3
       Discover the advantages and disadvantages of homeowner-ship.

   2   How Much House Can You Afford?   15
       Find out how much home you qualify for and understand the role your credit plays.

   3   Understanding the Up-Front Costs of Buying a Home   33
       Find out just how much money you need for a down payment and other costs.

   4   Buying a Home with an Agent   43
       Learn what an agent can do for you as well as how to select the "right" agent.

   5   Selecting a Mortgage Lender   59
       You're the customer. Find a lender who will treat you like one.

Part 2:   **Choosing the Home for You**   69

   6   Deciding Where You Want to Live   71
       Use your likes and dislikes, your dreams, and lifestyle to determine your ideal home and neighborhood.

   7   Defining Your Dream Home   81
       Have a good idea of what you need in a home? How many bedrooms? One story or two? Home office?

   8   How to Find Your New Home   95
       You know what your perfect house looks like, now where is it? Try one of several house-hunting tips from this chapter.

   9   Buying an Existing Home   105
       From bedrooms to kitchens to shower nozzles—try everything on for size when touring existing homes.

  10   Buying Other Types of Homes   117
       Condos, co-ops, townhouses, patio homes, and zero lot line homes can have their advantages. Is one right for you?

11 Building a New Home 129
If you want to start from the ground up, perhaps a new home is in your future. Find out how to get the most out of a new homebuilder.

Part 3:   Understanding Your Finance Options 151

12 Financing 101 153
This is your jumping-off point for understanding lending, mortgages, and your options.

13 Fixed-Rate Mortgages 167
If the interest rates are low (as they have been recently) or you will be in the home for a while, think about going fixed.

14 Adjustable-Rate Mortgages 175
If your credit's not so good, rates are high, or you won't be in the home long, consider going adjustable.

15 Getting Other Types of Financing 185
If your circumstances warrant a different type of financing, there are many kinds to choose from, including seller financing, VA loans, and others.

16 Applying for a Mortgage 197
They don't make you fill out all those forms for the fun of it—learn what they are for and what documents and information you'll need.

Part 4:   Getting the Best Deal 215

17 Making an Offer on a Home 217
This process can be an elaborate game of offer and counter-offer. Just remember that in the best negotiations, both sides win.

18 Working the Deal 231
Counteroffers are lobbed back and forth until you buy your home or someone cries "Okay!"

19 Choosing Insurance 241
Protect yourself from the 11 common house perils and more.

20 Having the Home Inspected 251
Make sure you don't get trapped in a money pit.

21 Handling the Closing: Buyer's Perspective 261
It's like a big party. Invite all your friends. Bring all your money.

Part 5: **Selling Your Home** **279**

22 Deciding to Sell Your Home 281
It's a tad more complicated than sticking a "For Sale" sign in your front yard. Be ready!

23 Selling Your Home Yourself 291
Strategy, pricing, marketing, negotiating—you'll need all of these skills if you plan to sell your home without an agent.

24 Selling Your Home with an Agent 305
An agent can help you in innumerable ways when selling your home; do some asking around to select one who's right for you.

25 Getting the Home Ready for Sale 317
Clean and repair, but don't go overboard on the remodeling.

26 Pricing and Marketing the Home 331
Discover common pitfalls in pricing and handy tips for marketing your home.

27 Dealing with Purchase Offers 343
Know your bottom line.

28 Handling the Closing: Seller's Perspective 353
It's that party again, but this time you get to keep some of the money.

Appendixes

A Glossary 367

B Resources 377

C Loan Payment Tables 383

Index 389

Contents

Part 1: Getting Started   1

1 The Dream of Owning a Home   3

The Great Things About Owning a Home 4

The Flipside: Some of the Drawbacks of Owning a Home..........6

    Bills To Pay *6*

    When Buying a Home Might Not Be Right *7*

Facts About Buying a Home 8

People You Work with When Buying a Home 10

What to Expect When You Buy a Home 11

What To Expect When You Sell Your Home 12

2 How Much House Can You Afford?   15

How Much You Make and How Much You Spend 16

    What If You're Self-Employed? *17*

    Keeping Track of Your Income..*17*

    Keeping Track of Your Expenses *18*

How Much Money Can You Borrow? 18

Understanding Lender Ratios..19

    What's Your Housing Ratio (a.k.a. Maximum Mortgage

        Payment)? *20*

    Don't Forget Taxes and Insurance! *21*

    Use This Example To "Get" This Concept....................................*21*

Prequalifying for a Loan 22

    What Do You Need to Prequalify? *23*

    Advantages and Drawbacks of Prequalifying................................*23*

Getting Preapproved for a Loan 24

Checking Your Credit 24

    Getting a Credit Report *25*

    What's on Your Credit Report?..*26*

    What's a FICO Credit Score?..*27*

    Are You a Risky Creditor? *28*

    Correcting a Mistake or Responding to Problems..........................*28*

    Strengthening Your Credit *29*

    Dealing with a Bad Credit Report *30*

Before All the Numbers Make You Dizzy 30

3 Understanding the Up-Front Costs of Buying a Home   33

Everything You Need to Know About Down Payments 33
How Much of a Down Payment Do You Need?...........34
Where Can You Get the Down Payment?...........34
What If You Don't Have Money for the Down Payment? 35
When Do You Fork Over the Down Payment? 35
Additional Costs You Pay When Buying a Home 36
Paying Lender Fees 36
Coughing Up Advance and Reserve Payments...........38
Paying Insurance on Your Mortgage 39
Still More Fees 40
Adding Up All the Costs 41

4 Buying a Home with an Agent   43

Understanding the Types of Agents 44
Agents Defined...........44
Brokers Defined 44
Realtors Defined 45
New-Home Agents Defined 45
Is the Agent Working for You or the Seller? 45
Using a Buyer's Agent 46
Using a Selling Agent 49
Using a Discount Broker 50
How Agents Can Help 50
Agents Can Navigate Financial Steps...........50
Agents Can Help Find the Right House 51
Agents Can Help Negotiate and Close the Deal...........52
Selecting a Good Agent...........53
Finding an Agent...........53
Putting an Agent to the Test...........54
Firing an Agent...........56
Working with "For Sale by Owner" Homes 56

5 Selecting a Mortgage Lender   59

Types of Lenders and Why They Matter...........60
Understanding the Secondary Loan Market 61
Uncle Sam Helps Out 61
Portfolio and Jumbo Loans 61

Where Can You Find a Lender? 62

Using Your Agent to Find a Lender 63

Reviewing a Mortgage Advertisement 63

Using the Internet to Find a Lender 64

Questions to Ask Lenders 65

Part 2:   Choosing the Home for You   69

6   Deciding Where You Want to Live   71

Where Do You Want to Live? 71

Home to Stay, or Home to Resell? 72

What Is Your Job Situation? 72

What Are Your Family's Needs? 73

What Are the Schools Like? 73

What Are the Taxes? 74

What About Emergencies? 75

What About Driving? 75

What About Fun? 75

Sources of Community and Neighborhood Information 76

Checking Out the Community 76

Ask Your Agent 77

Doing Your Own Neighborhood Assessment 77

Finding New Home Communities 78

7   Defining Your Dream Home   81

Rule #1: Keep an Open Mind 81

What Style of Home Suits You? 82

How Many Stories? 82

What Is the House Made Of? 83

Existing Home vs. New Home 83

*The Benefits of an Existing Home (or the Drawbacks of
a New Home)* 83

*The Drawbacks of an Existing Home (or the Benefits of
a New Home)* 84

Touring the Interior of the House 84

Casing the Kitchen 85

Touring the Bedrooms 85

Testing the Bathrooms 85

Looking at the Family/Living/Great Rooms 86

Do You Need a Home Office? 86

What About Storage? Attics and Basements 86

What About More Storage? Closets 87

Still Need Storage? Garages 87

Inspecting the Exterior of the House 88

And the Home Faces … 89

Heating and Cooling Systems 89

The Home's Landscaping 90

Extra Goodies Like a Pool 90

Summing Up Your Dream House Wish List 91

8   How to Find Your New Home   95

When Is the Best Time to Buy a Home? 95

Buyer's Market vs. Seller's Market 96

Seasonal Sales 97

Finding a Home 98

Drive Through Neighborhoods 98

Read the Local Papers 98

Read the MLS Listings 100

Ask Around 101

Shop Auctions and Foreclosures 101

Search Online Home Listings 102

9   Buying an Existing Home   105

How the Home Tour(s) Work 106

How Does the Home Measure Up? 107

Do You Like the House? 107

Does the House Have Everything You Need? 107

Can You Live in the House? 109

If You Don't Like Something, Can You Change It? 110

Is the House Well-Maintained? 111

Check the Exterior 111

Check the Home Systems 111

Check the Interior for Structure and Maintenance 113

Evaluating the Neighborhood 113

Define the Character of the Neighborhood 113

Visit the Neighborhood 114

Your Home Comparison Checklist 115

10   Buying Other Types of Homes   117

What Other Home Types Are Available? 118

Buying a Condominium 118

The Good (and Bad) Things About Condos *119*

The Condo Board Rules the Community! *120*

Selecting a Community..*121*

Making an Offer *122*

Buying a Co-Op...123

Selecting a Co-Op *123*

Financing Your Co-Op *124*

Vacation Homes, Fixer-Uppers, and More...............................125

Relocating to a New City *125*

Buying a Vacation Home *126*

Buying a Fixer-Upper *127*

11   Building a New Home   129

Considering the Pluses and Minuses of Buying

a New Home 130

New Homes Are Great Because … *130*

The Drawbacks of a New Home *130*

Selecting a Type of Home..131

Tract and Semi-Custom Homes *131*

Custom Homes *132*

Finding New Homes 133

Using an Agent *134*

Selecting a Subdivision *134*

Selecting a Good Builder *137*

Selecting a Home Plan *139*

Selecting a Good Lot *140*

Understanding the Sales Contract 141

Contract Terms *141*

Upgrades, Upgrades...*142*

Getting a Good Deal *145*

Including Home Extras in the Mortgage................................*146*

Getting a New Home Warranty 146

Avoiding New Home Problems 147

Part 3:   Understanding Your Finance Options   151

12 Financing 101   153

How Basic Lending Works 154
How Home Loan Lending Works 154
What's the Interest Rate? *154*
Other Fees: Paying Loan Points *155*
How Long Do You Make Payments?................................*156*
Different Loans for Different Folks 157
Fixed-Rate Mortgage Loans *157*
Adjustable-Rate Mortgage Loans *158*
Conventional Loans *158*
Government-Backed Loans...*159*
Conforming vs. Nonconforming Loans *160*
Still More Loan Types *160*
Your Loan May Require Mortgage Insurance 160
Paying Mortgage Insurance *161*
Canceling Mortgage Insurance *161*
How to Decide on the Type of Financing 162
How Much Can You Afford for a Down Payment? *163*
How Much Can You Afford for a Monthly Payment? *163*
How Long Will You Live in the Home? *164*
What's Your Risk Level?..*165*

13 Fixed-Rate Mortgages   167

The Advantages of a Fixed-Rate Mortgage 168
The Drawbacks of a Fixed-Rate Mortgage 168
Interest and Points for Fixed-Rate Mortgages 169
How Long Should You Pay on Your Fixed-Rate Loan? 170
Thirty-Year vs. Fifteen-Year vs. Biweekly *170*
Is the Shorter Term Better? *171*
Prepaying Your Mortgage 171

14 Adjustable-Rate Mortgages   175

The Pros and Cons of an Adjustable-Rate Mortgage 176
The Good Things About an ARM...................................*176*
The Bad Things About an ARM *176*
How an Adjustable-Rate Mortgage Works.....................177
What You Pay At First: The Initial or Teaser Rate *177*
How the Rate Is Figured: The Index..............................*178*

The Lenders Cut: The Margin *178*
How Often Payments Change: The Adjustment Interval............*179*
How High the Rate Can Go: The Rate Caps................*179*
Negative Amortization and ARMs 180
Selecting an ARM 180
What You Want (Ideally) in an ARM *180*
What You Should Ask When Shopping for an ARM................*182*
Looking at the Worst-Case Scenario *182*

15 Getting Other Types of Financing **185**
VA Loans 186
Taking Over the Seller's Mortgage, a.k.a. Assumptions............186
Start Small and Pay Later: Balloon Mortgages 187
Two Loans and One Down Payment: 80-10-10 or 80-15-5
  Loans 187
Getting a Lower Interest Rate Via a Buydown 188
Loan Help from Sellers with Carrybacks 188
Paying for Your Home with Layaway Payments 189
Fixed and Adjustable Rate Loans in One: Two-Step
  Mortgages 189
How to Do the Two-Step *190*
Is the Two-Step for You?..............................*191*
Leasing with Option to Buy 191
Still More Options...191
Loans for Those with Blemished Credit 192
Refinancing Your Loan 193
Reasons to Refinance....................................*193*
Using Your Refinance Money *194*
How Refinancing Saves You Money *194*
Shopping Around for Refinance Loans *195*

16 Applying for a Mortgage **197**
The Roster of Loan People....................................198
How the Lender Decides Whether to Lend You Money 198
Taking the Loan Application............................*199*
Verifying Information...................................*199*
Looking at Your Credit Report *199*
Getting an Appraisal on the Home *200*
Knowing What Lenders Look For........................*201*
Approving or Denying the Loan *201*

Applying for the Loan 202
  Spilling Your Financial Guts 202
  Locking in an Interest Rate 207
  Estimating Closing Costs 208
  Estimating Interest Rates 209
  Ensuring a Smooth Application Process 211
What to Do If You Can't Get a Loan...211
  Income Problems..212
  Credit Problems 212
  Appraisal Problems 213
  Discrimination Problems 213

Part 4:   Getting the Best Deal   215

17   Making an Offer on a Home   217

Writing an Offer 217
  What the Offer Should Include at the Minimum 218
  What Else Can Be Included in the Offer? 218
  Tips on Making an Offer 219
What Are You Willing to Pay? 222
  Comparing Other Sales Prices 222
  How Motivated Is the Seller? 223
  Asking the Seller to Pay Part 224
The Offer Is Contingent On … 224
  Getting Financing 224
  Receiving a Clear Deed and Title 225
  Having the Home Inspected 225
  Having the Home Appraised 226
  Other Contingencies to Consider 226
Specifying Other Offer Terms 226
  Setting Time Limits..226
  What Personal Property Is Included? 227
  Real vs. Personal Property 227
  Specifying the Condition of the Home at Settlement 228
  Prorating Tax and Other Payments 229
Making a Deposit..229

18   Working the Deal   231

Understanding the Offer Process 232
Using the Best Offer Strategies..232

Handling Counteroffers 233

Receiving a Counteroffer *234*

Responding to a Counteroffer *234*

Quitting and Moving On *236*

Having an Offer Accepted...236

Withdrawing an Offer 237

Do I Need a Real Estate Attorney? 238

19 Choosing Insurance   **241**

Understanding the Types of Insurance.................................242

Insuring Your Home 242

What Home Insurance Covers *243*

Types of Home Insurance *243*

How Much Insurance Do You Need?...................................*244*

Tips on Home Insurance *245*

Search the Web for Insurance Information *246*

How Insurance Payments Are Made...................................*247*

Comparing Insurance Policies *247*

Getting Title Insurance..248

The Title Search *248*

What Title Insurance Protects *249*

20 Having the Home Inspected   **251**

Seller Disclosure: It's the Law......................................251

Why Get an Inspection? 252

Scheduling an Inspection...252

What the Inspector Checks..253

What the Inspector Should Check *254*

What the Inspector Doesn't Check..................................*256*

What the Inspector Shouldn't Do *256*

Reading the Inspection Report 256

Handling Any Inspection Problems 257

Big Problems vs. Little Problems..................................*258*

Ways to Handle Problems *258*

21 Handling the Closing: Buyer's Perspective   **261**

What Has to Happen Before the Closing 261

Who Owns the Home? *262*

The Final Walkthrough *263*

What You Pay at Closing 264
Don't Forget the Down Payment 264
Closing Costs 264
Paid as Part of the Loan 265
Paid in Advance 266
Prepayments (Reserves) Held by the Lender 266
Title Charges 266
Government Recording and Transfer Charges 267
Still More Settlement Charges 267
Keeping a Reserve in an Escrow Account 267
And the Total Comes to … 268
What Happens at the Closing 268
What You Should Bring to the Closing 269
Signed, Sealed, Delivered 269
Exchanging Money 273
Statement Side 1: The Totals 273
Statement Side 2: The Closing Costs 273
The Passing of the Keys 273
Handling Problems 274
Walkthrough Problems 274
Money Problems 274
Loan Problems 275
Title Problems 275
Moving In! 275
Pre- and Post-Move Tips 275
Hiring a Professional Mover 276

Part 5: Selling Your Home   279

22 Deciding to Sell Your Home   281

Why Do You Want to Sell?..282
Tallying Your Likes, Dislikes, Wishes, and Wants 282
What Do You Hope to Gain by Selling? 283
Are You Ready to Sell? 284
Timing the Sale of Your Home: Sell First vs. Buy First 284
Buy First, Sell Later 284
Sell First, Buy Later 285
Buy and Sell Together 286
What Costs Are Involved in Selling a Home? 286

What to Expect When You Sell Your Home 287
    Step 1: Getting the Home Ready 287
    Step 2: Deciding Whether to Use an Agent...................287
    Step 3: Pricing and Marketing the Home 288
    Step 4: Negotiating Offers 288
    Step 5: Closing on the Home...................................288
    Step 6: Buying a New Home 288

23 Selling Your Home Yourself   **291**
FSBO: What to Expect 292
Pricing Your Home 292
    Figuring Your Net Proceeds 293
    Defining Acceptable Financial Terms 293
Marketing Your Home—Doing It Yourself 293
    Putting a Sign in Your Yard..................................293
    Taking Out an Ad 294
    Marketing Your Home Online 295
    Preparing Fact Sheets..295
Showing Your Home 296
    Handling Sales Calls 296
    Showing Your Home...297
    Holding Open Houses 297
Handling Buyer Financing 298
Negotiating an Offer 298
    Be Prepared 299
    Draw Up Offers...299
    Review Offers...299
Closing on the Home 300
Other Key Players Who Can Help You Sell Your Home 301
    Working with Agents 301
    Hiring an Attorney 302
    Using a HomeSelling Service 302
    Using an Escrow Company 302
What to Do if Your Home Doesn't Sell........................303

24 Selling Your Home with an Agent   **305**
Should You Use an Agent or Sell Alone? 306
Finding an Agent 307
    Quizzing the Agent 308
    Evaluating the Agent's Listing Presentation 309

Signing a Listing Contract 311
Types of Contracts..*311*
What the Listing Contract Should Include *314*
Getting Out of a Listing..*314*

25 Getting the Home Ready for Sale   317

Doing Home Repairs...318
Inspecting the Home Yourself *318*
Getting a Professional Inspection..*320*
Deciding What Repairs to Make...*321*
Do It Yourself or Hire Someone?..*321*
Should You Remodel? *322*
Cleaning Up the Home...322
First Impressions Count—Clean Up the Outside *323*
Clean the Inside *323*
Eliminating Clutter 324
Put Everything Away! *324*
Undecorating the Home *325*
Collecting Home Information 325
Understanding Seller Disclosure 326
Do You Have to Disclose? *326*
What Must You Disclose? *326*
Completing a Seller Disclosure Form *327*

26 Pricing and Marketing the Home   331

Setting the Listing Price 331
Studying Comparable Homes for Sale......................................*332*
Getting an Appraisal *334*
How the Market Affects Price...*335*
Deciding What Else to Offer 335
Figuring Your Net Proceeds 336
Marketing Your Home 337
Showing Your Home 338
Scheduling a Showing *339*
Getting the Home Ready for a Showing *339*
Dealing with Criticism...*340*
Holding an Open House *340*

27 Dealing with Purchase Offers   **343**

Dealing with Other Agents 343
Evaluating an Offer 344
What an Offer Should Include 345
What Price and at What Terms? 345
Checking the Contingencies...................................345
Checking the Time Limits 346
Making a Counteroffer 347
Accepting an Offer..348
What to Do If You Don't Get Any Offers 348
Should You Help with Financing? 350

28 Handling the Closing: Seller's Perspective   **353**

Knowing What to Expect at Closing 354
What You Have to Do...354
Handling Termites and Other Critters 355
Checking the Chain of Ownership...........................355
Collecting Documents 355
Hiring a Closing Orchestrator 356
Handling Problems with Closing 357
What Happens at Closing...358
Fees You Can Expect to Pay at Closing 358
The HUD-1 Statement—My Column or Yours? 359
Sign on the Dotted Line 362
Tax Implications for Home Sales 362
Reporting the Sale of Your Home 363
Figuring the Tax Basis..363
Moving Out! 364

Appendixes

A Glossary   **367**

B Resources   **377**

C Loan Payment Tables   **383**

Index   **389**

Foreword

Look in almost any newspaper's residential real estate section. (If you're reading this, chances are you probably already have. You've probably also been poring over the tangled maze of Internet sites related to buying and selling a home.) Notice anything peculiar about the newspaper sections? There basically are four types of articles:

- **Advice:** "A spec house—one built on a speculative basis, without an order on the books—can be fancy. But it could ultimately disappoint discerning buyers because it's not customized to their tastes."

- **Basics:** "Inspections get bugs out of sale deals."

- **Paid "advertorials":** Articles written by public relations professionals with one goal—to get you to buy a home. For example, "Just imagine …. Relax and unwind in this five-year-old Florida-style custom …"

- **Features:** "Family finds home with a heart."

Homeowners are sponges for advice. Something always needs to be fixed, something always needs to be replaced, something always could be improved—and nobody is an expert in everything. That's where those basics come in. (Can I fix this leaky faucet myself, or do I need a plumber?)

That promotional ad copy serves an important purpose, too, whether in the paper or on the Internet. Without it, you'd just have to drive around and look for Realtors' signs. And those feature stories—my specialty—help us all live vicariously through others who are living the "American dream" of homeownership. They help us see the possibilities in our own homes. They can stretch our own thinking, showing us new possibilities. They can inspire.

But right now, you're looking for the first two: advice and the basics. Inside *The Complete Idiot's Guide to Buying and Selling a Home, Fourth Edition,* you'll find it, all in one volume. It's in language that is easy to understand. It's in bite-size portions, suitable for the experienced needing a refresher course, as well as those needing a broad introduction to the nuts and bolts—the infrastructure, if you will—that upholds the dream for all of us.

Forgive the sugar. My colleagues in the newspaper business can be a cynical lot. But I'm not. It truly is a remarkable thing to own your own home. It truly will change your life.

Buying or selling a home isn't a leisure activity. It's a form of work. That doesn't mean it won't be enjoyable. It's kind of like the "work" a gardener spends in a garden. Likewise, what you're doing right now isn't reading for leisure. It's reading for a reason. So read on. Bend the pages. Mark them up. Be prepared. You're headed home.

Richard Mize
Real Estate Editor
The Daily Oklahoman

Introduction

You're an expert in your own field. You have your own lingo and specialized knowledge that you use everyday. But when it comes to real estate, you just might feel overwhelmed. The terms are confusing, and it may seem that the real estate agents, lenders, and others involved in the process of buying or selling your home don't want you to understand. For instance, if you are buying a home, your lender may say "You'll want to consider a conventional ARM with a 90LTV for that home. The qualifying ratios used are 28/36." What?

You don't need a degree in real estate law to make sense of such jargon, nor to know how to determine what kind of home will best suit your needs—and how to find it. You just need someone to tell you what you need to know and what's important. That's what this book does.

So You Want to Buy a Home

Owning a home is probably the quintessential American dream. In 2002, close to 70 percent of Americans owned their home. Homeownership is at an all-time high! Are you ready to take the plunge?

The Complete Idiot's Guide to Buying and Selling a Home, Fourth Edition, strives to make understanding the homebuying and homeselling process easy. The book is divided into five parts. The first four parts focus on the homebuying process; the last part covers selling your home:

Part 1, "Getting Started," explains what you need to do to get your finances in order before you call a Realtor and what to expect once you pick up the phone. In addition, this part walks you through choosing an agent (if you want one) and picking a mortgage lender. Think of homebuying as a team effort. Because you probably will be working closely with an agent and a lender, selecting the "right" team members is key.

Part 2, "Choosing the Home for You," helps you determine where you want to live and what type of home you want to live in. This is the fun part—where you get to dream, dream, dream. What does your dream home look like? Does it have a huge country kitchen? A master suite? A nice yard for gardening? Knowing what you want and need helps you find a house that is perfect for you.

Part 3, "Understanding Your Finance Options," focuses on the next step in the homebuying process: getting financing so you can pay for the home. This part covers, in simple terms, the financial options available for purchasing your home.

Part 4, "Getting the Best Deal," brings you to the final step: closing on the home. Once you find the home you want, you have to convince the sellers to sell it to you at the price you want to pay. This part covers how to make an offer, review a counter-offer, and get an offer accepted. Before you can move in, you have to do a few more things, such as have the home inspected and insure it. Then there's the closing, when you sign a couple hundred documents, turn over your money, and—finally—get the keys to your new home.

If you've already been through the homebuying process and want to sell your home and purchase a new one, **Part 5, "Selling Your Home,"** walks you through all the necessary steps—making the decision to sell, getting the home ready, deciding whether to use an agent or sell by owner, pricing and marketing the home, negotiating offers, and closing on the home.

Extras

In addition to clear explanations and advice, this book offers vital information that can help you accomplish a difficult task more easily, or caution you about a common pitfall. These tips are splashed generously throughout the book and are easily recognizable with the following icons:

Buyer Beware

To avoid common mistakes, look for this pitiful note. Here you'll find warnings and cautions against potential problems or misunderstandings.

Bet You Didn't Know

These handy sidebars contain useful information that isn't obvious or readily available.

Real Deal

These are tips that mention a better way to accomplish a task, a way to save money, a way to get a better deal, or some shortcut. Read these tips to get short bits of advice on buying and selling a home.

Real Estate Terms

These notes introduce you to the mysterious lingo used in real estate. After reading these notes, you'll be able to throw around terms such as **LTV** and **settlement** sheet like the pros.

Acknowledgments

Thanks to Renee Wilmeth for arranging the revision and for her insightful comments, to Jennifer Moore for her smooth handling of the editorial review, to Doug Jones for his technical review, and finally, to Christina Smith for her fine editing of the chapters.

Special Thanks to the Technical Reviewer

The Complete Idiot's Guide to Buying and Selling a Home, Fourth Edition was reviewed by an expert who double-checked the accuracy of what you'll learn here, to help us ensure that this book gives you everything you need to know about buying or selling your house. Special thanks are extended to Doug Jones.

Trademarks

All terms mentioned in this book that are known to be or are suspected of being trademarks or service marks have been appropriately capitalized. Alpha Books and Penguin Group (USA) Inc. cannot attest to the accuracy of this information. Use of a term in this book should not be regarded as affecting the validity of any trademark or service mark.

Part 1

Getting Started

Owning a home is the American Dream! It can provide you with many benefits, including the pride of homeownership, tax savings, and a place to call your own. Your first step when purchasing a home is deciding "Yes! I want to own my own home."

Once you make that decision, you need to become financially prepared to make the commitment. You want to find out how big a down payment you can afford and how much you can spend for a home. In addition, you need to decide if you want to work with an agent and find a lender that will help you purchase your dream home. Part 1 covers all these basic steps on the road to homeownership.

The Dream of Owning a Home

In This Chapter

- Discovering the many advantages of owning a home
- Understanding the drawbacks of owning a home
- Learning who all the real estate people are
- Reviewing the buying and selling process

Almost everyone imagines owning his or her own home. After all, that's part of the American dream. For generations, most Americans have been driven to own a piece of America. Whether it be a new home in the suburbs, a co-op in the city, or a condo for retirees, everyone wants his or her own place to put up their feet and call home.

Owning a home is still as enticing as it ever was, but is it right for everyone? Is it right for you? You may, after reviewing the information in this chapter, decide buying isn't right at this time. This chapter helps you make that decision by explaining the advantages and disadvantages of buying a home. In addition, you learn about all the people you will be working with if you do pursue a home purchase. Finally, this chapter provides a solid overview of the homebuying process so you know what to expect. Let's get started!

The Great Things About Owning a Home

The first—and best—advantages of owning a home are intangible—the control and autonomy that ownership affords you and the sense of pride in that ownership. There's just something special about owning your own place. In addition, homeownership offers many financial and commonsense advantages.

As an example, Uncle Sam likes to encourage homeownership, because you get a big tax break when you own your own home. You can deduct some, if not all, of the interest you pay on the loan, as well as some of the costs involved in financing your home. Your property taxes are also deductible. On a modest home, you may be able to deduct, for example, $8,000 or more per year. That can translate into thousands of dollars of tax savings, depending on your tax bracket.

Homeownership also brings with it the advantage of enforced savings. Unlike a rent payment, which goes bye-bye once you pay it, some of the money you pay on your home goes toward building up your *equity*. You can take out a loan against your equity, and you can get back the equity when you sell your home.

Suppose you sell your home for $150,000, the real estate agent's fees (6 percent) come to $9,000, and you still have $130,000 left to pay on the principal payment to the mortgage company. This means that you will probably receive a check for $11,000 for the sale of your home ($150,000 – 9,000 – 130,000 = $11,000), minus any selling costs you incur.

Equity is the percentage of the home you own. When you first purchase a home, the bank owns most of it. This is most likely because you only had a small percentage to put toward the down payment on the home. When you start making payments, most of the payment goes toward the interest on the loan (of course, the mortgage company gets its money first), but a drop or two goes into the equity bucket.

Real Estate Terms

Equity is the financial interest or cash value of your home, minus the current loan balance, minus any costs incurred in selling the home.

As you pay off more of the loan, more drops go into the equity bucket. When you sell your home, that bucket is yours.

If you want to build equity in your home faster than simply paying your monthly mortgage, you can usually make additional payments toward the principal of your home loan. If you aren't sure whether you can do this, check with your mortgage company and ask if your loan has any prepayment or additional payment penalties. Refer to the "Prepaying Your Mortgage" section in Chapter 13 for more information.

Bet You Didn't Know

Another interesting note is that if you make the payments for 30 years on a home with a 30-year mortgage, you will likely pay two to three times the original amount you borrowed to purchase your home (depending on your interest rate). That's simply part and parcel of the loan process. When you apply for a loan, the lender will provide an approximation of the amount of the loan over its term (for instance, 30 years). It can be scary to think about. But real estate is usually a good investment, and your home most likely will have appreciated (gone up in value) considerably over those 30 years. Think of it this way: It would have probably taken you twice that long just to save that much money, and if you paid cash, you don't get as many tax breaks. Also, don't forget that you have your nice home to live in all the while.

If you rent an apartment or home, you don't have much control over the rent. Landlords can raise the rent—sometimes as much as they want. As a homeowner, on the other hand, you have the advantage of fixed housing costs. If you pay $800 the first month of a 30-year fixed mortgage, you'll pay $800 the last month, for principal and interest. Ask your parents how much their house payments were—probably between $50 and $500. Thank goodness for the time value of money. If you get an adjustable-rate mortgage, however, the payments may vary somewhat. The types of financing are covered in Part 3.

Most homes appreciate—or increase in value—over time. Your home is likely to be worth more when you sell it than when you purchase it; this is known as *building equity*. You can use the money you make on the sale of your home to finance a bigger and better home or to finance your retirement. (Keep in mind that not all homes appreciate in value.)

Bet You Didn't Know

You can paint all the rooms in your home chartreuse and knock out walls to remodel if you want. It's your home, and you can do anything you want. Well, almost anything. Keep in mind that many communities require you to secure a building permit for substantial structural changes to your home. In addition, you might have to get "permission" from your neighborhood homeowners association to make improvements or add particular items to the outside of your home. If you are thinking about doing some remodeling to a home you plan to purchase, be sure to ask about any restrictions or covenants before you sign on the dotted line.

The Flipside: Some of the Drawbacks of Owning a Home

When the roof is leaking, your mortgage payment is late, and your new neighbors move in with a 90-pound German shepherd that likes to howl at the moon every night, you may seriously start to realize that for all the advantages associated with owning a home, there will be some drawbacks.

Real Estate Terms _____

When someone fails to make payments on a home, the mortgage company may force payment by seizing and selling the property. This proceeding is known as **foreclosure**.

The downside of buying a home is that you must make the monthly mortgage payments; if you don't, the lender can *foreclose* on the home, meaning that the lender can take your home away from you.

In addition to the actual loan, you will have property taxes, homeowners insurance, and possibly even mortgage insurance fees to pay that depend on your down payment amount (refer to Chapter 12 for more information on mortgage insurance).

Bills To Pay

Other expenses that you probably don't have as a renter are as follows:

◆ All the utility bills. Landlords usually cover some of the utilities for apartment dwellers, like water and sewage, and maybe even your electric or gas use.

◆ Maintenance and upkeep on the home and property. For instance, as a home-owner, you are responsible for fixing the leaky roof, mowing the grass, painting the garage, spraying for insects, and so on.

◆ Homeowners association fees. Many new homes, condominiums, co-ops, and townhouses have association fees you must pay in order to live in a particular area.

Finally, you can't pull up stakes and leave as easily if you own a home. If you're a renter, you can give your notice and take off. You don't have any financial responsibilities to the landlord. When you have a home, on the other hand, you have commitments you must settle before moving on.

When Buying a Home Might Not Be Right

In some cases, buying a home isn't the best idea. Here are some scenarios of when you are probably better off not buying.

◆ **You know you're going to keep the home for only a short time.** For instance, if you may be transferred to a new job or get married and move, you may want to consider renting rather than buying. When you haven't owned a home for very long, it's difficult to break even, let alone make a profit, when you sell it. You don't have much equity built up, plus you have all the costs of selling the home to consider. So be sure you are going to stay put at least long enough to break even when you sell.

◆ **You aren't sure that you're going to like the area where you're considering a purchase.** Do your homework first. Don't just jump in and buy a home because it's, say, close to where you work. Try visiting the local supermarket or taking your kids to the neighborhood park—anything that will allow you to get to know some of the neighbors and get a "feel" for the area. This is especially true if you are moving to a new city. You may want to rent first to get a good sense of the lifestyles of the various neighborhoods. And then buy when you can make a more informed decision.

◆ **You cannot count on a steady income to make your payments.** The lender may not approve you for a loan. If you're approved and you cannot make the payments, the lender may foreclose. You will lose all the money you have invested, and your credit rating will be severely tarnished. If you have an unsteady income, you may want to wait until you're sure you can make the long-term financial commitment of buying a home.

◆ **You don't have the money for a down payment.** The rest of the chapters in this part cover the costs of purchasing a home, and while there are a lot of workarounds for coming up with a down payment, you probably should seriously consider whether you can make the house payments on a home (see the preceding bullet). You may want to wait until you are more financially secure. This book gives you a good overview of where you need to be financially, so don't despair if you don't have a big wad of cash; homeownership is possible. Simply keep in mind that not

CAUTION

Buyer Beware

You can find programs for no down payment or low down payments, but you most likely pay a premium for this type of loan agreement. If you do look into no or low down payment options, be sure to understand the costs associated with them. It might be worth your while to wait and start a savings program for a down payment.

just the down payment, but also consistent monthly payments are required for homeownership.

- ◆ **You're buying a home to live in solely as an investment.** You should be aware that, although most homes do appreciate in value, appreciation is not guaranteed. Many things that you have no control over affect the value of your home—local economy, national economy, abandoned buildings or new businesses in the neighborhood, a landfill, or even tacky neighbors who paint their homes chartreuse.

Don't let the drawbacks get you down, though. Owning a home is quite satisfying and a great learning experience.

Facts About Buying a Home

On your quest to purchase a home, you will find that everyone has an opinion and some little tidbit of information to share with you. Your best bet is to do your own research and ask lots of questions. This book is a good place to start, along with all of the websites it suggests. If you have questions, make sure you find an answer, preferably from a reliable source (not your neighbor's cousin who just sold his home back in Omaha).

There is a lot to learn about real estate and owning a home. Here are some pieces of information that will help you be better prepared:

- ◆ **Everything will vary.** You'll find that there aren't many tried, true, and trusted facts about the homebuying and homeselling process. Every homebuyer and homeseller's experience varies wildly. One person may sell his home in the first week it is on the market; it may take another person six months. One person may feel an adjustable mortgage is the only way to finance. Another person may say it's insane to gamble like that and insist on a fixed-rate mortgage. Everything varies according to your situation and what you want.

- ◆ **Everything will change.** Laws about what tax benefits you get, laws about what the seller must tell you, and real estate practices can change at any time.

Real Deal

You can learn a lot from this book about buying and selling a home, but remember to ask friends and colleagues about their experiences. And when dealing with agents and homeowners, don't be afraid to ask them about everything.

◆ **There is no perfect time to buy.** Some buyers get caught in the "I'll wait until I can afford my dream home" trap. These buyers wait and wait until they think the market is perfect, they find the home they've always wanted, or they can afford the home they've always wanted. Unless you have a compelling reason to wait, you shouldn't. The perfect market, perfect home, or perfect price may not come along. Buy what you can afford and then trade up. Or buy something close to what you want and remodel. One of the biggest advantages when shopping for a home is to see the so-called "diamond in the rough." If you can look beyond the tiger wallpaper and the black velvet drapes, you can see the real potential of a property.

◆ **Almost everything is negotiable.** From the price you pay for the home to the date you can move in, negotiate, negotiate, negotiate. When you make an offer, you can and should ask for the moon if that's what you want. This book provides many tips and ideas on how to negotiate the best deal.

Bet You Didn't Know

Keep your eyes and ears open for changes in interest rates. Factors like how well the stock market is doing, what the unemployment rate is, the price of gas and fuels, and other business and economic issues affect the interest rates (like the Federal Reserve altering interest rates). In 2002, for instance, rates hovered consistently at low rates. Why? The government wanted to give the economy a boost, so the Federal Reserve cut interest rates. That trend is likely to continue, but your best bet is to do your research.

You can get more information about the current financial market by reading publications like *The Wall Street Journal.* You can also try numerous websites. Check out www. bankrate.com for up-to-date information on all things financial.

◆ **Negotiate to win-win.** A lot of people think that a successful deal happens only when they impose their will on another and get their way entirely (a win-lose situation). The best deals, though, are when both negotiating parties are happy (a win-win situation). If you buy a home at the price you want and the terms you want, and the sellers also get the price they want at acceptable terms, you both benefit.

◆ **The little-known physics Law of Expanding Possessions.** If you're moving from a small home to a larger home, be prepared for the Law of Expanding Possessions. Physicists have yet to understand what causes this phenomenon, which simply stated says, "If you have a two-bedroom home full of junk and move to a four-bedroom home, you will have a four-bedroom home full of junk."

◆ **The redecorating cycle.** Be prepared for the redecorating cycle. When you move in to your new home, you'll probably find that the couch isn't going to go with the carpet in the living room. Then when you recarpet, the recliner is going to look shabby, so you're going to need a new recliner. And while you're getting the recliner, you might as well pick out a new coffee table, which will bring you full circle back to the couch, which now doesn't seem to fit in with the new carpet, recliner, and coffee table. And after you paint the room to go with the new couch, carpet, recliner, and coffee table, the dining room will need work. Rest assured that one day everything will be perfect. That's the day you put the "For Sale" sign up and hope to recoup all your redecorating dollars.

Now that you have a better idea of what to expect, you are probably wondering who all the people are who will help you along the way.

People You Work with When Buying a Home

Are you ready to get started? Then let me introduce the cast of characters you will most likely work with to make your dream of owning a home a reality.

◆ **Realtor (or agent).** If you want to buy a home, it is a good idea to have a Realtor working for you. This is the person who will help you find your dream home and help you get the best deal. Notice that I didn't say, "get you the best price." I said "deal" because sometimes there are other things you can negotiate for that will make the deal "sweeter." You can find out more about selecting an agent in Chapter 4.

Real Deal _____

If you know people in the real estate business, contact them and pick their brains for the name of a good Realtor; referrals are usually your best bet. The same goes for finding a mortgage company. If you know someone who has successfully closed on a home with a particular lender (and broker), that is a good place to start.

◆ **Sales associate (or new-home consultant).** If you are trying to build or buy a newly constructed home, you might be dealing with a sales associate who is serving as the broker for the new homebuilder.

◆ **Lender (or mortgage broker).** Unless you have the cash lying around to pay for your new home, you will be financing your home with a mortgage company. If you are working with a mortgage broker, that person serves as the liaison between you and the mortgage company that he or she has set up for you to work with.

◆ **Escrow officer (loan officer).** When that fateful day arrives when you must sign on the dotted line, this is the person who walks you through the process.

◆ **Seller.** This is who you are buying the home from or the company you are having build your new home (or that built your new home). This also might be you, if you are selling your home.

◆ **Buyer.** This is you and your partner, if you are purchasing the home with someone. Or, this might be the people who are buying your home from you, if you are selling your home.

Now that you are a little more familiar with all the parties involved in the purchase and sale of a home, let's move on to the actual steps involved.

What to Expect When You Buy a Home

You have decided that you are tired of living in your apartment or rental home, or maybe Mom and Dad are trying to push you out of the nest. You want to become one of the millions of Americans who have embarked upon homeownership. Now what do you do?

Here is a (best-case scenario, mind you) quick-and-dirty, step-by-step process for purchasing a home:

1. Take a look at your finances and credit history, and determine (on your own) how much home you think you can afford. (Also pay close attention to Chapter 2.)

2. Obtain financing from an approved lender. This means you need to get prequalified or, better yet, preapproved. (Refer to the "Getting Preapproved for a Loan" section in Chapter 2.)

3. Narrow your criteria for the type of home you are looking for.

4. Start a savings plan (if you don't already have one) for the down payment and closing costs associated with purchasing a home.

5. Find a real estate agent you feel comfortable with who listens to your wants/ needs and will work *for* you. If you don't want to work with an agent, skip to step 6.

6. Start looking for your dream home, whether it be a current home for sale or a new build.

7. Read and understand everything you can about your financing options. This can be confusing, but it is a very important part of the homebuying process.

8. Make an offer on a home, possibly a counteroffer, and close on the deal.

Along the way, you will find it necessary to choose a homeowners insurance company, get the home inspected, perform a walkthrough, and take care of other odds and ends that must happen before the keys are turned over to you. Don't worry. This book covers all the necessary steps, providing background information and tips for each.

What To Expect When You Sell Your Home

If you own a home that you need to sell, you will want to pay close attention to Part 5. Most likely, you will perform the tasks required to sell your home right along with (or before) closing on your new home.

Here is a (best-case scenario again) quick-and-dirty, step-by-step process for selling your home:

1. Find a real estate agent you feel comfortable with who listens to your wants/needs and will work *for* you. If you don't want to work with an agent, skip to step 2.

2. Get the home ready for people to view; possibly move out.

3. Price the home realistically and market it strategically.

4. Deal with the different purchase offers you receive (hopefully at least one or more).

5. Close on the home and hand over the keys.

It all may sound a little scary, and it may seem like you will never get everything to happen when it is supposed to happen. Well, that is what this book will help you with. And you will get there soon!

The Least You Need to Know

◆ There are many advantages to buying a home, including having a place to call your own, tax savings, appreciation in the value of your home, and enforced savings.

◆ You should carefully consider the wisdom of purchasing a home if you don't plan to live in the area for long, you're not sure you are going to like the area, you do not have a steady income, or you are unable to come up with a down payment *and* money for monthly house payments.

◆ Learn who all the different people are who will be helping you purchase your home. Make sure they are reliable and that they are willing to work for you. The best way to ensure this: Ask others for referrals.

◆ The process of purchasing a home can appear complicated; learn as much as you can about each step along the way and ask lots of questions. Use this book as your guide.

◆ The process of selling a home can take a few days, months, or even years, depending on many factors you decide on along the way. Part 5 of this book hopefully helps speed this process.

Chapter 2

How Much House Can You Afford?

In This Chapter

- ◆ Calculating your total income and monthly expenses
- ◆ Finding your appropriate price range
- ◆ Getting prequalified and preapproved
- ◆ Checking your credit history

If you had enough money to pay cash for your home, buying a home would be easy—simply write a check. Unfortunately, few people can pay cash for a home. Around 99 percent of homebuyers borrow money to buy their home. You probably fall into this 99 percent. Even if you did have enough money to purchase a home outright, you might not want to do so because of the tax benefits.

The critical question is *how much can you afford to borrow?*

All lenders are going to take a close look at your financial situation. This chapter covers the upfront costs of buying a home and then helps you take a close, perhaps painful, look at your financial and credit situation.

How Much You Make and How Much You Spend

Before lenders will give you a loan, they will carefully review the money you make and the money you spend. The first thing you should do in figuring out how much money you can spend on a home is to determine your yearly and monthly gross income.

Your monthly *gross income* is the amount you earn each month *before* taxes. For example, if you earn $36,000 per year, you gross $3,000 each month (36 ÷ 12 = 3). If you and your partner combine your gross income to earn $60,000 per year, you gross $5,000 each month (60 ÷ 12 = 5). Your *net income* is a completely different story.

To begin, gather all your check stubs and income information. If you will be buying the home with a partner, gather income information for this person as well. Make sure you also locate pay stubs and past income tax forms; you can expect to show them when requesting a loan from the bank.

Real Estate Terms

What's the difference between net and gross income? **Gross income** is the amount you earn before taxes; **net income** is the amount you make after taxes and other expenses. A good way to remember the difference between gross and net is to picture a fishing net; the net amount is what is left after part of the gross amount falls through.

If you have other income from freelance work or the sale of furniture that you make in your woodshop, gather that information also. Make sure that this additional income is money that you have paid taxes on; otherwise, the lender will not consider it.

If you have other income from bonuses, know that bonuses don't always count. This is because bonus money is not always guaranteed. If you want to have your bonus money considered as part of your gross salary, you need to prove that bonuses are a regular part of your pay. You must show a track record of receiving bonuses for two years. Your employer, for instance, may be able to write a letter saying that the bonus is dependable.

If you receive alimony or child support, you can include this money in your total, if you want. You must show that this is a dependable source of income and will be continuing for a minimum of three years. You may need a settlement statement from your divorce that states the amount you receive. Most lenders will consider only income that can be verified—from your employer or past tax returns.

Keep in mind that lenders will look for an average income. They will want to evaluate your income from the past two years to make sure it has been steady, and they will take into consideration any seasonal jumps. Usually two years of continuous employment proves to lenders that you have a steady income. If you have had multiple jobs in the past two years, lenders may require that you write a letter as to why you have switched jobs often. In addition, if you're recently out of college, lenders may take into consideration your future earning power.

What If You're Self-Employed?

Back in the day, banks sometimes looked unfavorably at people who were considered to be "self-employed." They were considered a risk and had no guarantee of getting approved for a loan. Nowadays, consultants and small businesses are popping up all over, and those who are self-employed are treated almost like people with "real jobs."

If you're self-employed, the lender will usually consider as gross income the amount of money on which you paid taxes. For instance, if your business grossed $100,000, but you paid taxes on only $35,000, the lender will consider $35,000 as your gross annual income. You will have to show two years of tax returns to verify your income.

If your self-employed income fluctuates from year to year, you might be asked to provide a letter as to why your income went down from one year to the next. Of course, no letter is necessary if your income goes up. Lenders like consistency—although they don't have a problem if your income keeps going up. Also note that if you grossed $50,000 one year and $100,000 the next year, the bank will average the two years to come up with an average gross income of $75,000.

If you don't have two or more years of tax returns and your business is mainly freelance or contract work, it can help to show the lender copies of contracts you have for current and future work.

Keeping Track of Your Income

Use the following worksheet to record your yearly gross income. To calculate your monthly gross income, divide this figure by 12.

Calculate your gross income.

Income (yearly)	You	Co-Purchaser
Gross Salary	$ _____	$ _____
Bonuses	$ _____	$ _____
Interest	$ _____	$ _____
Dividends	$ _____	$ _____
Social Security/Pension	$ _____	$ _____
Child Support	$ _____	$ _____
Other _____	$ _____	$ _____
Sub Total (add above lines)	$ _____	$ _____
Yearly Gross Income (add Columns)	$ _____	
Monthly Gross Income (divide by 12)	$ _____	

You now know how much money you and your partner make each year and each month. You will use these figures along with your monthly expenses to calculate how much you can borrow in the section, "What's Your Ratio?"

Keeping Track of Your Expenses

You know the money that is coming in. Now you need to figure the total money that is going out. Lenders consider this your monthly expense. You might be surprised to find out how much money you have (or don't have) left over at the end of the month after paying all your bills.

Real Deal

If you have fewer than 10 months left on an installment loan, don't include it in your total monthly debt payments. If you're close to 10 months, consider paying off the loan enough to bring it under the 10-month mark. Then you don't have to count it.

You need to collect all your required monthly payments and total them. This includes car loans or leases, student loans, minimum monthly payments on any and all credit cards, and so on. Use the following worksheet to record your monthly expenses. Adjust the categories as needed to suit your particular expenses.

Make a note of your total expenses; you will use this total in the next section to compare some lending ratios.

Calculate your monthly expenses.

Expenses (monthly)	You	Co-Purchaser
Car Payment	$ _____	$ _____
Student Loan	$ _____	$ _____
Credit Card #1	$ _____	$ _____
Credit Card #2	$ _____	$ _____
Credit Card #3	$ _____	$ _____
Other Loan	$ _____	$ _____
Child Support	$ _____	$ _____
Alimony	$ _____	$ _____
Other _____	$ _____	$ _____
Sub Total (add above lines)	$ _____	$ _____
Monthly Expense (add columns)	$ _____	

How Much Money Can You Borrow?

The first part of the loan equation is complete: You know how much you make and how much you spend. The next step is to figure out how much you can borrow.

If you're getting tired of all the number crunching, you can use a ballpark method for figuring out how much you can borrow. Roughly, you can borrow up to 2 to 2½ times your annual gross salary (sometimes more). If you and your partner make $50,000, you might be able to buy a home in the $100,000 to $125,000 price range.

Lenders and agents are a little leery of the ballpark method. For one thing, this method is too easy, and if they allow things to look too easy, you may figure out you don't need them. More important, rough estimates can't take into consideration individual circumstances. For example, if one couple with a $50,000 income has $20,000 in savings and no car payment, they may be able to afford an even more expensive home than a ballpark figure would indicate. If another couple with a $50,000 income has two car payments, maxed-out credit cards, and intend to get their down payment by winning the lottery, they might not qualify for a home in any price range.

Understanding Lender Ratios

Lenders compare your income and monthly payments to certain qualifying ratios—the most common of which is the debt-to-income ratio. If you have a particular lender in mind, call the lender and ask what ratios it uses. You will see these ratios expressed like this:

◆ 28/36 (the ratios most often used for conventional loans)

◆ 29/41 (ratios used for FHA loans)

The first number, sometimes called the front-end ratio or *housing expense ratio*, is the percentage of your income that you can spend on housing. For example, most lenders say your monthly house payment (including loan payment, property taxes, and insurance) shouldn't total more than 28 percent of your gross monthly income (that is, your gross annual income divided by 12). The ratio used depends on the amount of money you put down on the home as your down payment.

The second number, the back-end or *overall debt ratio*, totals your housing expenses plus your long-term monthly debt, then figures this total as a percentage of your monthly gross income. For example, most lenders say your housing expenses plus your monthly debt should not be more than 36 percent of your monthly income.

Real Estate Terms

The **housing expense ratio** (front-end) is the percentage of gross monthly income that goes toward paying a mortgage or rent on a home. The **overall debt ratio** (back-end) is your total monthly expenses, including housing, credit cards, loans, and all other debt.

How do lenders come up with these ratios? Lenders don't like guesses, but that's basically what the ratios are. The lenders feel if they follow these guidelines, homeowners will be able to pay off their loans. The ratios are arbitrary, though, and are based on studies done in the 1930s and 1940s by the Federal Housing Administration. Most lenders sell the loans to a secondary market, and, therefore, follow the guidelines set by the agencies that purchase the loans. The ratios will vary depending on the area. Also, the bigger your down payment, the less significant the ratios become.

What's Your Housing Ratio (a.k.a. Maximum Mortgage Payment)?

To figure out your housing ratio (maximum mortgage payment), use the following worksheet and these steps:

1. Enter your monthly gross income.

2. Multiply this amount by 28 percent (.28). The resulting figure is what you can conservatively afford for a monthly mortgage payment.

Calculating your maximum mortgage payment housing ratio.

Monthly Gross Income	$ _____
	X .28
Maximum Mortgage Payment	$ _____

To figure out your overall debt ratio (maximum mortgage payment), use the worksheet and follow these steps:

1. Enter your monthly gross income.

2. Multiply this amount by 36 percent (.36). This figure is the total amount of money you can spend on all debts—housing and other.

3. Write in your present monthly debts.

4. Subtract your present debt from your maximum monthly debt to find out how much you have left over for your mortgage payment.

Translating this monthly payment into a loan amount can be tricky. Your housing expenses include what is known as PITI (principal, interest, taxes, and insurance—pronounced "pity").

The principal and interest will vary depending on the amount of the loan, type of loan, and interest rate. You can use the tables in Appendix C to look up the principal and interest amount for different loans and interest rates.

Monthly Gross Income	$ _____
	X .36
Maximum Monthly Debt	$ _____
Present Monthly Debt	$ _____
Maximum Mortgage Payment	$ _____
Overall Debt	$ _____

Calculating your maximum mortgage payment overall debt ratio.

Don't Forget Taxes and Insurance!

Just because a lender says you can afford house payments of $1,200 doesn't mean you actually can. On top of the principal and interest, you need to add taxes and insurance. Taxes will vary depending on where you live, and insurance will vary depending on the policy you purchase.

You can ask your real estate agent to give you estimates of these payments. You might also be responsible for an association fee, which is a fee you pay toward the maintenance of common areas in your neighborhood, like a playground, trees and grass, and athletic courts.

Use This Example To "Get" This Concept

The following shows the yearly gross income and monthly payments for our sample couple, Nancy and Sid Lewis. The combined income of the couple totals $55,250. Their monthly gross income, then, is $4,604.

Income (yearly)	Sid	Nancy
Gross Salary	$ _____30,000	$ _____25,000
Bonuses	$ _____	$ _____
Interest	$ _____	$ _____
Dividends	$ _____	$ _____250
Social Security/Pension	$ _____	$ _____
Child Support	$ _____	$ _____
Other _____	$ _____	$ _____
Sub Total (add above lines)	$ _____30,000	$ _____25,250
Yearly Gross Income (add columns)	$ _____55,250	
Monthly Gross Income (divide by 12)	$ _____4,604	

Gross income.

If you apply the first ratio (housing expense), you can see that the Lewis family can afford a maximum payment of $1,289.

Monthly expenses.

Expenses (monthly)	Sid	Nancy
Car Payment	$ _____240	$ _____325
Student Loan	$ _____85	$ _____
Credit Card #1	$ _____	$ _____25
Credit Card #2	$ _____	$ _____
Credit Card #3	$ _____	$ _____
Other Loan	$ _____	$ _____
Child Support	$ _____	$ _____
Alimony	$ _____	$ _____
Other _____	$ _____	$ _____
Sub Total (add above lines)	$ _____325	$ _____350
Monthly Expense (add columns)	$ _____675	

A maximum mortgage payment housing ratio.

Monthly Gross Income	$ _____4,604
	X .28
Maximum Mortgage Payment	$ _____1,289

If you use the second ratio (overall debt), you can see that the Lewis family can afford a maximum payment of $983. The lender will use the lowest figure, which is $983, when qualifying the loan.

A maximum mortgage payment overall debt ratio.

Monthly Gross Income	$ _____4,604
	X .36
Maximum Monthly Debt	$ _____1,658
Present Monthly Debt	$ _____(675)
Maximum Mortgage Payment	$ _____983

Prequalifying for a Loan

If you have followed all the worksheets in this chapter, you have prequalified yourself. You should feel pretty confident about what you can afford, and you should know your financial situation.

If you choose not to do the worksheets, you may want to have a lender prequalify you. (You also may want to do this in addition to qualifying yourself so you're sure your figures are accurate.)

What Do You Need to Prequalify?

Once you find a company to qualify you, you can either schedule an appointment or sometimes be qualified right over the phone (or via the Internet). You will be asked to provide the following:

◆ **Social Security number.** Lenders will use this to pull your credit report, which will give them a synopsis of your credit history (if you have any) and a credit score. The credit history will contain any and all credit cards (yes, even the Gap card), bank or car loans, and any type of credit you have had within the past seven years or that you currently have.

◆ **Name and addresses for the past three years.** Lenders will use this information to determine how "stable" you are. Do you move from place to place often, or have you lived in the same location for a while?

◆ **Employment history.** This shows whether you have a track record for working with a company for only a short period of time, or if you have worked for the same company for many years.

◆ **Current income.** This is how much money you make on a monthly basis. Are you paid weekly, bimonthly, or monthly? Are you paid a salary or do you work on a commission basis? Are you self-employed?

◆ **Current expenses.** Lenders will look at how much money you spend each month on a regular basis—for example, your monthly car payment and monthly credit card payments.

◆ **Current bank account balances.** Lenders also want to know how much money you have in the bank. If you have $12.53, how do you think it looks compared to $12,530?

You can prequalify informally, or you can go one step further and actually get preapproved for a mortgage.

Advantages and Drawbacks of Prequalifying

When you prequalify informally, you don't pay a fee. You usually spend 20 to 30 minutes on the phone with a lender. The lender will ask you questions about your income and monthly debt (similar to the earnings and expenses covered in this chapter). Then the lender will do some quick calculations to let you know how much you can finance. This type of prequalifying is good when you want a very rough estimate.

Keep in mind that the lender is not guaranteeing you a loan; you will still have to go through a formal qualification. Also, lenders base their estimate on what you tell them. If you exaggerate your income, make up an amount because you don't know, or forget about monthly payments, you won't get an accurate figure.

Sellers like to know that when you make an offer, you can actually get a loan for the home. If you have informally prequalified, you don't really have any advantage in the negotiating. If you are preapproved (covered in the next section), sellers may look more favorably on your offer because they know you have a secure bid. Compared to other bids that might not be secure, your offer may look better.

Getting Preapproved for a Loan

The preapproval process is one step further than prequalification. If you are preapproved, it means that the lender has verified your credit, reviewed your tax returns, and verified your employment, earnings, and assets. The lender will then give you a letter stating that it is willing to grant you a mortgage for a specified amount within a certain time period (usually 60 days).

It will also state the maximum loan amount and any stipulations regarding the loan (for example, you have to sell or rent your current home first). This documentation proves that you have been approved for that loan and that an underwriter has checked and guaranteed the loan.

Real Deal

A preapproval letter can make quite an impact with sellers if they know you are preapproved and are extending an offer on their home. If you had two offers on your home for sale, one that is preapproved and one is not, who would you think has the logical advantage?

Sellers like buyers who have been formally preapproved because they know that the buyer will not (or should not) have problems purchasing their home.

Keep in mind that when you get preapproved by a lender, you're guaranteed a loan with that particular lender. Another lender may offer better terms (for example, fewer fees or a better mortgage product), and if you want to use that lender, you will have to go through getting approved with them. As you learn in Chapter 5, you will probably want to shop around and select a lender with the most favorable terms. You'll learn more on lending in Part 3.

Checking Your Credit

When you qualify for a loan, the lender will check your credit to ensure that you don't have any credit problems. If you have had a history of credit problems, you will probably want to get your credit report and be prepared to respond to any questions or problems on the report.

If you haven't been late or missed any payments, you probably don't have to worry about getting a bad credit report. But mistakes do happen, and sometimes your report may include something that is wrong or a problem that has been resolved. You may want to get a copy of your credit report just to double-check.

Getting a Credit Report

Federal law requires that you have access to any information in your credit files. You can obtain a credit report from a local credit report agency or a national credit bureau. Three of the best-known credit bureaus are Equifax, Experian, and Trans Union.

The fee for a report ranges from $2 to $10 (depending on the state you live in). You must send the credit bureau a letter that includes your full name, date of birth, Social Security number, and present and past addresses. You may also need to send a copy of your driver's license or a phone or utility bill to verify your current address. Don't forget to personally sign the request letter, because your signature is a requirement to obtain the credit report.

> **Bet You Didn't Know**
>
> The Internet includes many financial sources, including numerous mortgage companies (for example, www.mortgage.com). You can visit sites not only to get information about the financing process, but also to prequalify and get a rough estimate of how much you can borrow. (Make sure you understand whether you are prequalifying or getting preapproved. Remember, there's a difference!)

Equifax
P.O. Box 105873
Atlanta, GA 30348
1-800-685-1111

Experian
P.O. Box 2104
Allen, TX 75013-2104
1-888-682-7654

Trans Union
P.O. Box 390
Springfield, PA 19064-390
Credit Report Request: 1-800-888-4213
Credit Report Disputes: 1-800-916-8800
Fraud Victims Assistance: 1-800-680-7289

> **Real Deal**
>
> For more information about credit reporting or to view sample reports and access company information online, visit the websites of the three major credit reporters: Equifax (www.equifax), Experian (www.experian.com), and Trans Union (www.transunion.com).

You can also request your spouse or partner's report at the same time, but you must supply all the same information and include both your signatures.

Get the report two to three months before you apply for the loan so you'll have time to resolve any problems that turn up.

If you have been turned down for credit, the creditor must furnish you with a copy of the declination letter (why you were declined) and a copy of the credit report (free of charge, if you ask for it).

What's on Your Credit Report?

Once you receive your credit report, you might be curious as to what all of the information means. Each of the credit reporting bureaus use different codes and a different format for a typical consumer credit report, but the following information will be on all of the reports:

◆ **Identifying information.** This includes your name, any former names (maiden or married names), current and previous addresses, your Social Security number, date of birth, and current and previous employer information. All of this information is tracked from any credit applications you have ever had to fill out. So make sure you fill out credit forms completely, accurately, and consistently each time.

◆ **Credit information.** This includes any and all information about credit accounts opened, the assigned credit limit, loan amounts, current balances, monthly payments, and the pattern that you have paid your credit for the past years. In addition, any names of individuals who are on your accounts (for example, a spouse or even ex-spouse or co-signer) will be listed. The companies that you do business with provide this information.

◆ **Public record information.** This includes federal district bankruptcy records, state and county court records, tax liens and monetary judgments, and in some states, overdue child support payments. This information comes from public records.

◆ **Inquiries.** This includes the names of those who have obtained a copy of your credit report for any reason. For example, if you ever receive credit card offers in the mail, those companies will most likely be listed on your report, because they obtained your credit information. This information comes from the credit reporting agency, and it remains available for as long as two years, according to federal law.

All this information is used to calculate a FICO score—a scoring system derived in part from your past credit history. This score is calculated each time the credit report is requested.

What's a FICO Credit Score?

The FICO score is a number between 300 and 800. Most lenders will tell you that a score higher than 660 is considered "good." If your score falls between 620 and 660, you will probably have to write more explanation letters and work harder to convince a lender to give you a loan. You also might be looking at a higher interest rate on the loan right out of the gate.

Your FICO credit score is influenced by five characteristics that help lenders determine your credit risk. Each of the following are taken into account, in descending order of importance:

- **Past delinquencies.** If you have made late payments in the past, you are more likely to repeat this in the future, and you are more of a risk. See the next section, "Are You a Risky Creditor?" for examples.

- **Use of credit.** If you max out your credit cards or keep them close to the limit, you are more of a risk because of your spending habits.

- **Credit file length.** If you have a short credit history, the FICO system assumes you are more of a risk because you are inexperienced with handling credit.

Real Deal

Note that there isn't a big difference between "good credit" and "great credit." If you have a great credit score, in the 700+ range, you might be able to qualify for specific loan opportunities that lenders offer. But don't be disappointed when your interest rates aren't much better than those that would be offered to individuals with good credit.

- **Number of times asked for credit.** If you initiate multiple requests for credit cards, loans, or other debt instruments in a short period of time, you are more of a risk.

- **Mix of credit.** If you only have credit cards (revolving loans), you are considered more of a risk than someone who has a combination of installment (for example, car loans) and revolving loans. On an installment loan, money is borrowed once and fixed payments are made until the balance is gone; revolving credit has borrowers making regular payments, which frees up the access to more money.

The FICO system also looks for patterns and whether any problems appear to be ongoing. If your score falls below 620, you have a chance of getting a loan, but you will really have to work for it and will definitely pay for it in your loan interest rate (refer to the section, "Loans for Those with Blemished Credit" in Chapter 15). In recent years, more of these types of loans have been granted, and certain lenders specialize in dealing with individuals who have this type of credit rating.

Are You a Risky Creditor?

You will be considered a higher credit risk if your credit report shows that you have more late payments and slow payments than listed for the following types of credit:

- **Housing debt.** An example of this type of credit is your current mortgage or rent. You should have no payments past due.

- **Installment credit.** An example of this type of credit is a car loan. You should have no payments that are 60 days or more past due and no more than two payments that are 30 days past due.

Real Estate Terms

A **subprime** borrower has either missed payments on a debt or has been late with payments. Lenders will charge a higher interest rate to compensate for the potential losses from customers who may run into trouble or default on the loan.

- **Revolving credit.** An example of this type of credit is a credit card. You should have no payments that are 60 days or more past due and no more than two payments that are 30 days past due.

If you have some of these types of risk, you might be considered a *subprime* borrower. This is a person with a less-than-perfect credit report. Again, it doesn't mean you will never find a lender, it just means that you will have to work a little harder to find a match.

Correcting a Mistake or Responding to Problems

If your credit report doesn't show any problems, you can rest assured that your loan won't be turned down because of your credit report. If your report does include a problem, you should correct it (if it is in error) or resolve it. A mortgage lender can also get an agent from a credit bureau to help correct any errors.

If you have any outstanding debt, resolve it by contacting the creditor. Be sure to send a letter to the creditor requesting they notify you and all three reporting services that the problem has been fixed. If you cannot resolve the problem, document your explanation. The credit agency must include your explanation of the problem in the credit report.

If you pay your bills, but pay them late, you may think that you don't have a bad record. Slow pays (late payments) are almost as bad as no pays, and they reflect poorly on your credit record. You should document or explain any late payments, especially any late rent or mortgage payments. Perhaps you moved or got a divorce and the bill arrived too late.

If your report has a mistake, you need to get *each* reporting agency to correct it. This is harder than actually clearing an outstanding debt! Write a complaint letter; call the local office. If you can't get resolution, call the bureau manager. If you write in, include the questions you have about your credit report and the actions you would like to take. Then include your name, address for the past five years, Social Security number, date of birth, current employer, phone number, and signature.

> **Real Deal**
>
> If you find that your credit is in a lot worse shape than you anticipated, you can contact one of the personal credit counseling organizations for help. For example, you can contact Consumer Credit Counseling Services at 1-800-577-2227. They might be able to help you sort out your credit problems for a small fee or possibly even at no charge.

Strengthening Your Credit

If you know you have a low score due to slow pays or because you haven't established credit in your name, there are a few things that you can do to strengthen your credit.

Finding out that you have no credit history can happen whether you are young or not so young. Many married baby boomers have been taking care of their family for years, only to find out that their credit cards and credit history are actually established in their spouse's name only. Because of their lack of employment history and being the secondary person on bank accounts, they haven't established a credit history.

Even if your name is on all the accounts, it doesn't mean that you have established credit. Apply for a department store card or gas card in your name (because they are relatively easy to apply for) and pay the bills on time, of course. Another option might be to open a bank account with your name as the primary person on the account and then secure a credit card against the deposit amount. These are a few sure-fire ways to build or perhaps rebuild your credit.

If you have had bad credit, work to build new, positive credit references. As mentioned in a recent article in the *Indianapolis Star*, "One of the main factors that will determine your ability to purchase a home is your credit rating." Create a budget and stick to it. Pay off any past due debt. And again, know what your credit report says so that you aren't broadsided.

Dealing with a Bad Credit Report

How long will you be haunted by bad debt? Suppose that in the past you had some credit problems, but now they are all resolved. How long does bad debt stay on your record? Seven years. After that time, the unfavorable credit information should be dropped from your file. If you file for bankruptcy, this information stays on your record for 10 years. Lenders really only look at the last two years, though.

If you have a bad credit report, does that mean that you will never own a home? No. It may mean that you have to search harder to find a lender, and you may pay a higher rate for the loan. Lenders will work with you, and you can always refinance the loan to get a better rate once you have established a better credit report.

Real Deal

If you have several credit cards, get rid of most of them before you apply for a loan. Having too many credit cards may be looked on unfavorably by lenders. With easy access to credit, you could get yourself into trouble.

Another option to consider is looking for homes where the sellers are willing to carry some or all of the loan. When this happens, the seller serves as the mortgage company or bank, and you make payments directly to the seller. This way, if you cannot make the payments and the home must be foreclosed upon, the home ownership goes right back to the seller. To some sellers, this is worth the trouble of carrying the loan. But if you keep making the payments without any problems, the home is yours.

Before All the Numbers Make You Dizzy

This chapter is heavy on number crunching—figuring this, subtracting that, multiplying by 28 percent, and so on. If you like to work with numbers, it should be easy to figure out the amount of loan you can afford. Basically, you're prequalifying yourself.

If you don't want to wade through all the worksheets, you can ask your mortgage officer to give you an estimate of how much home you can afford and what the upfront costs will be. You can also go to a lender and be prequalified or even preapproved.

Keep in mind that if you ask your mortgage officer to estimate how much home you can afford, that person will tell you exactly how much home that translates to. You might actually be able to afford a $300,000 home, but that doesn't mean that is how much you are looking to spend.

Be sure your real estate agent understands the price range you want to stay within. If agents start to show you homes out of the range you feel comfortable with, let them know. Remember that agents are still sales-oriented individuals. They make a commission off the price of the home you purchase and stand to make a lot more money on a $200,000 home than a $100,000 home ($6,000 vs. $3,000).

The Least You Need to Know

- ◆ Lenders look at two ratios when deciding whether you qualify for a loan. The front-end or housing expense ratio requires that your mortgage payment not exceed a certain percentage (usually 28 percent) of your monthly income. The back-end or debt-to-income ratio requires that your mortgage payment plus your debt payments do not exceed a certain percentage (usually 36 percent) of your monthly income.

- ◆ Mortgage payments consist of the principal, interest, taxes, and insurance. You will see this abbreviated as PITI.

- ◆ To find out how much you can borrow, talk with a lender and prequalify either formally or informally, or you can prequalify yourself.

- ◆ To prequalify yourself, divide your gross yearly income by 12 to get your gross monthly income, and then subtract your total monthly payments.

- ◆ You may be able to get preapproved by documenting all of your income and debt with a lender.

- ◆ It's a good idea to check your credit record to ensure that you don't have any credit problems. If you do, resolve the problem or have your record corrected before you apply for a loan.

- ◆ Just because you can prequalify to purchase a $300,000 home doesn't mean you have to spend that much.

Chapter 3

Understanding the Up-Front Costs of Buying a Home

In This Chapter

- ◆ Deciding on a down payment source and amount
- ◆ Determining what closing costs you have to pay
- ◆ Totaling the up-front costs of buying a home

To acquire most anything, you need money. The same holds true when you buy a home. You should expect to pay out two big amounts—one for the down payment and one for the closing costs. How much you pay for each depends on your particular situation. This chapter gives you an overview of what you can expect.

Everything You Need to Know About Down Payments

You may see no-money-down deals advertised or $1,300 move-in specials. Although you need to carefully scrutinize these types of deals, they can sometimes be a great way to go.

In most instances, you're going to have to (or want to) put some money down to purchase a house. Lenders don't like to give out loans that are risky to them. Borrowers who don't have any money invested in a property may be more likely to default on the loan. The more money borrowers put down, the happier (and more lenient) the lenders are.

How Much of a Down Payment Do You Need?

The down payment is usually figured as a percentage of the purchase price. The percentage you must pay depends on the type of financing you receive. Conventional financing offers programs with as little as 3 or 5 percent down. With this type of down payment, you would also be required to pay mortgage insurance (more in the section "Your Loan May Require Mortgage Insurance" in Chapter 12). Mortgage insurance reduces the risk to the mortgage company when there is less than 20 percent equity invested by the borrowers.

Real Deal _____

Veterans may be eligible for no-money-down loans. For information on VA loans, see Chapter 15.

Real Estate Terms _____

You may hear lenders use the term **loan-to-value** or **LTV**. If you put down 10 percent and finance 90 percent, that's called a 90 percent LTV loan.

For a conservative example, let's use a down payment of 20 percent of the purchase price. If you're buying a home for $100,000, you'd be expected to pay $20,000 down with an 80 percent *loan-to value* or *LTV.* Other types of loans—for example, government-assisted loans—require a smaller down payment. For this type of loan, you may need to put down only 5 percent or less.

Where Can You Get the Down Payment?

Where can you look for the money for a down payment? Well, in the best of circumstances, you have been saving for a home purchase, and you have money in your savings account.

If that's not the case, you may need to do some creative thinking for the down payment funds. For instance, you may have assets that you aren't even aware of. For instance, perhaps you have a stamp collection that you can sell. Or perhaps you have a life insurance policy with some cash value. Consider all sources of income, such as your tax refund or end-of-the-year bonus.

What If You Don't Have Money for the Down Payment?

If you don't have the money for a down payment, you can try one of the following strategies for getting the money:

- Start a savings program and wait until you have 3 to 5 percent of the purchase price saved. If you don't have any savings, you probably aren't ready to buy a home. You should have at least some savings for the down payment. Also, you should be sure that you can afford the monthly payments. Open a savings account now and start saving.

- When you're thinking about buying a home, you may want to create a budget and try to stick to it. Take some time to analyze where your money is going and look for places to save. Make your savings a basic expense; don't just save what is left over every month from your paycheck.

- Consider asking your parents or a relative for a cash gift for the down payment. If your parents are in a position to help, they can be a valuable resource when you're just starting out. Keep in mind that with gifts, the lenders require certain documentation or circumstances. For instance, most lenders require a gift letter stating that the money was a gift and does not have to be repaid. If you are getting a conventional loan, at least 5 percent of the down payment has to come from your money. The gift can be used for the closing costs or reserves (two months of house payments). The Federal Housing Administration (FHA), on the other hand, allows a gift for the entire down payment and closing costs.

- If you're purchasing a new home, look for a builder who will consider *sweat equity*. In exchange for doing some of the work on the house (painting the interior, for example), the builder may apply credit toward the closing fees.

- Consider using a different type of financing—for instance, seller carrybacks (where the seller acts as the financer) or assuming a mortgage. These alternative strategies are covered in Chapter 15.

When Do You Fork Over the Down Payment?

When you make an offer on the house, you're going to have to show the seller that you're sincere. An earnest smile and firm handshake won't do it. The seller will want a deposit on the house, sometimes called *earnest money*. The amount of money required for the deposit will vary depending on the local practices, the offer you're making on the house, and the market (whether it's a buyer's or a seller's market). The nuances of making an offer are covered in Chapter 17.

The earnest money will go toward your down payment. The down payment is payable at the closing. See Chapter 21 for closing strategies from the buyer's perspective.

Additional Costs You Pay When Buying a Home

In addition to the down payment, you also have to pay settlement or closing costs when you close on the loan. When you apply for a loan, the lender will give you an estimate of the closing costs, and you will probably feel like crying when you see the total. Typically, closing costs depend on the local costs and loan arrangements.

Before you give up, keep in mind that the costs you're required to pay will vary depending on your situation. You may be required to pay some costs; the seller may pick up other costs. Remember to bargain. Depending on how motivated the sellers are, you could get them to pick up quite a bit of the closing costs. Also, with some types of loans, you can finance some of the closing costs (that is, you can add them to your loan amount). The following sections describe some of the fees you can expect to pay at closing and also help you scrutinize your fees to avoid paying any "junk" fees.

Paying Lender Fees

A lot of money you pay in closing goes into the lender's pocket. Lenders are the money people; therefore, a lot of the closing costs are lender fees. It's a good idea to make sure you understand the fees you pay to the lender:

> **Bet You Didn't Know**
>
> One of the most confusing concepts for homebuyers is points. Basically, a point is prepaid interest. You pay more money upfront (at the closing) for a lower interest rate over the term of the loan. The value of a point is 1 percent of the loan. So if you have to pay 1 point on a $150,000 loan, you'd pay $1,500. Two points would total $3,000.

◆ **Points.** A prepayment of interest. One point is equal to 1 percent of the mortgage or loan amount. Depending on the type of loan you get and the current mortgage market, you may have to pay points. For example, you may get an 8 percent loan with two points. If you're financing $100,000, 1 point would be equal to $1,000. Two points would total $2,000. Points are tax deductible in the year they are paid (unless it is a rental investment property—then you have to depreciate the amount over a certain period of time, usually 20 years). You can keep your points down in two ways. First, you can shop for a loan with the lowest number of points and interest rates. Rates and points will vary from lender to lender. Second, you can ask the seller to pay points. Points can often be used as part of your negotiating strategy (asking buyers to pay points).

◆ **Loan origination fee.** This fee covers the costs of the time for finalizing and reviewing the loan. Although it is basically a prepaid point, or 1 percent of the loan amount, it is not tax deductible. (In some areas, points and origination fees are synonymous.)

◆ **Loan application fee.** Though this fee is almost never charged, it is usually around $200 to $300 and is payable when you apply for the loan. The lender uses it immediately to cover the costs of verifying your income, checking your credit, getting an appraisal, and so on. Be sure to inquire about this fee when you apply for the loan (see Chapter 16).

◆ **Interest payment.** Depending on when you close on your home, you may have to pay interest for that month. Many buyers are confused about how house payments are paid and why interest is due at closing in some cases. When you rent an apartment, you pay in advance. On August 1, you pay the rent for the month of August. When you purchase a house, you pay in *arrears*, or back pay on the house. For instance, your payment for August 1 pays for the month of July. (Chapter 16 gives you some tips on timing the closing of your sale to lessen interest payments.)

◆ **Document preparation fee.** Some lenders charge you an additional amount for preparing the loan documents. This may be a fluff fee of around $150. In addition, there might be a processing/underwriting fee of $350. When you're shopping around for a lender, ask about these fees.

◆ **Credit check fee.** As part of the loan application process, you may be charged a fee for running a credit check. It's usually around $20 to $60. This fee doesn't actually go into the lender's pocket. The lender has to pay it out to have the credit check done (although that usually costs less than $20).

◆ **Appraisal fee.** Before a lender will approve a loan, the house will need to be appraised. The lender wants to protect itself and know that you are not paying too much for the house. The lender usually arranges the appraisal, but you may have to pay the fee. Expect to pay $250 or more. Again, the lender has to pay this fee to the appraiser. See the "Getting an Appraisal on the Home" section in Chapter 16 to learn more about appraisals. (You can request a copy of the appraisal for your records. This is also convenient if you want to obtain a home equity loan or a line of credit in the future.)

◆ **First payment.** When you close on a house, you need to pay for the part of the month that you will be living in the house. If you close on July 29, you have to pay for July 29, 30, and 31. You're then paid up for that month. Your next payment won't be until September 1; this payment will cover the month of August.

Real Deal _____

Sometimes you can ask your lender to pay all your closing costs and instead charge you points. This way, the fees are deductible in the first year you pay them. Check with your accountant as to what home purchase expenses are deductible and if there are any stipulations to doing this. For example, you can only write off the number of points that are "generally acceptable in your area." This means that you cannot pay 10 points instead of your down payment and try to write them all off, if only 2 points paid by lenders is most common in your area.

There are almost always additional fees when you get to the closing. Make sure you tell your mortgage officer that you want to be prepared; have them give you a Good Faith Estimate (see Chapter 21 for more information).

Coughing Up Advance and Reserve Payments

In addition to lender fees, you have to pay some other fees up front, including your insurance. You also have to set aside some money for your *escrow account.*

All lenders require that the home you purchase be insured. If your spouse sneaks a cigarette in the garage and burns the house down, the lender wants to be sure the damage is covered (more on insurance in Chapter 19). You usually have to pay insurance upfront and show a receipt and a one-year policy. You also will be required to place two months' worth of insurance payments into the escrow account.

Buyer Beware _____

You may also have to pay for flood insurance if you live in a flood zone, and having to do so can be quite a shock. First, many areas are designated as flood zones. Flood insurance is an assignment by the U.S. Corps of Engineers. Second, the designation is nearly impossible to change. Finally, you can purchase flood insurance only from the federal government; you can't shop around. You can, however, tweak your deductible to lower your payment. Ask your real estate agent.

Depending on where you live, you may also need other types of insurance, including earthquake insurance. See Chapter 19 for more information on insurance.

You may be required to place two to six months' worth of property taxes in an *escrow account* as well. If you opt not to do that, you must have 20 percent equity and pay a fee. In this case, you arrange for a tax service. Basically, you sign a contract, hiring a company to watch your taxes and make sure that you pay them. If you don't, the lender is alerted, pays the taxes, adds the amount to your mortgage, and may foreclose. The municipality (your local government) can also foreclose for delinquent taxes.

Property taxes are included as part of your monthly mortgage payment. Ask your agent to give you an estimate of taxes in the area in which you're looking. When you're considering a particular house, the listing should give you an exact amount for current taxes, but if you have any questions, you should check with the local tax assessor's office to be sure.

Real Estate Terms

An **escrow account** is established because the lender doesn't trust you to save the money to pay taxes and insurance when they come due. So the lender requires you to pay $\frac{1}{12}$ of your insurance and tax amount each month. This money is kept in an escrow account. When the tax and insurance bills come due, your lender pays them from this account.

If you are building a new home, your taxes might be based on the unimproved land. Until the taxes are reassessed with your home on the land, your payment might be significantly lower for up to the first couple years (depending on your area).

Paying Insurance on Your Mortgage

If you put down less than 20 percent for a down payment, you will probably be required to pay *private mortgage insurance* (*PMI*). This is also sometimes known as a *mortgage insurance premium* (*MIP*) if you have an FHA loan (more on that in Part 3). This insurance protects the lender in case you default on the loan. If you default on the loan, the banks try to recoup some of the expenses lost for having to resell the home by charging you a mortgage insurance payment each month. For some loans, you must pay this insurance fee up front. For other types of loans, you pay a monthly fee (sometimes in addition to the upfront fee) as part of your mortgage payment. Mortgage insurance can add around 0.25 to 0.75 percent to your interest rate. (The rates can vary depending on the loan-to-value, type of loan, and other

Real Deal

After you've lived in your home a few years and have built your equity, you can cancel your PMI and perhaps receive a refund. This is a little-advertised option and isn't done automatically when you qualify, so keep it in mind and check up on your mortgage insurance periodically to see whether you still need it (more on this in Chapter 19).

issues.) Chapter 19 discusses this type of insurance. For some loans, you may be able to finance the cost of mortgage insurance.

Still *More* Fees

I can hear the groan. Yes, there are a lot of costs for buying a home. There's simply no getting around it. In addition to the preceding, you may also be charged for other miscellaneous fees. If you have hired an attorney to handle the transaction, you will have an attorney fee. You should negotiate this fee with your attorney. Also, sometimes the lender charges you an attorney fee for its attorney, who ensures that local, state, and federal regulations are adhered to.

You'll pay an escrow fee ($200 to $350) to ensure that no outstanding liens, unpaid loans, or other claims exist against the property. This fee also goes toward closing on the home mortgage. This fee varies according to the price you paid for the house. Title insurance is required and guarantees the title search if any claims or discrepancies pop up. The cost of title insurance varies depending on the price of the house, but count on several hundred dollars. Usually the buyer pays a portion of it and the seller pays the balance.

You're also charged a fee for recording the sale with the proper county courthouse. Usually this fee is split by the buyer and seller, but this varies from state to state. You may also have to pay fees for an inspection and survey. The inspector will check for pests; roof damage; and problems with the plumbing, wiring, heating, water, structure, and more. Inspections are covered in Chapter 20. There may be other government fees, such as tax stamps, transfer taxes, and other fees due upon the sale. These fees vary by area.

Other fees that people sometimes forget about are the homeowners association fees that you might have to pay to live in a particular neighborhood, or perhaps you are purchasing a condominium and there is a monthly maintenance fee.

Real Deal

In addition, depending on what part of the country your home is in, you will most likely be charged a flood certification fee of around $20. This is insurance that compensates for physical property damage resulting from rising water. It is required for properties located in federally designated flood areas. You might be charged this fee even if you are nowhere near water—sometimes you are in a flood plain and you don't even realize it (it might have flooded back in 1905).

Adding Up All the Costs

The following table shows an example of what you might pay up front for buying a home. Keep in mind that each of these figures will vary—the sales price, the required down payment, the closing costs … everything. This table should give you a rough idea of what to expect. Some fees will appear on your estimate and some won't. Get the fees in writing from your mortgage lender, called a Good Faith Estimate (see Chapter 16 for more information).

Estimate of Up-Front Costs

Purchase price	$100,000
Interest rate	8 percent
Total amount financed	$95,000

Type of Fee	Amount	Description
Down payment	$5,000	5% of purchase price
Loan origination fee	$950	1% of loan amount
Points	$950	1 point or 1% of loan amount
Appraisal fee	$300	
Credit report	$60	
Insurance	$350	
Mortgage insurance	varies	
Insurance reserve	$58	2 months—$(350 \div 12) \times 2$
Tax reserve	$280	2 months at 140
Attorney fees	$300	
Escrow fees	$300	
Title policy	$300	
Processing/Underwriting	$350	
Document preparation	$150	
Recording fees	$20	
Survey	$125	
Tax Service	$75	
Flood certification	$20	
Total	$9,588	

The Least You Need to Know

- ◆ You will be required to make a down payment of 3 percent or more, depending on the type of financing you get.

- ◆ You will also have to pay closing costs, which can run from 3 to 6 percent or more of the sales price.

- ◆ Keep in mind that closing costs can be negotiable. You can ask the seller to pay some, or you can shop around for a lender that doesn't charge a lot of closing costs. For some loans, you can finance the closing costs.

Buying a Home with an Agent

In This Chapter

- Understanding the various types of agents
- Determining who pays the agent
- Learning how an agent can help
- Selecting an agent
- Working with "for sale by owner" homes

When you announce your desire to purchase a house, you may be surprised at the number of real estate people who want to represent you. Agents come out of the woodwork, calling you, sending you information, knocking on your door. It may seem like every other person you know turns out to be a real estate agent or knows an agent (maybe several). Your neighbor tells you, "I only work at Pizza Hut part-time. I'm actually a real estate agent." Your mother calls and tells you that the Senior Citizen Center has sponsored a real estate class and your grandmother now has her real estate license.

You won't have to worry too much about finding an agent—you do need to worry about finding a good one. Because this person is going to play an integral role in helping you buy a home, you want to first understand the types of agents to choose from and then select an agent whom you like to work with and who has the experience you need.

Understanding the Types of Agents

If you look at the terms used in the real estate business, you may think that you have wandered into the world of spies. There are agents and selling agents, brokers and associates, and finally Realtors—with a capital R! Understanding who does what in the process of buying a home can help you avoid any confusion.

Agents Defined

The person you will most likely deal with is the agent. This person handles the buying and selling of homes and may also be called a sales associate. An agent is always associated with a broker, sometimes as an employee but more often as an independent contractor. For example, Ray Lewis works at Dan Schwarz Realty Inc.; Dan Schwarz is the broker and Ray Lewis is one of the agents.

Remember that a broker can also be considered an agent, so to keep things straight, I'll use *broker* when I mean the principal broker (someone you are not likely to deal with) and *agent* for the person who will help you find your home.

The agent who puts the house on the market or lists the house is often called the *listing agent*. Your agent, the agent who shows the house and handles the buyer, is often called a *selling agent*. (You'll learn more about selling agents later in the "Using a Selling Agent" section.)

Buyer Beware

If you meet an agent at an open house and choose to be represented by that agent, make sure that the agent knows you want to be represented by a buyer's agent.

Brokers Defined

The principal broker is the big chief, the head honcho, the queen bee—the person licensed by the state to conduct a real estate business. All the other worker bees center around the principal broker. Having a broker's license means that the person can start and run a real estate office, but not all brokers do. Many brokers are agents and do both sales and management.

Sometimes the broker is associated with a franchise, such as Century 21. If you select a franchised broker, you have the advantage of national name recognition and usually a strong national advertising campaign. Keep in mind, though, how a franchise works. Each franchise is individually owned and operated. That means you aren't guaranteed a great agent just because you selected a well-known real estate franchise. You should select a firm based on that office's reputation—not the reputation of the national firm.

Realtors Defined

If an agent is an agent, then who is a Realtor? Are agents also Realtors? Why the capital *R?* What's the penalty for not capitalizing the *R?* Realtor is a trademark designation, hence the capitalization, and the penalty for not remembering to capitalize the *R* is death by beheading. Just kidding.

A Realtor is a broker or agent who belongs to the local or state Board of Realtors, which has an affiliation with the National Association of Realtors (NAR). These members follow a code of ethics beyond state license laws. More important, Realtors sponsor the *Multiple Listing System* (*MLS*), which is used to list houses for sale. You'll see more on this topic later in the "Is the Agent Working for You Or the Seller?" section as well as in Chapter 7.

New-Home Agents Defined

If you purchase a new home, the person selling the home (the builder or builder representative) may offer to be your broker and handle all the details of purchasing the home. (This is kind of like the fox guarding the henhouse.) You can use this person as your "agent," or you can be represented by a separate agent. For more information on the advantages of having an agent in a new home sale, see Chapter 11.

Is the Agent Working for You or the Seller?

In the past when you bought a home, everyone worked for the seller—the broker, the agent, the Realtor, the person showing you homes and working with you to find a home. All of these people represented the seller and were paid by the seller. This sometimes came as quite a shock to people buying a home.

The trend has changed, though, and now you can select how you're represented— with a selling agent, a dual agent, or a buyer's agent. Most likely you will use a buyer's agent.

Bet You Didn't Know

Real estate is one of the few professional fields that allow the agent to represent both sides in a deal. Many other professionals consider the dual representation of some agents (those that represent the seller, but aid the buyer) to be unethical. For instance, lawyers and accountants both are forbidden by their code of ethics to represent two opposing parties. Yes, the profession has changed with the addition of specific buyers agents to allay some of these concerns, but you still need to be careful. Is the profession likely to change? Nope. The practice is too profitable for the agents.

Using a Buyer's Agent

The real estate practice of agency has evolved, and now it is most common to find a different type of agent—a buyer's agent. This type of agent represents you, the buyer. The agent can make recommendations to you on what price and terms to offer. When buyers' agents negotiate a deal, they negotiate it with only your interests in mind. Anything you tell these agents is confidential; they will not pass the information along to the seller.

How a buyer's agent is paid depends on the agreement you reach with the agent. Most get a flat fee or a commission based on the purchase price. Some require a retainer that may or may not be applied to the total fee. Some require a minimum fee. Sometimes you pay the fee, and sometimes the seller pays the fee.

Real Deal _____

If you use a buyer's agent from a brokerage firm, be sure to ask how conflicts of interest are handled. Remember that the firm has both buyer's agents and selling agents. Also, check into the disclosure rules. Will the firm tell you whether it is a dual agency, meaning is it representing both parties?

If the agent is paid based on purchase price, you will want to inquire who pays this fee. Sometimes the buyer's agent can negotiate for the seller to pay the commission fee. Or the buyer's agent can help you negotiate a better purchase price, perhaps enough to cover the commission fee. The seller should be motivated to do this, because the seller will only have to pay the listing agent's commission. The listing agent will probably be amenable also, because the listing agent most likely will still get a commission.

If you have a buyer's agent who shows you a property listed by the same company, you have a *dual agency*. The buyer's agent should tell you when this occurs.

You will probably be asked to sign an exclusivity agreement that says you will work only with that agent for the time specified (usually 60 to 90 days). The two forms that follow are examples of the contract a buyer must sign when procuring a buyer's agent (buyer's agency selection form), and the contract the buyer and seller must sign granting permission for an agent to act as a dual agent (dual agency disclosure agreement).

BUYER'S AGENCY SELECTION FORM

(Disclosure of A. H. M. Graves Company, Inc.'s policy on broker cooperation, compensation, and conflict of interest.)

A. H. M. GRAVES COMPANY, INC. (Graves) offers assistance to

Paul & Paula Pierce (Buyer) in locating property to purchase with

either of the following types of representation:

(Where the word "seller" appears, it shall also mean "lessor," "landlord" etc., if applicable. "Sale" or "sold" shall also mean "lease" or "leased." "Buyer" shall mean "lessee." The obligation of the broker shall also apply to any associated salesperson.)

_____ **Sub-Agent**
Sub-Agents are brokers and salespersons who procure buyers for the Seller's property and represent the interest of the Seller. A Sub-Agent is compensated from the sales transaction by the Seller and receives a portion of the commission Seller pays to listing broker.

OR

__X__ **Buyer-Agent**
Buyer-Agents are brokers and salespersons who procure buyers for the Seller's property and who represent the interests of the Buyer. Representations which Buyer-Agents make about Seller's property are not made as the agent of the Seller. A Buyer-Agent is compensated from the sales transaction by the Seller and receives a portion of the commission Seller pays to listing broker. If Seller or Seller's listing broker elects to reduce compensation to Buyer's Agent, such reduction may limit the range of properties that Graves may show to Buyer.

BUYER CHOOSES TO HAVE GRAVES SERVE IN THE MANNER CHECK MARKED ABOVE.

Disclosure of Potential Dual Agency

Graves owes certain duties to Buyer when acting as Buyer's agent. Graves owes similar duties to a seller when acting as agent for the Seller under a Listing Contract. A Graves represented buyer may be interested in seeing a property listed by Graves. This situation creates a dual-agency and in such event Graves will have a potential conflict of interest. As such, Graves will not be able to represent both Seller and Buyer without the written consent of both parties. It is highly probable that Buyer will want to see a property listed by Graves. Buyer hereby consents to Graves acting as dual agent in such an event.

Paul Pierce _____   _Maris Bluester_ _____
Buyer   Date   Agent/Salesperson   Date

Paula Pierce _____
Buyer   Date

Form P-227A 8/2/93

An example of a buyer's agency selection form.

DUAL AGENCY DISCLOSURE AGREEMENT

1. This Dual Agency Disclosure Agreement ("Agreement") is entered into on *July 10*_____, 19*00*.

2. by and between *Graves Realtors*_____ ("Broker")

3. *Mr + Mrs Seller*_____ ("Seller"), *Bess Manager*_____ ("Listing Salesperson"),

4. *Mr + Mrs. Buyer*_____ ("Buyer"), and *Newer Agent*_____ ("Selling Salesperson").

5. A. The Broker has a Listing Contract with Seller dated *6/30/00*_____

6.   whereby the Broker is appointed as the Seller's Agent to sell real estate commonly known as_____

7. *8169 Ashwood Ct*_____ in *Indpls*_____,

8. Indiana, *46268*___ Zip Code.

9. B. The Broker also has a Buyer/Broker Contract with Buyer whereby Broker is appointed as the Buyer's Agent to
10.   assist in the purchase of real estate.

11. C. Seller wishes to sell said real estate to Buyer, and Buyer wishes to purchase Seller's real estate.

12. D. Seller and Buyer both wish to use the services of Broker who is a Dual Agent in this transaction.

13. E. Seller and Buyer understand that it can be unlawful for an agent to act as a Dual Agent, because (1) there is
14.   an inherent possibility of a conflict of interest and/or breach of a fiduciary duty which (2) might cause damage
15.   to a Seller or Buyer. A Dual Agent is not acting unlawfully if a Seller and Buyer agree that their agent can act
16.   as a Dual Agent, and represent them both in a transaction.

17. F. The Broker/Dual Agent wishes to disclose to Seller and Buyer the nature of an agent's position when serving
18.   two principals, so that Seller and Buyer can make an informed decision whether they want the Dual Agent to
19.   serve them both in the aforesaid transaction. Since the Broker has agency duties to both the Buyer and Seller,
20.   the Broker would represent both the Buyer and the Seller in the transaction only with consent.

21.   In this dual agency relationship, the Broker's fiduciary duty will be limited by not disclosing confidential
22.   information. Confidential information includes the possibility that the Seller will accept a price less than the
23.   listing price, that the Buyer will pay a price greater than the price offered, or any other information that could
24.   adversely affect either party's negotiating position. However, nothing would prevent the Broker from disclosing
25.   to the Buyer any known material facts about the real estate.

26. G. Seller and Buyer agree that Broker is hereby empowered to act as their Dual Agent in this real estate
27.   transaction; and that Seller and Buyer waive any claim they now have or may have in the future against
28.   Broker for acting as a Dual Agent in said transaction.

29.   This Agreement may be executed simultaneously or in two or more counterparts, each of which shall be
30.   deemed an original, but all of which together shall constitute one and the same instrument. Delivery of this
31.   document may be accomplished by electronic facsimile reproduction (FAX); if FAX delivery is utilized, the
32.   original document shall be promptly executed and/or delivered, if requested.

33. **SELLER**

34. *John Seller*_____ Dated:_____

35. *Irma Seller*_____ Dated:_____

36. **BUYER**

37. *Diane Brooks*_____ Dated:_____

38. *Tom Brooks*_____ Dated:_____

39. **DUAL AGENT**

40. *Bess Manager*_____ Dated:_____
41.   Listing Salesperson

42. *Newer Agent*_____ Dated:_____
43.   Selling Salesperson

44. Accepted by: *Graves Realtors*_____ Dated:_____
45.   REALTOR / BROKER

An example of a dual agency disclosure agreement.

Using a Selling Agent

In the past, most agents were selling agents with certain responsibilities to the seller. The agent must follow the seller's instructions (unless the instructions are illegal). The agent must be loyal to the seller and must work to get the highest selling price (which is also in the agent's interest, because this means a bigger commission).

The selling agent must not divulge any confidential seller information. The agent, for instance, cannot tell you that the sellers are desperate and that they are willing to accept a lower bid, unless doing so is in the sellers' best interest.

The selling agent cannot tell you what to offer for a particular house and cannot point out certain undisclosed defects of a house (unless they are hidden defects). However, the agent must pass along any information of interest that you might mention. For example, if you say that you're going to offer $90,000 for the house but are willing to go to $100,000, the selling agent can pass along this information to the seller.

In addition, the selling agent is paid by the seller. Here's how it works: When a house is put on the market, the seller agrees to pay a percent of the sales price to the agent(s) involved in selling the house. Six percent is common. So suppose that a house sells for $100,000. The commission on the house totals $6,000. That money is divided into two parts. The agent who listed the house gets part of the money. (The amount will vary—sometimes the agent gets only half the money and sometimes a certain percentage.) This agent splits that amount with his principal broker.

The agent who sells the house gets the other half and usually splits that commission with his principal broker. If the listing agent both lists and sells the house, the listing agent and his principal broker split the entire commission.

If you work with a selling agent to buy a house, you should not tell that agent how much you're willing to pay. Your agent must certainly know the price range you can afford, but don't tell the agent the highest you will pay for a property. Don't reveal any special terms you would consider offering the seller. Don't tell your selling agent anything you wouldn't want the seller to know.

Real Deal

If you are both listing your house and looking for a new house, the sales commission may be negotiable. Ask your agent. Agents may be willing to lower the commission if they both list and sell the house.

Using a Discount Broker

In recent years, another type of broker has emerged—the discount broker. When you use this type of agent, you get access to the MLS listings and do most of the legwork yourself. You can view the houses alone (although in some states this isn't allowed), draw up your own contract, arrange for financing, and so on. In exchange for this, you don't pay the entire commission.

You want to be sure to completely understand what you can do, what break you will get on the commission, and what extras the broker charges for. For instance, the broker may charge you for making calls, arranging showings, and so on.

Also, you may find agents in your area that offer flat rate fees for certain services such as drawing up an offer. If you are fairly knowledgeable about the homebuying process, you may consider doing most of the work yourself and hiring out only those parts that you are not comfortable doing (or are not allowed by law to do).

How Agents Can Help

Do you need an agent? Probably. The next sections explain some of the benefits you can expect from using an agent.

Agents Can Navigate Financial Steps

It would be great if by "financial help" I meant that the agent is willing to lend or, better yet, give you the money to buy the house. That would make using an agent worthwhile! Unfortunately, I mean a different kind of financial help. A real estate agent can help you financially in these ways:

- **Analyze your financial situation.** Your agent can help you answer these questions: How much home can I afford? How much down payment can I afford? What can I do to be in a better situation to afford a home? Chapter 2 explains all the details about prequalifying and getting preapproved for a loan. Your agent can navigate you through these processes.

- **Estimate the costs of home ownership.** In addition to analyzing your financial situation, your agent should be able to prepare you for the costs of owning a home (mortgage, taxes, insurance, and so on, all covered in Chapter 3). Also, the agent should be able to translate a mortgage amount into monthly payments. For example, if you purchase a $100,000 home, what (roughly) will your monthly payments be?

◆ **Educate you about the types of financing.** An agent should be knowledgeable not only about real estate but also about financing. He or she should be able to explain the different types of financing available as well as what might be appropriate for your situation. If the agent can't answer all your financial questions, he or she should be able to put you in touch with a mortgage officer who can.

Buyer Beware _____

If you are not comfortable with the homes your agent is showing you (perhaps they are not in your price range, or you feel as if the agent is not listening to what you like), be sure to speak up. Tell the agent you are not happy. Also, don't ever let an agent pressure you into considering a home that you don't really want. If you get really uncomfortable, you can always drop the agent. See the "Firing an Agent" section later in this chapter.

You can save a great deal of money by shopping around for a lender, so an agent can be critical in helping you select the "best" lender for your situation. Some agents can recommend a particular lender and tell you what to expect when you apply for a loan. Some agents may even go with you and help you through the loan application process. (Ours did.) Some may help you shop for a loan with the best terms.

Agents Can Help Find the Right House

In addition to financial assistance, the agent's key role is in helping you find a house. Using an agent has several advantages over just looking by yourself:

◆ An agent can help you define what type of house you want by asking you a lot of questions. How big of a house do you need? Do you plan to resell the house? What's your family and job situation? Do you have children? Plan to have children? Will you be transferred to another job? By being nosy, an agent can help you get a good idea of what you want.

◆ An agent has access to the Multiple Listing System (MLS), which lists detailed information about most homes for sale in your area. Without an agent, it may be difficult to get access to this information. (However, times are changing! The automation of listing systems will make MLS information more accessible to the general public. This topic is discussed in Chapter 8.)

◆ A good agent plays the role of matchmaker by listening to what you want and then helping you find the right house. An agent can search for houses within a particular area, within a particular price range, or with certain characteristics.

A good agent will keep up to date on the current listings and show you new properties as they are listed. Usually an agent has a jump on listings and knows when a house is coming on the market or when a house is listed. If you rely on traditional home-finding tactics, such as open houses or the real estate section of the newspaper, especially in a seller's market, you may not get to the house(s) fast enough.

♦ An agent knows information about the community or city. If you're moving to a new city, an agent will be extremely valuable. The agent can recommend certain areas; give you an estimate of taxes; and tell you about the local school system, community services, hospitals, police, and so on.

♦ An agent will arrange appointments for you to visit houses and will tour them with you. From the listing, the agent can tell you a lot about the house—age, lot size, square footage of the entire house as well as each room, listing price, and more. The agent also has the experience of looking at many, many homes and can help you evaluate the quality of the home compared to the price.

Real Deal

An agent can really be beneficial if you are relocating to another city. First, most homebuyers are relocating with a deadline—for instance, starting a new job. So an agent can help the buyer find a house quickly. Second, agents can provide a wealth of information about the new city. Some agents here in Indiana (and probably elsewhere) provide a packet of information about the city that includes Chamber of Commerce information, a list of public and private schools, local and national school rankings, utility information, public services, and entertainment. They also know about market value and lifestyles in the various neighborhoods. If your agent doesn't offer this information, ask. They can probably dig it up for you.

Agents Can Help Negotiate and Close the Deal

An agent can be especially helpful in making an offer and negotiating the deal. The agent will help you prepare the sales agreement that lists the critical terms of the sale—selling price, terms, contingencies, and so on. The agent will represent your offer favorably and will help you handle any counteroffers. Chapter 17 covers the details of making an offer.

The agent will be able to evaluate the property and has access to information about other similar properties. For instance, your agent can tell you the selling prices of other houses in the area. Often you can use this knowledge as a bargaining tool. Agents also will know about the resale value of homes, something to consider if this is your first house and you plan to trade up in the future.

Sellers take buyers represented by agents more seriously, because they realize the agent has probably already prequalified them. The seller doesn't have to be nervous about wasting time on a buyer who can't afford the home.

Even after the offer is accepted, the agent will help guide you through the rest of the process—getting the loan, having an inspection done, responding to any problems, and handling the closing. If any problems pop up during the process, your agent will help you through them.

Selecting a Good Agent

As with most sales jobs, the 80/20 rule applies to real estate. Twenty percent of the agents sell 80 percent of the homes. When you're selecting an agent, you want one of the 20 percent. You want someone with experience. This section helps you find an agent you can be comfortable with.

Finding an Agent

If you've ever gone to an *open house*, you know how quickly you're besieged with offers to help you find your dream house. The open house agent may follow you around the house, trying to become your agent. Sometimes the agent is more interested in soliciting clients than in showing you the house. You may easily find yourself hooked up with an agent when you had no intention whatsoever of doing so. It's better to put some thought into selecting an agent. Don't necessarily sign up with the first person who promises you your dream home.

Here are some strategies for finding a good agent:

- **Ask others for recommendations.** The best sources of recommendations are family, friends, and co-workers who have recently purchased houses. If someone worked with an agent and had a good experience, chances are the agent is pretty good.

- **Ask the broker for recommendations.** The broker should be knowledgeable about all of his or her agents. Ask the broker for the agent who has sold the most in the office. Ask the broker to recommend an agent familiar with the area and price range you want.

- **Check the agent's background as well as the firm he or she represents.** What is the reputation of the firm? Has the firm sold a lot of houses? Does the firm have a lot of agents? Is the support staff friendly? Ask for the agent's resumé. Finally, call some of the agent's references. Real-life experiences of a sale or purchase go way beyond the facts on a resume.

- **Check the agent's history.** How long has the agent been in business? How long has he or she been working full time selling real estate? (Some agents work only part-time.) How many properties has the agent listed? (The more, the better.) How many properties has he or she sold in the past few months? Be sure that the agent has access to the MLS listings.

- **Investigate problems.** Ask the local real estate board whether there have been any problems with the agent.

Another source for agent information is the Internet. You can search for agents from several sites. Some agents even have their own web pages.

Look for local real estate companies around the area you are interested in. Usually, they will advertise their web address if they have one. Also, you may find links or locators on general real estate pages. For example, the Prudential Real Estate page includes an agent locator that you can use to find an agent. The address for this site is www.prudential.com/realestate.

Putting an Agent to the Test

Once you select an agent, be sure you enjoy working with that person. You're going to find that the more comfortable you are with your agent, the more pleasant the whole home-buying process is. Take this agent-comfort test to be sure you're working with an agent you like.

Yes	No	
❏	❏	Is the agent easily accessible by fax, pager, cell phone, and so on? Does your agent return your calls? Is your agent pleasant and helpful when you call, or harried and annoyed?
❏	❏	Does the agent have time for you? Or does he or she rush you?
❏	❏	Is the agent somewhat organized? Does he or she provide information that is helpful such as detailed listing and home information for the homes you view?
❏	❏	Does your agent explain things so that you can understand? Does your agent welcome questions? Does the agent seem to have a good knowledge about the industry? Or are the answers you receive vague?

❏   ❏   Does your agent explain different financing options? Does the agent have information available for many lenders, or does he or she steer you to one lender only? You want an agent that has good relationships with many lenders.

❏   ❏   Does your agent explain the implications of contracts? You want an agent who first knows the answers and second can explain the answers so that you can understand. You don't want an agent who glosses over the answers, explains things so that you end up more confused, or tells you not to worry about the answers, because he or she will take care of it.

❏   ❏   Is your agent interested in your needs? You can gauge this by how well the homes you are shown match what you've told the agent.

❏   ❏   Does your agent listen to you? You want an agent who listens—not one who is just interested in making a sale. If you have stressed to the agent that you want a one-story house, but all he or she shows you are two-story houses, your agent may not be listening.

Real Deal

You definitely want an agent who listens, but you also want an agent who is creative and challenges you when necessary. An agent may help you see beyond the shag carpet and avocado appliances. You may find that you have narrowed your "dream home" description too much, and your agent may need to pry open the other possibilities that are available.

❏   ❏   Does the agent ask you personal questions about your financial situation? You may think the right answer is *no*, but the correct answer is *yes*. If you find your dream home and can't afford it, what good is it? An agent should first help you figure out what you can afford and then help you find houses within that range. If an agent doesn't first investigate your financial situation, you may find yourself in over your head.

❏   ❏   When the agent takes you to look at houses, do the houses seem to match what you're looking for?

❏   ❏   Does the agent know the area well? Some agents are more familiar with or even specialize in a certain area. You want an agent who knows the area in which you are looking—that is, he or she knows what houses have sold for in the area, the taxes, community, and so on.

❏   ❏   Does the agent show only houses listed with his or her firm? If so, you might inquire whether the agent gets an incentive when selling a house with his or her firm. You want an agent who isn't steering you to certain properties for his or her own benefit.

❏   ❏   Do you like the agent? It's an involved process, so it's best to select an agent that suits your personality. You may prefer someone with a sense of humor (a must for me). You may prefer someone that is no-nonsense. Because you will be sharing information and working together, you want someone that you respect and feel comfortable with.

Armed with these questions, you can find an agent to help you find your dream house.

Firing an Agent

Just because you selected one agent doesn't mean you're stuck with that person for the rest of your housebuying life. You might have signed up with an agent spontaneously and then realized this person isn't right for you. Maybe an agent is too busy? Or too pushy?

If you're uncomfortable with an agent, you should say so as soon as possible. You probably had to sign an exclusivity contract for 30 to 60 days, but if you make it apparent to the agent that he or she will be wasting time with you, you may be able to get out of the contract.

Be polite but firm. Tell the agent why the relationship isn't working out. Perhaps the agent isn't showing homes in your price range. Perhaps he or she doesn't know enough about the area you have targeted. Firing an agent doesn't have to be ugly if you stick to the reasons and provide feedback in a helpful way.

Working with "For Sale by Owner" Homes

When you're looking for a house, you may see a lot of "for sale by owner" homes, abbreviated FSBO and pronounced *fizz-bo*. In this case, the seller is *not* using an agent and has decided to sell the house directly to you.

Dealing with a FSBO can be tricky. You can decide to deal directly with the seller, or in some cases, you can persuade the seller to accept your agent. If you decide to deal directly, you will have to handle all the negotiations between you and the seller, and you will lack the experience of an agent in helping you write a good contract, get financing, negotiate, and close. Be careful. You need to be sure not to forget something critical. In fact, you should probably hire a lawyer to look over all the paperwork.

Real Deal

Chapter 23 is entirely dedicated to selling a FSBO home. It would be a good idea to read that chapter, because all the information will apply if you purchase a home from people selling their home themselves.

The seller should be prepared to help you with arranging financing and should handle the closing. The seller may also have a sales contract you can use. But can you trust the seller? If he's handily prepared a contract for you, are you sure he's not salivating and stifling a giggle as you sign your first-born child away? Look over the contract carefully. Consider using an agent, perhaps on a flat-fee price, to review the contract.

Also, be sure that you can handle the stress of dealing face-to-face with the seller. Sometimes you lose your leverage without a go-between. Face-to-face negotiating can be tough. (That's another benefit of using an agent. It's much easier for him or her to convey to the owner that the house smells like cats and you'd like to have the carpet replaced or deduct the cost for new carpeting from the sale.)

Finally, you have to know where your leverage is. For example, the seller, if he sells directly to you, is going to save 6 percent of the sales price. On a $100,000 home, that's $6,000. Who's getting that savings? If the seller wants to pocket the entire savings, what's your benefit? You should be able to negotiate a lower selling price. Or you may want to insist on using your agent and having the seller pay the 3 percent commission fee, or you could negotiate to have your agent do the paperwork for a flat fee. Ask your agent for an estimate.

The Least You Need to Know

♦ Most commonly, you will use a buyer's agent to represent you in your search for a house. This agent can assist you in every way a "regular" agent can but will have your best interests in mind, not the seller's.

♦ An agent can help you prepare financially to buy a house, has access to house listings, and can help you negotiate and close the deal.

◆ You want to select an agent who is active (sells and lists many homes) and knowledgeable, with whom you feel comfortable, and who listens to you.

◆ You shouldn't avoid FSBOs, but you should be prepared to handle some of the special situations they present, such as creating a sales contract and arranging financing.

Selecting a Mortgage Lender

In This Chapter

◆ Understanding the different types of lenders

◆ Finding a lender

◆ Asking a lender questions

◆ Comparing fixed-rate and adjustable-rate mortgage loans

I think a lot of buyers are so grateful that someone is willing to lend them the money to buy a home that they don't realize they need to shop around for a lender. Although a lender may make you feel differently, you are a customer. You're giving them your business, and as such, you should be sure to select the lender that offers you the best deal and best service. The mortgage process can make or break a transaction.

Purchasing a home can be exciting, or it can be a nightmare. The mortgage process determines which it will be. This chapter teaches you how to select a lender so that your homebuying experience will be a dream come true.

Types of Lenders and Why They Matter

Who has money to lend? Who will lend it to you? There are many sources of loans in the United States. It can get confusing when you apply for a loan, because you can be dealing with any number of types of lenders. Perhaps you have a mortgage broker who takes your paperwork but then submits it to another lender. Perhaps you use your local town bank and secure a loan from this source. Here are some common sources of loans:

- **Savings and loans.** S&Ls are responsible for more than half of all mortgage loans in the United States.

- **Commercial banks.** Though they make loans mostly for commercial ventures, in some cases, a commercial bank may lend money for real estate sales, especially in a small town where the bank knows whether the borrower is good for the loan.

Real Estate Terms

Originate means to process a loan, gathering all the paperwork. Once the paperwork is collected, it is sent to the underwriter, who decides whether to give the loan. To **underwrite** is the same as to approve.

- **Credit unions.** These are another good source of loans. Because of your affiliation and accounts with a credit union, you might have access to a loan with fewer fees and a lower interest rate. If you aren't already associated with a credit union, look into it.

- **Mortgage brokers.** Acting as a middleman, a mortgage broker takes your loan application, processes the papers, and then submits the loan to a lender, who *underwrites* and closes the loan.

- **Mortgage bankers.** Different from a broker, a mortgage banker both *originates* the loan directly and closes the loan.

- **Builders and developers.** Some builders and developers also provide loans. Doing so makes it easy to sell and finance the home in one process.

- **Government agencies.** Government agencies, such as the Federal Housing Administration (FHA) and Veterans' Administration (VA), don't actually give you a loan, but they do encourage loans that don't meet the conventional loan standards. Doing so makes you, as a potential borrower, more attractive to the lender.

Understanding the Secondary Loan Market

Most investors aren't interested in your $100,000 home mortgage. That's not enough for them to trifle with. But if you put several $100,000 loans together, that makes quite an attractive package. And that's what some lenders do. They combine several mortgages into a package, or bundle, and then sell the bundle to a secondary market. The secondary market is a group of investors who invest in mortgages. Banks, pension funds, and insurance companies, for example, often invest in mortgages.

If the lender where you apply for a loan plans to sell your loan on the secondary market, it will let you know. It doesn't mean too much to you as the borrower, just that you may be dealing with a different mortgage company at some time during the term of your loan. In some cases, the original lender continues to service the loan (sends you your payment books). In other cases, the new lender takes over servicing; you'll receive a letter telling you where to send new payments.

Uncle Sam Helps Out

The government has set up agencies specifically for buying mortgages. Some of these agencies are

- ◆ Fannie Mae (Federal National Mortgage Association)
- ◆ Freddie Mac (Federal Home Loan Mortgage Corporation)
- ◆ Ginnie Mae (Government National Mortgage Association)

Because the original lender is interested in selling the loan packages, and because Fannie Mae and the gang are avid purchasers, lenders follow the guidelines set out by the government agencies. This means that most lenders have the same limits on the amount they'll lend, and most check over your income using the same criteria—the criteria set forth by the government agency.

 Real Deal _____

You can get more information about Fannie Mae, Freddie Mac, and Ginnie Mae at their websites: www.fanniemae. com, www.freddiemac.com, and www.ginniemae.gov (note that this is a government extension).

Portfolio and Jumbo Loans

In some cases, the rules of Fannie Mae and crew can cause you problems. For instance, your loan amount may be beyond the limits set by these agencies. When this happens, you may have to find a different type of lender. You're shopping for a lender that provides a portfolio loan. Portfolio loans aren't structured to be sold to the secondary market, so they don't have to meet the requirements.

If the amount of money you want to borrow is beyond the limit of Fannie Mae, Freddie Mac, and/or Ginnie Mae, you need to find a lender that offers jumbo loans. A jumbo mortgage loan is larger than the limits set by Fannie Mae and Freddie Mac ($322,700 in the year 2003, and 50 percent higher than that in Alaska and Hawaii). A jumbo mortgage will carry a higher interest rate than a conventional mortgage, because greater risk is associated with the loan being paid back in full.

Where Can You Find a Lender?

Depending on the market, you may have to look hard to find a lender, or the lender may be calling you! In a down market where money is tight, a lender has many customers vying for loans. In this type of market, the lender doesn't have to chase the customer.

In an up market where money is moving, a lender is more aggressive in searching out clients. You might, for instance, get calls asking you if you want to refinance your house or offering to give you a home equity loan (refer to Chapter 15). These calls indicate that the lender is looking for customers.

No matter what the market, you can find lenders from several sources. Your real estate agent may recommend a lender or may be able to help you locate a lender. You can also ask friends and relatives to recommend a lender. Perhaps someone in your family or someone you work with has recently purchased a home. Ask these people what their experiences were with the lender.

Read the paper. Many lenders advertise their current lending rates. You can call and interview the lenders yourself. Later in this chapter, the section "Questions to Ask Lenders" will help you with this interview. The later section "Reviewing a Mortgage Advertisement" explains how to read an advertisement. Ads are often deceptive. The advertised rates may no longer be available when you call. Don't choose a lender solely based on advertised rates.

Check your local banks, savings and loans, and credit unions. They may offer real estate loans, and if they do, they probably have some free literature that explains the services they provide.

You can enlist the help of a mortgage search company. This type of company uses a computerized network to find the best loan opportunities in your area. The search company will take your financial information and match it with the available lending services. One firm, HSH Associates, will provide a survey of 20 to 50 lenders in the area for a fee of around $20.

Using Your Agent to Find a Lender

Since 1974, it has been illegal for a real estate broker to receive a kickback or finder's fee from referrals. If your agent sends you to a particular lender, you don't have to worry that the agent does so because he is receiving a payment for the referral.

Recently the Department of Housing and Urban Development (HUD) has allowed the rules to change. If an agent searches out potential lenders by a computerized database, the agent can charge for the service. Advocates insist that this service will provide the convenience of one-stop shopping for buyers.

Others don't agree. For example, the rule does not say how many lenders have to be included in the database and how much the agent can charge. Also, new HUD provisions allow a brokerage to pay agents who recommend loan companies or settlement companies owned by the brokerage. This means you could be charged a fee that is too high for a "service" that the agent is being paid to do anyway. Also, the recommended company might not be the one with the best deal.

Buyer Beware

If your agent offers to help you find a lender, be sure you understand what the agent gains from doing so. Some have always checked for loans and are doing so as a courtesy. If the agents are charging a fee, make sure you know that up front.

Reviewing a Mortgage Advertisement

You may find a large advertisement in the real estate section of the paper that lists mortgage companies as well as their interest rates (see the following table). To decode the ads, remember that a fixed-rate loan is interest plus points. In comparing adjustable-rate mortgages, you want to know the initial rate, true rate, adjustment intervals, caps, and points.

The ad will list the name of the mortgage company, the phone number, and maybe the address.

Sample Advertisement

Capitol Mortgage				1-800-555-0991
30 yr FIX	5.75	0/.5	5%	$0/325
15 yr FIX	5.25	0/0	5%	$0/325
3/1 yr ARM	3.65	0/.2	20%	$35/$325
5/1 yr ARM	4.625	1/0	20%	$35/$325
30 yr Jumbo	5.25	4/0	20%	$35/$325

The ad usually lists the term of the mortgage (30 or 15 year), the interest rate, the number of points (both the discount and origination points), the down payment required, and the credit report and the application fee. In the example, Capital Mortgage has a 30-year mortgage at 5.75 percent interest. This loan requires no discount points, but you must pay a .5 origination point. Five percent down is required. The credit report is free, and the application fee is $325.

You'll see variations of these loans (such as 30-year FHA or 15-year Jumbo). Part 4 of this book covers all the various types of finance options in complete detail. Here you just want to get an idea of how to review the available information.

Buyer Beware

If you fill out any personal information online, be careful. First, make sure that the site is secure. (Look for a closed lock or other security indicator in the status bar of your browser window.) Second, make sure you know what you are agreeing to. Are you required to use one of the lenders found by the site? Are there any fees associated with the loan search?

Using the Internet to Find a Lender

If you have an Internet connection, you can also visit and get information from many mortgage market websites. For instance, at Mortgage Market Information Services (www.interest.com), you can look up mortgage rates and search for lenders by state. You can also learn more about mortgages and read news about trends and market directions. Also, don't forget to visit the government loan sites such as Fannie Mae (www.fanniemae.com) for the latest rates and requirements for this type of loan.

You can also find sites such as LendingTree (www.lendingtree.com) or Select Lenders (www.selectlenders. com). Many of these sites allow you to apply online as well as provide you with several loan options that fit your circumstances.

In addition to these sites, try using a web search site such as Google, Yahoo!, or Excite to find other sites related to mortgages and home loans.

Real Deal

Many sites provide handy tools such as an online calculator. Use this tool to play around with the loan information (price, interest rate, number of payments, additional fees, and so on) and calculate monthly mortgage payments. By changing the rate or term, you can see how the loan type/rate affects your payment.

Questions to Ask Lenders

When you do your loan research, be prepared to interview the lenders. You'll need to find out what types of loans they offer, at what interest, and with what terms. Even if you let your agent shop for you, you may want to call lenders to be sure you are comfortable with them. You want a lender you can trust. You should be prepared to tell the lender the selling price of the home, the down payment you can afford, and any other financial information needed to give the lender a general idea of your situation.

Here are some questions to ask a potential lender or to find out by reading advertisements:

♦ What types of loans are offered? Fixed-rate and adjustable-rate? Other types? What payment schedules are offered? Does the lender offer, for instance, 15-year loans or biweekly payment schedules?

♦ What is the current interest rate for a 30-year, fixed-rate loan? For a one-year adjustable? Keep in mind that rates vary daily. When you're shopping for a home, you may want to keep your eye on the paper and watch the rates. When you're ready to apply for the loan, the rate for that day applies. You can lock in the rate or *float the rate* until closing. Also, you may want to tailor this question for the specific type of loan you're interested in. Most lenders have numerous loan packages to choose from.

♦ How many points are charged for a particular rate? If you pay one more point, how much does the interest rate decrease? If you pay one less point, how much does the rate increase? Points also fluctuate. Does the lender charge an origination fee? You can get a good idea of the points charged by calling the lender or by looking at advertisements. Again, the points you pay will depend on when you apply and which package you select.

Real Estate Terms

If a lender allows you to **float the rate,** it means that you can lock in the current interest rate on a mortgage for a specified period of time, and also "float" the interest rate down to a better rate if market conditions improve before closing. Most likely you will only be allowed to float the rate down one time during the specified timeframe.

◆ What application fees are charged? How much is the application fee? Credit report fee? Does the lender charge a loan origination fee? What nonstandard fees does the lender charge? These fees many be included in loan ads. Keep in mind that you can save some money by shopping around for a lender with good rates *and* reasonable fees.

◆ Does the loan require mortgage insurance? If so, how much does it cost? Can you finance the insurance? How long is the insurance required? If it is required only until a set time or until equity reaches a certain point, what is the process for dropping the insurance?

◆ Can you lock in the rates? If so, when are the rates locked—at application or approval? How long is the lock? Does the lock include both the interest rate and the points? Is there a charge for locking in a rate? If the rates drop and you're locked in at a higher rate, can you close at the lower rate?

◆ Can you prepay on a loan without prepayment penalties? What is the fee for late payments?

◆ What are the escrow requirements? How many months' worth of insurance must you prepay? How many months of property taxes do you have to prepay?

◆ What is the processing time for the loan? An average processing time is 21 to 60 days. If you're working under a set deadline, you might ask whether the loan can be closed by a certain date.

◆ If you have a problem or question, whom should you call? You don't want to select a lender based just on the best deal. You also want a lender that is service-oriented.

The bottom line is this: Most mortgage lenders have access to the same money and similar interest rates as other lenders. Where they differ is the loan package options as well as where fees are charged and how much they charge.

The Least You Need to Know

◆ Buyers can find many sources for loans, including savings and loans, credit unions, mortgage brokers, and mortgage bankers.

◆ Many lenders combine loans into a package and then sell the package to a secondary market (investors). Several government agencies were set up specifically to purchase home loans—Fannie Mae, Freddie Mac, and Ginnie Mae.

◆ You can find a lender by asking your real estate agent for a referral, by checking your local paper, by asking friends and family for recommendations, or by searching online.

◆ When shopping for a loan, ask the lender about the rate, points charged, and fees for processing the loan. You may also want to ask about the processing time as well as other factors, such as whether you can lock in the interest rate.

Part 2

Choosing the Home for You

Once you define a price range, you can start looking at homes until you find one that you like. You may fall in love with the first one, or you may look at home after home after home. Somewhere out there, though, you'll find the home for you.

It all depends on where you want to live, the type of community you want to be a part of, and the type of home you are looking for.

Chapter 6

Deciding Where You Want to Live

In This Chapter

- Determining your neighborhood needs
- Researching communities and neighborhoods
- Finding a new home community

An important aspect of any dream home is its location. That location describes the state, city, neighborhood, and possibly even the subdivision where you ideally would like to live.

As a buyer, you have many considerations for selecting a location, including your lifestyle (parents of school age children? empty nesters?) and your desires (convenient shopping? out in the country?). Consider this chapter your guide to cruising neighborhoods.

Where Do You Want to Live?

The three most important factors in buying a home are location, location, and location. This statement isn't very original, but it's true.

Suppose that you find a beautiful five-bedroom home with four baths, a three-car garage, a marble fireplace, and a huge kitchen—everything you could want. What is that home worth? If you picture it in an idyllic neighborhood, the home is worth a lot. Now imagine that same home smack dab next to a garbage dump or in the middle of a high-crime area. What's it worth now? Get the picture?

Buyer Beware

When you move to a new area, sometimes it's a good idea to try to live in an apartment or rental home first to get used to the community, traffic patterns, and all the little things that you take for granted when you know a place.

Your decision regarding what area or areas you'd like to live in will be influenced by your lifestyle. For example, a retired couple, a single parent, a newlywed couple, a large family, and a single adult shopping for a home will have entirely different sets of needs. But whether you're moving downtown, to the suburbs, or to a medium-size or small town, you have lots of options for finding a distinctive community that meets your needs. The following sections discuss the issues you'll want to consider when exploring communities and neighborhoods.

Home to Stay, or Home to Resell?

How long do you plan to stay in the home? I know this is a tough question. If it's your first home, you might be thinking that you could live there forever. Chances are, however, that you won't. (Most people stay in a home no longer than seven years.)

Real Deal

If your primary consideration is resale value, look for a community that is about to have a growth spurt—one where the resale value of the home is likely to go up. You can spot promising growth by looking for the construction of new homes, new roads, new community services, and new businesses.

If you know that you'll eventually be moving, you should consider the resale value of the home as you look at houses.

On the other hand, if you're shopping for a home that you plan to live in for a long, long time, you want to first be sure that it will accommodate you for that long, long time. In this case, you may not be as concerned about what the house would sell for if you put it back on the market.

What Is Your Job Situation?

If you're planning to stay in the same job at the same location, consider how long a drive it will be from your new house to work. What's the maximum commute time you find acceptable? While the commute may not seem like a big deal initially, over time you may regret living so far from your place of work. Do you have access to public transportation if you need it? Is it easy to access the interstate? The location of your workplace may narrow your location choices for your home.

If you're not planning to stay at the same job and location, you need to think about another set of considerations. How will purchasing a home affect your job situation? If you may be transferred soon, will you be able to resell the house quickly? Will you be able to make a profit or at least break even if you have to sell the house? If not, you may consider renting.

Also consider your income potential. Will your income go up? Down? Stay the same? Your income not only affects the price of homes you can afford but also may be a consideration in the type of loan you apply for. For instance, if you know your income is likely to rise, you might consider getting an adjustable-rate mortgage to have a lower interest rate at the start. Then if your mortgage payments go up, you shouldn't be in a bind since your income should also be increasing.

What Are Your Family's Needs?

Don't forget to take your family's needs into consideration. Do you have children? Do you plan to have children? If so, you'll want to be sure you have a house large enough to accommodate them. Think not only about right now, but the future. That adorable eight-year-old is going to be a teenager before you know it. Is the floor plan suitable for a teenager? Where will the kids park once they get that coveted/dreaded driver's license?

If you have children, you will also want to consider the location of nearby parks or playgrounds. If your children are older, they'll probably be leaving the nest soon. Once they do, will your housing needs be the same? And what about your parents? You may want to live close to them or even have them move in with you.

Take into consideration your pets as well. If you have a dog, for instance, is the yard fenced or will you have to add this? Does the pet have enough room to play? Are there parks nearby, perhaps even a dog park? Pets live in the home, also! Consider all possibilities and be sure you feel you can accommodate these possibilities with your new house.

What Are the Schools Like?

Investigating the school district will be important if you have children. And even if you don't have children, living in a good district can increase the resale value of your home. Here are some strategies for making sure the schools make the grade:

◆ Figure out which school district you would like to be in and which schools are available in that district. You can then look for homes within those school districts. Are there private as well as public schools in the area? Find out how the children get to school. Do they walk? Ride a bus?

Real Deal _____

Check into the standardized testing scores for the schools and see how your school placed overall. Look at a few years' worth of information to see whether the rates are on the rise, consistent, or falling.

◆ Visit the schools. Examine curriculum, class load, and school policies. Talk to the principals and the teachers. Ask a lot of questions. What is the average class size? How do students rate on the standardized tests? How many students graduate? How many go on to college? What is the per-pupil expenditure? What extracurricular activities are supported?

◆ Talk to other parents in the area. How involved are they? What do the parents like and dislike about the school? What is the general reputation of the school? You might want to attend a parent-teacher meeting, if possible.

Bet You Didn't Know

You can get a detailed report on a particular school district by visiting www.theschoolreport.com. You can view a list of available schools in an area, as well as statistical information such as the grades, the number of students, and so on. You can also access a detailed report that lists SAT scores, percentage of graduates going to college from a particular high school, and other awards and achievements.

You can also access this site as well as view crime information with the Relocation Crime Lab at www.homefair.com.

If you have preschool age children, don't forget to look into daycare facilities in the area.

What Are the Taxes?

Your agent or the homeowners should provide you with the general taxes for the area. The amount of the taxes will have an effect on what you pay each month. The lender will also consider the tax amount in determining what you can afford to pay each month. Chapter 3, as you may recall, covered all of the up-front costs including tax payments that are required for purchasing a home.

Find out when taxes are reassessed. In some places, taxes are reassessed every so many years. If you're due for a reassessment, there's a good chance that the taxes will be raised. In other places, taxes are reassessed when a property is sold. In this case, you might have to come up with more money for the closing as well as for the taxes.

What About Emergencies?

Unless you like the sound of screaming sirens, you probably don't want to live right next door to a hospital. But you will want to know where the closest medical facility is and make sure it's up to your standards. While you're at it, find out where the nearest fire and police stations are.

Once you find the police station, drop in and ask about crime statistics in the area. You can also get a good sense of local crime by reading the "Police Blotter" section of the local paper—while it won't provide you with comprehensive statistics, it will give you a good idea of what kind of crimes are typical for that area. Vandalism and public intoxication are certainly less troubling than burglary, assault, and murder!

Buyer Beware _____

Investigate any new plans for the community, especially if you don't want to finance the new school gymnasium or end up living next to a Taco Bell. Find out what improvements are planned, how will they be financed, and if there are any zoning changes coming up. Check local papers or neighborhood associations.

Real Deal _____

Think also about the medical needs of your family. You will want to find a doctor, dentist, and possibly veterinarian to serve your family's needs.

What About Driving?

Look at the traffic pattern in the community. If you have small children, you may not want to live on a busy street. What are the speed limits and safety precautions in the area? If you have to commute, you'll want a quick, reliable route to your place of work.

Think also of your parking needs. Do you park in a garage? Driveway? On the street? What about parking at the grocery? Shopping? Workplace? Are the parking and garage facilities adequate?

What About Fun?

In addition to looking into the public services provided in a community, you may also want to see what recreational facilities are available. For example …

- Does the community have a local library?

- Is there a swimming pool nearby? Some communities have free public pools in the neighborhood. Others may require you to join a country club. Check into the various facilities and their associated fees.

- Are there public golf courses? Private golf courses? If you are an avid golfer, again, you may consider a country club.

- Are there public tennis courts? Private tennis courts?

- Does the area have well-kept parks? If you have pets, does the neighborhood have places to walk and play with the pet? If you enjoy running, is there some-place in your neighborhood or close by where you can run?

- Are the facilities easy to get to? Are they overcrowded?

- What about malls, grocery stores, bars, and restaurants? If you are single, these may be the most important factors you consider.

- Is the neighborhood technologically up-to-date? For instance, can you get Internet, cable, or other broadband connection? This is important if you work from your home. Also, look into other entertainment features such as digital cable or satellite TV.

Think about what you like to do and then be sure you will have the means to do it.

Sources of Community and Neighborhood Information

A neighborhood is more than the sum of its parts. So while the information on schools, parks, crime, taxes, and traffic you gathered in the previous sections will tell you a lot about the neighborhood, you'll also want to take some time to get a more general feel for the community.

Checking Out the Community

The local paper and residents are the best sources of information about a community. When looking at various communities, consider the following sources of information:

- Subscribe to a local newspaper and review the articles and advertisements. What types of stories are covered? What is the attitude of the paper? What about Letters to the Editor? What are the views of the community leaders? Finding out this information can help you decide whether you will feel comfortable in a particular community.

- Review the classified ads to get a sense of the homes for sale and rent as well as the job market for a particular area.

- Visit local stores, libraries, and community centers. Are the stores prosperous? Inviting? Are the people pleasant?

- Talk to local residents. Do the residents work in the area, or do they commute to another location? What do they like about the community? What do they dislike? How long have they lived in the area? The community is really a reflection of its residents, so the more you know about the residents, the better sense you will get of the community.

- Check with the Chamber of Commerce and other associations. You may be able to find information about population and income trends. For instance, you can check with the Homebuilders Association to find out which areas of the town have seen the most growth.

In addition, you can visit the www. chamberofcommerce.com website and find all types of information on relocating to a specific city.

Ask Your Agent

In addition to community resources, ask your agent about various areas. Your agent should be able to give you information about particular communities—statistics about home sales, crime rates, schools, taxes, and more.

> **CAUTION**
>
> **Buyer Beware**
>
> Agents have to be careful when characterizing a neighborhood. Steering you to a particular neighborhood based on the buyer's race, color, religion, country of origin, age, or sex is discriminatory and against the law. If you think you have encountered discrimination, see Appendix B for the U.S. Department of Housing and Urban Development customer service hotline.

Doing Your Own Neighborhood Assessment

In addition to collecting information, drive around the neighborhood and consider the following questions:

- Are there a lot of homes for sale in the neighborhood? A lot of homes for sale could be a good sign—a hot market. Or it could be a bad sign—people trying to get out.

- Are the homes well maintained, or are they in need of repair?

- Does the neighborhood have access to public transportation? For instance, is it near a bus stop, train station, or park-and-ride stop?

◆ Can you characterize the lifestyle of the neighborhood? If so, do you fit in? If you have kids, for instance, you may want to select a neighborhood with other young families. Are there a lot of swing sets or bicycles? If you're swinging single, you may want to find a neighborhood where the singles swing.

◆ Do you see any problems in the neighborhood? Look for any negative aspects of the neighborhood—heavy traffic, graffiti, unkempt houses, pollution. Drive through a neighborhood at night, as well as during the day; you may see a dramatic difference in activity.

Finding New Home Communities

In addition to targeting a few communities and neighborhoods, you should also consider whether you want to purchase an existing home or build a new home. (Chapter 7 covers the key factors when comparing a new home vs. an existing home.) Or you may purchase a condo, co-op, or townhouse (this topic is covered in Chapter 10).

Bet You Didn't Know

If you decide that you want to live in a planned community, you usually pay a homeowner association (HOA) fee each month as long as you own your home. The fees can be anywhere from $25 to $250 and up (and they can increase), depending on the location, neighborhood, and amount of common areas.

Keep in mind that your decision will also help you narrow your choice of neighborhoods. If you want a new home, for instance, you need to find a neighborhood where new homes are being built.

If you want to purchase a new home, you most likely will look into one of the planned communities in your city. Planned communities are like little neighborhoods within a city; they are designed to accommodate a large number of newly built homes and maintain the areas that surround the neighborhood. For example, most planned communities have multiple new-home builders who all have homes available.

CAUTION

Buyer Beware _____

Homebuyers in planned communities often complain about the set of rules enforced by the homeowners association. You may need to get permission to add certain features to your property, such as a greenhouse or swimming pool. You may be limited in the type of fence you can add or the color you can paint your house. When shopping for a new home community, think about any changes you plan to make and check out the homeowners association rules *beforehand*.

Often, homeowners living within planned communities share certain areas. For example, homeowners in that community may share a park, green belt, community center, playground, coded entry gate, or even things like basic cable or homes wired with fiber-optic networks. Find out which areas are shared. If possible, tour them or ask to see the plans.

Also check out how improvements are handled. Usually, the individual homeowners in an area meet and decide on improvements that need to be made. For example, if the nearby park starts to look run-down or the basketball goal is broken, the association pays for the repair and maintenance of these types of common areas. Ask about this process.

New planned communities often have model homes available. You can visit these model homes, walk through each of them, obtain floor plans, and see what upgrades are available. (You can read more on this in Chapter 11.)

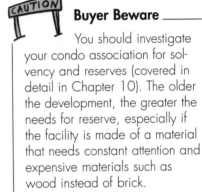

Buyer Beware

You should investigate your condo association for solvency and reserves (covered in detail in Chapter 10). The older the development, the greater the needs for reserve, especially if the facility is made of a material that needs constant attention and expensive materials such as wood instead of brick.

The Least You Need to Know

- Think about what your lifestyle is like now and what it will be like in the future when considering a neighborhood.

- Factors such as whether you may be transferred to another job or whether you plan to have children will affect your housing decisions.

- Find out what the taxes are and what the schools are like.

- For sources of information, check out local publications, the police station, residents, and businesses. Also, ask your agent.

- Do your own tour of the neighborhood, noting the upkeep and lifestyle choices of its residents.

- If you're considering buying a new home, look into planned communities, which are designed to accommodate a large number of newly built homes and to maintain shared areas and services for the homeowners.

Chapter **7**

Defining Your Dream Home

In This Chapter

◆ Selecting a home style

◆ Comparing new homes vs. existing homes

◆ Considering the interior of the home

◆ Considering the exterior of the home

◆ Creating your dream home wish list

When you shop for anything, it's good to have a rough idea of what you want to buy. If you went out to buy a car but had no idea what type of car you wanted, you could spend weeks or even months making a decision. Sports car? Van? Jeep? Luxury car? Station wagon? Truck? Minivan? Or maybe a motorcycle?

It's the same way with buying a home. Before you start shopping, you should think about what you need and what you want in your home.

Rule #1: Keep an Open Mind

This chapter should give you an idea of what elements to consider when you're searching for a home. You shouldn't, though, use this chapter to narrow your home-hunting to a specific home—a split-level red brick home with four bedrooms, two baths (one with a hot tub), country kitchen with pot rack and blue-flowered wallpaper, dining room with chair rail, marble fireplace, entertainment room, two-car garage, asphalt driveway, swimming pool, and a yard with a privacy fence. If you do this, you may not find a home in your price range that matches exactly, and you could miss other homes that you may have liked better.

Instead, use this chapter to picture what you ideally would like. Try to keep in mind that you're probably going to have to compromise. What features are essential? What are extras?

Also, if you are planning to purchase the home with another person, it is a good idea to get "on the same page" with that person. Try to decide what is important to both of you and make a list on paper. Perhaps one person really wants a large yard, but the other person doesn't care one way or the other. Or perhaps one person really hates the kitchen being at the front of the home.

Real Deal

A good agent (one who listens to what you need and what you want) might recommend looking at homes that vary from your specifications. Be willing to consider some of these homes. One of them could turn out to be your dream home!

Finally, rank the items on your list as to matter of importance to you both and be realistic about things that you can and can't live without. Rarely do two people like all the same things that one home has to offer.

When you go out looking at homes, do so with an open mind. Consider what you like and don't like about the home and compare how well it matches up to what you absolutely must have in a home.

What Style of Home Suits You?

You'll find many styles of homes available—from a Cape Cod with a white picket fence to a ranch. You may prefer a certain style, but more commonly you look at the other issues that are part and parcel of the style. For instance, the style of the house may not matter as long as it is one story. Or you may not care whether the home is a Greek Revival or a Colonial as long as it is made of brick. This section describes the key elements that help you define your ideal house style.

Real Deal

You can find information about purchasing a condo, co-op, or other home type in Chapter 10. For information on buying a new home, see Chapter 11.

How Many Stories?

When you look at homes, you will find many different styles: one-story, two-story, three-story, split-level, ranch, and so on and so on. What you want and like is up to you. For example, if you're a retired person, you may want a one-story home so that you don't have to worry about going up and down steps. If you have children, you may want a two-story home so that you can send the kids upstairs and you can hide out downstairs. Or you may want the children on the same level as you. You will have to weigh privacy vs. safety.

What Is the House Made Of?

Another element that defines the style of the home is what the home is made of. Is it a wood frame home? A combination brick and frame? Aluminum siding? Stucco? Hay? Sticks? Brick?

Again, selecting what you want will depend on what you like and how much maintenance you want to do. Also consider the cost of maintenance. Frame homes will require painting; brick homes do not. However, sometimes brick homes need to be "repointed" (fixing the bricks), which can be expensive. Price will also be a factor. For example, a brick home may cost more than a similar frame home.

As long as the home has been well maintained, you shouldn't have too many worries. You should inquire about the maintenance and keep in mind what you will have to do to keep up the exterior.

Existing Home vs. New Home

When you're shopping for homes, you will want to decide whether you want an existing home or a new home. You may also want to consider purchasing a condominium, townhouse, duplex, co-op, patio/garden home, or a mobile home (all of which are covered in Chapter 11).

This section discusses the benefits and drawbacks of a new home compared to an existing home. This information gives you a rationale for your choice, but often the decision is based on personal preference. Some people *love* new homes; some people hate them. Some people prefer older neighborhoods; some don't.

The Benefits of an Existing Home (or the Drawbacks of a New Home)

According to a recent publication of the *Fannie Mae Guide to Homeownership*, 8 out of 10 homebuyers purchase an existing home rather than a new home. There are many good reasons to purchase an existing home.

Most existing homes are in an established neighborhood, usually closer to the city. You can expect to find trees and sometimes larger yards. Also, the yard may already be landscaped.

An older home tends to have more personality. In a new subdivision, you may see several different home styles, but the homes may all look alike. (This will vary depending on the subdivision and the type of new homes.) In an older neighborhood, the style and size of the homes will differ. You might have a colonial brick home next to a frame Cape Cod next to a ranch.

The older home may also have nice amenities, such as hardwood floors or built-in cabinets, which may be costly to include in a new home.

You'll usually find that the ceilings are higher and the rooms may be bigger than in a new home. Also, the home may have a basement, which can greatly add to the size of the house. Consider also that the price of adding a basement to a new home can run anywhere from $15,000 to $65,000 and up.

The Drawbacks of an Existing Home (or the Benefits of a New Home)

You should also consider some negative factors when buying an existing home. Newer homes usually have a better traffic flow and provide a better use of space. As one example, think closets. Either women back when existing homes were built didn't have as many shoes as they do now, or they had no say in the design of the home, because most older homes have little tiny closets that will hold about three pairs of pants, three shirts, one coat, and three pairs of shoes. And that's for both you and your spouse. You may also find that the bathrooms are small or too few.

As the home gets older, it is going to require more maintenance. You may need to paint the home, fix the plumbing, rewire, and more. That is, unless the seller has done some major maintenance work, like replacing the roof, furnace, air conditioning, and so on. In a new home, all these features are brand new and the home will likely also include all new appliances.

Real Deal

Getting a good inspection (covered in Chapter 20) on an existing home can help you be sure you aren't getting a home that will become a money pit. If repair work does need to be done, an inspection will inform you ahead of time.

You usually can select specific options in a new home. You might be able to select the wall color, the floor type, the cabinets, the hardware, and so on. With these options, you get just what you want from the start and don't need to think about remodeling or repairs as quickly as you might with an existing home.

Touring the Interior of the House

So far you should have thought about how long you want to live in the home, who's going to live in the home with you, where you want to live, and what type of home you want. Finally, it's time to think about the home itself. This section covers the key indoor features to review and think about.

Casing the Kitchen

The most important area of the home is probably the kitchen. Everybody has to eat. If you like to cook or entertain, you may want to put a big kitchen on the top of your "have-to-have list." (I don't know what it is about a kitchen, but at parties, people are drawn to it. Maybe the appliances are magnetized or something.)

If you have children, you may also want to have an eat-in kitchen where Junior can throw his Spaghetti-Os as far and as often as he wants without ruining the dining room carpet and table.

In addition to a kitchen, you may want a dining room. (Sometimes the kitchen is both.) The size and style of the dining room will depend on what you like. Do you want a more formal dining room area, or do you want an eat-in kitchen that opens to the great room?

Touring the Bedrooms

What's the first thing you want to do after eating a big meal? Take a nap. The number and size of bedrooms is next on the list of things to consider in a home. Bedrooms are for more than just sleeping. They can provide office space, storage space, hobby rooms, whatever. How many bedrooms do you want? How big do you want them? I've been in a "four-bedroom" home where the fourth bedroom was so small you'd have to sleep standing up.

When you consider the number of bedrooms, remember your family situation. Do you have children? Will you have children? Will you have more children? Will you need to take in a parent sometime down the road? Do you have guests frequently?

Testing the Bathrooms

The "big three" for home selection are kitchen, bedrooms, and bathrooms. The more bathrooms, the better! You will want to decide on the minimum number of bathrooms you need. One? (Good luck!) One and a half? Be sure the half is big enough for at least one person. Sometimes people convert a closet into a bathroom. If you can barely fit four outfits in the closet, how do you expect to fit a 5-foot, 11-inch person? Two? Two is the recommended minimum. Three or more? You're living like royalty.

Looking at the Family/Living/Great Rooms

You eat, you sleep, and you go to the bathroom. What else do you do in your home? You will want to be sure you have an area in which to relax, entertain, work, work out, and so on.

Most homes have a living room. Sometimes this is a formal room where no one actually does any living and the furniture is covered with plastic. It looks good, but no one is actually allowed in the living room. Sometimes the living room is a living/family room where you watch TV, entertain, and lie on the couch.

Some homes have both a living room and a family room or a combination living/family or living/dining room. The family room may be called different names—great room, rec room, or den. The family room may be used for watching TV, or it may be used as an office. (Sometimes a spare bedroom is converted into a home office.) You will want to consider the number and size of the living rooms you need.

Do You Need a Home Office?

If you work from home or bring work home with you, you may want to purchase a home that includes room for a home office. This may be an actual office, a library, a converted bedroom, or a basement area. If you require a home office, make sure you not only have someplace to hang your diploma(s), but also check the cable and electrical access in the room. We converted our back porch into an office, and while I enjoy the view, I can't change the layout of the furniture because only one wall has electrical outlets.

> **Bet You Didn't Know**
>
> According to a 2002 survey by the National Association of Home Builders, 44 percent of those surveyed have set aside a separate room for a home office.

What About Storage? Attics and Basements

When you're thinking about your home, think about where you're going to put all your stuff. Do you need a basement? Basements can add up to 50 percent more room to a two-story home and almost 100 percent more room to a ranch home (unless you only have a half basement). The basement can serve as a storage area, a place to put your washer and dryer, or a place to stick your teenager until he outgrows puberty. Many people move only because they lack a basement. And a basement can add to the resale value of the home.

As for attics, most homes have them, but what you need to determine is if you can realistically store things in them. If the attic only has a tiny opening accessible from the garage ceiling, you might consider doing the following:

- Installing an attic cover that unfolds a stairway leading upward when you open it.

- Placing plywood boards over the rafters to provide a storage area.

- Checking the attic ventilation to see if items you are storing in the attic get to 100°F and up and –30°F or colder.

- Installing an attic light if there isn't one already there for HVAC (home ventilation and air conditioning) repair.

If a home has a completely separate attic that you access through an upstairs room, it most likely has a lot of storage space, unless Junior wants to convert the room into a workout area.

What About More Storage? Closets

A hundred years ago, most people had only a set of work clothes and a set of church clothes, so closets were understandably small. Nowadays, we all have so many clothes and things that our closets are overflowing and we want bigger ones—and more of them! When we talk about closets, we also are referring to storage closets—you know, the kind in the hallway or outside the main bathroom that will allow you to store linens and boxes of old stuff.

Look at all of the closets in the house. Picture where you will place all of your storage items. If there's not room, you might need to add storage space, get rid of stuff, or lease a storage unit.

Real Deal _____

If you are looking at a two-story home, check to see if it has a storage closet under the stairs. These are great places to store items that you rarely use or use only once a year (Christmas trees and so on). If a home you are looking at doesn't have a closet under the stairs, and you think the home is short on storage space, check with an inspector to see if the space under the stairs can be converted into a closet.

Still Need Storage? Garages

When you think of a garage, you probably think of a structure with a garage door. Well, homes can have any of the following:

- A single-car garage attached to a condominium, townhouse, duplex, co-op, patio/garden home, or mobile home unit

- A multiple-car garage attached to a home

♦ A carport open to the elements attached to a home

♦ A completely separate structure located away from the home

♦ No garage at all

People also have garages built for their mobile homes, golf carts, boats, jet skis, and automobiles they work on and repair.

Garages are usually a bonus with most homes—the more, the better. Depending on the age of the home, a garage might be considered "finished" or "unfinished." An unfinished garage (like an unfinished basement) is not painted, nor does it usually have much insulation or built-in shelving. Consider all these things when purchasing a home, because the after-the-fact costs of adding a garage will be expensive.

Inspecting the Exterior of the House

By now, you should have a good idea of what the inside of the home should look like. Now let's take a walk around the outside of the home. What's important to you here? Consider these questions:

♦ Do you want a little yard, big yard, no yard? I've been in homes with no back-yards, with the backyard on the side of the home, and with a backyard as big as a football field.

♦ Does the home have a nice view? A good view can provide you and your family with many years of pleasure, as well as increase the value of the home.

> **Bet You Didn't Know**
>
> Many homeowners associations don't allow you to have items in your backyard that show above a standard fence line. It would be "too annoying" to other residents. Keep this and similar neighborhood covenants and restrictions in mind when you are considering a home. Think about what types of things you might want in your backyard and make sure your community will accommodate them.

♦ Is the yard fenced in? Do you need a fence to keep Xie, your 110-pound Doberman, in the yard? Do you need one to keep your kids in the yard? Do you want a fence just for decoration, such as a split-rail fence, or for privacy, such as a 10-foot fence around your swimming pool? Can you add a fence? Is it against local zoning laws, neighborhood covenants, or ordinances?

♦ Is there room for the kids to play? Will there be room for their swing set, tree house, and ump-teen bicycles and scooters?

♦ Do you like to garden? If so, is there room for one? Is the terrain right for a garden? Is it too rocky? Too sloped?

♦ Where will you park? On the street? In a driveway? In a garage? How big is the garage? Can you use the garage to store all the stuff that won't fit in your basement—bicycles, sports equipment, yard and gardening tools?

♦ Does the home have a driveway? Is the driveway gravel? Paved? Does it need to be paved? Is it flat or on a hill? Think about driving down or up the driveway after an ice storm. Can you add a basketball hoop?

And the Home Faces ...

Does your home face north, south, east, or west? This is an interesting consideration if you are worried about high heating and cooling bills or warming up a swimming pool. For example, if your home has most of its bedrooms and the family room at the back of the home, you might want to be wary of a home where the back part gets the long afternoon sun (an east/west facing home). Or perhaps the swimming pool you want to add will only get sun early in the morning and then be shaded by the home the rest of the afternoon (a north/south facing home), meaning a cold pool.

These considerations aren't as dramatic with a new home, because most are built with dual-pane windows, high-level *SEER* rated heating and cooling systems, and new and improved insulation.

Heating and Cooling Systems

You will also want to think about heating and cooling.

You may prefer a certain kind of heating system. For instance, is it important to you whether the home has gas or electric heat, radiators or steam? Are the systems in good working order? (An inspection can also help determine the state of current systems.) What do the utility bills run? You can ask the home seller to show you various utility bills to check out the usual cost of running that system. If you are building a new home, the builders should have a general idea of what the heating and cooling bills will be.

As another consideration, think about how the home is cooled. Do you want air conditioning? Central air or wall units? If the home doesn't have central air, how expensive would it be to add it? Or in this case, can you rely on window air conditioners to cool the home?

Real Estate Terms

The **SEER**, or **Seasonal Energy Efficiency Ratio**, rating is similar to miles per gallon in the automotive industry. The SEER gives an indication of the performance efficiency of the system. The higher the SEER, the more efficient the unit. And, the more efficient the unit, the lower the operating costs (utility bills).

Look also at the water heating system. How many gallons does the water heater hold? Is it in good shape, or does it need to be replaced?

The Home's Landscaping

What is the current state of the home's landscaping? Does the home have a nice lawn and trees, or do trees need to be cut down and the lawn resodded? What about flowers?

Real Deal

Another consideration about a home is whether the water is city water or well water. Also, is the water very hard? If so, you might need to consider a water softener. In addition, who picks up the trash in the neighborhood? Do they recycle? What days do you put out the garbage? Will the homeowners association fine you if you leave your garbage containers on the street too long?

Think also about any future plans you have. Do you want to add a garden? If so, do you have a place for the garden?

Finally, keep in mind that some neighborhoods have rules over the changes you can make to the outside of the home. For example:

♦ Do you have to have grass in the front yard?

♦ Are there certain types of trees that you cannot grow?

♦ Do you need to keep all external buildings (sheds, for example) looking exactly like your home?

♦ Do you have to put up a fence?

It is better to know before you purchase the home and get fined by your homeowners association for having a birdfeeder in your front yard. Yes, homeowners associations will warn and sometimes fine you for "breaking the rules."

Extra Goodies Like a Pool

Consider any amenities that you would like the home to have:

♦ Does the home have a deck? Can you build one?

♦ How about a hot tub? Swimming pool? Tennis court?

♦ Do you want a fireplace? Are there burning regulations in your town?

♦ Hardwood floors? All over the home, or only in parts?

♦ Built-in cabinets? Whitewashed or natural wood?

♦ Prewired security system? Stereo system?

If the home doesn't have these items, can you add them? Are there any restrictions or rules that govern these additions?

In addition to thinking about what you want, also think about what you don't want. Remember that some of the things you hate can be changed. Just because you hate the living room wallpaper doesn't mean you shouldn't buy a home that you otherwise like. On the other hand, it is usually not wise to buy a three-bedroom home when you need a four-bedroom, thinking it will be easy to "knock this wall out and add another room right here." Be sure to consider the difficulty and expense of the changes you'll want to make.

Bet You Didn't Know

If you are thinking about buying a historic home, note that the city may have ordinances for what you can and cannot fix/alter on your own home. For example, if you have ever watched the television program *This Old House*, you probably already know that historic districts can require you to get numerous permits to alter, repair, or simply paint a historic district home. On the one hand, this is good because the city is trying to maintain a particular classic look and feel. They don't want you to come in, tear the home down, and put up an A-frame. On the other hand, it is your home, and it can be quite annoying when you cannot do what you want to it. You will have to decide what is important to you—the historic value or the creative freedom.

Summing Up Your Dream House Wish List

Use the following checklist to help you define what you do and don't want in your dream home.

Checklist

Style of Home

❏ One story	❏ Ranch	❏ Doesn't matter
❏ Two story	❏ Split level	❏ Other

Construction

❏ Wood frame	❏ Brick and frame	❏ Doesn't matter
❏ Brick	❏ Concrete, brick	❏ Other
❏ Stone	❏ Vinyl/aluminum siding	

Type of Kitchen

❑ Eat-in   ❑ Country   ❑ Doesn't matter
❑ Pantry   ❑ Gourmet   ❑ Center island

Number of Bedrooms

❑ 1   ❑ 3   ❑ 5 or more
❑ 2   ❑ 4   ❑ Doesn't matter

Number of Bathrooms

❑ 1   ❑ 1 ½   ❑ 3
❑ 2 ½   ❑ 3   ❑ Doesn't matter

Features	Really Need	Really Want	Would Trade	Definitely Don't Want
Living room	❑	❑	❑	❑
Great room	❑	❑	❑	❑
Dining room	❑	❑	❑	❑
Family room	❑	❑	❑	❑
Basement	❑	❑	❑	❑
Finished basement	❑	❑	❑	❑
Workout room	❑	❑	❑	❑
Office	❑	❑	❑	❑
Screened porch	❑	❑	❑	❑
Big closets	❑	❑	❑	❑
Fireplace	❑	❑	❑	❑
Central air	❑	❑	❑	❑
Built-in cabinets	❑	❑	❑	❑
Big yard	❑	❑	❑	❑
Room for a garden	❑	❑	❑	❑
Garage	❑	❑	❑	❑
Paved driveway	❑	❑	❑	❑
Deck	❑	❑	❑	❑
Swimming pool	❑	❑	❑	❑
Hot tub	❑	❑	❑	❑
Other	❑	❑	❑	❑

The worst decision you can make is to buy a home and think you will just make do until something better is available. It takes time and money to move, and you may end up stuck in that home for longer than you think. Be sure you are happy with the home.

The Least You Need to Know

- Have a general idea of the type of home you want and a specific list of features you like. But be willing to consider other home styles and types.

- Buying an existing home usually means a more established neighborhood and unique home design. On the downside, expect to have less closet space and higher maintenance costs.

- The three most important types of rooms to consider when looking at a home's interior are the kitchen, bedrooms, and bathrooms.

- Don't focus only on the interior of a home. Make sure you consider the outside of the home for utility bills, landscaping, and potential future additions and repairs.

Chapter 8

How to Find Your New Home

In This Chapter

◆ Deciding the best time to buy a home

◆ Using several sources for finding homes

◆ Understanding the Multiple Listing System (MLS)

◆ Searching the Internet for online home listings

For Sale signs are like wildflowers: They pop up all over the place every spring. You can almost hear them as you drive through the neighborhoods in your city—*pop, pop, pop.*

Why do a lot of homes go on the market in the spring? Is that the best time to shop? Find out the answers to these questions and more right here in this chapter.

When Is the Best Time to Buy a Home?

Finding the right home is a lot like dating. The first one could be your dream home. Or you could have to go through a lot of duds before you find your princely estate. The entire process of looking, making an offer, financing, and moving can take anywhere from a couple of days to over a year. Simply realizing that finding a home may take some time will help ease the pressure. Relax and enjoy yourself! Otherwise, you may end up frustrated, tired, and unmotivated.

One factor to consider when looking for a home is the general state of the real estate market. Is it a buyer's market (lots of homes at good prices) or a seller's market (few homes for sale and selling at a higher price)? Another factor to consider is seasonal high and low sales periods. You can get a sense of how to best time your home purchase in this section.

Real Deal

If you're selling your home, you should probably put it on the market before you start looking for your next home. If you find a home you want, the seller might not take you seriously if your home is not already on the market or sold.

If you find a new home before you sell yours, you may lose it to a buyer who can close immediately. On the other hand, if you sell your home before you find a home and the buyers want to move in right away, you'll have to arrange for temporary housing. It's nice to sell your current home and buy your new home at the same time so that you can move directly from your old home to your new home, but in reality the sell/buy decision is a balancing act.

Buyer's Market vs. Seller's Market

Depending on the economy, you may find yourself in a buyer's market (the buyers get the best deals) or a seller's market (the sellers get the upper hand). Sometimes you'll find yourself somewhere in between.

In a buyer's market, there are a lot of homes on the market, and they may take a while to sell. To sell a home, the seller might need to offer a really good price, plus additional incentives, such as help with financing. If you're buying a home in this type of market, you can take your time looking and can usually strike a pretty good deal.

In a seller's market, homes aren't on the market for long. In fact, they may sell before they are even listed. Because the market is so strong, many owners will decide to sell their homes themselves; you'll see a lot of "for sale by owner" homes in this type of market. If you're selling a home in this market, you're lucky. You'll probably get many good offers and not need to offer any additional incentives. If you're buying a home in this market, you may have to work hard to find a home that you like and can make an offer on before it is sold (see "Finding a Home," later in this chapter).

To have the best chance of getting your offer accepted, you should be financially ready (preapproved). Also, don't expect to submit and have accepted a contract with a lot of contingencies. You may find yourself in a bidding war and have to pay more than the seller is asking.

Real Deal

When planning a move, keep in mind the time it takes to do so and how that will mesh with your life. You may want to try to time the move with your children's school schedules. You may want to avoid moving during the holidays. Think about the best and worst scenarios of a move and try to plan accordingly.

What determines the market type? Factors that affect the general economy—inflation rate, interest rates, unemployment statistics, and stock market activity. For instance, in the opening months of 2000, the home market was strong because of low interest rates. A record 67.8 percent of Americans owned their homes in 2002.

Keep in mind that general economic aspects affect sales, but each community is different. Some popular communities may always give the edge to the seller. For instance, in Indianapolis, homes in the popular Meridian-Kessler area usually sell quickly and at a higher price than comparable homes in other areas. People are willing to pay extra to live in this neighborhood.

Another determining factor is the availability of homes in that area. Think about the economic truth of supply and demand. If the area has lots of homes for sale, you usually have more bargaining power. Fewer houses for sale may mean higher prices.

Seasonal Sales

If you chart the sales of homes for the months of January to December, you will probably find that the sales follow the traditional bell pattern. Sales are slow at the start and end (January and December) and peak in the middle (May and June).

If you think about these seasonal peaks, you will see they make sense. Most people don't want to move or be bothered with moving around the holidays (November to January), so there may not be a lot of homes on the market during this time. Plus, homes don't look as appealing in the dreary days of winter. The trees are bare and the skies are dark.

If you're looking for a bargain, consider shopping during the down time. You may find that homes on the market in this season have to be sold. Otherwise, why wouldn't the sellers wait for a better time?

After January 1, sales pick up. People are thinking about New Year's resolutions, getting cabin fever, and may be thinking of a change. Also, homes look nice in the spring, and it's easy to work on repairs at this time. So you'll see lots of folks out on ladders and lots of homes for sale from March through April. The peak of homebuying occurs somewhere around May and June—that's a good time to move if you have children in school, but it also may be the worst time to buy. You have a good selection, but the market moves fast.

Sales tend to drop off at the end of the summer—again, children are heading back to school, and parents may not want to uproot them. Also, it's hot! You may see an increase in sales during September and October, but once the holidays arrive, sales drop.

If you have the luxury of shopping when you want, you may be able to use these sale seasons to your advantage.

Finding a Home

Now that you have a better idea of where you want to live (covered in Chapter 6) and are pretty sure about the type of home you want (covered in Chapter 7), how do you find the right home? There are many ways, as the following section describes.

Drive Through Neighborhoods

As you take a look at the community and neighborhoods you like, you should keep your eyes open for homes for sale. Most homes on the market include a For Sale sign in the yard. You can watch for these signs as you search for the neighborhood you want. Jot down the address and listing Realtor of any homes that catch your eye. Some sites may even have brochures that you can pick up, a phone number with a prerecorded message, or even a radio station that you can tune to for more information on that particular home. Some may enable you to take a virtual tour of the home via the Internet. In addition to Realtor-listed homes, write down the numbers of any "for sale by owner" properties.

Read the Local Papers

You can also find homes by reading the local paper, which probably has a section advertising homes for sale. Because many sellers hold open houses on Saturdays and Sundays, either the Saturday or Sunday paper usually has an entire section devoted to real estate.

You can read through the paper and mark homes that sound interesting. If you're just starting to look, you may want to visit a few open houses in the area in which you think you want to live. The following figure shows how cryptic some ads can be. The following table will help you decipher the codes.

Power/Baseline 3BR+den, 2BA, RV gate, no HOA, CNR LT, GR, MBR down, 3CG, Owner will carry $152K 6935 E. Mille Ave, Open Sat/Sun 10-5

A typical ad in a local newspaper.

The first few times you read an advertisement for a home, you may think you're playing a round of Wheel of Fortune. What happened to all the vowels? Pretty soon you'll recognize the terms and abbreviations used.

Abbreviation	What It Means
BA	Bath
BR	Bedroom
MBR	Master bedroom (perhaps listing "up" or "down," if two-story)
LR	Living room
DR	Dining room
GR	Great room
FR	Family room
CA or C/A	Central air
2CG	Two-car garage
BSMT	Basement
HOA	Homeowners association
CNR LT	Corner lot
FP or FRPLC	Fireplace

If you're searching for a bargain, look for words such as *reduced* or *motivated sellers*. These terms may indicate the home has been on the market for a while. Ask your agent to find out how long the home has been listed. This information can help you find homes that may be ripe for purchase. Also, ask your agent if the price has been lowered during the time the home has been on the market.

Words and phrases such as *fixer-upper*, *TLC needed*, *handyman special*, and *needs updating* should clue you in to the fact that the home isn't in the best condition. If you're looking for a fixer-upper, then watch for these phrases. If you don't want to worry about repairs and redecorating, look for homes described as being in *move-in condition*. Chapter 10 has a section on special home types, including fixer-uppers.

Read the MLS Listings

Ninety-five percent of all homes on the market are listed with an agent. When a home is listed with an agent, information about the home is entered into a computer system known as the Multiple Listing System or MLS (see the following figure of a sample MLS listing).

```
                                                07/11/00 17:02:58
                        #:408295 RES Active    LP:    $109,900
                          8169 N  ASHWOOD CT
                        Town:INDIANAPOLIS      Area:49 02              Section A
                        Township:PIKE TOWNSHIP  Zip:46268
                        Lg :CROOKED CREEK          L131      S3
                        Map: N-81   W-30
                        ------------------------------------------
                                 L F W              L F W    Sq Ft
                        LR:15x14 M C N  2B:12x10 U C N 3:       0
                        GR:             3B:12x10 U C N 1:       0
                        DR:12x10 M C N  4B:10x13 U C N 2:       0
                        KT:13x10 M V N  5B:          B:         0
                        BK:             LU:06x05 M V N
Bath-M:.5    U:2    L:0    Bd: 4 FB: 2 FR:19x12 M C N  BR:
LS:103X175         YB:0       HB: 1 MB:13x13 U C N                     Section B
Tax ID:6012377                     School:PIKE TWP    Approx SqFt:    0
Mngmnt Company:                    Completion Date:      Status:R
1M :        0    Taxes :  666 SW:N Assumption:N  Appr:N
1P :        0    Tax Yr:1999       Assumption Fee :    0 EQ:  $109,900
Yrs: 0           Tax Ex:N          Assumption Rate: 0.00
2nd:N            Mandatory Fee:   0/
------------------------------------------------------------------
Dir:86TH AND MICHIGAN WEST TO PAYNE ROAD-SOUTH TO OIL CREEK-WEST TO ASHWOOD DR
    RIGHT TO ASHWOOD CT.
Rem:WOODED CUL-DE-SAC SETTING FOR FOUR BEDROOM-2 STORY-FRESHLY PAINTED-NEW      Section C
    CARPET AND HOT WATER HEATER-MOVE RIGHT IN-GREAT LOCATION-NEAR 86TH STREET
    SHOPPING!!!!!

--------------------------------------------------------------------
  STYLE -Traditionl   LVL/RM-2 LEVEL    LVL/RM-Eight Rms  EXTERI-Brick
  EXTERI-Sid-Alumin   BATHS -2.5 Baths  AREAS -Covrd Prch AREAS -Laundry Rm
  AREAS -Family Rm    AREAS -Sml Entry  DINING-Sep. Room  DINING-Dining L
  DINING-Etin Ktchn   DINING-Pantry     EQUIPM-Rng/Ov Ele EQUIPM-Refrigratr
  EQUIPM-Dishwasher   EQUIPM-Disposal   EQUIPM-Rng Hd Fan REQ DI-Defects-NN
  INTR A-Metl Wndow   INTR A-Scrn Compl INTR A-Strm Compl INTR A-Wlkin Clst     Section D
  INTR A-MBR Suite    FIREPL-No Frplace WTER H-Electric   HEATIN-Heat Pump
  COOLIN-Cntrl-Elec   BASEME-Slab       GARAGE-Attach 2   GARAGE-G Door Opn
  LOT IN-Wooded       LOT IN-Mature Tre LOT IN-Cul-de-Sac LOT IN-<.5 ACRE
  UTILIT-Mun Wtr Cn   UTILIT-Mun Swr Cn XTERIO-Sidewalks  XTERIO-Concrte Dr
  EXTRAS-No Extras    SCHOOL-Pike TWP   PRES F-NotApplica PSSBLE-Conv/Icon
  POSSES-At Closing   FEE IN-NotApplica MISC. -Take Photo
--------------------------------------------------------------------
251     BLUESTEIN, MARIS    AP:846-7870 2P:290-7870 SAC:3.5   VRC:N LD:03/29/94
GRAV08 A.H.M. GRAVES CO., REALTORS   OP:844-9941 BAC:3.5   TYP:ER XD:09/30/94   Section E
        *** Information deemed reliable, but not guaranteed.***
```

A sample MLS listing.

Your agent will use the MLS listing to tell you key aspects about the home. The agent will understand the format, abbreviations, and information included. Basically, the MLS listing includes the address and listing price as well as the township. The listing also includes information about the types and sizes of the rooms in the house. You can also find out the tax information and school district. The MLS listing may also include a description of the property.

If you're working with an agent, the agent should be able to provide you with lists of homes in a particular price range and in a particular area. Most likely your agent will pull several listings from the system and take you by the homes. If you're interested in a home, the agent will set up an appointment to tour it.

Most often the agent will want to accompany you—even when you're just driving by the homes. Sometimes you can convince the agent to give you the listings so that you can drive by yourself. Keep in mind that when you take the agent with you, she can get a good idea of what you like and what you don't like and better tailor your home search to find a match.

Ask Around

In a seller's market, homes may sell even before they are listed in the computer system. In this type of market, you may have to be more aggressive in finding a home. The best time to purchase a home is before it is put on the market—when the seller is thinking about selling. If you can catch the seller at this critical point, you may be able to negotiate a good deal. The seller will avoid the hassle of putting the home on the market, and you will get the home you want.

To find homes about to be put on the market, tell family, friends, co-workers, and acquaintances that you're looking. Any one of these people may know of a home about to be sold. For instance, your friend Pam might know that your mutual friend Steve is getting a divorce and will be selling his home soon. Your mother might know that cousin Billy is about to be transferred to Akron, Ohio, and will be putting his home on the market.

 **Real Deal**

You can get the best deal when the seller is highly motivated to sell—for instance, in special situations such as transfers, divorce, and so on. You can't come right out and ask these questions, but be on the lookout for certain clues. One neighbor in our area put up a Divorce is Final sign in her yard!

Shop Auctions and Foreclosures

If you're really on a hunt for a bargain, you may want to actively search for an "as-is" or foreclosed property. Usually this type of home is sold directly by the lender. Look for advertisements in the paper. Or call some local lenders and ask whether they handle foreclosed properties, and if so, how you can get information about the homes. Foreclosure notices are also posted in the county courthouse.

Real Estate Terms

A **lien** is a legal hold or claim from one person on the property of another. The lien placed by a first mortgage is special; it is called the first lien and takes precedence over others.

If you're thinking about buying this type of property, you will want to be sure to do a title search. Find out before you close if any back taxes are due or if there are any *liens* against the property.

Foreclosed properties may not have been well maintained; therefore, be sure to have a careful, professional inspection done so that you know about any problems or costly repairs that are needed.

When you're at an auction, be sure that you understand the rules. You may be required to have a certified check ready for the deposit, and you will most likely need to be prequalified for a loan. Your bidding card may include information about the maximum financing for which you're qualified. Also be sure you understand when the sale is final. Some auctions take the highest bid—no matter what. Other auctions have a minimum bid. Some auctions require for the sale to be confirmed by the seller before it is final.

Be careful not to overbid. Do your homework and decide on the market value for the home as well as how high you will bid. If you get into a bidding war, stop at your maximum price. Otherwise, you may end up paying far more for the home than you intended.

Search Online Home Listings

In addition to the traditional means of finding a house, the Internet has opened up a whole new arena for finding homes. You can view homes for sale online, sometimes even taking a virtual tour of the home. All from your desk! This method is especially handy if you are relocating to another city.

You can find many nationwide as well as local home listing sites. Look for advertisements in the real estate section or on For Sale signs. Read stories about the local real estate market and note any popular brokerages; most of the brokerages have websites.

You can also search for home sites using any of the many Internet search tools, including google.com, yahoo.com, altavista.com, and others. In addition to these, here are the addresses of just a few of the nationwide listing sites you might want to try:

- **The National Association of Realtors (NAR)** site. www.realtor.com. This site lists more than 2 million homes for sale. You can also search for a Realtor and get home-buying advice from this site.

◆ **Yahoo! Real Estate.** list.realestate.yahoo.com. Similar to the NAR site, you can enter search criteria as well as get information on other related real estate topics.

◆ **HomeGain.** www.homegain.com. Narrow your search by selecting a state and then an area. You can also get tips and troubleshooting advice from this site.

◆ **HomeSeekers.** www.homeseekers.com. Search for homes as well as get market reports for a particular area at HomeSeekers.com.

◆ **Cyberhomes.** www.cyberhomes.com. An online research service for homebuyers and sellers that provides access to listings of residential real estate for sale on the Multiple Listing System.

◆ **International Real Estate Directory.** www.ired.com. This site calls itself "the source for independent real estate information." While you cannot find home listings, you can use the links to get detailed information on all aspects of the real estate industry.

Real Deal ⎯⎯⎯

Many of these sites provide access to other handy home-buying tools. You may be able to research neighborhoods, for instance, or calculate mortgage payments. You may be able to get information about the real estate market. Keep these sites in mind for both general and specific home-buying information.

◆ **Homebuilder.com.** www.homebuilder. com. This site helps you find new homes, manufactured homes, and custom homes, as well as provides resources for learning about financing and mortgages.

The Least You Need to Know

◆ To buy a home, you need to go through four steps: find the home, have an offer accepted, finance the purchase, and close. There's no set time limit for these steps—it varies widely.

◆ In a buyer's market, there are a lot of homes on the market, and they may take a while to sell.

◆ In a seller's market, homes aren't on the market for long. In fact, they may sell before they are even listed.

◆ If you're searching for a bargain in the newspaper ads, look for words such as *reduced* or *motivated sellers*. These terms may indicate that the home has been on the market for a while and the seller is willing to negotiate.

◆ You can find homes on the market through your agent, by reading the local paper, by driving through neighborhoods you like, by word of mouth, and by searching online listings.

Chapter 9

Buying an Existing Home

In This Chapter

- ◆ Knowing what to expect when touring homes
- ◆ Comparing the home to your list of needs (and wants!)
- ◆ Making sure the house is well-maintained and the neighborhood is acceptable
- ◆ Using a summary checklist to remember homes

If you have done your homework and gotten prequalified (or even preapproved), hired an agent, and made a list of the requirements for your new home, you have all the tools you need to find *and* evaluate potential homes.

When you're looking, how can you keep all the homes straight? What are you looking at in each of these homes? This chapter gives you some strategies for taking a good, thorough look at a house, using your needs as the scale to measure the home and check the neighborhood.

While not all of the information in this chapter will pertain to you if you are considering a condominium or other type of home, you can use this chapter as a guide for evaluating the property. You can also find additional issues for this type of home in the next chapter.

How the Home Tour(s) Work

Your agent will do her best to match your needs to houses currently on the market. The agent may drive you by some homes and then set up appointments for the ones you find appealing. Or she may set up appointments for houses she thinks you will like. You could have several appointments in one evening or day. When scheduling appointments, your agent should take into consideration your schedule as well as the style and location of your "dream" home.

When you tour a home, the agent will accompany you. (The homeowners may or may not be in the house.) The agent will also provide you with an information sheet that tells you the age of the house, its square footage, size of rooms, property taxes, utility bills, and so on. The information sheet may also include a picture. (You can see an example of an MLS listing in Chapter 8. The information sheet may be the same as this listing.)

Bet You Didn't Know

It's a good idea to view just a few houses at a time. If you view 10 or more, the homes will quickly become a blur. Pick a nickname for the house you want to remember. Maybe it's the "baby blue," the "cat house," the "new baby home." If you have a video camera, take it along and videotape the home. Be sure to get permission to do so first.

If you have any questions about the home, ask your agent. If the agent does not know, he or she can usually find out. For instance, you might ask when the roof was replaced or what type of plumbing is in the house.

As you tour the house, you may want to jot down notes to yourself. You can use the checklist at the end of this chapter to record your impressions of the house. Or you may want to jot down notes on the information sheet. If you're moving from another town and cannot easily return, you may want to take a camera and snap pictures or sketch floor plans.

Real Deal

You may think that there's just one home that is perfect for you, but there are probably several. Keep your perspective. If a deal doesn't go through on that perfect home, rest assured that you will find another one that you will like just as well or even better!

As another strategy for keeping track of homes, pick one house that is the house to beat—the best house you have seen so far—and forget all the others. As you view a new home, compare it to the top-runner. If the home doesn't hold up, forget about it. If you compare a house and it is better, forget about the first one.

After you look at several houses, you may find that there's one you want to return to. You can set up an appointment to see a house a second time.

How Does the Home Measure Up?

While touring the house, use your checklist of "must haves." Also, ask yourself some common sense questions such as "Do you like the house? Can you imagine living *happily* in the house?" The rest of this chapter gives you some suggestions on what to look for as you tour.

Do You Like the House?

If everyone had the same tastes, all the homes on your street would look the same. Instead, all homes are different, and each person has different likes and dislikes. The first thing you have to decide about a house is if you like it.

Sometimes you will have an immediate reaction to a house. It just *feels* right. "This is my house," you may think. Sometimes you may take a while to warm up to the house. As you go through it, you may hear a little voice saying "Yeah, yeah." Other times you will immediately hate a house.

Why the intense emotions? Because your home is a reflection of you. Some houses will fit, some won't. There's no way to predict any individual's reaction. You just have to gauge yours.

Does the House Have Everything You Need?

After noting the emotional appeal of the house, you need to check out what the house has and what it lacks. Walk through each of the rooms and compare the features to the "dream-home wish list" you created in Chapter 7. Keep in mind that you're going to have to be flexible and compromise on some features. You may decide the house doesn't have to be one level if you find a two-story house with a kitchen that's ideal.

When evaluating the home, here are some questions to consider:

◆ Does the house have enough bedrooms to accommodate your family now? Don't forget to also think about five years from now. Imagine how your family needs might change. Also, if needed, can you add on?

◆ Does the house have enough bathrooms? Are the bathrooms big enough? Can you add a bathroom? If so, what would be the cost to add or upgrade?

◆ Is the kitchen adequate for your needs? Is there enough counter space? Cupboard space? Are the range and refrigerator included in the sale of the home? If so, are they in good condition? Does the kitchen have a dishwasher? Is it included? All built-in appliances are usually included; others are negotiable.

◆ Does the house have enough living space in which to watch TV? Relax? Can the living space be adapted to meet your needs in the next five years? For instance, if you're planning to have a child, will there be room for the child to play?

Real Deal

Not all homes will advertise a "home office," so if this room type is not listed, don't despair. Look for homes with a finished basement or a bonus room. As another alternative, you can convert one of the bedrooms into an office. If the home has both a family room and a living room, the living room might work as an office or study/library.

◆ Does the home have an office or room that you can convert to an office? As more people work from home either part-time or all the time, the importance of an office may be key. Be sure to also ensure the room has the proper electrical and other hookups (such as cable) for your office.

◆ Does the house have enough storage space? Check the attic, basement, garage, and closets. Are they clean? Accessible? Protected from extreme temperatures? Like Goldilocks, you don't want the storage space—for instance, the attic—to be too cold or too hot.

◆ Are the yard and landscaping acceptable? Is the lawn overgrown or bare? Will it require work? Do you care how the lawn looks? Do your neighbors care? Remember that some communities have restrictions about the outside features of a home.

◆ Does the home have the amenities that you want? Hardwood floors? Built-in cabinets? Fireplace? Deck? Patio? Pool? If not, can you add them? Again, consider not only whether the property will allow for the addition but also check into any neighborhood covenants or restrictions.

◆ What personal property is included with the house? The washer? Dryer? Dishwasher? If these items are included, are they in good shape? If they aren't included, keep in mind that you may need to purchase the items separately. You might use the lack or quality of appliances as a negotiating point, perhaps asking for allowances to replace the outdated or dysfunctional items.

Can You Live in the House?

The best home isn't necessarily the home equipped with everything you want; the best home is the one you like living in. Once you are sure the home has the basic features you need, imagine living in the house. For example, you might think the house is okay because it has four bedrooms, and you need four. But how are the four bedrooms situated? Are they right next to each other so that you can hear your 14-year-old's headbanger music from your room? Are the bedrooms big enough? Can your eight-year-old fit her entire Barbie collection in her room? As you walk through the home, imagine it's *your* home. Think about the things you'll do in the home:

◆ Imagine your daily routine. Where will you sleep? Watch TV? Cook? Eat? Work?

◆ Imagine your entire family in the house. Where will your children sleep? Are their rooms close enough to yours that they feel safe, but far enough away to have some peace? Where will your children do their homework? Watch TV? Where will your spouse or you work?

◆ Walk through the house and check the traffic pattern. Do you have to walk through five rooms to get to the family room? Is the entrance inviting? Are the bathrooms easily accessible for you and any guests you may have over? Or will your guests have to traipse through your bedroom to get to the bathroom?

◆ Look at the lighting in each of the rooms. Is there enough natural light? Enough overhead or built-in lighting? You may find that some rooms are too bright while others are too gloomy.

◆ Think about your lifestyle. Will you have enough privacy? Do you like to entertain? If so, where will you entertain? If you have guests over, where will they sleep? Ideally, you want a mix of both public areas for entertaining as well as cozy, private areas for snuggling in.

◆ Think about all your possessions. Where will they fit? Where will you keep your 50+ pairs of shoes? Your tool collection?

◆ Think about your household chores. What work will need to be done routinely around the house? What big home repair or improvement projects need to be done and what will they cost? Where will you do laundry? Where will you put the groceries when you come in? Where will you put mops, brooms, a vacuum cleaner?

◆ Imagine your furniture in this house. Do you prefer this home with your old furniture, or your old home with new furniture? You may dislike your current home for reasons you don't realize. Maybe all you need is a new sofa!

◆ Does the home provide adequate entertainment, security, and technological features? For instance, you may have a home entertainment system. Will it fit/work in your new home? Does this home have a security system? Can you add one? What about access to broadband Internet? Or a home network? As homes become more technologically savvy, expect these features to be more common and to play a bigger role in evaluating a home.

Bet You Didn't Know

You may have heard about the "home of the future" and smart appliances. While these aren't currently mainstream, expect them to become more critical. Microsoft, for instance, has built Microsoft Home, and this home challenges visitors to imagine the possibilities of automated homes. Some features include being able to turn systems on or off and adjust them by speaking or via the Internet. For instance, you can walk into a room and give the command to turn on the local news. Or you might start the oven from your office.

Appliances may tell you when they need to be serviced. Automated homes also offer the possibility of checking up on your home while you are away or checking in on other homes such as your vacation home.

While some of these features are currently available, many others won't be available for several more years. And like any new technology, expect to pay more for new "toys." Expect prices to become more affordable when the technology is accepted into the mainstream market.

If You Don't Like Something, Can You Change It?

Keep in mind that certain aspects of the house are not easily altered. You can't move the garage to the other side of the house, at least not without major work and cost.

Real Deal

Some changes are fairly simple. For instance, if you find yourself in love with a house that has a showerhead positioned at your belly button, you can always install a showerhead on a hose (it takes about 15 minutes). If you're really ambitious, you can even raise the position of the pipe.

You can't change where the house is located. (Well, I suppose you can if you want to go to the trouble of moving the house, but it's not likely.) You can't readily change the style of the home.

Other things are changeable. If you don't like the carpeting, for instance, you can have it replaced. Wallpapering, paint, and curtains can all be changed. Sometimes when you're looking at a home, you have to look past the decorating to see the actual home underneath. Be sure to keep an open mind and look at the home's potential.

At the same time, though, if you do envision changes, keep in mind the cost of any redecorating or remodeling. Sure, you can redo the kitchen so that it has just the layout, cabinets, and flooring you want, but at what price?

Is the House Well-Maintained?

You love the house. It has charm, character, and all the features you could want. Are you ready to make an offer? Better wait. Behind that beautiful facade could be a cracking, leaking, sinking mess.

Check the Exterior

When you look at a house, you will also want to consider its structure—particularly the exterior. Here are some things to check:

◆ Check the placement of the house on its lot. Does it "fit?" Do the materials used to build the home flow with its setting? Do the home and yard have a favorable layout, or is the backyard a steep incline with an irrigation ditch running through it?

◆ Look closely at the exterior of the home to see whether it is well-maintained. Do you see peeling paint? Missing shingles? What construction materials were used to build the house? Are they of good quality? What type of maintenance and upkeep does the exterior require?

◆ Check the roof. An inspector will check the roof more carefully, but you may be able to spot problems right away. Moss on the roof usually indicates moisture. Cracked, curled, or missing shingles may indicate that the roof needs repair. If it's winter and all the other houses have snow on the roof and this one doesn't, you probably are looking at a poorly insulated house.

◆ Check the gutters to be sure they are intact and attached.

◆ Is there a fence? If so, what material is it made of? What maintenance does it require? Is the fence in good shape? If there's not a fence, do you need one? Does the community have any restrictions on fencing? Again, thinking ahead can save you a lot of heartache later.

Check the Home Systems

In addition to what you can see, look also at what you can't see. That is, be sure to inspect yourself (and have a professional inspect) the main systems of the home, including the following:

◆ Check the heating and cooling systems. How is the house heated? Is the house air-conditioned? If so, how—central air or window units? Is the air conditioning sufficient? What's the monthly heating bill?

◆ Check the energy rating of the home and its appliances. Look for homes with efficient energy systems and appliances. The U.S. Environmental Protection Agency and the U.S. Department of Energy endorse the Energy Star label. Homes and products with the Energy Star label use 30 percent less energy than their standard counterparts. Typically, homes designated as Energy Star homes have good insulation, high-performance windows, and high-efficiency heating and cooling systems. You not only use less energy, but you also save money on utility bills and do your part to protect the environment when you are energy-conscious.

CAUTION

Buyer Beware

If you see a tangle of extension cords in a room, it probably means that the room doesn't have adequate wall outlets.

◆ Check the electricity. Again, an inspector will carefully check the electricity, but you may want to be sure outlets are placed conveniently in all the rooms. Also find out what the electric bill runs each month. You can usually get this information from the agent or directly from the electric company with just the address of the house.

◆ Check the insulation. Check the attic to see if the home is properly insulated. Also ask the agent or seller if the home contains urea-formaldehyde insulation, which can be hazardous. Make sure the storm windows are in good shape. Are they even there? Are they broken or bent?

◆ Check the local utilities. Is trash collection included as part of the taxes? Do you use city water and city sewers? If so, what's the fee? Are there any underground fuel storage tanks? Any contamination in the area?

Bet You Didn't Know

Taste the water, flush the toilet, and stand in the shower. These are three things I routinely do when I visit a house. First, water tastes different depending on whether it's city water or well water. And water varies from city to city. You probably don't want to buy a house where you hate the water. Also, I stand in the shower. Why? Because my sister lives in a house where the shower nozzle is right about at chin level. When I have to take a shower there, I have to do a backbend to get the shampoo out of my hair. Which reminds me of another thing: Check the water pressure. There's nothing worse than taking a shower when the water drip … drip … drips out.

Check the Interior for Structure and Maintenance

Finally, be sure you look beyond the number of bedrooms and bathrooms to the condition of the rooms themselves. In particular, check the following:

♦ Check the interior walls and ceilings. Are they drywall? Plaster? Are the interior walls in good shape? Any cracks? Keep in mind that some cracks will appear as a normal result of the house settling—it doesn't mean the house is going to fall in, but you will want the inspector to take a close look at structure.

♦ Check the condition of the flooring. Is the carpet in good shape? Are the floors level? Is the tile or linoleum cracked or dirty? Do the floors creak? There are remedies for these problems, but it is best to know about them ahead of time.

♦ Look at the window treatments. Are they adequate? Do they provide enough privacy? Block enough light? Are all of the treatments included with the sale of the home? Window treatments can be pricey, especially if you have to have custom blinds made or install not only curtains but window hardware as well.

♦ Check the basement. Is it dry? Any indication of water damage? If the home-owners store a lot of stuff on the basement floor, it probably means it's dry.

♦ Ask the seller for any disclosure information. Most states require the seller to disclose any defects in the property. In some states, a seller disclosure form is mandatory. Even if the form is not required by law, you may ask the seller to provide this form anyway.

Evaluating the Neighborhood

In addition to looking at the interior and exterior of the house, consider also the neighborhood. Chapter 6 gave you the various neighborhood features to consider, so you should have some idea beforehand of what you want. Then simply compare how this area stacks up to your ideal community wish list. This section reminds you of what elements to consider closely.

Define the Character of the Neighborhood

Take a look at your house and the surrounding neighborhood. Does it fit in? A modest house in a more expensive area has the highest resale value. The most expensive house in a modest area has the lowest resale value but could be the best buy. You may get a lot of free space and amenities.

Look at other houses in the neighborhood. Are they well-maintained? Are there lots of homes for sale?

Visit the Neighborhood

Even if you find your dream home, you aren't going to be happy if your next-door neighbors have a garage band called Eardrum Explosions and practice every night. You will want to take a close look at your neighbors, your neighborhood, and your community. Here are some avenues to explore:

◆ Drive around the immediate area. Do you notice any "bad" neighbors? Loud dogs? Unsightly homes? Are there a lot of rental properties? You will have to define for yourself the type of neighbor you'll be comfortable with. Once when we were looking at a house, the next-door neighbor came over and told us how his brother, who also lived there, was arrested the night before for beating his wife. Not my idea of someone I'd borrow a cup of sugar from.

Real Deal

Check the resale values of homes in the area. Most people stay in a home an average of seven years, so thinking ahead to selling this home can help you make a sound investment. Ask your agent for listings of home sales in that area. Are the prices declining or on the rise? Check the local news for information about any planned improvements or zoning changes in the area.

Buyer Beware

Read up on the local news. Any major loss of employment in a community can adversely affect the value of the homes in that area.

◆ Walk around the neighborhood. You may not see all of the neighborhood by driving. If there's an alley, walk down the alley. Walking around the neighborhood also gives you a good feel for the area.

◆ Visit the home at different hours. The awful headbanger band probably doesn't practice at three in the afternoon, so be sure to visit the house at different times—in the morning, after work, at night. See who's around and how they live.

◆ Consider your routine. Where will you shop? How far a drive is it if you have to run out for a six-pack of Coke? How far is it to your office? What's the traffic like?

◆ Drive around the city. What's downtown like? Are the businesses well-kept or is it a ghost town? Are the people friendly?

◆ Find out whether the neighborhood has a homeowners association and what the fees are. Also, look into any restrictions. If you like to work in your garage but this isn't permitted in that neighborhood, you might reconsider. Find out if the association imposes fines and for what reasons. Also, if the fees are high and the neighborhood common areas are not well-kept, you may consider a different area.

Your Home Comparison Checklist

To keep track of the houses you view, consider making copies of the following checklist to carry with you as you view homes. Use it to make notes about the homes you see and like.

Address: _____

Price: $ _____

Type of house: _____

Construction (frame, brick, etc.): _____

Style: _____

Condition of house: _____

Inside

❏ Kitchen Notes: _____

❏ Dining Room Notes: _____

❏ Bedrooms. No.: _____ Notes: _____

❏ Family Room Notes: _____

❏ Bathrooms. No.: ___ Notes: _____

❏ Basement Notes: _____

❏ Finished   ❏ Unfinished

Outside

Lot size: _____

❏ Fence   ❏ Landscaping

❏ Garage   ❏ Driveway

Notes: _____

Amenities

❑ Deck

❑ Hardwood floors

❑ Screened-in patio

❑ Fireplace

❑ Hot Tub

❑ Ceramic tile

❑ Crown moldings

❑ Built-in cabinets

❑ Pool

❑ Other:

Notes: _____

Utilities

❑ Heating

❑ Electricity

❑ Air conditioning

❑ Water

❑ Plumbing

Notes: _____

Personal Property

❑ Refrigerator

❑ Dryer

❑ Washer

❑ Dishwasher

❑ Stove

Notes: _____

The Least You Need to Know

◆ Your agent will set up appointments for you to tour different homes and will accompany you on the tour. You should ask your agent a lot of questions; after all, she is the expert. Ask her opinion of the home.

◆ When you tour the home, ask yourself these questions: *Do I like the house? Does the house meet my needs? Can I live in the house?*

◆ Keep in mind that some things cannot be changed and some things can. For example, don't rule out a house just because you hate the wallpaper.

◆ You will want to have the house thoroughly inspected by a professional, but as you tour the home, be sure to look at the structure—plumbing, wiring, heating, exterior, interior, and so on.

◆ To keep track of the homes you tour, especially if you tour many, take notes or pictures. You may even consider videotaping the home tour. (If so, get permission from the homeowners first.)

Buying Other Types of Homes

In This Chapter

- ◆ Learning about different types of homes
- ◆ Selecting a condominium
- ◆ Purchasing and financing a cooperative
- ◆ Moving to another city
- ◆ Purchasing a vacation home or fixer-upper

Hate to do lawn work? Want to live someplace where someone else cuts the grass and takes care of maintenance, but you still have your own place? If so, you may want to buy a different kind of home—a condominium, townhouse, patio home, zero lot line home, or cooperative. This chapter explains each of these types of residences, as well as how to make a smart purchase decision if you decide this style of living is for you.

In addition, this chapter covers some special types of home purchases, including a fixer-upper and a vacation home. You'll see what special issues you need to consider when purchasing these types of homes.

What Other Home Types Are Available?

When people start talking about different types of homes, the subtle differences can get pretty confusing. Here is a breakdown of a few common types of homes that you might have heard of and be interested in purchasing:

- ◆ **Condominium (condo).** This actually refers to a style of ownership in which the property is divided between individual living units and common areas such as parking lots, community rooms, and recreational areas. An owner holds title to the interior space of a unit, while the common areas are jointly owned and maintained by all the owners. These will be covered in detail in the later section, "Buying a Condominium."

- ◆ **Townhouse.** This is an attached home that is not a condominium. An owner holds title to the space above (to the sky) and below (to China), as well as the unit space. Townhouse owners may also own their lot.

- ◆ **Patio home.** This is a home where owners take care of the interior and exterior portions of the home and enjoy a yard for which an association fee is paid to have the yard work done. Some communities also have swimming pools, tennis courts, and clubhouses similar to condos.

- ◆ **Zero lot line homes.** Single-family subdivisions where all the homes are shifted to one side of the lot. The homes are built on the property line with the yard (if any at all) on one side. This creates more usable yard space for each homeowner.

- ◆ **Cooperative (co-op).** A type of multiple ownership in which the residents of a multiunit housing complex own shares in a cooperative corporation that owns the property, giving each resident the right to occupy a specific apartment or unit. Co-ops are covered in detail in the later section, "Buying a Co-Op."

The preceding types of homes all share things in common and are variations on the same basic idea; you own part of the home and share parts of the building or community.

Buying a Condominium

When you purchase a condominium (often called simply a "condo"), you own the airspace inside the walls of the building and a portion of the shared or common elements—for instance, sidewalks, pool, elevator, and so on. You do not own the walls, ceiling, or floor of your residence. You own what's inside the walls and ceilings.

You still get a tax break, like other homeowners, but you don't have to worry about home maintenance. Usually you pay a condo fee for the upkeep of the grounds and the building.

The Good (and Bad) Things About Condos

As with everything, there are advantages and disadvantages of condo living. Here are some of the potential advantages:

- You can deduct your property taxes and interest paid on the condo. Condo ownership is just like home ownership in this regard.

- Unlike an apartment that you pay rent for, when you own a condominium, you build equity during the time you live in the condo. You can sell the condo just like you can sell your house. Any equity in your home is your potential profit.

- You have less maintenance to worry about, because exterior repair and maintenance work is taken care of by the condominium association. (Interior maintenance is still up to you.) For this reason, condos are often popular with empty nesters and retirees. They can downsize not only to a small, more manageable home, but they also don't have to worry about the upkeep of the outside and the yard. Singles often find condos suitable to their lifestyles as well. They own a home, but don't have to spend a lot of time maintaining and working on that home.

- Your condominium may include recreational facilities—a swimming pool, tennis courts, recreation room, and more.

- If you want to live in a certain area, a condominium may be your only option. For instance, in large cities such as Chicago, you may find a better selection of condos than single-family homes in certain areas.

- In some cases, you may pay less for a condo than for a single-family home.

> **CAUTION**
>
> **Buyer Beware**
>
> Be sure to include the monthly fees for a condominium when figuring the monthly payments. In addition to PITI (payment, interest, taxes, insurance), you will pay a monthly maintenance fee.

Here are some of the potential disadvantages of owning a condo:

- In a slow market, condo prices are usually the first to suffer and the last to rebound. That means if you have to sell during a downtime, you may not get the price you want, and it may take longer to sell the condo.

♦ You are living in a community, and as such, you must abide by the rules set up in that community. The board, for instance, decides which improvements you can make. See the following section "The Condo Board Rules the Community!"

♦ You may have less space and less privacy in a condo than in a single-family dwelling.

Bet You Didn't Know

In 2001 and 2002, condominium sales were very strong. Reasons for the strong market included low interest rates attracting first-time buyers, the lower price tag for a condo (yet at the same time strong sales of this type of home indicating a strong market), and the increase in the number of empty nesters and retirees.

Prices for condos are on the rise because of the market demand. Prices are rising faster than for single-family homes, but most condos (excluding the luxury condo) are still less expensive than a single-family home.

The Condo Board Rules the Community!

When a condominium community is established, a condo association is formed. This association then elects the board. As a member of the condominium community, you can vote for board members and other issues. The number of votes you have may vary depending on certain factors, such as the size, location, view, or floor plan of your condominium. The better-placed condos may have more votes, for example. Or the votes may be assigned one vote per unit.

Once the board is created, it establishes a budget and assumes the responsibility of collecting fees, enforcing rules, deciding which repairs and improvements to make, and overseeing repairs and improvements. The board will most likely hire a management company to run the condo community, but the board will oversee this management.

Real Deal

Become a board member of the condo association. Doing so enables you to keep up on what's going on in your community, plus you have a say in the decision-making process.

The board is, in effect, a mini-government. It may create guidelines for changes you can make to your condominium. If you don't make your payments on time, the board can put a lien against your property. What does this mean to you? A couple of things. Before you buy a condo, be sure you understand the authority of the board and that you are comfortable with this structure. If it bothers you that you have to get permission to redo your bathroom, you may be frustrated with condominium living.

If you decide to purchase a condominium, it's a good idea to get to know the board members. The board members reflect the values and opinions of the other residents. Keep in mind that you will be living in a close community with these residents. Are you comfortable with the philosophy? Do you fit in?

Be sure you understand all the financial obligations that come with owning a condominium. The section "Making an Offer," later in this chapter, discusses this topic in more detail. For instance, you might want to find out about plans for improvements or major repairs. In some cases, the board can make the residents pay a special assessment fee for repairs and improvements.

Selecting a Community

If you are considering a condo, the first aspect you should check out is the community. Here are some points to consider:

- Is the condo association financially sound? You don't want to purchase a condo in a community where the treasurer has just absconded with all the condo fees. The association should keep a reserve of funds for repairs and improvements. If that reserve is empty, you as a condo owner can be charged a special assessment for any repairs that have to be made, such as a new roof for your unit. Ask how many special assessments have been made in the past few years. Ask about any planned improvements or repairs and how they will be financed.

- Is the condo well managed? Remember that one of the benefits of living in a condo is leaving the maintenance up to the condo association. If that association isn't responsive and your grass grows up to your waist, what's the benefit? What routine maintenance do they do? Can you request certain maintenance?

- How many condos are sold? Vacant? Rented? If many of the condos are sold, it may indicate a solid community. If many are vacant, you should wonder why. Also, if many are vacant, that means there is less money in the maintenance kitty. Finally, the percentage of rentals may control the type of financing that is available.

- Which facilities are part of the community? Is there a gym, a swimming pool, meeting rooms? Are you part owner of

Real Deal

Some rules are good! You may want your freedom, but you'll quickly find that a few rules are necessary when a family with 17 children, 2 aunts, an uncle, 2 grandpas, 4 dogs, and a cat moves in next door, and they all think that fireworks every night are a great way to keep the kids entertained. Rules will help keep peace in the community.

the facilities, or do you have to pay a fee to use them? Make sure the facilities are adequate for the community. That pool may look nice now, but when all 200 kids from the community pile in, the pool isn't going to look so fun.

♦ What are the bylaws and restrictions that you must abide by? Can you have a dog? Can you paint your garage a different color? You should look closely at the master deed, which should list the conditions, covenants, and restrictions. Read the bylaws to see who's responsible for what. What authority does the board have?

♦ What are the monthly charges for the condo association fees? What percent of this payment is deductible? What do these fees pay for?

In addition to looking at the community, you should carefully check out the unit itself. Is it well maintained? What is the square footage? What amenities are included? Do you like the floor plan? In what condition are the windows, walls, carpets? What are your neighbors like? You will be glad to find these things out before you make an offer.

Real Deal _____

Another thing you may want to check into about your co-op or condo are any restrictions on renting the unit. Are you allowed to sublet? Are there any restrictions? Do the renters have to go through any formal approval process? Check the bylaws or ask specifically about rental procedures if you think you might rent your unit in the future.

You may also want to find out the procedure for listing a condo or co-op for sale. Are you allowed to sell it on the open market?

Making an Offer

Before you make an offer on a condo, you should review the master deed, bylaws, and house rules carefully with your agent and/or attorney. If you do not review these documents before making the offer, you should make the review and acceptance of these documents a contingency in the contract.

The sales contract is similar to a single-family home contract. The contract includes the offer price, the terms, and any contingencies. (You can find information on drawing up and negotiating a contract in Chapters 17 and 18.)

Getting financing on a condominium is similar to getting financing on a house. One difference is that the lender will include your monthly condo association fee as part of your PITI . Also, you may be required to make a larger down payment. Finally, some lenders may make loans only for "approved" condos—those that qualify for Federal Housing Administration (FHA) financing.

Bet You Didn't Know

Two new trends with condos are the concept of a luxury condo (on one end) and simplified living (on the other end). Luxury condos, considered a status symbol and often located in or near the downtown areas of major cities, are growing in popularity for empty nesters who prefer condo living. These types of condos include swank lobbies, exercise facilities, top-of-the-line furnishings, and other luxuries. Some communities include gourmet restaurants, a concierge, room service, maids, and limos!

On the other end, many first-time buyers, including singles and young families, prefer the simplicity of condo living. You can expect newer condo designs to emphasize simplicity as well as technology. Newer condos, for instance, are wired for Internet and other digital access.

Buying a Co-Op

In some ways, a cooperative (or co-op) is similar to a condominium. The key difference is in the structure of ownership. Rather than owning real estate, you buy shares in a corporation that owns the building. When you purchase a certain amount of shares, you then have the right to live in a particular unit. This is called a *proprietary lease*. Unlike a condominium, where you can buy it if you have the money, you must be "approved" by the board before you can purchase a co-op. The board members must vote you in before your purchase is approved. Sound snobby? It can be.

Most co-ops are located in New York City, but you may find this type of living arrangement in other large cities, such as Boston or San Francisco. Like the increase in sales of condos, 2001 and 2002 showed an increase also in the co-op market for the same reasons—the (usually) lower price of this type of home as well as the independent lifestyle.

Selecting a Co-Op

Selecting a co-op is similar to selecting a condominium. You should investigate the building and management carefully. You should review the proprietary lease, bylaws, and financial statements of the corporation. Here are some items to consider:

- ◆ Is the co-op financially sound? Does it meet all the expenses for running the co-op? Does it have reserves to cover renovations and repairs?

- What is the age and condition of the building? Does it need repairs? A new roof? New elevators? You may want to have the co-op professionally inspected.

- What are the covenants, conditions, and regulations you have to observe? You should know the rules you must follow. You should also investigate whether you can sublet the unit.

- Can you resell your co-op? If so, what is the process? Because all buyers must usually be board-approved, selling a co-op can take longer and be more of a hassle than say, selling a condo. You had to provide references and impeccable credit to buy originally; the board will require the same criteria of any potential buyers. Just keep in mind that you don't have total freedom in the sale; your potential buyer may not be up to snuff. Therefore, you may have to look harder to find a buyer.

Financing Your Co-Op

Before 1984, if you wanted to buy a co-op, you had to pay cash or take out a personal loan. Then in 1984, Fannie Mae agreed to buy co-op loans. (For more information about Fannie Mae, see the section "Government-Backed Loans" in Chapter 12.) Once Fannie Mae started buying the loans, lenders started making the loans. One of the largest co-op lenders is National Cooperative Bank (NCB).

How is the financial situation for a co-op different? Because you do not own real estate, you do not get the same tax deductions as a condo owner or homeowner. That doesn't mean you don't get any tax breaks; you just have a different tax situation. If you are thinking about buying a co-op, you may want to talk to your accountant about the type and amount of tax deductions you will be allowed to take.

To get approval on most co-op loans, the lender requires that the participating co-op meet certain standards: structural soundness, restricted commercial use, a fiscally responsible budget, and good management. You can expect to pay a higher interest rate on a co-op, but the closing costs may be less.

Your monthly payment includes your monthly maintenance fee. A lender will probably include this fee in your total monthly payment when qualifying you for a loan.

In addition to satisfying the lender's criteria, you will have to pass inspection from the board members. You may need to submit personal references and financial statements. The board may also interview you.

Vacation Homes, Fixer-Uppers, and More

Condo and co-op sales, as you have seen, require special considerations. In addition, there are some homebuying situations with special buying considerations, as covered here.

Relocating to a New City

If you are in the process of moving out of town and are looking to purchase a home in your new town, you have a very different set of questions than people moving within the same town.

For example …

- Are you familiar with the cities and towns near where you are moving?

- Do you know anyone where you are moving?

- Will your new employer help you find a place to live? Will they pay moving expenses?

- Should you rent a home or apartment before you choose a home to purchase?

- Are you working within a particular time frame for the move?

- Do you need to be out of your current home or have it sold before you close on a new home? Does your company provide any help if your current home does not sell?

When moving to another city or state (or even country), the role of your real estate agent will be even more critical. Your agent should be able to listen to your needs and suggest various neighborhoods in your new city in which to look. You may visit your new town and have to schedule all your visits in a day or so. You may do some of the viewing and narrowing down using methods (like virtual tours or looking up school district information on the Internet) that you can do from your current home. You may want to select an agent who has the experience of dealing with out-of-towners.

Similar strategies work for scoping out a new neighborhood in a new city. Read the local paper. Visit shops and businesses in the areas of interest. Drive around the city. Ask your agent lots of questions about different areas such as the resale value of homes and the reputation of the school district.

Real Deal _____

The HomeFair website (www. homefair.com) includes a moving calculator that helps you compare the cost of living in two different cities.

Finally, do some research on the cost of living. Is it higher than your current city? Comparable? Ask what provisions your company will make for your move. Will they provide for a rental property until you find a home? Will they pay for moving expenses? Do they have real estate agents that they work with for corporate moves?

Buying a Vacation Home

A vacation home also requires special considerations. Sure, it's a dream come true to own a house *and* a vacation property. But keep in mind these additional factors:

- ◆ What is the upkeep for the second home? Will you close it down for most of the year? Who will handle the maintenance and upkeep during the "off-season?"

- ◆ What are the tax implications of this second home? You most likely need to consult an accountant to understand what you can and cannot deduct; the deductions for a second home are not the same as for your primary home.

- ◆ Do you plan to rent the home or property? If so, will you handle this yourself, or use a rental management company? If you plan to use a rental management company, what do they charge? What services (for instance, maintenance, damage by tenants, and so on) do they provide?

- ◆ If you plan to rent, are you counting on a certain amount of rental income to pay for the home? Be sure you can afford to make the payments without relying too much on renting, which is not guaranteed income.

- ◆ Check into insurance rates on this second home. You may need special insurance if you plan to rent.

Buyer Beware

You can find many timeshare units for sale. Basically, you own one or more weeks of time at a vacation property. These are often not a solid investment (although they may work for your vacation needs). You pay a much higher price for that one week; timeshares have an incredibly high markup.

Also, you must keep up on the maintenance and ownership of the property as well as pay pretty high maintenance fees. It's hard to know what's going on in your unit in Acapulco all the way from Boston. Turnover rates and maintenance can be a nightmare. (It'd be much easier to simply rent a condo for your vacation and avoid the hassle of ownership.) Ask other property owners what their experience has been. Tread very carefully when considering this type of vacation "home."

Buying a Fixer-Upper

A fixer-upper home is attractive to those that aren't daunted by hard work and can see beyond the current home to its potential. Perhaps you cannot afford a "perfect" home in a neighborhood, but you can purchase the ugly duckling in the area. Ideally, you then work to transform the ugly duckling into the beautiful swan. You may purchase a fixer-upper to live in or to sell (hopefully at a profit).

Remember these considerations before you purchase a fixer-upper:

- Be sure you know what needs to be done. Perhaps the house just requires a paint job and a few fixes. If the home, on the other hand, requires new plumbing, a new roof, foundation work, or other heavy duty work, make sure you know this *before* you purchase the house.

- Realistically consider how much money you'll need to bring the house up to your standards (if you plan to live there). If you plan to rent or sell the home, be sure to weigh the amount you need to spend vs. any profits. What are homes in that area selling for? Is it a decent neighborhood? What are comparable rental properties getting?

- Make sure you are getting the house at a reasonable price. A good rule of thumb is that the selling price should be 20 to 30 percent lower than the value of the house after you fix it up.

- Who will do the work on the home? If it's you, make sure you have the time available. It's easy to *say* you can reroof the house in a weekend; it's another thing to actually want to and do the work. A common mistake is to greatly underestimate the time and money it will take to improve the house.

- If you are going to hire others to do the work, be sure you know how much you can expect to pay for the repairs. You may want

Real Deal

You may need to do some detective work to find this kind of house. Look for other "names" for fixer-upper, such as "handyman's special" or "needs TLC." Also, some homes in this category may not even be listed for sale; they may be vacant. You might need to call the tax collector office to get the address of the current owner.

Buyer Beware

Traditionally, real estate has proven to be a strong investment, but a return is not guaranteed. Before you purchase a home strictly for an investment, know what's involved. Check out *The Complete Idiot's Guide to Real Estate Investing, Second Edition,* by Stuart Leland Rider for additional investment information.

to get bids and estimates on the work, especially any major work such as a new roof.

◆ Like "regular" homes, be sure to make the sale contingent on an inspection. Even though you know the inspector is going to find problems, you want to get a good idea of *all* the problems, not just those you can see. If unforeseen problems pop up, you have this contingency clause to help you renegotiate the price or even back out of the sale if needed.

◆ Consult a tax attorney to ensure you get all the allowable tax breaks. You may be eligible for a tax break if you live in the house two of the five years before its sale.

The Least You Need to Know

◆ Understand the distinction between owning a condominium, townhouse, patio home, zero lot line home, and a cooperative; they each have their subtle differences.

◆ When you own a condo, you don't own the walls, floor, or ceiling of your unit. Instead, you own the airspace within those walls. You may also own a part of the community's common facilities.

◆ If you live in a condominium, you don't have to worry about maintenance. Instead you pay a monthly fee, and the maintenance of the property is taken care of for you.

◆ When you purchase a co-op, you don't own property. Instead you own shares in the corporation that owns the co-op. In return for the shares, the corporation grants you a proprietary lease, which gives you the right to live in a certain unit.

◆ Be sure to check out the condominium or co-op bylaws, rules, restrictions, and other management and financial information. You should select a community that is financially sound and well managed.

Chapter 11

Building a New Home

In This Chapter

- ◆ Understanding the pros and cons of buying a new home
- ◆ Deciding on a type of new home
- ◆ Finding a new home
- ◆ Negotiating a contract
- ◆ Getting a home warranty
- ◆ Avoiding problems

Perhaps you are one of the millions of people who want a brand new home in a brand new neighborhood with brand new carpeting, brand new appliances, brand new everything. There's something thrilling about newness.

Buying a new home and buying an existing home are similar in some aspects. The process of finding a home, making an offer, getting financing, and closing are basically the same. So most of the material in this book pertains to both new and existing homes. There are, however, some variations when it comes to finding a "good" home and in making a "good" offer, as covered in this chapter.

Considering the Pluses and Minuses of Buying a New Home

As your city expands, you will find that new communities pop up all over town with brand new homes and big closets. Chapter 7 helps you compare and contrast the benefits of existing homes vs. new homes. This section gives you an overview of the advantages and disadvantages of a new home.

New Homes Are Great Because ...

New homes offer many benefits. Because the heating, plumbing, wiring, air conditioning, and so on are all new, you will have the advantage of low maintenance costs. Also, the home may be more energy efficient, and the builder will most likely offer a warranty for the home's major components.

Builders must have perked up and listened to what people want in a home, because most new home designs include *big closets* and lots of cabinet space. New homes also usually include a well-designed floor plan—big kitchen, special amenities such as a master suite, and so on.

Real Deal

Look for an Energy Star rating on a new home. Homes and products with the Energy Star label (endorsed by the Environmental Protection Agency) use 30 percent less energy than their standard counterparts.

When you purchase an existing home, you either have to keep the red velvet wallpaper and green shag carpet or pay the price to redo them. With a new home, you have *more choices*. The builder will usually let you pick the color and type of floor coverings and wall coverings. You may also be able to choose your appliances, hardware, and other home elements.

Many new subdivisions include extra amenities for the community, such as a clubhouse, swimming pool, tennis courts, and other fun things.

The Drawbacks of a New Home

If you're thinking of purchasing a new home, you will also want to consider the disadvantages. New homes are being built farther out in the suburbs than existing neighborhoods. You may have a longer commute, and you may have to deal with more traffic.

Land is expensive. Builders want to fit as big a home on as small a lot as possible. If you hate to mow your lawn, you're in luck. If you don't want to sit on your deck and stare directly into your neighbor's kitchen, you may be out of luck. *Small yards* are part of the bargain with a new home.

New homes may also lack decent landscaping—at least until the trees and grass grow in. Many people are put off by this barren look. You may have to put some work into actually getting a yard by reseeding and watering until a decent lawn grows in.

If you have your home custom designed and custom built, you can select any type of home you want. However, most new homes are predesigned by the builders. You can select home A, B, or C. That means there will be several homes in your neighborhood that look exactly like yours—at least from the outside. This *lack of personality* has kept many people in the existing-home market. Special features such as crown molding or built-in cabinets are more common in existing homes. To add them to a new home, you may have to pay a considerable upgrade price.

The neighborhood may have covenants that limit what you can and cannot do with your home. For example, you may not be able to have a storage shed or perhaps you can't paint your home that lovely color of chartreuse you picked out. You may not be able to park your semi-trailer on the street. You may also have homeowners association fees that can add to your home budget.

In some cases, a new home costs more than an equivalent existing home. Also, you may have less bargaining power on the price when you buy a new home.

Selecting a Type of Home

If you know you want to build a new home, one of your decisions is the type of new home you want. Most of this chapter deals with tract and semi-custom homes, but you will find some advice on building a custom home.

Tract and Semi-Custom Homes

You commonly find tract homes in the planned communities that are springing up everywhere. The homes are standardized to minimize the cost of materials and labor (also called "production homes"). Therefore, you select the particular home model you like.

You can upgrade or add preselected features that the builder allows, which helps you quickly narrow and make your selections (as opposed to picking from among thousands of selections say, for your faucet). You may be able to make some changes. For example, you may be able to select a bay window instead of a regular window. Or you might change a bedroom into an office and ask for additional outlets.

You most likely will not be able to make any significant structural changes to the home. This is usually because unplanned changes are expensive and time-consuming (they must get approval from each city where the home will be built). The builder's goal is to provide affordable home options with minimal changes within a specified amount of time.

If you want more control over the design of the house, you may choose a semi-custom home. You are allowed to choose a home only from a set of their pre-determined floor plans. But, you can move windows, doors, or anything you like within reason. Of course, all of this is usually for a price.

Buyer Beware

One of the reasons that tract homes are less expensive than custom or semi-custom homes is that the builder can hire contractors at a better price because of the quantity of work they need completed. In addition, if there are only four floor plans to build, many of the materials can be purchased in bulk and at a better price. This can also mean that the materials and labor are not as high in quality. Ask around, check with your local Registrar of Contractors, and see how many people are dissatisfied with the builder's work. This can quickly tell you how reputable builders are and if they take pride in their work.

Custom Homes

If you want to have a unique home (and you have the money to build this type of home), you may decide to build a custom home. With this type of home, you start with a blank page and design all of the elements from floor plan to house style, from kitchen layout to the knobs used on your cabinets. While you have a great deal of control, expect also for your home to be much more expensive and to take much longer to build than a tract or semi-custom home.

When building a custom home, you start by purchasing a lot. Like tract housing, you can find many subdivisions which offer only custom designed homes. You may purchase your lot beforehand, or your builder may have some lots available.

Next, select a builder. Because you will be working closely with the builder, pick someone who can not only complete the job, but someone with whom you feel comfortable and whose advice you will trust. You will be making a lot of decisions! The section "Select a Builder" gives advice for custom as well as tract homebuilders. Reputation and past work experience are key.

To make the process go smoothly, consider the following tips:

◆ Have a very good idea of what you like. You will be asked lots of questions about big things like what the outside of the house is to be made of to little things such as the type of fixtures used in the bathroom. Collect samples, pictures, drawings, and other items that you like to give your builder some idea of your desires.

◆ Drive around and note the addresses of home styles that you like. The builder can use these homes to see what styles and materials appeal to you.

◆ Take advantage of design centers, talking with interior decorators and looking at installations of various ideas. You can find independent centers. Some homebuilders also have a design center for concepts, materials, and plans that they use. Finally, use the Internet to find design ideas.

◆ Rely on your builder for advice. Also, the builder may be able to get items at a discounted price. Ask the builder which design and home stores he or she recommends.

Real Deal

Many builders provide a homeowner manual that guides you through the process of building a custom home. If this is available, use it as a resource. You may also compare the manuals of different builders when you are trying to decide which builder to use.

◆ Think ahead. While you may not consider selling your home, you should think about how your choices will fly if you do resell. Avoid anything that is too trendy, difficult to change, or too customized. Doing so will make your home easier to get ready when and if you sell. Also, think about what types of features add value to the home. For instance, a killer kitchen always plays well.

◆ Look over the contract and warranty carefully. The later sections in this chapter on these topics pertain to both custom and tract homes.

◆ Know when and if you can change your mind on details. Doing so after a product has been ordered or work has begun will be costly. If you find something you like better, make sure you have enough time to implement your change (or the money to pay for the change order).

Finding New Homes

Finding a newly built home is in some ways similar to finding an existing home. First, you want to select a good location and a floor plan that meets your needs. You want to select a good quality home. When you look at existing homes, you can see what you are getting. When you buy a new home (especially if it hasn't been built yet), you want to investigate the builder. This section explains all the items to consider in finding and building a new home.

Using an Agent

Many states have laws that regulate visiting new-home developments. These laws have been instituted to protect you as the homebuyer and the agent working for you. If you have an agent whom you like, make sure you tell him or her that you are interested in looking at new homes. The agent will most likely make you aware that he or she must accompany you on your first visit to a new-home subdivision. The agent will also have to fill out a form indicating that he or she is your agent, even if you don't end up interested in the homes. If your agent isn't with you and you find your dream home, the builder's rep may get the full commission on the home. That's like the wolf being the three little pigs' insurance salesperson.

The builder should accept working with your agent and pay for the agent's commission. You pay the same price regardless of whether or not you use an agent. In many cases, builders are happy to get buyers with agents; then the builders know these buyers are serious and qualified.

Buyer Beware

If you don't work with an agent, be sure to have an attorney look over all the contracts. Also be sure you are getting something in return. Whose pocket does the saved commission go into?

If the new-home builder won't allow you to use an agent in conjunction with building their home (meaning, they don't allow co-brokering), then you have to use the builder's rep. The builder might pay their rep a salary instead of a commission or only a partial commission, supposedly to pass the savings on to you the homebuilder.

Most builder representatives are helpful and informative, but remember that they are salespeople and have sales goals; their job is not necessarily to make sure you are doing the right thing in buying a new home.

Selecting a Subdivision

Finding a new home may be easier or harder than finding an existing home, depending on how you look at it. On the plus side, most new homes are built in new subdivisions (sometimes referred to as *PUDs*). The developers and builders are likely to advertise these new developments in the real estate section of the paper. You may also spot subdivisions as you drive around the city.

Many times tract homebuilders have multiple subdivisions that they are building at the same time. So, if you find your dream home on the west side, but really want to live on the east side, ask them if they are (or are going to be) building in a different location.

On the minus side, most new subdivisions are located outside the city, where there is room to expand. In this case, you may have to look a little harder to find a subdivision that is in an area acceptable to you. Keep in mind the questions from Chapter 6 about your community and neighborhoods. As you look at the subdivision, consider the following questions:

- Is the area around the subdivision acceptable? If the subdivision is within an existing neighborhood, you can check out the neighborhood. If the subdivision is surrounded by land, you may want to investigate the plans for the area. For instance, you probably won't want to move into a subdivision if the surrounding area is planned for commercial growth. Contact the local city government.

- Are there any homes available that you can move right in to (usually referred to as *spec homes*), or do you have to wait a certain number of months (around three to nine months) for the home to be built?

- Where are the *easements* in a particular neighborhood? Are they along the sidewalk in front of the home or in the back yard where you want to plant things?

- How much is the homeowners association fee? *Is* there a fee? What facilities and maintenance does the fee include? How often is the fee raised? Homeowners associations are usually run by the individual homeowners, but early on in a development there aren't enough owners, so the association decisions remain with the builder. Ask how long it will be before the association decisions return to the individually elected homeowners.

- What are the CCRs (community covenants and restrictions) involved with the neighborhood? The CCRs can be very demanding when it comes to what you can do in your own front yard and how your home looks. For example, you might not be able to leave your garage door open for a certain length of time.

Real Estate Terms

A **PUD (planned unit development)** is a type of real estate project that gives each unit owner the title to a residential lot and building, and a nonexclusive *easement* allowing access to the project's common areas. An **easement** gives someone the right to limited use of another's property; the most common easements are for utility lines.

Buyer Beware _____

Ask how conflicts are handled and how restrictions are enforced. Most often, the association as well as individual homeowners can file a complaint if one of the neighbors breaks a covenant. Keep in mind, though, that the covenant must be enforced routinely.

Read all the restrictions before you sign a purchase agreement to build a new home.

◆ Are there any airports or other facilities nearby that will affect your neighborhood? New developments are supposed to disclose information about airports, toxic waste dumps, and the like to potential homebuyers so that after they move in, they don't discover their property values have plummeted after the airport decides to increase in size and fly 200,000 cargo flights per year. Translation: lots of loud planes. It happens; make sure you ask about things like this.

◆ What types of structures are being built near the neighborhood? You want to know if a massive shopping mall is going to be built right behind your home, or if a new elementary school will be built across the street.

◆ How long before all the homes in the neighborhood are supposed to be sold? This can impact you if for some reason you are relocated and need to sell your home. It might be harder to sell your home if prospective homebuyers can simply buy a new home for the same price. Many people don't like to build new homes, however, or perhaps need to move in right away.

◆ Do you have to obtain your mortgage with one of the builder's preselected lenders? Will it cost you extra if you want to use your own lender? Are there any points or monies toward your new home in upgrades if you work with the builder's specific lender?

◆ What will the taxes be? Will you have to pay for any special assessments—for instance, to install the sewer lines or sidewalks? Is there any difference in taxation between a new home and a resale?

◆ What is the likelihood that the subdivision will be completed with like-quality homes? How many homes are sold in the subdivision? How many are planned? Make sure you have a good idea of how the entire planned community will look. Many communities have detailed maps, perhaps even scale models, so that you can get a sense of how things will turn out.

This may sound like a lot to think about. Well, it is. Just ask lots of questions and visit a neighborhood numerous times. You might even consider talking to some of the people who are already in their new homes (if there are any) and ask them about the neighborhood and the builder. Which leads us to the next section on choosing a builder.

Buyer Beware _____

Some new homebuilders will offer special discounts if you use the in-house mortgage lender or title service. Just because they say it's discounted doesn't mean it is; check around with other lenders. Be sure that you are not paying more for interest, loan fees, and other fees. With all the fees and documents, it's easy to overlook an item in the list. But you should look closely at every fee listed. Is it a fair price? Higher? Also, if you don't know what a particular fee is, ask. You'd be surprised that the various official sounding fees are sometimes included in the loan package. Part 3 of this book covers financing options and helps you understand the usual fees.

Selecting a Good Builder

When you think about selecting a home, think about the three little pigs. You don't want to purchase a home that a huff and a puff will blow over. The quality of the homes depends a lot on the builder.

Many subdivisions will include homes built by several different builders, so you can select a builder you like. You may want to tour several homes in the subdivision to see which homes you like. Try to focus on the quality of the home—not the "wow!" factor or the price.

Investigate the sales of homes in the subdivision. Which are the best-selling homes? Why? Are they better quality? Better price?

If you have a friend who works in home construction or home maintenance, ask that person for recommendations. He or she may be able to tell you that homes by SlapEmUp Homes are a nightmare and which builders have the worst and best reputations.

Ask the builder reps why one home is better than another. Of course, they are going to give you a sales pitch, but look for concrete details. Do they use better roofing materials? Do they include other extras as part of the deal (for instance, landscaping)?

Determine what the basics and extras are for a given home. Find out the costs for upgrading. Builders make most of their money from upgrades. For example, if one builder offers more extras in a home or charges less for upgrades, you may want to consider that builder. Take a look at the following upgrade comparison table.

New-Home Upgrade Comparison

Feature	Builder #1	Builder #2
Base price of home	$129,900	$124,900
Back patio cover	Included	3,500
Landscaping	Included	2,000
Upgraded carpet pad	Included	1,000
Fireplace	Included	3,000
Upgraded carpet	4,500	4,500
Total	**$134,400**	**$138,900**

Buyer Beware

If you move into your new home while the rest of the subdivision is still under construction, you should be prepared for a lot of construction noise.

Real Deal

Most people stay in their homes an average of seven years. Therefore, think about the resale value of a home even as you are just having it built. Check into the resale of other homes by this builder. Ask your agent about resale values within your selected area. Investigate any future plans for the community that might affect the home sales.

Notice that the base price for Builder #1 starts out higher but includes more upgrades in the home, which proves to be less expensive than Builder #2 in the long run. Make sure you consider more than just the home base price when deciding on which builder to go with.

Visit homes built by the builder and talk to homeowners. You can visit recently built homes. These owners may be able to tell you about any problems they've had. You may also want to visit a more established subdivision where the builder has built homes. These homeowners can tell you how the homes have stood up over the long term. Ask the homeowners what they like and what they dislike. Which builders have good resale track records? Do the homes appreciate? Do they sell quickly once placed on the market, or is there something that keeps buyers away?

Check out the reputation of the builder. How long has the builder been constructing new homes? Is the builder solidly financed? Check with the Better Business Bureau and other consumer groups to see whether any complaints have been made against the builder.

Consider using a builder that adheres to the Quality Assurance Builder Standards. Affiliated builders follow guidelines and standards for residential construction (as well as remodeling). In Indiana, these rules are set forth by the Builders Association of Greater Indianapolis (BAGI). In your area, check with your city or area builders association.

Ask your Realtor, who may know which builders have a good reputation and which homes have a good resale value.

Selecting a Home Plan

After you decide on a particular builder, you can focus on the fun part—selecting the home you want. Many builders have several styles of homes that you can choose from. Do you want the Cape Cod style? Or are you more of a Colonial person? The homes may vary in style, size, amenities, and other aspects. You should tour the various styles of homes to see which one you prefer.

If possible, it's a good idea to buy a home that is already built—you know exactly what you are getting, and you know the home is ready. If you have the home built, you may be able to select some aspects of the home, but you can't be sure it will turn out exactly how you envision it, and you will probably encounter delays.

When you look at the floor plans, think about you and your family's needs now and five years from now. Consider these questions:

◆ How many bedrooms do you need? How many bathrooms? How large are the rooms?

◆ What "living" rooms are included—great room, living room, den, dining room, and so on? Do you like the placement of the rooms in the home—that is, the traffic pattern?

◆ What type of kitchen does the plan include? An eat-in kitchen? A country kitchen? What items in the kitchen can you select? The appliances? Tile? Cabinets? What do you have to pay extra for?

◆ Does the home include a home office? Can you change another room into an office? If so, does the room have enough outlets and other connections needed for your work?

- How big is the yard? Is landscaping included? Is a fence included, or do you have to pay extra for it? Is the patio or deck included? How big is the standard patio and deck? Can you get a bigger one? For what price?

- Is a garage standard? Is it finished or unfinished?

- Does the home have a basement? How much will it cost you to have a full basement? Half basement? Finished? Unfinished?

- How is the home heated? Does it use the most energy-efficient heating source? What about central air? Insulation?

- Which decorating options do you get to select? Can you pick the floor coverings? Wall coverings? Window treatments? If so, compare the quality and selection of each of these options. Do you have to pay more to upgrade the carpet or other decorating features?

- What's included in the sale, and what's extra? For instance, are the appliances included? Many builders give you an appliance allowance. You can use this allowance to select the type and brand of appliances. You may want to shop around to make sure the allowance covers the appliances you need.

Real Deal

Keep in mind that the model home has the top-quality carpet, cabinets, tiles, appliances, and so on. Your home may not include the same features. If you are touring the model home, be sure to ask whether you will get the exact carpet, exact tile, and so on. If not, check out the quality of the materials that will be used for your home. If you want to upgrade, inquire about the costs.

Selecting a Good Lot

You've got your home and neighborhood. Now you have to plunk that home down somewhere in that neighborhood. Where? You may be able to select any location you want in the subdivision. The best lot isn't the largest lot; it's the one with a view. Keep in mind that you may have to pay more for the home, depending on the lot you select. In some cases, you may not have a wide selection for the placement of the home. The builder may have only a few lots left.

When you select a lot, be sure to consider the traffic pattern in the neighborhood. Does everyone in that neighborhood have to drive by your home to get to their home? Will the street be busy? Does the home back up to a main road? Consider your view. Does the home back up to trees? Is your lot next to a schoolyard or church?

CAUTION **Buyer Beware** _____

Picture how the neighborhood will look when complete. When there are no homes, it may look like you have an entire plantation! But once the homes start going up, the view is going to be different. Take a look at the plans for the development and see where homes will be built. Note also how close to each other the homes will be placed.

Understanding the Sales Contract

When you talk to a builder, you may get the impression that nothing is negotiable: The price is fixed. In most cases, the builder will hold firm to the price. That's because the builder has fixed costs that can't be avoided. The lumber is going to cost so much, the electrical work is going to cost so much, and so on. Most builders operate on a slim margin, so they don't usually give you too much of a break on the price. But there can still be some room for negotiation—it can't hurt to ask. See the following example of a home purchase agreement for a new home.

Make sure you read this document carefully. You will find that when you initially sign the contract to build a home, many of the things you are agreeing to might come back to haunt you later if you don't thoroughly understand them.

Also find out whether you can use any lender you want. Being able to select a lender is to your benefit and can save you money. Mortgage companies (and their representatives) make thousands of dollars when you choose them as your lender; be sure to refer to Chapter 5 when you select a mortgage lender.

Contract Terms

One area that is open for negotiation is the terms of the contract (see the following home purchase agreement for a new home). For example, maybe the builder offers you $3,000 in upgrades if you build a new home with them. Perhaps instead you can ask the builder if they will *buy down* the mortgage. (See Chapter 15 for information on this type of financing.) Or you can ask the builder to provide help with the closing costs. You may ask to do some of the work yourself in exchange for a break on price or features (known as sweat equity). Your agent can help you negotiate a favorable contract.

Upgrades, Upgrades

What you see in the model home and what you get are two different things. The carpeting, wall covering, cabinets, tile, fixtures, and so on used in your home may vary, but for a price, you can upgrade to the better stuff. Consider the price and inclusion of any of the following upgrades:

- Better quality floor and wall coverings (carpet, tile, vinyl, and so on).

- Better quality appliances. Find out what appliances are included as part of the deal. Often you get an allowance for appliances; you then select the brands and types of appliances you want. If the appliances are included, look at the models. Are they of the quality you need and want? If not, what is the price to upgrade?

- Better quality or more amenities. How much is the fireplace? Is the deck included?

- Better quality outside materials (roofing and exterior walls).

- Better quality landscaping. In some cases, the covenants, conditions, and restrictions of the area may require a certain type of front yard, and in this case, the landscaping may be included as part of the price.

You will find out that upgrades are "gravy" to new homebuilders; this is where they make lots of money. They can charge you $500 to add a soft water loop (to have a water softener installed) when in actuality it only costs them $25 in parts and labor. Consider upgrading your home after it is built, and then have multiple contractors bid for your project, instead of paying the builder's marked-up price.

Davis
H O M E S, L P   **HOME PURCHASE AGREEMENT**

Davis Homes, LP, an Indiana corporation having its principal office at 3755 East 82nd Street, Suite 120, Indianapolis, Indiana 46240 ("Builder"), and _____ ("Purchaser") hereby convenant and agree as follows:

1. **Description of Home.** Builder agrees to build and Purchaser agrees to purchase from Builder a custom built home, model _____, elevation _____, to be constructed on lot number _____, in the _____ Subdivision, _____ County, Indiana. The custom built home will include the lot referred to above and will be constructed in substantial compliance with the General Specifications described on **Exhibit A**, which is attached hereto and incorporated herein by this reference.

2. **Purchase Price.** For the real property and improvements described above, Purchaser agrees to pay Builder the sum of $_____ payable as follows:

Earnest money due at signing	$ _____
Down payment due at mortgage approval or authorization to begin construction	$ _____
Mortgage Amount	$ _____
Cash payment due at Closing	$ _____

3. **Mortgage Application.** Within five (5) days after the date of this Agreement, Purchaser shall make formal application to a mortgage lender for a commitment for a mortgage loan of at least $_____. Purchaser agrees to use his best efforts to obtain the mortgage loan commitment and to provide all supplementary information requested by the mortgage lender in connection with such application. Purchaser agrees not to increase his present indebtedness such that it impairs Purchaser's current ability to secure financing of the above amounts. Purchaser understands and agrees any increase in indebtedness which impairs his ability to obtain financing shall constitute a violation of Purchaser's promise to use his best efforts to obtain a mortgage loan commitment. Purchaser agrees any failure by Purchaser to respond to a request for information or assistance from a potential mortgage loan lender within five (5) days of the request shall constitute a violation of Purchaser's promise to use his best efforts to obtain a mortgage loan commitment. Purchaser acknowledges that interest rates, terms and closing cost payable by Purchaser in connection with a mortgage loan are set by the mortgage lender and that Builder is not responsible for fluctuations in interest rates, terms or fees. In the event that Purchaser is unable to obtain a mortgage loan commitment in the amount stated above (or such lesser amount as Purchaser deems sufficient to proceed) within sixty (60) days after the date of this Agreement, Purchaser shall give Builder written notice of Purchaser's inability to obtain financing and send a written request to the mortgage lender requesting the mortgage lender verify the failure to obtain financing, and reasons therefor, to Builder. Upon Purchaser's written notice to Builder that despite Purchaser's best efforts he has failed to obtain such a commitment, Builder shall have the option to either cancel the Agreement and refund all earnest monies to Purchaser or to attempt to procure a mortgage commitment for and on behalf of Purchaser. However, if Purchaser's failure to obtain a financing commitment has been caused in whole or part by Purchaser's failure to use his best efforts to obtain a mortgage loan commitment, Purchaser understands and agrees Builder will retain all earnest money deposited and may also pursue all other legal remedies or relief. In the event Builder does not obtain a mortgage commitment for Purchaser within sixty (60) days after Builder's receipt of such notice, Builder or Purchaser may cancel the Agreement by delivering a written notice of cancellation to the other party, and Builder shall return Purchaser's earnest money deposit. Until one of the parties cancels the Agreement, both may continue to attempt to obtain a financing commitment, and upon receipt of such a commitment, the Agreement shall become non-cancellable. Prior to any cancellation, Purchaser agrees to cooperate with Builder and execute any and all necessary applications and provide all information required to obtain such loan. Purchaser understands and agrees that any job transfer, or other change in employment status, will not release Purchaser from his duties and obligations as contained in this Agreement. In the event any such change in employment status occurs which prevents Purchaser from obtaining the required financing to complete this Agreement, Purchaser understands and agrees that Builder will retain all funds received and may also pursue all other remedies and relief.

4. **Color Selections.** Within ten (10) days after the date of this Agreement, Purchaser shall deliver to Builder a completed Color Selection sheet which shall become a part of this Agreement. If prior to the start of construction, Builder determines that any item or color requested is or will be unavailable, then Purchaser shall select a substitute item or color within seven (7) days after receipt of written notice from Builder of such unavailability. If Purchaser fails to make any choice within the above time limit, Builder shall make such choice for Purchaser.

5. **Mortgage Commitment.** Within sixty (60) days after the date of this Agreement Purchaser shall deliver to Builder (a) a written commitment letter from a mortgage lender, or other evidence of sufficient cash to complete this transaction in a form acceptable to Builder and (b) all sums due as a down payment prior to start of construction under Paragraph 3. If Builder does not receive the above documents and sums, he will have no obligation to proceed and may, at his option, cancel this Agreement and refund all earnest monies to the Purchaser less any actual out-of-pocket expenses incurred by Builder on account of Purchaser.

6. **Change Orders.** Any changes or alterations requested by Purchaser in the General Specifications or Color Selections must be approved in writing by Builder and, in the case of General Specification, by F.H.A., V.A., or other mortgage lender. Such changes or alterations shall not be valid unless Purchaser provides the above mentioned parties with a written change order on a form provided by Builder setting forth the description and additional cost of the change. Purchaser shall pay such additional costs at the time such change order is signed by the appropriate parties, plus any applicable processing fees pursuant to Builder's change order policy. No change orders will be accepted after Builder has received Purchaser's mortgage commitment or other authorization to begin construction.

7. **Construction, Schedule, Delays.** Builder estimates that all work to be performed by it under this Agreement will be completed within _____ (_____) days after the start of construction, but, Builder does not guarantee a firm completion date. The start of framing on the house will constitute the start of construction. Builder will make reasonable and diligent efforts to meet the estimated construction schedule, but Builder will not be obligated to provide or compensate for any accomodations to Purchaser as a result of unavoidable construction delays, including, but not limited to, Builder's inability to convey clear title; the act, neglect or default of Purchaser; damage by fire, earthquake, weather or other casualty; and delay caused by strike, walkout, or any other act by employees of suppliers of labor or materials. Such delays shall not serve to cancel, amend, or diminish any of the Purchaser's obligations under this Agreement. If such delay occurs, the time fixed for completion of the construction shall be extended for a period equal to the time lost by reason of such delay. In the event of late completion not caused by the aforementioned delays, Builder will pay to Purchaser at closing a sum equal to Ten Dollars ($10) for each day Builder's work is incomplete after expiration of completion date, which shall constitute liquidated damages to Purchaser, and shall be the only recovery for delay to which Purchaser shall be entitled. If after the start of construction Builder is unable to obtain the materials specified on the General Specifications or the Color Selections, Builder shall have the right to substitute materials of similar pattern, design and quality.

8. **Permits, Insurance and Assessments.** Builder shall secure building permits as required; and shall maintain workmen's compensation and liability insurance during the construction period; and shall pay any special assessments or improvement bonds, including those payable in the future, for the work covered by this Agreement.

9. **Construction Liens.** Builder agrees to indemnify and hold Purchaser harmless from any and all liens which may be filed in connection with Builder's construction under this Agreement. Purchaser agrees as a condition precedent to Builder's obligation under this Paragraph, to notify Builder in writing of the existence of any such lien within ten (10) days from the date on which Purchaser receives notice of the intention to hold such lien.

10. **Disputes.** Should any dispute arise between Purchaser and Builder with respect to the meaning of the General Specifications or the quality of materials or work required by this Agreement, the dispute shall be reviewed by two qualified persons chosen by Purchaser and Builder, respectively, and if these two persons are unable to agree on the disputed matters, they shall name a third person as umpire, and the decision of the majority of the three persons shall be binding on both Purchaser and Builder. If such persons determine that the work or materials were not finished in good workmanlike manner, they shall specify the additional work or materials to be furnished by Builder and Builder shall complete the work to their specifications within a reasonable time. If, in the sole opinion of Builder, a dispute is unlikely to be resolved pursuant to this Paragraph, Builder may, at its election, cancel this Agreement by written notice to Purchaser accompanied by Builder's check refunding all monies previously paid to Builder by Purchaser, plus interest at the rate of six percent (6%) per annum; whereupon, this Agreement shall terminate, and neither party shall have any further liability to the other party hereunder whatsoever.

11. **Builder's Control of Premises.** The real property described in Paragraph 1 shall be under the Builder's control and possession from the commencement of the work thereon until the Builder receives payment in full pursuant to Paragraph 2 including any amounts due for changes or alterations. Purchaser further convenants and agrees that he will not occupy or take possession of such real property until he has fully inspected and accepted it, all sums due Builder under this Agreement have been paid in full, and title has been conveyed to him.

12. **Closing.** Purchaser and Builder agree that an acceptable final inspection by V.A., F.H.A., or other lender shall constitute evidence of completion of Builder's obligation under this Agreement. Purchaser agrees to close within five (5) days after such inspection. In the event that Purchaser fails to close within five (5) days after final inspection, the Purchaser will be deemed to be in default of this Agreement. In such case, Builder may, at his option, extend the time for closing for successive periods of thirty (30) days, provided that Purchaser pays to Builder a fee of 1½% of the sales price in advance for each extension period; or Builder may, at his option, elect not to offer any such extension, retain all sums paid by Purchaser as liquidated damages and seek to enforce any of his legal remedies under this Agreement.

P _____

Initials B _____

A sample purchase agreement, page 1.

13. **Deed and Title Insurance.** Builder will convey fee simple title to Purchaser by Corporate Warranty Deed at closing and shall deliver an Owner's Policy of Title Insurance in an amount equal to the total price as specified in Paragraph 2. Purchaser will assume and agree to pay the first installment of real estate taxes which will become due and payable after closing.

_____ (Initial if applicable)   14.   **F.H.A. Amendatory Clause.**   The following clause is applicable only if this Agreement is contingent upon Purchaser's securing an F.H.A. insured loan: "It is expressly agreed that, notwithstanding any other provision of this Agreement, the Purchaser shall not be obligated to complete the purchase of the property described herein or to incur any penalty by forfeiture of earnest money deposits or otherwise unless Builder has delivered to the Purchaser a written statement issued by the Federal Housing Commissioner setting forth the appraised value of the property for mortgage insurance purposes of not less than _____ ($_____). Builder hereby agrees to deliver the above statement to the Purchaser promptly after such appraised value statement is received by Builder. The Purchaser shall, however, have the privilege and option of proceeding with the consummation of this Agreement without regard to the amount of the appraised valuation made by the Federal Housing Commissioner."

_____ (Initial if applicable)   15.   **V.A. Amendatory Clause.**   The following clause is applicable only if this Agreement is contingent upon Purchaser's securing a V.A. guaranteed loan: "It is expressly agreed that, notwithstanding any other provision of this Agreement, the Purchaser shall not incur any penalty by forfeiture of earnest money or otherwise be obligated to complete the purchase of property described herein, if the Agreement price exceeds the reasonable value of the property established by the Veterans Administration. The Purchaser shall, however, have the privilege and option of proceeding with consummation of this Agreement without regard to the amount of the reasonable value established by the Veterans Administration."

16.   **Warranty.**   Upon full payment by Purchaser to Builder of the price as specified in Paragraph 2, including any charges or alterations requested by Purchaser, Builder will enroll Purchaser in the "2-10 Home Buyers Warranty" program, providing Purchaser with up to two (2) years of warranty protection on certain components of the custom built home. THE 2-10 HOME BUYERS WARRANTY IS THE SOLE WARRANTY MADE BY BUILDER AND IS SUBJECT TO PURCHASER PROPERLY MAINTAINING ALL ITEMS CONNECTED WITH HOME AND PROPERTY OWNERSHIP. THIS IS A LIMITED WARRANTY AND DOES NOT COVER ANY CONSEQUENTIAL DAMAGES. BUILDER MAKES NO OTHER WARRANTIES, EXPRESSED OR IMPLIED, INCLUDING NO IMPLIED WARRANTY OF HABITABILITY, MERCHANTABILITY OR FITNESS FOR PARTICULAR PURPOSE. IF ANY WARRANTY IS IMPLIED FROM THIS AGREEMENT, IT SHALL NOT HAVE A DURATION LONGER THAN THE EXPRESSED WARRANTY IN THE 2-10 HOME BUYERS WARRANTY AGREEMENT. Purchaser shall give Builder a written notice of any claim under the 2-10 Home Buyers Warranty agreement. Builder shall have sixty (60) days after receipt of such notice to inspect the custom built home and, if such inspection shows defects covered by the home warranty agreement, Builder shall make necessary repairs or adjustments without cost to the Purchasers within ninety (90) days (weather, labor, and supply conditions permitting). Purchaser agrees to allow a "break-in" period of six (6) months after occupancy before requesting repairs of or adjustments except of emergency matters.

17.   **Mortgage and Closing Costs.**   Mortgage application fees, legal closing costs and pre-paid interest, taxes and insurance required in connection with this transaction shall be allocated between Builder and Purchaser as shown on the attached Closing Costs Addendum to Home Purchase Agreement.

18.   **Utilities.**   Purchaser agrees that all utilities to be billed to the custom built home will be changed from Builder's name no later than three (3) days after closing. Other connections of utilities shall be in Purchaser's name and will be at the expense of Purchaser.

19.   **Purchaser's Acknowledgement.**   Purchaser acknowledges receipt of a true copy of this Agreement and acknowledges that he has read and understands the contents thereof.

20.   **Miscellaneous.**   This Agreement shall be binding upon the heirs, administrators, executors, and the assigns of the respective parties hereto. If any provision of this Agreement is held to be invalid by any court of competent jurisdiction, the invalidity of such provision shall not affect any other provision of this Agreement. The headings of this Agreement are intended solely for convenience of reference and shall be given no effect in the construction or interpretation of this Agreement. This Agreement constitutes the entire understanding and agreement between the parties concerning the subject matter of this Agreement and may not be amended, supplemented or modified except by a written document signed by all parties. Any and all previous agreements, whether written or oral, between the parties concerning the subject matter of this Agreement are hereby cancelled and superseded by this Agreement. The failure of any party to insist upon performance of any of the provisions of this Agreement shall not be construed as a waiver of such provisions. This Agreement shall in all respects be interpreted and construed in accordance with and governed by the laws of the State of Indiana. This Agreement or any notice thereof is not recordable in any public record.

21.   Purchaser understands and agrees that all desired features and specifications must be included on the final signed blueprints which will determine the course of construction of the home. Purchaser understands and agrees that any feature, specification, or other construction detail not clearly specified in the final signed blueprints will be determined by Builder.

22.   Builder's obligation hereunder is conditioned on its ability to obtain all necessary permits and licenses including, but not limited to, a building permit to allow for construction of the home. This includes plotting of the subdivision and improvements to be made thereon. If Builder is unable to obtain all such permits within ninety (90) days from date, Builder shall have the right in its sole discretion to cancel this contract by written notice to Purchaser, accompanied by a refund of all amounts paid Builder by Purchaser together with interest at six (6%) percent per annum; whereupon, this agreement shall terminate without further liability or rights hereunder.

23.   **Further Specifications, Conditions and Options.**   _____

_____

_____

_____

IN WITNESS WHEREOF, the parties hereto subscribe their names, this_____ day of _____, 19____.

PURCHASER(S) _____   _____

                ADDRESS _____

                CITY/STATE/ZIP _____

                HOME PHONE_____

                BUSINESS PHONE: HIS _____

                                          HERS _____

BUILDER ACCEPTANCE   DAVIS HOMES, LP

Date_____   By _____
                                                                    Title

★ ★

MORTGAGE LENDER _____   TYPE FINANCING _____
CO-OP REALTOR _____   REALTY COMPANY_____
ADDRESS_____
CITY/STATE/ZIP _____
PHONE _____

A sample purchase agreement, page 2.

Getting a Good Deal

Keep in mind that builders are motivated to sell. Unlike a seller that has lived in a home, the builder doesn't have any emotional ties to the home. The builder's motivation determines the flexibility in sales terms. In some instances, you may be able to negotiate a better deal. Also, keep in mind that you are the customer, and you should be treated as such.

The following scenarios provide some examples of getting a good deal:

♦ **Buy early in the development process.** When a subdivision has homes that have been sold and are lived in, it makes the area more appealing to new buyers. The builders want to be able to say that *x* number of homes have sold. They want to give other buyers the illusion that they had better buy now or be locked out of the swanky neighborhood forever. For this reason, builders may be more willing to deal if you are one of the first buyers.

♦ **Buy before the increase.** Most builder reps will tell you that the base model price is going to increase soon. This may be true, but it is also their way of getting you to make a decision sooner. Don't let any price increase force you into making a decision that is not sound.

♦ **Negotiate to buy the model.** The model will include top-quality furnishings, plus you can see exactly what you are getting. You may arrange for the builder to sell you the model and then rent the home to the builder until the development is complete.

♦ **Think carefully about upgrades and extras.** Do you really need the upgrade now? If it's more expensive to have the work done after the house is complete, then yes, go for the upgrade. If it's something that you can change later, then consider waiting. You may be able to make the change at a later date and at a better price because you can shop around for someone to do the work. Likewise, consider whether all the work has to be done. It might be better to have the builder frame the basement but leave it unfinished. You can then later hire someone to finish the basement or possibly even do the work yourself.

♦ **Buy in a down market.** If new-home sales are slow, builders may want to unload the excess units. If they don't, they have to pay the costs to maintain and promote these empty units. Also, they have sunk a great deal of money into supplies and labor (they have to pay the subcontractors whether the home sells or not), so builders in a bind may be willing to sell a home for what they have invested in it, just so they can pay off their bills.

♦ **Buy the last unit.** As more and more homes in the subdivision sell, the builders get more and more profit. They may be less worried about meeting expenses and may be flexible on price. Plus, the builders are likely to want to move on to the next development and may be motivated to sell the last home.

Including Home Extras in the Mortgage

When you build a new home, it might or might not come with a pool, landscaping, window treatments (blinds), or other big-purchase items that you have to buy after the home is built. If you want these items to be completed while the home is being built, you must check with your builder.

If you want these items completed after you close on the home with a separate contractor, ask your lender about a *mortgage holdback*. This is where you add the price of the purchase to the mortgage and the lender holds the money to pay the company when they complete the job.

> **Bet You Didn't Know**
>
> Some homebuilders will only allow a particular pool builder to build you a pool while they are building your home. You might be able to choose any pool builder you like, but they cannot start building your pool until you have closed on the home.

This will usually cost you a fee to the lender (big surprise). Make sure you ask your contractor if they will allow this type of financing, and whether they charge you a fee to do it as well.

Sometimes you can purchase items like window treatments through a new homebuilder's design center (at quite an elevated price, usually). The design center is where you pick out your flooring, colors, doorknobs, appliances, interior and exterior lights, and all the little extras in your home. Refer to the "Upgrades, Upgrades" section earlier in this chapter for things you can have your builder add.

Getting a New Home Warranty

A *warranty* is a guarantee that a product will function for a certain period of time. For example, your toaster may come with a 30-day warranty. If the toaster doesn't toast, you can get a new toaster or have it repaired. Home warranties work the same way.

On a new home, there are different types of warranties. All homes come with an *implied warranty* from the builder. This means that the builder should replace or repair anything that threatens the home—the structure, soundness, and function of the home and its components. In addition, some homes come with an expressed *builder's warranty*. This warranty explicitly lists which features are covered and for how long.

Some builder's warranties are backed by insurance. If the builder defaults, the insurance company will guarantee the claim. For example, a homeowner's warranty, or HOW, includes the following coverage:

> **Year one:** Covers defects in workmanship and materials; structural defects; flaws in electrical, plumbing, heating, cooling, ventilating, and mechanical systems. Does not cover appliances, fixtures, and equipment.

> **Year two:** Covers major structural defects and certain major electrical, plumbing, heating, cooling, ventilating, and mechanical systems. No longer covers defects in materials and workmanship.

> **Years three through ten:** Covers certain major structural defects.

A good warranty should include the following information:

- ◆ The name of the person who holds the warranty and a statement telling whether the warranty can be transferred.

- ◆ The length of the warranty.

- ◆ An exact explanation of what is covered and what is not. The appliances? The roof? The plumbing?

- ◆ A description of what will happen if a problem occurs. Will the problem be fixed? By whom? In what time frame? How do you file a claim? Do you have to pay a deductible? If so, how much?

- ◆ Any limitations on damages. If the ceiling leaks and ruins your stamp collection, is the collection covered?

If you are using an agent, ask him or her to look over your warranty and make sure it provides good coverage.

Avoiding New Home Problems

Buying a new home probably doesn't have any more or any fewer hassles than buying an existing home. But you will encounter a different set of problems. Use this section to anticipate and head off any potential problems.

You are trusting the builder to complete a job. To make sure you have some recourse if you are not satisfied with the completed home, you may want to include the following information in your sales contract:

- **Insist on a final walkthrough inspection.** Insist that any incomplete, missing, or broken items be fixed. If possible, don't close until the changes and final repairs are made. A builder who has been paid may not be motivated to fix the dripping sink. If the money is still held in escrow until that drip is fixed, you have some leverage to ensure that the repairs are made.

- **Make sure that your home is built to the standards of the model you visited.** In some cases, the builder may make changes—for instance, if the housing market changes. Builders have very set routines for clients that are building new houses. The buyers are required to make choices along the way and monitor and sign off on progress. Therefore, you shouldn't encounter any surprises. Just make sure you understand how the particular building process is mapped out and stay involved.

- **Ask for ongoing inspections.** If you know someone with home-building experience, have that person check out the home during its building phases. It's easier to spot shoddy electrical work—and have it fixed—when the work is being done. Obtain a Customer Communication Form from your builder and start keeping a paper trail (faxing them) on all the things that are incorrect or need to be rectified in your home *while it is being built.*

- **Hire a home inspector.** For a well-earned fee, they will review the home as it is being built, make sure it is up to standards, and accompany you on your final walkthrough (usually bringing many imperfections to the builder's attention that you might never have noticed). Also, consider making the sale contingent on a final professional inspection before you close.

Finally, prepare for delays. The builder may take longer to build the home than planned. This can cause problems if you don't have anywhere to live or if you have locked in the interest rate. First, make sure you have a place to stay if the home isn't built on time. Second, consider locking in the rate until the closing date. You may ask for this if you are using the builder or mortgage company for financing. Third, check up on the progress. If four months have gone by since you made an offer and they haven't started the basement yet, you're in trouble.

The Least You Need to Know

- ◆ The key items to consider when purchasing a new home are the area, builder, plot, and plan.

- ◆ Check out the builder's reputation. Talk to homeowners already living in homes built by the same builder. Check with the Better Business Bureau. Ask those acquainted with homebuilders for their opinions.

- ◆ Builders may not be too flexible on price, but you might be able to negotiate for upgrades to the carpeting, roof, yard, and so on. You can also negotiate on the terms of the contract.

- ◆ There are three types of new-home warranties: an implied warranty, a builder's warranty, and an insurance-backed warranty. You should get all three.

- ◆ If you are having the home built (rather than buying a newly built home), keep tabs on the progress and have any problems corrected as the home is built. Also, expect and be prepared for delays.

Part 3

Understanding Your Finance Options

After looking at home after home until all the rooms merge into one never-ending maze of homes, you find the home you want and the sellers accept your offer. Now you can relax, right?

Wrong! The next maze is the financial maze—finding the right type of financing for you. Put on your blue suit and get ready to play banker because this part explains all the financial options available for purchasing a home.

Financing 101

In This Chapter

- ◆ Understanding how lending works
- ◆ Understanding the components of a mortgage loan
- ◆ Knowing the different types of financing
- ◆ Factoring in mortgage insurance
- ◆ Deciding which type of financing is most appropriate for you

When you think about securing financing, think about a high school dance. The lenders are on one side of the room, and the buyers are on the other. Getting together requires agreement by both sides. For example, which lender do you want to dance with? And will that lender dance with you?

This chapter helps you decide which dance partner is right for you.

How Basic Lending Works

Bankers aren't in the business because they like to handle money; they like to *make* money. Banking is a business, just like any other business. What bankers "sell" is money.

Here's how it works. Your Aunt Betty deposits $500 in her savings account, and the bank agrees to pay her 5 percent interest on that money. The bankers then take Aunt Betty's $500 and loan it to you. In exchange for letting you use "their" money, the bank charges you 9 percent interest.

The 9 percent interest rate you pay covers the 5 percent the bank has to pay Aunt Betty, any costs for moving the money around, and of course, a profit for the bank. The difference between the savings interest and lending interest is called the *spread.*

When money is tight, more people want money. Lenders can be picky about who gets the money and can charge a higher rate to those who borrow the money. When money isn't tight, there is more money than there are borrowers. Lenders want to make the loans attractive, so rates go down.

How Home Loan Lending Works

How much you pay on a home loan depends on the factors used for your particular loan package. These concepts include the interest rate, the discount or origination points, and the term, all handily covered in this section.

What's the Interest Rate?

If all the banks offered money to all buyers at the same rates, selecting a lender would be easy. Instead, lenders differ in how much they charge you to use their money. This charge is called the *interest rate* and will vary depending on the lender, the economy, the type of loan, and other factors. Interest rates can range from 4 percent to 15 percent or higher. The interest rate has a huge effect on how much you pay for an item. Consider the following example.

If you borrow $100,000 at 8 percent for 30 years, your monthly payment will be $733. If you borrow the same amount of money for the same amount of time but at a higher interest rate, your payment increases significantly. The following table compares a loan at 8 percent to a loan at 13 percent. The monthly principal and interest payment amount difference is $372!

How Interest Rate Affects Payments—Principal and Interest

Example 1		Example 2	
Loan amount	$100,000	Loan amount	$100,000
Interest rate	8%	Interest rate	13%
Term	30	Term	30
Monthly payment	$733.76	Monthly payment	$1,106.20
Difference: $372.44 a month!			

When a lending institution makes a loan, it *amortizes* the loan—that is, it calculates the loan amount plus interest and then divides that total by the number of months you are paying on the loan (the term). The interest is front-loaded, so for the first few years of payments, you are paying mostly interest. (The bank gets its money first.)

The interest rate quoted and the interest rate you actually pay will be different, because the real interest rate will include points, application fees, and other fees you pay for the loan. The real interest rate is called the *APR* or *annual percentage rate*. When you apply for a loan, the lender will tell you the true APR.

Bet You Didn't Know

If you have a spreadsheet application (Microsoft Excel, for example), you can calculate a monthly mortgage payment using the Paste Function. Simply click the Paste Function button on the toolbar (it looks like an "f" with a small "x" next to it). Click the PMT option under the Financial Function category and click OK. Type in the Rate (the percent interest rate in decimal form ÷ 12 months); the Nper (loan years times 12 equals the number of periods); the Pv present value (amount you are borrowing now); and click OK. The payment amount will appear in the cell. As an example, borrowing $100,000 (-100,000Pv) at a 7.5 percent interest rate (.00625Rate) for 30 years (360Nper) equals a principal and interest payment of $699.21.

Other Fees: Paying Loan Points

In addition to the interest rate, you may also be required to pay points. One point is equal to 1 percent of the loan. A lender uses points to trick you into thinking you are getting a lower rate than you really are. The points are sometimes called *discount points*. Usually the lower the rate, the more points you have to pay. For example, a lender may offer a loan for 6 percent with zero points. Or you can get a lower rate (5.25 percent) by paying two points up front, known as "buying down" the rate.

Fewer points means less money up front but a higher rate. More points may mean a lower rate, but you will have to come up with more money at the closing.

The number of points will vary depending on the lender and the mortgage package. You pay points at the closing. Keep in mind, though, that if interest rates are high and you think you will be in your home for a long time, it might be a good idea to buy down the interest rate by paying points. When you pay points on the close of your home, you are allowed to deduct them on your taxes in the year that you paid them. So if you pay 2 points on a $100,000 home, you can deduct $2,000 on your taxes. Check with a tax accountant to verify your particular situation.

Real Deal

Because points are usually tax-deductible, consider the tax savings when thinking about whether to get a loan with points. Check with a tax accountant for your particular situation and area. As an example, your mortgage lender might be able to pay all your closing costs and instead charge you points on the loan. This might enable you to deduct some of your closing costs (that is, the points) on your taxes.

How Long Do You Make Payments?

Buyer Beware

Check out any restrictions regarding prepaying on the loan amount. Most lenders allow you to prepay, but you should check to be sure this is allowed. When you prepay on a loan, you simply send an additional amount (usually on a separate check) toward the principal amount on your loan. The *principal* is the amount you originally borrowed, not the interest you are paying on the loan.

Loans vary depending on how long you make payments. You can get a 30-year loan, a 15-year loan, or a loan on which you make 26 payments a year (every other week). The length of time you pay is called the *term*.

Most lenders today allow you to prepay on the loan amount. Prepaying on a loan will pay off the loan earlier and can save you a lot of money in interest. For example, if you make an additional $1,000 payment on your mortgage per year, depending on the amount of your loan, it can shave years off your mortgage term. Refer to the "Prepaying Your Mortgage" section in Chapter 13 for more information.

Now that you have a good idea of the different elements that factor into a home loan payment, let's take a look at the different types of financing.

Different Loans for Different Folks

My mom and dad live in the same home that I grew up in. They paid on the home for 30 years and paid the same monthly payment that they did in 1965 all the way up to 1995. (Their payment is less than most car payments!) Back when they purchased their home, most people selected this type of financing, which is called *fixed-rate financing*. Most people expected to stay in their homes for 30 years and wanted the stability of fixed payments.

Times have changed! First, people don't stay in the same spot as long, and second, lenders have gotten more creative with the financing they offer. Now you can shop around for different types of loans.

As mentioned earlier, loans differ in the interest rate and points charged. Loans also vary depending on how the payments are structured. The two most common structures are *fixed-rate mortgages* and *adjustable-rate mortgages*.

Loans also can vary depending on who offers the loans and how they are backed. The two most common types of loans are *conventional* and *government-backed*. You can get your loan from Bill Banker or from Bill Banker with Uncle Sam backing you.

Real Deal

Remember, the term *mortgage* doesn't refer to the payments you make on your home. A mortgage is the lien or claim against your property.

You get an overview of the various loan types in this section. Other chapters in this part cover each loan type in more detail.

Fixed-Rate Mortgage Loans

Until 1970 or so, like my parents' case, almost all loans made for homes were fixed-rate mortgages. On a fixed-rate mortgage, your monthly payment never varies. You pay the same amount for the first payment as you do for the last. If interest rates go up, it doesn't matter; your payment stays the same. Likewise, if interest rates go down, your payment still stays the same. Fixed-rate mortgage loans are covered in Chapter 13.

Real Deal _____

If you have a fixed-rate mortgage loan, you may not be stuck with that loan for the rest of your life. You can refinance the loan to get a better interest rate. Generally, it's a good idea to refinance if interest rates drop by 1 percent or more. Because of the dramatic drop in interest rates since 2000, the home loan market has experienced a refinancing boom.

Calculate the costs to see how long you must have the new loan in order to break even on the closing costs you will have to pay. Chapter 15 covers refinancing.

Adjustable-Rate Mortgage Loans

Before 1972, interest rates were low (around 7 percent), and lenders were doing okay. Then the U.S. economy hit a rough spot. From 1972 to 1980, interest rates skyrocketed, at one point reaching 20 percent. Lenders lost money because they had to pay a high interest rate on savings accounts, but borrowers with fixed-rate mortgages were still paying them the low rate they had secured before the spike in rates. The lenders, of course, didn't like this, so they decided to have borrowers share in the risk in future loans made. Hence the adjustable-rate mortgage, or ARM.

When you get an ARM loan, you usually pay a lower rate initially than on a fixed-rate mortgage. The interest rate on the ARM loan is tied to an index that reflects the current money market. If the interest rates go up on your renewal date, your payments go up. If the interest rates go down, your payments go down. Chapter 14 covers ARM loans in detail.

Conventional Loans

In addition to the different loan types, loans vary depending on who backs them. The most common loan backers: conventional, government-backed, and nonconventional.

Conventional loans are secured from a lender—usually a bank, mortgage broker, or savings and loan institution. (Chapter 13 discusses sources of conventional loans.) Conventional loans usually require 3 to 20 percent for a down payment. You can put down less than 20 percent, but if you do, most lenders will require that you purchase private mortgage insurance (PMI). This insurance increases the costs to you because you have to pay to protect the lender in case you default on the loan (because you were allowed a smaller down payment).

Government-Backed Loans

To make homeownership more affordable, the government got involved in the loan business and decided it would back home loans. The lender still makes the loan, but the government backs, or insures, the loan.

The two most common types of government loans are FHA (Federal Housing Authority), which are insured by the federal government, and VA (Veterans' Administration), which are guaranteed. VA loans are covered in Chapter 15.

FHA loans offer many benefits to first-time buyers. Because the FHA insures the loan, the lender will accept a smaller down payment. On an FHA loan, for instance, you may be able to put just 3 to 5 percent down. A lower down payment helps new buyers who don't have a lot of up-front cash to afford a home. But on the other hand, you may pay a higher interest rate.

You can finance some of your closing costs. Again, this feature helps first-time buyers who don't have a lot of up-front money. The monthly payments on the loan will be more because the amount financed is more, but you don't have to come up with the money when you purchase the home.

FHA loans are attractive because they are *assumable* (someone else can take over the payments). Assumable loans may be an added attraction when you sell your home. (Assumptions are covered in Chapter 15.) In the past, some FHA loans were freely assumable, meaning the buyers did not have to qualify. Newer FHA loans are *qualified assumptions*, meaning that the buyers must qualify to take over the loan.

There are no penalties for prepaying an FHA loan.

 Real Deal

Many buyers think that they can qualify for an FHA loan only on their first home. That's not true. You don't have to be a first-time buyer to get an FHA loan. Your loan amount must be within a certain range to qualify, and you may not have another FHA loan outstanding.

Flip the coin, and there are drawbacks to an FHA loan. You are required to put less down on the home, so you have less up-front money invested. To balance this, you are required to pay a mortgage insurance premium (MIP) up front. This fee is usually 2.25 percent. You can finance the insurance, but keep in mind that your monthly payment will be higher. See "Your Loan May Require Mortgage Insurance" later in this chapter for more information.

The home you want to finance must be appraised by FHA appraisers. Sometimes the FHA will require certain repairs before approving the loan. FHA loans will finance homes that cost up to a certain amount. The amount varies depending on the area and is usually based on the average cost of housing in the region.

Conforming vs. Nonconforming Loans

Fannie Mae and Freddie Mac are government-backed companies that purchase loans. Loans that meet the guidelines set by these companies are often called conforming loans. Fannie and Freddie purchase loans only up to a certain amount ($322,700 in the year 2003 for all states except Alaska and Hawaii); often loans over this amount are nonconforming loans or jumbo loans.

Real Deal

Check the Fannie Mae (www.fanniemae.com) or Freddie Mac (www.freddiemac.com) websites for current information on loan qualifications and limits.

For a nonconforming or jumbo loan, you may be required to pay a higher interest rate, and you may have to follow different guidelines. These types of loans are covered in Chapter 15.

Still More Loan Types

In addition to this menagerie of loan types, there are still other ways to finance the purchase of a home. You can assume someone else's mortgage. You can ask the seller for financing. Other loan arrangements are the topic of Chapter 15.

Your Loan May Require Mortgage Insurance

Mortgage insurance is required by lenders if you get an FHA loan or make a down payment of less than 20 percent. Some states have laws that prohibit an LTV (loan-to-value) ratio of more than 80 percent without insurance. Also, the secondary market (explained in Chapter 5) may not purchase this type of loan without insurance. Your lender will set up and purchase this type of insurance.

Buyer Beware

Don't confuse this type of mortgage insurance with the kind that pays off the home in the event of the death of the purchaser. You'll be bombarded with offers of this type of insurance when you close on the home. Don't be tempted—there is usually a better and cheaper way to provide the same protection.

For FHA loans, your loan is backed by an insurance program; this means you must pay the insurance premium. This type of mortgage is called a mortgage insurance premium (MIP) or mutual mortgage insurance (MMI).

Conventional loans require private mortgage insurance, or PMI, when you put less than 20 percent down. MIPs, MMI, and PMI work the same way; they help the lender recover the cost of selling your home if you default on the loan.

Paying Mortgage Insurance

With an FHA loan, you pay 2.25 percent of the loan amount at the closing plus a monthly fee. This premium provides insurance for the life of the loan and can be financed. If you sell or refinance an FHA loan, you may be entitled to a refund. Ask your lender or contact the U.S. Department of Housing and Urban Development (HUD) (www.hud.gov) for more information.

For private mortgage insurance, you usually pay two months' worth at close, plus a monthly charge, or you can pay a lump-sum payment. The amount depends on the down payment, the coverage required by the lender, and the type of loan (fixed or ARM). The premium may be higher for ARMs, for example.

The insurance is added to your monthly mortgage. In the following example, if you borrow $100,000, the premium is $500 at 0.5 percent. This fee is divided by 12 and added to your monthly payment. The following table breaks down the costs of private mortgage insurance.

Real Deal

Although there are only a few PMI companies, ask your lender to shop around on rates for private mortgage insurance. The cheapest is best for you!

The Cost of Private Mortgage Insurance

Description	Amount
Loan amount	$100,000
Yearly premium (0.5%)	$500 ÷ 12
Added to monthly payment	$42

Canceling Mortgage Insurance

Depending on the loan agreement, you may be able to cancel the insurance once you reach a certain amount of equity. If you have 20 percent equity (80 percent loan-to-value), you may be able to stop paying insurance. Your loan-to-value ratio may change sooner if you add capital improvements to the home, if your home appreciates in value quickly, or if you have paid down your mortgage (paid a larger monthly payment).

Real Deal _____

The increase of value in a home is called market value appreciation. In 2001, the nationwide average for home appreciation was 6 percent.

Check with the lender about how and when you can cancel PMI. The lender may require an appraisal if the property has been improved, a clean payment history on the loan (for instance, no more than one 30-days-late payment in 24 months and one 15-days-late payment in 12 months), and a minimum payment history on the loan (for example, two years). Finally, the property must still be occupied by the original owner.

Another way to get the PMI payment taken off your loan payment is to have your home appraised by your lender's approved appraiser (in case the value of your home increases dramatically in a short period of time). If you go this route, the lender will require you to have 25 percent equity (75 percent loan-to-value), and usually you must have had the loan for at least 12 months.

Bet You Didn't Know

A federal loan enacted after July 1999 requires PMI cancellation when the loan-to-value ratio drops to 78 percent, which takes on average 10 to 15 years for the borrowers. But many homes appreciate in value faster than that, sometimes reaching this loan-to-value ratio in four years.

Your lender has no incentive and no program in place to automatically cancel your mortgage insurance. So it's your responsibility to keep on top of your home value and to look into canceling this fee when possible.

Depending on the lender, the cancellation process can be relatively easy. For instance, if your loan is owned or serviced by Fannie Mae and Freddie Mac, you can cancel if you have an on-time monthly mortgage payment, your mortgage is at least two years old, and your loan-to-value ratio drops below 80 percent.

Other lenders may require more work. Ask what they require (an appraisal, for instance), get it, and be persistent.

How to Decide on the Type of Financing

You've now surveyed the market; you know what your options are when shopping for a loan. How do you pick one? Unfortunately, there's no one right answer. Which loan is right for you will depend on your current financial situation, your future plans, and other factors. This section helps you narrow down your choices.

How Much Can You Afford for a Down Payment?

Money, as usual, is the first consideration. If you have piles and piles of money sitting in your closet, you can pick and choose among the different lending options. If you are like most people, though, you probably lack those piles of money. You may have just one pile, and that pile will affect which type of loan you can get.

For example, conventional loans require a 10 to 20 percent down payment. If you can't come up with that amount, you have to consider a different loan type—perhaps an FHA loan.

Buyer Beware

Deciding which type of loan you take will depend on several factors. This section includes some simple summary tables. Keep in mind that these tables summarize general circumstances. Your own situation will depend on all the factors—not just one.

Down Payment	Loan Type
20% or more	Conventional
3% to 19%	Insured conventional (with PMI/MIP/MMI)
Less than 3%	FHA or VA
0%	Nonconforming

How Much Can You Afford for a Monthly Payment?

In addition to the down payment, you should take into consideration how much you can afford—and how much the lender thinks you can afford—for a monthly payment. Deciding how much you can afford is covered extensively in Chapter 2. Chapter 2 explains the ratios the lender uses to qualify you for a loan amount.

Remember that lenders calculate your monthly home payment as a percentage of your income. Also keep in mind that your monthly home payment will depend on the interest rate. You may want to select a loan type with the lowest initial interest rate in order to qualify for the home.

Suppose that you can afford $700 for monthly payments. This payment amount includes principal, interest, taxes, and insurance. If the fixed-rate mortgage loan for a $100,000 home charges 8 percent, the payment on the principal and interest alone is $733. You won't qualify for this type of loan.

On the other hand, if the initial rate for an ARM loan is 6 percent, the monthly payment for principal and interest on a $100,000 home is $600. You could qualify for this type of loan. This type of loan, for example, is a good idea if you need more home than you can afford on a fixed rate and you have a higher earning potential—that is, your income is likely to rise.

How Long Will You Live in the Home?

Another factor to consider when selecting a loan type is how long you plan to live in the home. A recent survey shows that most people stay in a home an average of five to seven years.

If you plan to stay in the home five years or so, you may want to consider an adjustable-rate mortgage. The first few years of the loan will be at the lowest rate, or teaser rate. The following years will be adjusted according to the market. The payments could go up or down, but even if they go up, most can jump up only a certain amount each year. If you have one year at the teaser rate and then two years with a rate cap, you may find the interest rate has only risen 2 percent. This type of financing might be much more advantageous than a fixed-rate mortgage.

Consider this example:

Fixed-Rate	ARM
Year 1 at 6%	Year 1 (initial rate) 4.25%
Year 2 at 6%	Year 2 (+1%) 5.25%
Year 3 at 6%	Year 3 (+1%) 6.25%

If this were your situation, you would have had two years below the fixed rate and one year at about the same rate. In this case, the ARM is definitely a better choice.

Buyer Beware

The current interest rates are also a factor to consider when deciding on a loan type. If the rates are high, you may only qualify for an ARM loan. If rates are low, as they have been recently, you may want to lock into the low rate over the life of the loan.

Keep in mind that ARMs differ in the way they are structured. Not all include rate caps, or the rate cap may work differently. Chapter 14 discusses what to look for in an adjustable-rate mortgage.

On the other hand, if you plan to live in your home for the next 10 or 20 years, you may want to lock into a fixed-rate mortgage. Doing so ensures that your payments will remain the same. In the long run, you may benefit from the fixed rate. As a rule of thumb, if you plan to stay in a home five years or less, consider an ARM. If you plan to stay five years or more, consider a fixed-rate mortgage.

What's Your Risk Level?

Finally, you will want to consider your own personality. If you enjoy taking risks, having a mortgage that could get more and more expensive may not cause you to lose any sleep. If you are a worrier, you may not want to get an adjustable-rate mortgage, even if it is a better deal. The added worry of rising payments may not be worth the added savings in money.

The Least You Need to Know

- Loans vary on the amount the lender charges. You can expect two types of charges: an interest rate that you pay over the life of the loan and points that you pay up front.

- One point is equal to 1 percent of the loan amount. Interest rates and points are usually tied together. The lower the interest rate, the higher the points.

- FHA loans usually allow for a lower down payment, but you have to pay mortgage insurance. FHA loans aren't just available to first-time buyers.

- When you get a fixed-rate loan, your first payment and last payment are the same—that is, the payment never varies. Fixed-rate loans are a good idea when the interest rates are low, when you plan to stay in your home for a while, or if you do not like taking risks.

- With an adjustable-rate mortgage (ARM), the payment varies over the life of the loan. This type of rate is good when rates are high, and you may not qualify for a fixed-rate loan; when you will only stay in a home five to seven years; or when you don't mind taking risks.

- Depending on the loan-to-value ratio, you may be required to pay mortgage insurance. This applies both to FHA loans as well as conventional loans.

Fixed-Rate Mortgages

In This Chapter

- ◆ Understanding the advantages and disadvantages of a fixed-rate mortgage
- ◆ Checking interest rates and points for this loan
- ◆ Choosing a loan term
- ◆ Prepaying a mortgage

You've probably picked up on the theme of this book: good and bad, advantages and disadvantages, benefits and drawbacks, pluses and minuses. That's because there is no easy answer. For every situation, there's something beneficial about it and something not so beneficial. You have to weigh the pros and cons to decide which decision is right for you.

Here the decision being weighed is whether a fixed-rate mortgage is best for you.

Not a risk-taker? Then you'll probably be most comfortable with a fixed-rate mortgage. Fixed rates are a good idea in many circumstances. Which ones? Read this chapter to find out. Also read Chapter 14 and Chapter 15 to get an idea of the other types of financing, just so you know all your options.

The Advantages of a Fixed-Rate Mortgage

A fixed-rate mortgage was about the only type of mortgage available before the 1970s. If you had a mortgage then, you most likely had a fixed-rate mortgage. That's probably the kind of mortgage your parents have if they have lived in their home for some time. What that means is that your parents are likely to say "fixed-rate" all the way.

In some cases, your parents are right. A fixed-rate mortgage gives you the benefit of knowing your exact payment for the life of the loan. What you pay in 2003 will be the same amount you pay in 2033. To some buyers, the financial security of having a set payment greatly outweighs any cost savings they might gain from getting another type of mortgage.

Fixed-rate mortgages are especially sensible when interest rates are as low as they have been in the past few years. Why take the chance of playing "spin the interest rate" when you can lock into a favorable rate now?

If you plan to stay in your home for a long time, a fixed-rate mortgage becomes even more desirable. You gain most of the benefits of an adjustable-rate mortgage during the first few years of the loan. After that, you may end up paying a higher rate. As stated before, if you know you will be moving on to a different city, job, or house in a few years, the ARM makes sense, but if you are moving to your dream house to stay, a fixed-rate mortgage is the mortgage for you.

Real Deal

If you have an adjustable-rate mortgage or a high fixed-rate mortgage and the rates on fixed-rate loans drop, you may want to refinance and lock in at this lower rate. There are some charges for refinancing, but you can save money in the long run by refinancing. Chapter 15 covers refinancing.

Finally, you'll want to keep in mind that if your income is likely to rise, the burden of making payments will not be as great. When you are making twice the money, your house payments will still be at the original payment amount. That's a plus. And if your income is likely to decrease or remain steady (for instance, if you are retiring), a fixed-rate mortgage might also be the best bet. Your payments will be the same, so you can plan accordingly.

The Drawbacks of a Fixed-Rate Mortgage

When interest rates are high, the picture changes. In this case, the rates for a fixed-rate mortgage may be so high that you cannot qualify for a fixed-rate loan. Also, why lock into a high rate for the life of the loan? Instead, consider an adjustable-rate mortgage, which is usually offered at a lower "teaser" rate with a cap that will ensure your rate stays low for the first few years. After that, if you find that the economy has shifted and interest rates are low again, you have the option of refinancing at a lower, fixed rate.

CAUTION

Buyer Beware _____

If you decide on a loan based on the notion of refinancing later, keep in mind that some refinances may require you to pay an origination fee of 1 percent of the refinanced amount. Also note that refinanced points paid must be deducted from your taxes over a 20-year period, not the year of the refinance.

Interest and Points for Fixed-Rate Mortgages

When shopping around for a fixed-rate mortgage, you'll want to look at the interest rates that are offered and the points you have to pay. Keep in mind that the lender may offer a lower interest rate but have higher closing costs and points. You'll want to carefully compare the different loans offered.

Suppose that you are purchasing a home for $100,000. The lender offers two rates: 6 percent with no points, and 5.25 percent with two points (see the following table). Which is better? The answer depends on your situation.

The Price of Paying Points

Description	Amount
Price of home	$100,000
Price of two points	$2,000
Monthly payment at 6%	$600
Monthly payment at 5.25%	$552
Minimum savings	$48
Months to recoup points cost	41

If you can't come up with the additional $2,000 for the points, you'll want the option with zero points.

If you are going to live in the house longer than five years, you'll probably benefit from paying down the rate. Here's why. The difference between your monthly payments for the 6 percent rate and the 5.25 percent rate is $48 a month. If you divide the up-front costs of the points ($2,000), you can see that it will take you around 41 months (roughly 3 ½ years) to recoup that expense. After that, the $48 is the amount you save each month (that's over $15,000 in savings over the life of the loan).

If you are going to live in the house for less than five years, you won't recoup the expense of the up-front points. You end up paying more, even though you have a lower interest rate and lower monthly payments.

Ideally, you want the lowest rate with the lowest points. When you have to decide (higher rate, fewer points or lower rate, more points), first decide whether you can afford the extra expense of points. If you can, be sure you'll live in the house long enough to gain the cost savings from the lower interest rate.

How Long Should You Pay on Your Fixed-Rate Loan?

Fixed rates come in various sizes, or *terms*. The term is the length of time you make payments. Which term is right for you? Read this section to decide.

Thirty-Year vs. Fifteen-Year vs. Biweekly

The most common term is the 30-year fixed rate. Your payments are amortized over 360 months, or 30 years.

You can also get a shorter term—for instance, a 15-year mortgage. In this type of mortgage, your monthly payment is more (around 20 to 30 percent higher), but you pay off the interest and principal faster. You end up paying less. You can also get a 10-year or 20-year mortgage.

Remember that you can always pay more than your house payment and have that extra money go toward your principal. By prepaying or paying down the principal, you save money but aren't locked into always having to pay extra. See the section "Prepaying Your Mortgage," later in this chapter.

An additional option is a biweekly payment, available on a 30-year mortgage. With this type of mortgage, you make a payment every other week. You make 26 payments a year—basically an extra month's payment a year. Again, because you are paying off the mortgage faster, you end up paying less. With this type of mortgage, you'll pay off the loan in less than 24 years.

CAUTION

Buyer Beware

Biweekly payments can save you a lot of money, but they may also be more of a headache. You have to make twice as many payments, and some lenders charge a handling fee for this type of mortgage. You'll want to consider this fee against any cost savings.

The following table compares the total payments for a 30-year and 15-year mortgage for the same amount ($150,000) and same interest (6 percent).

Comparing Mortgages

	30-Year	15-Year
Interest rate	6%	6%
Payment	$900	$1,266
Principal paid	150,000	150,000
Interest paid	173,760	77,840
Total amount paid	323,760	227,240

Notice that you can save a lot of money when you choose the 15-year mortgage—close to $100,000 in interest savings. And in 15 years, you'll own your house free and clear.

Is the Shorter Term Better?

Some real estate professionals advise that the 15-year mortgage is a smart investment. You end up saving a considerable sum if you stay in the home for a long period of time. Also, the interest rate on a 15-year mortgage may be slightly lower than for a 30-year mortgage.

Other experts disagree. These experts say that you may not want to tie up your money for housing expenses. You can always make double payments on the 30-year loan, but then if you find yourself in a financial bind, you're not locked in to these higher payments. (See the next section, "Prepaying Your Mortgage.") Or you can put the extra money in a savings account or mutual fund that earns more money than your mortgage rate. This leaves the money readily available in case of an emergency.

Whether or not to go with a shorter-term loan is primarily up to you. If you cannot afford or don't qualify for the higher payments of a 15-year loan, you could consider a 20- or 25-year loan. If you still do not qualify, though, you're limited to the traditional 30-year loan. You'll still get to decide, though, how often you'd like to make those payments.

Prepaying Your Mortgage

When you are shopping around for a mortgage, you'll want to inquire whether you can prepay on the mortgage without penalty. Why prepay?

Remember that the lenders want their money first, so most of your money in the first few years of the loan goes toward interest. Take a look at the following table to see the amortization schedule of the first 12 months of a 30-year loan for $150,000 at 6 percent interest.

Amortization Table for the First 12 Months of a Loan

Loan Amount		Interest	Term	Payment
$150,000		6%	30	$900

Payment #	Payment Amt	Principal	Interest	Balance
1	$900.00	$150.00	$(750.00)	$149,850.00
2	$900.00	$151.00	$749.00	$149,699.00
3	$900.00	$151.00	$749.00	$149,548.00
4	$900.00	$152.00	$748.00	$149,396.00
5	$900.00	$153.00	$747.00	$149,243.00
6	$900.00	$154.00	$746.00	$149,089.00
7	$900.00	$155.00	$745.00	$148,934.00
8	$900.00	$155.00	$745.00	$148,779.00
9	$900.00	$156.00	$744.00	$148,623.00
10	$900.00	$157.00	$743.00	$148,466.00
11	$900.00	$158.00	$742.00	$148,308.00
12	$900.00	$158.00	$742.00	$148,150.00
TOTAL	$10,800.00	$1,850.00	$7,450.00	

In the first year, you pay around $11,000 in monthly payments, but less than $2,000 of that goes toward the principal. After one year, you still owe $148,150.

Buyer Beware

Keep in mind that prepaying does not reduce your monthly payment obligations. You can't tell the lender that you paid an extra $1,000 last year, so this year you are going to skip the first few payments. You *must* still make the regular payments.

Here's where prepaying can be beneficial. When you prepay, the money goes directly to the principal. If you have an extra $1,000 after paying your monthly bills (yeah, right), you can pay that $1,000 toward the mortgage. That money goes directly toward reducing the principal.

Again, financial experts disagree on whether prepaying the mortgage is beneficial. It does reduce the amount of money you pay for the home. You'll pay off the home more quickly if you prepay. Even if you make one extra payment a year, you can pay off your loan more quickly and save money.

Advocates against prepaying argue that you can put your extra money to better use. For example, if you prepay that $1,000, you get no tax benefit. If you put that money into a retirement account, you'll get a tax break. If you put the money into a savings account, you'll have access to it if you need it. If your mortgage rate is 6 percent, and you invest in a mutual fund paying 8 percent, you can make 2 percent on your money.

The Least You Need to Know

 ◆ Fixed-rate mortgages offer you the security of having a fixed payment over the life of the loan. If interest rates are low, you may want to lock into the low rate. If interest rates are high, you may want to consider a different type of mortgage.

 ◆ Many lenders will offer a lower interest rate in exchange for paying points up front. Whether this is a good decision depends on how long you plan to stay in the house. Figure out how much you'll save per month with the lower interest rate, and then figure out how many months it will take you to recoup the points.

 ◆ You can select a 30-year, 15-year, or biweekly fixed-rate mortgage. Your lender may also offer 10- or 20-year mortgages. The shorter the term, the less you pay in interest over the life of the loan, but the larger the monthly payment.

 ◆ When shopping for a fixed-rate mortgage, be sure to ask whether you can pre-pay on the loan without penalty. Prepaying reduces the principal (the amount you owe) more quickly than just making regular payments.

Chapter 14

Adjustable-Rate Mortgages

In This Chapter

- ◆ Weighing the pros and cons of an adjustable-rate mortgage
- ◆ Understanding how an adjustable-rate mortgage works
- ◆ Shopping for an adjustable-rate mortgage

Are you a gambler? Fancy yourself a risk-taker? If so, you may want to finance your home with an adjustable-rate mortgage (ARM). With an ARM, you're gambling that the interest rates can go down, so your payments will go down; the interest rates can go up, but you'll sell before your adjustable rate catches up with the current fixed rate; or you'll switch to a fixed-rate mortgage before your rate catches up.

Shopping for an adjustable rate is trickier than shopping for a fixed rate. You have to study the details of the loan—sort of like studying the tip sheets for racing horses. This chapter explains how an ARM works and how to select a good one.

The Pros and Cons of an Adjustable-Rate Mortgage

What do you gain by getting an ARM? What can you lose? This section helps you tally up the wins/losses for ARMs.

The Good Things About an ARM

The basic benefit of an ARM is that you pay a lower interest rate at the start of the loan. This means you pay a lower monthly payment and that may help for your loan process. Here is a list of ARM pros:

♦ You may have an easier time qualifying for an ARM loan. Remember that a lender will qualify you for a loan by comparing your monthly gross income to your monthly house payment (principal, interest, taxes, and insurance). If your payments are initially low because of the lower ARM rate), you can more easily make the grade.

♦ Different lenders look at different factors when qualifying you for a loan. Some lenders may use a different qualifying test. Again, you may qualify for an ARM, but not a fixed-rate mortgage.

♦ If you're just starting out, you're gambling that your income will rise. Even if your payments do increase, you may be in a better situation to afford the increased payments. Your spouse may go back to work, for example, or your children may finish college.

♦ If you plan to stay in the home only a few years, you'll gain the most benefit from an ARM. During the first few years is when you get the breaks on payments. You can sell before your rate rises and catches up with the current fixed rate. Also, if you need a bigger house than you can afford, you may consider an ARM to keep your payments within the range you can afford.

♦ If the current fixed rates are extremely high, an ARM may be the only type of loan you can qualify for. Also, if interest rates are high, you may gamble that they will go down sometime in the future. Finally, the principal and interest are recalculated at each term. If you prepay, you have more control.

The Bad Things About an ARM

ARMs, just like fixed-rate mortgages, aren't always the best option. Here are some of the disadvantages to consider:

♦ If there's not much difference between the fixed-rate mortgage and the ARM, or if the fixed rates are low, you may want to lock into the low rate rather than have your payments bob up and down. This has been the case for the past few years.

♦ If you aren't a risk-taker, you may worry too much about your house payments going up. You may want to get a fixed-rate mortgage for the peace of mind of knowing you have one payment that will not vary.

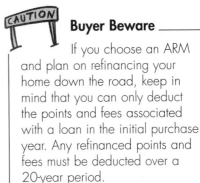

Buyer Beware

If you choose an ARM and plan on refinancing your home down the road, keep in mind that you can only deduct the points and fees associated with a loan in the initial purchase year. Any refinanced points and fees must be deducted over a 20-year period.

♦ If you plan to stay in the house for a long time, you may want to lock in to a fixed-rate mortgage (unless that rate is incredibly high).

♦ You may decide to choose an ARM and then refinance later during the term of the loan. (Refinancing is covered in Chapter 15.)

How an Adjustable-Rate Mortgage Works

Think about two football teams. The Bears have won all 10 of their games this season. The Colts haven't won any. Which team would you bet on? Probably the Bears—if all things are equal.

Now consider a different situation. To make the gambling more competitive, the bookie makes the Colts more attractive by giving you points. Instead of making the bet contingent on winning or losing, the bookie makes the bet also contingent on the number of points the winning team wins by. If the Bears win by 14 or more, they are the winners. But if the Bears lose, or they win by 13 or less, the Colts are the winners. Now, which is the best bet is not so clear-cut.

ARMs work in the same way. First, lenders make this type of loan more attractive by making its rates more competitive. Second, lenders use different methods for figuring out the spread—the difference in the rates charged. This section explains how an ARM works.

What You Pay At First: The Initial or Teaser Rate

To get you interested in an ARM, lenders usually offer a really low initial rate. This rate, often called the *teaser rate*, is usually good for a limited period of time—sometimes six months, sometimes one or two years.

Buyer Beware

The initial rate may be well below the current true rate, which means your rate will rise, even if the index does not. Be sure to find out what the current true rate is.

If you're looking through the advertised rates, you may see one loan for 5 percent and another for 6.25 percent. The 5 percent rate is most likely an ARM, while the higher rate is most likely for a fixed-rate mortgage.

The risk is that the initial or low rate is only available for a short period of time. Then the rate will adjust. How it adjusts depends on the index.

How the Rate Is Figured: The Index

All ARMs are tied to a certain economic index—some national indicator of current rates that is not controlled by the lenders. Different lenders tie the ARM to different indexes. Here are some common indexes:

- The rate of sales on Treasury notes and bills (six-month, one-year, three-year, or five-year T-bills)
- The average rate for loans closed, called *the Federal Housing Finance Board's National Average Contract Mortgage Rate*
- The average rate paid on jumbo CDs (certificates of deposit)
- The cost of funds for the lender

These indexes are usually printed in the newspaper so that you can see what the current rate is. When you are investigating ARMs, find out the index used and where the current rate is published.

The Lenders Cut: The Margin

The index isn't the rate used to determine your interest rate. It is the first part in the calculation. The lender adds something on top of the current index rate. This is called the *margin* and can run from 1 to 5 percent. The lender uses this formula to calculate the rate you'll pay:

Index Rate + Margin = Your Rate

For example, if the index used for your ARM is 4 percent and the margin is 2 percent, your interest rate will be 6 percent. The margin is usually fixed for the life of the loan and should be included in the contract.

How Often Payments Change: The Adjustment Interval

If you get an ARM, you understand your payment will then be adjusted according to the index used. How often it is adjusted varies.

For example, if you get a one-year ARM, your payments will stay the same for the first year and then be adjusted every year for the remainder of the loan (for example, each year for the next 29 years if it is a 30-year mortgage). At the end of each year (usually the anniversary date of your loan or the date stated in your contract), the lender will calculate the new interest rate, and you'll make payments accordingly until the next adjustment period, a year later.

You can also get a three-year ARM, five-year ARM, or seven-year ARM, or whatever the interval. This means that the initial rate will remain the same for three, five, or seven years, and then adjust every year thereafter. The adjustment interval will vary depending on the lender and should be included in the contract.

ARMs are recalculated at each adjustment period, and payments are based on the outstanding balance of the loan. This can be convenient if you plan to make additional payments toward the principal. You automatically get the additional amount adjusted into your payment with an ARM, whereas with a fixed-rate mortgage, you would have to refinance the loan to have a lower payment based on the additional amount paid.

CAUTION

Buyer Beware

Lenders can make mistakes. Know how to check their calculations so that you can be sure the payment amount is adjusted correctly.

How High the Rate Can Go: The Rate Caps

Your interest rate (and hence your payments) is like a tethered balloon. It can go up; it can go down—but only so far. Many lenders put a limit, or cap, on the increases and decreases. There are two types of caps: *rate caps* and *payment caps*.

A rate cap limits how much the interest rate can increase or decrease during the adjustment period (called a *periodic cap*) and during the life of the loan (called a *lifetime cap*). For example, an ARM may have a 2 percent periodic cap with a 6 percent lifetime cap. If your rate started at 5 percent, your interest rate could only raise 2 percent each period and would max out at 11 percent.

A payment cap limits how much your payment can increase during the adjustment period. Payment caps may sound reassuring because your payments will be within a certain limit, but this type of cap can cause problems—in particular, negative amortization, the topic of the next section.

Negative Amortization and ARMs

If you want your loan balance to go down (which you do), you must make a certain minimum payment to cover the interest with enough left over to pay off some of the principal, or balance. If your payment doesn't cover the interest (which can happen if you have a payment cap), the unpaid interest is added to the principle.

For example, say your initial payment is $850 and interest rates skyrocket. Perhaps your payment increases to $950 after the payment is adjusted, but you have a payment cap of $900. This means that for each monthly payment, you are required to pay $900, not the $950. This in turn means that all of your payment is going toward the interest—never any toward the principal balance on the loan. You never end up paying off the principal, and if you aren't covering the entire interest rate due with each payment (because of the payment cap), you owe more interest. You can make payment after payment and end up owing more than you initially borrowed. This is called *negative amortization*. To get out from negative amortization, you may be able to negotiate a new mortgage or prepay enough to cover the cost of interest and principal. The bottom line: With an ARM, you need to pay careful attention to your payments and how they fluctuate.

Selecting an ARM

When you're shopping for a fixed-rate mortgage, you need to look at one rate—the current interest rate plus any points paid.

Real Deal

If the rates go down, you may want to make the same (higher) monthly payment and apply the extra to the principal. Doing so will help you pay off the loan more quickly.

When you're shopping for an ARM, you need to look at several factors and consider the payments at various rates. You need to check out the initial rate, true rate, adjustment interval, caps, index, and margin. You can get some of the information—such as the rate and adjustment interval—from lender ads. You may need to call to confirm the finer details such as cap, index, and margin.

What You Want (Ideally) in an ARM

In addition to finding out the specifics of the rate, keep the following factors in mind when looking for an ARM:

- **Interest rates.** When you're comparing the rates of ARMs, don't get wooed by the teaser or come-on rate. This rate is temporary, and at the first adjustment period, your interest rate will go up. Instead, ask what the true rate is—what would the rate be today by adding the index and margin. You'll also want to find out if there is a minimum rate. Some lenders will charge a minimum rate even if the index goes below that rate.

> **Buyer Beware**
>
> Your lender should be able to tell you exactly what index is used. And this index should be keyed to some national indicator of current rates—beyond the control of the lender. It should also be a figure that you can check yourself. If this is not the case, don't use that lender.

- **Index.** Unless you can look into your crystal ball and predict what will happen with the economy, you probably aren't going to have much luck in picking the "best" index. You can try guessing which index will do what, but it's usually better to look at past performance. Ask for a chart that shows the changes in the particular index used for your loan. Look at a few years' worth of change so that you can see how stable or volatile the index has been.

- **Margins.** To compare ARMs that use the same index, look for the ARM with the lowest margin. Some lenders offer a lower initial rate but a higher margin. This structure enables them to increase the rate more quickly, depending on the annual cap.

- **Adjustment intervals.** As for adjustment intervals, keep in mind that the more frequent the adjustment, the more volatile your monthly payments. A longer interval is usually better, because your payments don't change as often. For example, suppose that you know you'll be moving within five years. In this case, you may want to get a five-year ARM, because you'll be moving sometime before the adjustment interval.

- **Lifetime cap.** A lifetime cap offers the most protection. If you have a lifetime cap of 5 percent, you know that your payments will never go more than 5 percent higher than the existing rate—no matter how high the rates go. Sometimes this cap also applies to how low the rate can go—that is, the rate cannot decrease more than 5 percent. Be sure to ask the lender.

- **Periodic cap.** You should also get an ARM with a periodic cap so that even if the rates do go to 12 percent, they can do so only a certain percentage at a time. FHA ARMs are capped at 1 percent per adjustment period. Conventional ARMs generally are capped at 2 percent. If you have a periodic cap and the rate jumps more than that cap, be sure to ask what happens. Is this extra percent added on to the next adjustment cycle, even if the rate hasn't gone up?

What You Should Ask When Shopping for an ARM

Armed with this information (sorry, couldn't resist!), ask the following questions to further research your ARM choices:

◆ In what situations could negative amortization occur with your loan terms? Ask whether the lender will alert you when this is a problem, and ask how the lender handles negative amortization.

◆ Can you convert the adjustable-rate mortgage to a fixed-rate mortgage? If the fixed rates are low, you may want to lock in at that rate. Be sure you know exactly what is involved in converting. Just finding out whether a loan is convertible isn't enough. The lender may charge a fee for the conversion and may also only allow you to lock into the current fixed rate, plus a margin. Also, you may be able to convert only on a certain date.

◆ What does the cap apply to—the initial rate or the true rate? If you get a low initial interest rate, you may calculate your highest rate at a certain percentage. For example, if the rate starts at 4 percent with a lifetime cap of 5 percent, you may think 9 percent is the tops. But if the cap is actually tied to the true rate, you have a totally different situation.

◆ If you sell the house, can the buyer assume the mortgage? Most mortgages are not assumable without lender approval.

◆ Can you prepay on the mortgage? If so, find out if there are any penalties.

> **Bet You Didn't Know**
>
> Some lenders have a new "one-way" ARM, in which you pay a higher initial interest rate, but the rate will never adjust up—only down. This can be convenient if you think that the rates will be going down soon. One of the drawbacks is that it is a higher interest rate (sometimes higher than a fixed-rate mortgage) and requires you to pay points. Again, be sure to ask your lender about all the potential hidden costs.

Looking at the Worst-Case Scenario

To understand how much your payments can rise, have the lender show you the worst-case scenario. Remember that lenders are trying to sell you something—the use of their money. They may stress the low initial payments.

Don't get caught up by the initial payments. Your payments are most likely going to go up. How much they go up and how much that means in monthly payments is something you should look at.

The following table shows the worst-case scenario for a one-year ARM for $150,000 at a teaser rate of 4 percent, a true rate of 6 percent, a periodic cap of 2 percent, and a lifetime cap of 6 percent.

A Worst-Case Scenario for an ARM

Evaluating an ARM			
Loan amount	$150,000		
Initial rate	4%		
Periodic cap	2%		
Lifetime cap	6%		

Year	Rate	Explanation	Monthly Payment
1	4%	Initial rate	$716
2	6%	Increase to periodic cap	$899
3	8%	Increase to periodic cap	$1,101
4	10%	Increase to lifetime cap	$1,316
5	10%	Increase to lifetime cap	$1,316

The Least You Need to Know

♦ An adjustable-rate mortgage (ARM) might be appropriate if you cannot qualify for a fixed-rate loan, if the interest rates are high, or if you plan to stay in your home only a short time (five to seven years).

♦ Many lenders offer a teaser rate to entice buyers to select an ARM. This low rate is only good for a short time; then your payments will most likely go up.

♦ The ARM rate is tied to an economic index (for example, the sale of T-bills) and is usually the index rate plus a margin. When the index goes up, your payments go up. When the index goes down, your payments go down.

♦ Depending on the loan, the ARM may have one or more types of caps: a lifetime cap, which limits the amount the rate can increase or decrease over the life of the loan; a periodic cap, which limits the amount the rate can increase or decrease within one adjustment period; and a payment cap, which limits the amount your payment can increase. Payment caps are not a good idea because they can allow negative amortization.

Getting Other Types of Financing

In This Chapter

- ◆ Qualifying for Veterans' Administration (VA) loans and assuming mortgages

- ◆ Understanding balloon mortgages and 80-10-10 or 80-15-5

- ◆ Using interest rate buydowns and carrybacks

- ◆ Considering a two-step mortgage

- ◆ Learning land contracts and leasing with the option to buy

- ◆ Looking into possible loans if you have less than stellar credit

- ◆ Refinancing your mortgage

The majority of residential loans are either fixed-rate or adjustable-rate mortgages. Other types of loans are available, though, depending on your circumstances. For example, if you're a veteran, you may qualify for a VA loan. If the seller is amenable, you could have the seller provide financing. These and other financial options are described in this chapter.

VA Loans

In addition to FHA (Federal Housing Administration) loans, the government sponsors another type of loan for veterans. These loans are guaranteed by the Veterans' Administration and are available to any veteran who has served 180 active days since September 16, 1940, or 90 days during a war. If you enlisted after September 7, 1980, you must have two years of service. If you are no longer with the armed forces, you must have received an honorable discharge. ROTC (Reserve Officers' Training Corps) members may also qualify. You must plan to live at the residence, and the property must pass a VA appraisal.

Real Deal

For more information about VA loans, contact the Veterans' Administration at the address listed in Appendix B, or visit their website at www. homeloans.va.gov.

Why are VA loans attractive? For one, you can get a VA loan with little or no down payment. You can expect to pay discount points; an appraisal fee; credit report, survey, title search, and recording fees; plus a VA funding fee, which adds to the closing costs. You should not be charged a brokerage fee.

You can get a VA loan for up to $240,000. You can prepay the loan without penalty, and the loan is assumable (with qualification of the new buyer).

Taking Over the Seller's Mortgage, a.k.a. Assumptions

Certain mortgages are *assumable*, which means the buyer can just assume the responsibilities of the mortgage. Some benefits of an assumable mortgage are that the buyer doesn't have all the expenses of obtaining a new mortgage, but the buyer usually needs to qualify with the current mortgage lender. If the current mortgage has a lower-than-market or reasonable interest rate, the buyer can save a lot of money on interest by assuming the current payment.

Buyer Beware

As the seller, check out the liability factors in allowing a purchaser to assume a loan. The person who originally received the loan (you if you are the seller) could be responsible if the new buyer defaults. Also, if you are purchasing a property for an investment and plan on renting it to tenants, you cannot assume an FHA loan (you would have to be the tenant).

Suppose that a seller has a 6 percent fixed-rate mortgage and has a buyer who is interested in assuming the payments on this loan. If the loan is freely assumable, the buyer can save the costs of applying for a loan and other associated costs; instead, an assumption agreement is made between the buyer and seller. (Most new loans are *qualified assumptions*, meaning that the buyer must still qualify for the loan.)

The buyer assumes payment on the existing mortgage and pays the difference between the mortgage balance and the selling price. For example, if the seller sold the home for $100,000 and still owed $80,000, the buyer would assume the $80,000 mortgage and pay the seller $20,000. You can see that even if you don't have the expense of closing on a loan, you may still have to come up with a considerable sum of cash.

You may not want to assume a mortgage, but you'll want to ask whether the mortgage you're securing is assumable. An assumable mortgage may be more attractive to buyers when you sell your home. However, this should be a small factor in your decision.

Start Small and Pay Later: Balloon Mortgages

A balloon mortgage is a type of financing that keeps the initial payments low for a certain period by financing the loan over a long term. The loan doesn't run the full term, though; instead, the full balance is due in one lump sum at the end of the initial period.

For example, you may secure a seven-year balloon mortgage for $115,000 at 7 percent. For the first seven years, your payments would be the same as if you secured a fixed-rate mortgage for 30 years. Nearly all of these payments go toward the interest; the principal is reduced some, but not a lot. You may owe, for instance, $103,500 at the end of the seven years. At this time, the remaining balance (the $103,500) is due. This is the balloon payment.

In most cases, the purchaser doesn't expect to receive a windfall for the balloon payment. Instead, the purchaser may secure another loan for the remaining balance. At this point, the buyer has some equity, plus a record of making payments. Or the buyer may decide to sell the house sometime before the balloon payment is due.

Two Loans and One Down Payment: 80-10-10 or 80-15-5 Loans

An 80-10-10 product is a combination of an 80 percent loan-to-value first mortgage, a 10 percent down payment, and a 10 percent second loan. This product can also be a combination of 80-15-5. This type of loan eliminates the need for private mortgage insurance, and for expensive homes, it can eliminate the need for a higher interest rate jumbo mortgage by reducing the first mortgage to a conventional mortgage. On a $250,000 home, an example could be broken down as follows:

80 percent of the loan is a regular mortgage (fixed rate or adjustable) = $200,000

15 percent of the loan is typically a balloon payment or a purchase money second (a bank loan, like a car loan) = $37,500

5 percent of the loan is the down payment = $12,500

Now, if any of you have ever gotten a car loan or a regular bank loan, you know that the interest rate is usually higher than a typical home mortgage interest rate. This is where the balloon payment or purchase money second part of the deal finds a slight catch. The interest rate on the second (15 percent) is at a higher rate than the regular mortgage (80 percent). For example, it might be around 9 percent for 25 years instead of 6 percent for 30. But, you can deduct the interest on your taxes as part of the mortgage interest. You cannot deduct any mortgage insurance (PMI or MIP) charges. In addition, you most likely can make additional payments to pay off the second loan (verify this with your lender). Then, you are only left with the 80 percent LTV loan, and you don't have to get an appraisal or refinance to remove the mortgage insurance.

Getting a Lower Interest Rate Via a Buydown

A buydown occurs when a seller pays a fee in order for the buyer to receive financing at a lower interest rate. This type of financing often occurs among builders or developers in a slow market.

Suppose that the interest rate is 8 percent, but you cannot qualify for a loan at this rate. Instead the seller pays the lender 2 percent to in effect "buy down" the loan for the agreed-upon term—say, two years. During those two years, you pay 6 percent interest. At the end of two years, you take over the entire 8 percent interest payment, or you can renegotiate the loan.

Who makes out on buydowns? Usually the sellers, because they most likely will increase the price of the home to cover the money they pay in interest, plus they'll make a profit or at least break even.

Loan Help from Sellers with Carrybacks

The sellers are most likely in a better position to secure financing than you are; after all, they own a home. For this reason, some sellers may be willing to provide the financing for you. This process is called different things depending on how the financing is arranged. For example, the seller may provide all the financing—this is called a *seller carryback*, a *seller takeback*, or a *purchase money mortgage*.

In a carryback situation, the seller agrees to carry back a mortgage for the purchase price of the home, minus the down payment. You, as buyer, agree to make monthly payments to the seller at a certain interest rate. Basically, the seller takes the role of the bank.

This type of financing can be beneficial to both the seller and the buyer. The seller sells the home and makes a decent return on the investment. The buyer buys the home and doesn't have to worry with the hassles and costs associated with securing a traditional loan. It is advantageous to people who might not otherwise qualify for a normal loan. In addition, if the buyer defaults on the loan, the home returns back to the seller instead of to a lender.

Buyer Beware

In any type of agreement between buyer and seller, you should have a real estate attorney review the details. You want to be sure you understand the agreement and that the agreement is not unfair to you.

Paying for Your Home with Layaway Payments

Land contracts may be appropriate for individuals who cannot secure a bank loan. A land contract works like a layaway plan. You live in the house, make payments to the seller, make repairs, and generally live in the home as if it were yours. But the home isn't yours until the deed is transferred.

Depending on the agreement, the title may be transferred when you make the last payment or when you have a certain amount of equity in the property. It's a good idea to hire a real estate attorney to carefully review the contract before you sign. It is best to have the deed completed initially and held until the title is transferred.

Buyer Beware

Remember that you don't hold the title to the property when you have a land contract. If you miss a payment, the lender can get back the property without any foreclosure.

Fixed and Adjustable Rate Loans in One: Two-Step Mortgages

The two-step mortgage is a combination adjustable-rate mortgage and fixed-rate mortgage. During the first step, you pay one interest rate for that loan period. During the second step, you pay another interest rate for the life of the loan.

Two-step mortgages currently come in two variations:

◆ **5/25.** With a 5/25 two-step mortgage, you pay one rate for the first five years. Then in the sixth year, the rate is reset for the remaining 25 years of the loan.

◆ **7/23.** A 7/23 mortgage works the same way, only the time frame is different. You pay one rate for the first seven years, and in the eighth year, the rate is recalculated for the remaining 23 years.

You may find other variations of this two-step mortgage, but they all basically work the same way.

How to Do the Two-Step

A two-step works like this. During the first term of the loan, you pay a low initial rate. This rate is fixed; that is, your payments do not vary during this initial term.

At the second step, your rate is adjusted and then may be fixed at that rate for the life of the loan. The new rate is tied to an economic index—usually the index plus the lender's margin—and sometimes has a rate cap (similar to an ARM). For some loans, the loan is converted to an ARM during the second period of the loan. Many loans have no caps after the initial term; instead, you pay the prevailing rate at that time.

With a two-step mortgage, the lender guarantees you the fixed-rate loan—that is, you don't have to requalify, and you don't have the expense of obtaining new financing at that time, although there is usually a conversion fee.

The following table shows an example of a 7/23 mortgage in which the buyer pays 6 percent for the initial seven years. Then the rate is adjusted, with a cap of 6 percent. The highest the payments could go (12 percent) is shown for years 8 to 23.

A 7/23 Mortgage

Evaluating a Two-Step Mortgage			
Loan amount	$115,000		
Initial rate	6%		
Lifetime cap	6%		

Year	Rate	Explanation	Monthly Payment
1–7	6%	Initial rate	$689.48
8–23	12%	Adjusted rate	$1,182.90

Is the Two-Step for You?

The two-step mortgage offers a few key benefits. Because the initial payments are low during the first term of the loan, you may have an easier time qualifying for the loan.

Also remember that the law of averages says that within five to seven years, you're likely to sell your home. In this case, you may sell or be ready to sell just at the point when the rate will increase. You have the benefit of paying the lower rate during the time you live in the house.

If you plan to move within a few years, the 5/25 or 7/23 might be ideal for your situation. If, on the other hand, you stay in your home longer than the five to seven years, you may end up paying more than the fixed rates. The rate for the second term usually runs 0.75 to 1 percent higher than the prevailing fixed rates.

Leasing with Option to Buy

A lease agreement is similar to a land contract. You live in the home and make the agreed-upon payments. Unlike a land contract, though, you're not obliged to buy the property. Usually you're given the right to purchase the home at a certain price within a certain time period. At that time, you can buy or continue to lease.

If you enter into one of these agreements, be sure to find out who pays for certain expenses. If the roof is damaged, who pays? Who pays for insurance?

Also, check to see whether the payments you make go toward the purchase price of the home. As with other types of creative financing, you should hire a real estate attorney to go over the contract carefully before signing this type of agreement. The terms of a lease contract can vary a great deal. You will want to make sure you understand all the provisions first.

You may also consider a lease purchase. You agree to purchase the property at a given time, but you pay rent in the interim. You may pay extra for this option.

Still More Options

Haven't found a match yet? You have still more options.

In rural areas, you can get a mortgage from the Rural Housing Service if your income is within a certain range. See Appendix B for the address of the Rural Housing Service.

You may secure a loan from a private individual—for instance, a family member. Keep in mind that the IRS discourages low- or no-interest loans. Generally, the IRS looks favorably on loans at the applicable federal rate, an index published by the government. If you secure a loan at a lower rate, the IRS may tax the lender on the interest that should have been received, even if it wasn't.

For some mortgages, you can arrange for a graduated payment plan, which allows you to make a lower payment for a certain period, then gradually make higher payments over the life of the loan. Your monthly payment increases at preset intervals. Beware: This type of mortgage allows for negative amortization. (See Chapter 14 for additional information.)

If you can secure the help of an investor, you may want to look into shared-equity mortgages. With this type of mortgage, an investor helps the buyer with a down payment and/or monthly payments. In return, the investor owns a percentage of the home or is entitled to a percentage of the profit when the home is sold. As a buyer, you pay the mortgage on your percentage of the loan, plus you may have to pay the investor rent on his percentage of the property.

If you cannot qualify for a loan by yourself, you may consider asking someone to co-sign with you. When an individual co-signs a loan, that person assumes the responsibility for repaying that loan. Some lenders will allow co-signers; some will place certain restrictions on the use of a co-signer. Keep in mind that the co-signer has to qualify just as the primary borrower does. And if the loan is defaulted on, both parties are responsible, and it affects both parties' credit.

To make housing available, many communities issue bond-backed or municipal mortgages. The government issues bonds, which are purchased by investors. The investors receive a good return on their investment, plus some tax advantages. The money raised by the bond sales then is made available to first-time homebuyers. For information about bond-backed mortgages, check with your local government agencies. You may also want to ask your agent.

Loans for Those with Blemished Credit

A subprime lender (also known as a nonconforming lender) loans money to a borrower who has less-than-perfect credit (on their credit report). Subprime borrowers have either missed payments on a debt or have been late with payments to creditors. Lenders charge a higher interest rate (an additional 1 to 4 percent on top of the traditional rate) to compensate for potential losses from customers who may run into trouble or default on the loan. In essence, if they make an extra $200 per month on your loan and you default after 10 months, they supposedly have an extra $2,000 "cushion" when they foreclose on the property and try to resell it.

A subprime mortgage isn't the same as mortgage insurance, which is removed when you have a loan-to-value ratio under 80 percent. The subprime mortgage interest rate stays with you for as long as you have the loan. If your credit improves over the years, you might want to look into refinancing your home in order to obtain a lower interest rate and save on your monthly payments. Refer to the next section for information on refinancing.

> **CAUTION**
>
> **Buyer Beware**
>
> Just because you have a bad credit record doesn't mean you should take any old loan that is offered. You may find that some non-conforming lenders are unscrupulous. That is, they may charge you a higher than required rate, as well as closing fees. Again, the key is to shop around and know what's available for your particular situation.

Refinancing Your Loan

When you refinance (also known as a "refi") your home, you are securing a new loan in order to pay off the existing mortgage or to gain access to the existing equity in your home.

In the years since 2000, interest rates have been at a historic low, fueling a refinance boom. Many homeowners took advantage of these rates and refinanced. Refinance loans in 2001, for instance, reached a record high volume at $1.1 *trillion*!

Some people refinance to pay for their kids' college, pay off credit card debt, or take that world cruise they have always dreamed of. Because the job market has also been tight during this time period (high unemployment, layoffs, corporate scandals), many used the equity in their home while looking for a new job or to manage living expenses.

Reasons to Refinance

Some of the most popular reasons to refinance include getting a lower interest rate and monthly payment, combining a first and second mortgage, getting rid of mortgage insurance, and changing mortgage lenders. Other reasons include switching from an ARM to a fixed-rate mortgage. This is especially beneficial if you can get a low fixed-rate of interest and not have to worry about the adjusting rates of an ARM. You may also refinance to switch to a shorter loan term (30 years to 15 years, for instance).

Using Your Refinance Money

In addition to the preceding reasons for refinancing, some homeowners take out a higher amount than the loan and use the extra money for personal expenses. For instance, they may use the extra money to pay off other loans, especially those with non-tax- deductible interest (such as credit cards), to refinance a home improvement, or to start or expand a business. In any case, you can see the many and varied benefits of refinancing.

Let's look at a good example of when you might want to consider refinancing your home. This section also covers how to shop around for the best refinance program.

How Refinancing Saves You Money

Say that you initially took out a home loan for $150,000 at 8 percent for 30 years. It probably cost you around $3,000 at the close with all the fees (which you were able to deduct on your income taxes for that year). Your principal and interest payment was $1100.65 and you probably had to pay for mortgage insurance (because your loan-to-value ratio was at 95 percent) at around $40 per month. Without taxes and insurance, you were at a monthly payment of $1140.65.

A few years have passed and your home is located in a hot market where homes have been appraising for $175,000 and the interest rates have dropped to 6 percent for a 30-year mortgage. Perhaps you have around $125,000 left to pay on the loan. With the new appraisal required to refinance your home, you are at a lower loan-to-value ratio. The lower loan-to-value ratio means that you don't need to carry mortgage insurance (saving you $40 per month), and the lower percentage rate takes your monthly payment down to $634.42. That is a savings of almost $241.32.

Real Deal _____

Many borrowers use a rule of thumb measurement between the current rate and the rate they are paying to calculate whether refinancing cuts cost. Usually, if the interest rate drops 2 points, it makes sense to refinance.

But with the current boom in the refinancing market and record low rates as well as low-cost to no-cost refinancing, that rule of thumb isn't accurate. Look to save at least half a percentage point or more.

You might be saying, "So, where is the catch?" Here it is. Refinancing your home isn't free; it will usually cost you 1 percentage point of the new loan amount (remember the origination fee) and numerous other fees that will probably add up to around

$2,000. You have to be in the home for roughly 10 months to start reaping the $241 per month benefit. If you plan on staying in the home, this is significant. If you might move in 6 months, it wouldn't be worth it.

Some lenders will allow you to "wrap" the refinance charges into the refinanced amount. Using the previous example, you would be refinancing $127,000 instead of $125,000. This is how they can call it a "no-money-down" refinance. This might be a good idea if again, you are planning to stay in your home for a while and the equity you have gained in your home (along with the lower interest rate) makes a significant change in your payment.

Shopping Around for Refinance Loans

Like securing a regular loan, you should shop around for rates and also closely compare lending fees. The lenders aren't giving you a loan out of their generosity; they are looking to make money off the transaction. Therefore, it's really important to know whom you are dealing with. For instance, we refinanced our loan; the first person we talked with was a broker who wanted to charge us a very high *brokerage fee*. (A mortgage broker takes the loan application and shops around with various lenders to get the best rate for the loan. The different players in the loan industry are covered in Chapter 5.) We declined and found a different loan company that did not charge this fee.

Also, take a close look at the fees. Some lenders tack on "junk fees" that add up. Look for generically named fees such as administration, management, warehousing, processing, or underwriting fees. Expect to pay 1 to 2 percent of the loan to cover all of your fees.

And finally, because of the boom, expect the loan process to take longer (four to eight weeks). (The bottleneck is home appraisal; there aren't enough home appraisers.)

Real Deal

Try to get a loan that does not charge points. Points on a refinance are not deductible in that year but are spread out over the life of the loan. For example, if you paid 1 point on a $100,000 30-year loan ($1,000), your tax savings would total only $33.33 a year.

The Least You Need to Know

◆ If you're a veteran, you may qualify for a VA loan.

◆ If the seller has an assumable loan, you can take over the mortgage and make payments on the loan as if you had secured it. Older loans may be freely assumable, while newer loans are qualified assumptions.

◆ With a balloon mortgage, payments are amortized over a long period of time so that your initial payments are low and go mostly toward interest. At the end of the term, the entire balance of the mortgage, the balloon payment, is due.

◆ Land contracts and lease purchase options enable you to live on a property and make payments. With a land contract, you don't get the deed to the property until you make all the payments or until you reach a certain equity amount. With a lease option, you're not obligated to buy the property, but at a certain time and price, you can buy the property.

◆ A two-step mortgage is like a fixed-rate and an adjustable-rate mortgage combined. During the first step (usually 5 or 7 years), the buyer has a fixed-rate mortgage for that period. After the initial period, there is a one-time rate adjustment based on an index, margin, and any caps in effect. For the remaining term of the loan, this rate is used.

◆ If you have had some credit problems, you may need to look for a subprime or non-conforming lender. You pay a higher interest rate with this type of mortgage.

◆ With record low interest rates, many homeowners are refinancing their loans.

Chapter 16

Applying for a Mortgage

In This Chapter

◆ Understanding who's who in the loan game

◆ Qualifying for a loan

◆ Applying for a loan

◆ Following up if you can't get a loan

Once you select a lender, you face the process of applying for the loan. It's not difficult, but it can be time-consuming.

To apply for a loan, you have to gather and complete so much information. You may think you need everything from your second grade report card to your library card in order to secure a loan. There are also lots of *i*'s to dot and *t*'s to cross, such as getting your future home appraised.

This chapter helps you prepare for what you need so that you aren't shocked when the lender asks for the equivalent of one file drawer full of documentation. You also get an overview of how the loan process works, what factors determine whether a particular buyer gets a loan, and what your options are if your loan request is denied.

The Roster of Loan People

Depending on the type of lender you get your mortgage from, you can expect to deal with any of several loan people. Here's the roster:

- **Loan originator or loan officer.** This person is responsible for taking down all your financial information and is usually your primary contact at the lending company. This person makes sure that all the needed information is ready for review.

- **Loan processor.** This person handles the processing of the loan, making sure all the steps are followed. For example, this person will order the appraisal, the credit report, and so on.

- **Underwriter.** This person is the decision-maker. He or she takes all the information the other two loan people have collected and decides whether you get the loan. (You don't have any contact with this person.)

- **Mortgage broker.** This person ensures a loan between a borrower and lender. The broker takes the loan and packages it for the lender. The next section explains how the underwriter decides whether you get the loan.

How the Lender Decides Whether to Lend You Money

How does an underwriter decide that Buyer A gets the loan, but Buyer B is rejected? The lender will look at a number of factors, including your current financial situation, your payment history, the current lending guidelines, and the property being purchased.

Here's the basic process the lender goes through:

1. Takes your application

2. Verifies your employment information, income information, and source of down payment

3. Orders and checks your credit report and appraisal

4. Approves or rejects the loan

Let's take a closer look at each of these steps.

Taking the Loan Application

In the application process, the lender will ask you to provide a lot of information about your financial situation, such as your current income, your current debt obligations, and more. (The section "Applying for the Loan," later in this chapter, explains in detail the documentation you'll be asked to provide.)

Buyer Beware

The mortgage lender is looking to be sure you're providing accurate and honest information. So if you want the loan, it's best to tell the truth about your finances and credit history.

Verifying Information

The lender then reviews and verifies your information. Have you been employed at the place you listed for the amount of time you said? Is your salary what you said it is? Do you have any serious criminal records? Do you have the money you said you do in your bank or other accounts?

Looking at Your Credit Report

In addition to verifying your income and employment, the lender will order a credit report. This report will tell the lender about your credit rating and credit history. How have you managed past debts? Have you recently filed for bankruptcy? The lender will look for any trouble signs, such as a history of late or missed payments, and will check to see whether you listed all your debts. Not including some debts on an application can raise a red flag to the lender. It's a good idea to check and clean up any credit problems before you apply for a loan. Chapter 2 includes complete information on checking and cleaning up your credit report.

Sometimes lenders run two credit checks—an initial check at the time of application and one later right before closing. For this reason, it's not a good idea to take on any new debt during the loan process. That debt is likely to show up on your second credit report.

Buyer Beware

Credit fraud is at an all-time high. This is all the more reason to double-check your credit rating. It's a good idea to do this once a year, regardless of whether you're applying for a loan.

The credit report will show not only all your accounts, credit limits, loan amounts, and balance history, but also will list anyone else that has looked at your credit history. Having too much credit is not a good thing because lenders think this is tempting. Be sure to close out old accounts.

Getting an Appraisal on the Home

In addition to checking out *you*, the lender will check out the property you intend to purchase. You may be silly enough to pay $125,000 for a house that's worth only $75,000, but the lender isn't going to loan you the money to do it. Why? Because the bank is likely to lose money if you default on the loan since the house isn't worth the price you are paying for it. All loans require an independent appraisal, which you as the buyer usually pays for. The appraiser determines the market value of the home.

Real Deal _____

Request a copy of the appraisal in writing from the lender at the time of the application. This appraisal can give you solid information that backs up the value of the home. Note that you cannot get the appraisal until the closing.

Buyer Beware _____

Scandals in the appraisal industry have been reported in recent years. In some cases, appraisers colluded with new home builders to appraise homes for far more than they were worth. In other instances, appraisers were "fixing" the appraisals on fixer-uppers. Always be sure to check the background of your appraiser and his or her company.

To determine the value, the appraiser will look at the neighborhood, especially similar homes in the area that have sold recently. She'll use these selling prices as a comparison. The agent will also look at how many homes are currently on the market. How desirable is the area? The appraiser will also look closely at the house—the condition of the home, the size and number of rooms, the type of construction, and the condition of the property. After reviewing the home and property, the appraiser will provide a value as well as supporting information on how that value was reached.

Usually the lender hires the services of the appraiser, and you pay for the appraisal through the lender. The house is appraised at least once but possibly more often during the loan process, depending on the lender and the situation. Appendix B lists the phone number for the American Society of Appraisers, which can give you a referral. You can also visit the website of the Appraisal Institute at www.appraisalinstitute.org (see the following figure).

Keep in mind that the appraiser only has to justify the price paid. If the home is worth $10,000 more than you're paying, the appraiser doesn't have to prove it. And because appraisers don't get paid extra for the effort, they usually stop at the price paid. That doesn't mean you didn't get a good deal.

Also, if the appraisal comes in too low, you aren't stuck. You can appeal the appraisal. Your agent may help you prepare comparisons for other homes to justify a higher appraisal price.

Bet You Didn't Know

Some lenders use a new method of performing an appraisal—a database and automated system. This process is quicker *and* cheaper, but there are some concerns. First, lenders may be tempted to charge you the higher "regular" fee, but use the shortcut method. The National Association of Realty (NAR) adopted a policy that requires lenders to tell you the method(s) used to appraise a property. Second, because many varying factors determine a property value, many lenders prefer the full appraisals. Ask your lender which type of appraisal will be used and the cost of the appraisal.

For newly constructed homes, you may not need an appraisal, especially if the lender is going to sell the loan to Fannie Mae. Fannie Mae has a new master residential appraisal process; an appraiser can examine the entire project site and provide a value for each model, rather than appraising each house individually.

Knowing What Lenders Look For

If you have ever shopped for a diamond, you may know that the four Cs determine a diamond's worth. (You can find more information about how the lender evaluates each of these factors in Chapter 2.) Lenders also use four Cs to qualify an individual for a loan:

◆ **Capacity.** Will you be able to repay the debt? Lenders base the answer to this question on your current income and employment record. Lenders also look at your other financial obligations.

◆ **Credit history.** Being *able* to repay the debt doesn't mean you *will* repay the debt. Lenders look at your record of making payments. Did you make them on time? Did you pay them consistently?

◆ **Capital.** How much money do you have right now? The lender will look at your assets. For instance, do you have money for the down payment? Will you have enough money after paying the down payment and closing costs, or will you have to scrape by for a few months?

◆ **Collateral.** What can the lender get from you if you default on the loan? The house, of course, but lenders want to ensure the house is worth the amount you're paying—hence the appraisal.

Approving or Denying the Loan

After all the details are in (your income information, credit history, appraisal, and so on), the loan underwriter will decide whether to give you the loan. The underwriter will also use the qualifying ratios (discussed in Chapter 2) to determine whether you're a good risk for the loan. If you require mortgage insurance, you'll also have to get the approval of the insurer.

If the loan is approved, you should receive a commitment letter stating the terms of the loan—the loan amount, the term or length of the loan, points, interest rates, and the monthly payment amount. If you agree to these terms, you sign the letter—that is, you accept all the terms and conditions of the loan. The letter will give you a set amount of time to sign and then close the loan. (Often you close very shortly after loan approval, and you don't get the letter until closing.) Read the commitment letter carefully. Lenders sometimes make mistakes. You'll want to be sure the terms are exactly as you intended. If the letter is not accurate, do not sign it.

If the loan is not approved, your loan officer will let you know. See the "What to Do If You Can't Get a Loan" section later in this chapter for more information about how to handle this situation.

Applying for the Loan

You now know what's going to happen once the wheel starts turning. This section explains how to get the wheel started—how to apply for the loan.

Spilling Your Financial Guts

When you apply for a loan, you'll most likely be interviewed by the loan officer. That officer will either ask you to complete the loan application or ask you questions and complete the application for you. You may do this in person, over the phone, or via fax.

In addition to the application, the loan officer will ask you to provide documentation. The requirements vary. Some lenders ask for more months' worth of pay stubs; others want different criteria on your credit. Just be sure that you understand what you need to provide for *your* loan process.

Here is a list of some of the things you will be expected to provide:

◆ Copies of all bank statements (savings and checking) for the past three months. If an account shows a large deposit in the past few months, be prepared to provide documentation of where this money came from.

◆ Copies of all stock accounts, 401Ks, IRAs, and other assets (life insurance, rental property agreements, and so on).

◆ Your most recent 30 days' worth of pay stubs, as well as the names and addresses of your past employers.

◆ Your W2 forms for the past two years.

◆ Your tax returns for the past two years. If you're self-employed or commissioned, you'll need to provide additional tax returns and all your schedules, including profit and loss statements for past years as well as year-to-date.

Real Deal _____

Shop around for lenders. Different lenders charge different fees. For example, you may find a lender that doesn't charge a loan origination fee. Or you may want to use a lender that has a cheaper application fee. Chapter 5 gives you some pointers on how to shop for the best lender.

◆ A copy of the purchase agreement for the house. You may also need a copy of the front and back of the check for the earnest money.

◆ A divorce decree or copies of support payments (if applicable).

◆ A check. You might have to pay some up-front fees for the application process—usually an application fee and possibly fees for the appraisal and credit report. Some lenders also charge a loan origination fee—a charge to prepare the loan.

Check to see whether any of the following considerations apply to you:

◆ If you're selling your residence, you need to bring a copy of the listing agreement.

◆ If you have sold your house, bring a copy of the purchase agreement.

◆ If you are keeping the home and are going to rent it to tenants, you need a copy of the signed lease agreement.

◆ If you're paying for the down payment with money given to you as a gift, you may be required to bring a gift letter, which states that the money is a gift and does not have to be repaid.

◆ If you're renting, bring in copies of rent checks for the last 12 months.

◆ If you have credit problems, be prepared to write an explanation.

See the following three-page loan application for an example.

Uniform Residential Loan Application

This application is designed to be completed by the applicant(s) with the lender's assistance. Applicants should complete this form as "Borrower" or "Co-Borrower", as applicable. Co-Borrower information must also be provided (and the appropriate box checked) when ☐ the income or assets of a person other than the "Borrower" (including the Borrower's spouse) will be used as a basis for loan qualification or ☐ the income or assets of the Borrower's spouse will not be used as a basis for loan qualification, but his or her liabilities must be considered because the Borrower resides in a community property state, the security property is located in a community property state, or the Borrower is relying on other property located in a community property state as a basis for repayment of the loan.

I. TYPE OF MORTGAGE AND TERMS OF LOAN

Mortgage Applied for:	☐ V.A. ☐ Conventional ☐ Other: ☐ FHA ☐ FmHA	Agency Case Number	Lender Case Number

Amount $	Interest Rate %	No. of Months	Amortization Type:	☐ Fixed Rate ☐ GPM	☐ Other (explain): ☐ ARM (type):

II. PROPERTY INFORMATION AND PURPOSE OF LOAN

Subject Property Address (street, city, state, ZIP)   No. of Units

Legal Description of Subject Property (attach description if necessary)   Year Built

Purpose of Loan	☐ Purchase ☐ Refinance	☐ Construction ☐ Construction-Permanent	☐ Other (explain):	Property will be: ☐ Primary Residence ☐ Secondary Residence ☐ Investment

Complete this line if construction or construction-permanent loan.

Year Lot Acquired	Original Cost $	Amount Existing Liens $	(a) Present Value of Lot $	(b) Cost of Improvements $	Total (a + b) $

Complete this line if this is a refinance loan.

Year Acquired	Original Cost $	Amount Existing Liens $	Purpose of Refinance	Describe Improvements ☐ made ☐ to be made
				Cost: $

Title will be held in what Name(s)   Manner in which Title will be held   Estate will be held in: ☐ Fee Simple ☐ Leasehold (show expiration date)

Source of Down Payment, Settlement Charges and/or Subordinate Financing (explain)

III. BORROWER INFORMATION

Borrower	Co-Borrower

Borrower's Name (include Jr. or Sr. if applicable)	Co-Borrower's Name (include Jr. or Sr. if applicable)

Social Security Number	Home Phone (incl. area code)	Age	Yrs. School	Social Security Number	Home Phone (incl. area code)	Age	Yrs. School

☐ Married ☐ Separated ☐ Unmarried (include single, divorced, widowed)	Dependents (not listed by Co-Borrower) no. ages	☐ Married ☐ Separated ☐ Unmarried (include single, divorced, widowed)	Dependents (not listed by Borrower) no. ages

Present Address (street, city, state, ZIP) ☐ Own ☐ Rent _____ No. Yrs.	Present Address (street, city, state, ZIP) ☐ Own ☐ Rent _____ No. Yrs.

If residing at present address for less than two years, complete the following:

Former Address (street, city, state, ZIP) ☐ Own ☐ Rent _____ No. Yrs.	Former Address (street, city, state, ZIP) ☐ Own ☐ Rent _____ No. Yrs.

Former Address (street, city, state, ZIP) ☐ Own ☐ Rent _____ No. Yrs.	Former Address (street, city, state, ZIP) ☐ Own ☐ Rent _____ No. Yrs.

IV. EMPLOYMENT INFORMATION

Borrower	Co-Borrower

Name & Address of Employer ☐ Self Employed	Yrs. on this job	Name & Address of Employer ☐ Self Employed	Yrs. on this job
	Yrs. employed in this line of work/profession		Yrs. employed in this line of work/profession

Position/Title/Type of Business	Business Phone (incl. area code)	Position/Title/Type of Business	Business Phone (incl. area code)

If employed in current position for less than two years or if currently employed in more than one position, complete the following:

Name & Address of Employer ☐ Self Employed	Dates (from - to)	Name & Address of Employer ☐ Self Employed	Dates (from - to)
	Monthly Income $		Monthly Income $

Position/Title/Type of Business	Business Phone (incl. area code)	Position/Title/Type of Business	Business Phone (incl. area code)

Name & Address of Employer ☐ Self Employed	Dates (from - to)	Name & Address of Employer ☐ Self Employed	Dates (from - to)
	Monthly Income $		Monthly Income $

Position/Title/Type of Business	Business Phone (incl. area code)	Position/Title/Type of Business	Business Phone (incl. area code)

Freddie Mac Form 65 10/92   Fannie Mae Form 1003 10/92

VMP-21 (9210)   Page 1 of 4   Printed on Recycled Paper

VMP MORTGAGE FORMS • (313)283 8100 • (800)521 7291

A typical loan application.

V. MONTHLY INCOME AND COMBINED HOUSING EXPENSE INFORMATION

Gross Monthly Income	Borrower	Co-Borrower	Total	Combined Monthly Housing Expense	Present	Proposed
Base Empl. Income *	$	$	$	Rent	$	
Overtime				First Mortgage (P&I)		$
Bonuses				Other Financing (P&I)		
Commissions				Hazard Insurance		
Dividends/Interest				Real Estate Taxes		
Net Rental Income				Mortgage Insurance		
Other (before completing, see the notice in "describe other income," below)				Homeowner Assn. Dues		
				Other:		
Total	$	$	$	**Total**	$	$

* Self Employed Borrower(s) may be required to provide additional documentation such as tax returns and financial statements.

Describe Other Income *Notice:* Alimony, child support, or separate maintenance income need not be revealed if the Borrower (B) or Co-Borrower (C) does not choose to have it considered for repaying this loan.

B/C		Monthly Amount
		$

VI. ASSETS AND LIABILITIES

This Statement and any applicable supporting schedules may be completed jointly by both married and unmarried Co-Borrowers if their assets and liabilities are sufficiently joined so that the Statement can be meaningfully and fairly presented on a combined basis; otherwise separate Statements and Schedules are required. If the Co-Borrower section was completed about a spouse, this Statement and supporting schedules must be completed about that spouse also.

Completed [ ] Jointly [ ] Not Jointly

ASSETS	Cash or Market Value	Liabilities and Pledged Assets.
Description		List the creditor's name, address and account number for all outstanding debts, including automobile loans, revolving charge accounts, real estate loans, alimony, child support, stock pledges, etc. Use continuation sheet, if necessary. Indicate by (*) those liabilities which will be satisfied upon sale of real estate owned or upon refinancing of the subject property.
Cash deposit toward purchase held by:	$	

LIABILITIES	Monthly Pmt. & Mos. Left to Pay	Unpaid Balance

ASSETS	Cash or Market Value
List checking and savings accounts below	
Name and address of Bank, S&L, or Credit Union	
Acct. no.	$
Name and address of Bank, S&L, or Credit Union	
Acct. no.	$
Name and address of Bank, S&L, or Credit Union	
Acct. no.	$
Name and address of Bank, S&L, or Credit Union	
Acct. no.	$
Stocks & Bonds (Company name/number & description)	$
Life insurance net cash value	$
Face amount: $	
Subtotal Liquid Assets	$
Real estate owned (enter market value from schedule of real estate owned)	$
Vested interest in retirement fund	$
Net worth of business(es) owned (attach financial statement)	$
Automobiles owned (make and year)	$
Other Assets (itemize)	$
Total Assets a.	$

Name and address of Company	$ Pmt./Mos.	$
Acct. no.		
Name and address of Company	$ Pmt./Mos.	$
Acct. no.		
Name and address of Company	$ Pmt./Mos.	$
Acct. no.		
Name and address of Company	$ Pmt./Mos.	$
Acct. no.		
Name and address of Company	$ Pmt./Mos.	$
Acct. no.		
Name and address of Company	$ Pmt./Mos.	$
Acct. no.		
Name and address of Company	$ Pmt./Mos.	$
Acct. no.		
Alimony/Child Support/Separate Maintenance Payments Owed to:	$	
Job Related Expense (child care, union dues, etc.)	$	
Total Monthly Payments	$	
Net Worth (a minus b) ►	$	**Total Liabilities b.** $

VI. ASSETS AND LIABILITIES (cont.)

Schedule of Real Estate Owned (If additional properties are owned, use continuation sheet.)

Property Address (enter S if sold, PS if pending sale or R if rental being held for income)	Type of Property	Present Market Value	Amount of Mortgages & Liens	Gross Rental Income	Mortgage Payments	Insurance, Maintenance, Taxes & Misc.	Net Rental Income
		$	$	$	$	$	$
Totals		$	$	$	$	$	$

List any additional names under which credit has previously been received and indicate appropriate creditor name(s) and account number(s):

Alternate Name	Creditor Name	Account Number

VII. DETAILS OF TRANSACTION		**VIII. DECLARATIONS**				
a. Purchase price	$	If you answer "Yes" to any questions a through i, please use continuation sheet for explanation.	Borrower Yes	Borrower No	Co-Borrower Yes	Co-Borrower No
b. Alterations, improvements, repairs						
c. Land (if acquired separately)		a. Are there any outstanding judgments against you?				
d. Refinance (incl. debts to be paid off)		b. Have you been declared bankrupt within the past 7 years?				
e. Estimated prepaid items		c. Have you had property foreclosed upon or given title or deed in lieu thereof in the last 7 years?				
f. Estimated closing costs						
g. PMI, MIP, Funding Fee		d. Are you a party to a lawsuit?				
h. Discount (if Borrower will pay)		e. Have you directly or indirectly been obligated on any loan which resulted in foreclosure, transfer of title in lieu of foreclosure, or judgment? (This would include such loans as home mortgage loans, SBA loans, home improvement loans, educational loans, manufactured (mobile) home loans, any mortgage, financial obligation, bond, or loan guarantee. If "Yes," provide details, including date, name and address of Lender, FHA or V.A. case number, if any, and reasons for the action.)				
i. Total Costs (add items a through h)						
j. Subordinate financing		f. Are you presently delinquent or in default on any Federal debt or any other loan, mortgage, financial obligation, bond, or loan guarantee? If "Yes," give details as described in the preceding question.				
k. Borrower's closing costs paid by Seller		g. Are you obligated to pay alimony, child support, or separate maintenance?				
l. Other Credits (explain)		h. Is any part of the down payment borrowed?				
		i. Are you a co-maker or endorser on a note?				
		j. Are you a U.S. citizen?				
		k. Are you a permanent resident alien?				
m. Loan amount (exclude PMI, MIP, Funding Fee financed)		l. Do you intend to occupy the property as your primary residence? If "Yes," complete question m below.				
n. PMI, MIP, Funding Fee financed		m. Have you had an ownership interest in a property in the last three years?				
o. Loan amount (add m & n)		(1) What type of property did you own—principal residence (PR), second home (SH), or investment property (IP)?				
p. Cash from/to Borrower (subtract j, k, l & o from i)		(2) How did you hold title to the home—solely by yourself (S), jointly with your spouse (SP), or jointly with another person (O)?				

IX. ACKNOWLEDGMENT AND AGREEMENT

The undersigned specifically acknowledge(s) and agree(s) that: (1) the loan requested by this application will be secured by a first mortgage or deed of trust on the property described herein; (2) the property will not be used for any illegal or prohibited purpose or use; (3) all statements made in this application are made for the purpose of obtaining the loan indicated herein; (4) occupation of the property will be as indicated above; (5) verification or reverification of any information contained in the application may be made at any time by the Lender, its agents, successors and assigns, either directly or through a credit reporting agency, from any source named in this application, and the original copy of this application will be retained by the Lender, even if the loan is not approved; (6) the Lender, its agents, successors and assigns will rely on the information contained in the application and I/we have a continuing obligation to amend and/or supplement the information provided in this application if any of the material facts which I/we have represented herein should change prior to closing; (7) in the event my/our payments on the loan indicated in this application become delinquent, the Lender, its agents, successors and assigns, may, in addition to all their other rights and remedies, report my/our name(s) and account information to a credit reporting agency; (8) ownership of the loan may be transferred to successor or assign of the Lender without notice to me and/or the administration of the loan account may be transferred to an agent, successor or assign of the Lender with prior notice to me; (9) the Lender, its agents, successors and assigns make no representations or warranties, express or implied, to the Borrower(s) regarding the property, the condition of the property, or the value of the property.

Certification: I/We certify that the information provided in this application is true and correct as of the date set forth opposite my/our signature(s) on this application and acknowledge my/our understanding that any intentional or negligent misrepresentation(s) of the information contained in this application may result in civil liability and/or criminal penalties including, but not limited to, fine or imprisonment or both under the provisions of Title 18, United States Code, Section 1001, et seq. and liability for monetary damages to the Lender, its agents, successors and assigns, insurers and any other person who may suffer any loss due to reliance upon any misrepresentation which I/we have made on this application.

Borrower's Signature	Date	Co-Borrower's Signature	Date
X		X	

X. INFORMATION FOR GOVERNMENT MONITORING PURPOSES

The following information is requested by the Federal Government for certain types of loans related to a dwelling, in order to monitor the Lender's compliance with equal credit opportunity, fair housing and home mortgage disclosure laws. You are not required to furnish this information, but are encouraged to do so. The law provides that a Lender may neither discriminate on the basis of this information, nor on whether you choose to furnish it. However, if you choose not to furnish it, under Federal regulations this Lender is required to note race and sex on the basis of visual observation or surname. If you do not wish to furnish the above information, please check the box below. (Lender must review the above material to assure that the disclosures satisfy all requirements to which the Lender is subject under applicable state law for the particular type of loan applied for.)

BORROWER   **CO-BORROWER**

Race/National Origin:	□ I do not wish to furnish this information □ American Indian or Alaskan Native □ Asian or Pacific Islander □ White, not of Hispanic Origin □ Black, not of Hispanic origin □ Hispanic □ Other (specify)	Race/National Origin: □ I do not wish to furnish this information □ American Indian or Alaskan Native □ Asian or Pacific Islander □ White, not of Hispanic Origin □ Black, not of Hispanic origin □ Hispanic □ Other (specify)
Sex:	□ Female □ Male	Sex: □ Female □ Male

To be Completed by Interviewer

This application was taken by:
□ face-to-face interview
□ by mail
□ by telephone

Interviewer's Name (print or type)

Interviewer's Signature   Date

Interviewer's Phone Number (incl. area code)

Locking in an Interest Rate

When you apply for the loan, you'll want to decide whether you want to lock in the interest rate or let it float. Interest rates change daily. A rate of 5.5 percent today could jump to 6 percent tomorrow or go down to 5 percent. Depending on the amount of your loan, this could mean a significant difference in your monthly payments.

If you're worried about the interest rates going up, locking in a rate may be a good idea. Locking in a rate guarantees that rate for a certain period of time. For example, you can lock in the 6 percent rate for 60 days.

If you do lock in the rate, you'll want to make sure of a few things. First, be sure to get the commitment in writing. Don't take the lender's word that the rate is locked. Make sure you do this, or you might be surprised what your rate is when you close on the home. Second, you'll want to be sure that the rate is locked for a long enough period of time for you to close on the loan. If you lock for five days but can't close within those five days, the lock is worthless. Most locks run 30 to 60 days. Third, you'll want to ask the lender whether you have to pay a fee for locking in the rate. Some lenders will charge a commitment fee. Finally, the lock should include both the rate and any points paid to obtain the rate.

Real Deal

Rates change daily. It would be wise to follow business and financial news closely during your loan application process, even if you don't normally pay attention to it. If you find that you've locked into a rate, and rates actually drop, you might try stalling until the lock expires so you can get the lower rate.

If you are building a new home and it will take around six months to close on the home, check with your lender to see what the longest rate lock is that the lender will allow for free. Many lenders will allow you to lock a rate at 30 or 60 days before the close, but to go beyond that time period, they will charge you a percentage of your loan amount as a lock fee. This fee might or might not be refundable (most likely not).

If you fear that rates will increase by the time your home is built and you close escrow, you might consider locking a rate. But just like the explanation of buying down interest rates (refer to Chapter 12), it might not be worth the extra expense of thousands of dollars to hold a rate, especially if you won't be in the home long or are obtaining an ARM.

If you're not worried about the interest rates changing or if you think the rates may drop, you may want to let the rate float (refer to the section "Questions to Ask Lenders" in Chapter 5 for more on floating the rate). You can float the rate until the time of settlement, or you may float and then lock in later, depending on your lender.

Estimating Closing Costs

As part of the loan application process, the lender is required by federal law (the Real Estate Settlement Procedures Act, or RESPA) to give you a *Good Faith Estimate* of closing costs (see the sample Good Faith Estimate in the following figure).

A Good Faith Estimate of closing costs.

The lender will estimate your closing costs based on his or her experience with that type of loan. The estimate should be close to what you really pay, but there's always a chance that it will be significantly different. The estimate will include costs for points, appraisal, title search, title insurance, survey, recording fees, attorney fees, and so on. The lender must give you this estimate within three business days of submitting the application. If you don't receive

Real Estate Terms

A **Good Faith Estimate** is a written estimate of closing costs. A lender must provide this to a prospective homebuyer within three days of submitting a mortgage loan application.

one, you should complain. You should also ask that a copy be sent to your real estate agent so that he or she can go over the charges. Chapter 3 explains some of the fees you can expect to pay. This can be a good way to compare different lenders with one another, as long as they are both comparing the same loan amount and interest rate (apples to apples). You will quickly be able to determine which lenders have extraneous fees. Don't be afraid to negotiate the fees. Many fees charged are fluff fees— unnecessary charges. Your agent can also help you sort out what you can expect to pay, what you don't have to pay, and what you can negotiate to *not* pay.

Estimating Interest Rates

In addition, the lender is required to send you a Truth-in-Lending statement that tells you the annual percentage rate (APR) for the loan. Remember that the rate you're quoted and the "real" rate are different. The APR takes into consideration all the costs of obtaining the loan—points, application fees, and so on (see the sample Truth-in-Lending statement in the following figure).

This statement should show the finance charge (amount you'll be expected to pay over the life of the loan), amount financed (mortgage amount minus any prepaid expenses you pay at or before closing), total of payments, schedule of payments, late-payment charges, and other information pertaining to the loan. If all the information is not available for the Truth-in-Lending statement, you'll receive an estimate from the lender. You'll then receive a second statement at the time of closing.

Finally, you should receive a government publication that discusses settlement, or closing, costs.

FEDERAL TRUTH-IN LENDING STATEMENT
(THIS IS NEITHER A CONTRACT NOR A COMMITMENT TO LEND)

Creditor:

Date: 07-13-00
Check box if applicable:

Loan Number:

ANNUAL PERCENTAGE RATE	FINANCE CHARGE	Amount Financed	Total of Payments	☐ Total Sale Price
The cost of your credit as a yearly rate.	The dollar amount the credit will cost you.	The amount of credit provided to you or on your behalf.	The amount you will have paid after you have made all payments as scheduled.	The Total cost of your purchase on credit including your down-payment of $
9.085* %	$ 133892.94*	$ 70319.00*	$ 204211.94*	$

☐ REQUIRED DEPOSIT: The annual percentage rate does not take into account your required deposit.
PAYMENTS: Your payment schedule will be:

Number of Payments	Amount of Payments	When Payments Are Due	Number of Payments	Amount of Payments	When Payments Are Due	Number of Payments	Amount of Payments	When Payments Are Due
		Monthly Beginning:			Monthly Beginning:			Monthly Beginning:
359	567.26	00-00-00						
1	565.60	11-00-29						

☐ DEMAND FEATURE: This obligation has a demand feature.
☐ VARIABLE RATE: This loan has a Variable Rate Feature. Variable Rate Disclosures have been provided to you earlier.

You are also required to pay 1/12th of the insurance & taxes in your monthly payment.
INSURANCE: The following insurance is required to obtain credit:
☐ Credit life insurance and credit disability ☒ Property Insurance $ 70500.00 ☐ Flood Insurance
You may obtain the insurance from anyone you want that is acceptable to creditor.
☐ If you purchase ☐ property ☐ flood insurance from creditor you will pay $ _____ for a one year term.
SECURITY: You are giving a security interest in: 126 E. 86TH ST. INDPLS. IN 46240
☒ The goods or property being purchased ☐ Real property you already own.
FILING FEES: $ 25.00
LATE CHARGE: If a payment is more than 15 days late, you will be charged 5.0 % of the payment.
PREPAYMENT: If you pay off early, you
☐ may ☒ will not have to pay a penalty.
☐ may ☒ will not be entitled to a refund of part of the finance charge.
ASSUMPTION: Someone buying your property
☐ may ☐ may, subject to conditions ☒ may not assume the remainder of your loan on the original terms:
See your contract documents for any additional information about nonpayment, default, any required repayment in full before the scheduled date and prepayment refunds and penalties.
* means an estimate ☒ all dates and numerical disclosures except the late payment disclosures are estimates.

The undersigned acknowledge receiving and reading a completed copy of this disclosure.
Neither you nor the creditor previously has become obligated to make or accept this loan, nor is any such obligation made by the delivery or signing of this disclosur

(Applicant) _____ (Date) _____ (Applicant) _____ (Date) _____

(Applicant) _____ (Date) _____ (Applicant) _____ (Date) _____

NOTE: Payments shown above do not include reserve deposits for taxes, assessments, and property or flood insurance.

VMP -784 (8807).02   KAR/KML   VMP MORTGAGE FORMS - (800)521-7291   7/88

A Truth-in-Lending statement.

Ensuring a Smooth Application Process

You may feel as if the entire loan process is out of your hands. That out-of-control feeling can be uncomfortable when so much is at stake. Here are some things you can do to ensure a smooth loan process:

◆ **Clean up your credit report.** Be sure to clear up any credit problems before you apply for a loan. If any problems turn up later, a lender won't want to hear your explanation after the fact. You can get help on cleaning up your report in Chapter 2.

◆ **Provide all the requested information quickly.** If the loan officer asks you for a pay stub, get the stub as quickly as possible. You can hold up the process if the loan processor is waiting on something from you.

◆ **Get copies of everything to protect yourself.** For instance, if you locked in a rate but have no proof of that, you're going to have a hard time if the lender says you *didn't* lock in a rate or that you locked in a different rate.

◆ **Call your loan officer periodically to check on the progress.** If there are problems, you'll want to know immediately, not at the end of 60 days. Perhaps the lender requires additional documentation. You should make sure that you are not responsible for any holdups.

◆ **Don't make any big purchases right before or during the loan process.** If you go out and buy a new car right before you apply for a loan, that debt is going to show up on your record. If you buy the car after you apply, the debt may also show up, because some lenders run *two* credit checks: one when you apply and one right before the closing. So if you're contemplating a big purchase, it's best to wait until after you close on the loan.

What to Do If You Can't Get a Loan

If you're denied a loan, the lender is required to explain the decision in writing. You should talk to the loan officer and find out what went wrong. If you can clear up the problem, you may be able to be reconsidered. If not, you may have to secure other financing.

Ask the loan officer for suggestions on how to improve your chances of getting approved. A loan officer has experience dealing with many successful and unsuccessful loans and may be able to give you some advice on improving your chances.

This section discusses some of the problems that can cause a loan to be denied.

Income Problems

If you don't have enough income to qualify for that loan, you can try the following to correct this situation:

◆ **Secure other financing.** If you cannot obtain financing through a traditional lender, you may want to try a different type of financing—for example, maybe the seller can help you with financing, or you can try a different loan program. For instance, you may be able to afford more with an ARM. Chapter 14 discusses the ARM loan and Chapter 15 discusses other types of financing. Also, you should ask your agent for suggestions.

◆ **Point out extenuating circumstances to the lender.** If you're about to get a raise, for example, you may ask your employer to give the lender a letter saying so. This may improve your financial picture enough to qualify.

◆ **Shop for a less-expensive home.** If you cannot qualify for the home of your dreams, perhaps you can qualify for a less-expensive home and then trade up when you're more financially secure.

◆ **Start a savings program.** If you don't have enough for the down payment, start saving now. You may not be able to afford a house today, but you don't want that to hold true forever.

◆ **Examine your current debts.** If that dream home is important enough to you, try lowering your existing debts by making some sacrifices. You could trade your car in for a less-expensive model; you could consolidate some outstanding loans— your debt would still be as high, but your monthly payments might be lower. Be creative and brutal. If you're spending a lot each month on concerts, movies, or eating out, cut back. You'll be surprised how quickly all of this adds up.

Buyer Beware

Bad credit is probably the number one hindrance to purchasing a home. Many people don't even know their credit rating, let alone realize how adversely it can affect buying a home. Don't be one of the herd! Check out your rating and get it cleaned up. Often a few small changes can make a big difference.

Credit Problems

If your credit report comes back with problems, you should ask to see a copy of the credit report. If there are errors, have them corrected. If there are blemishes in your credit history, add your explanation. Doing so may or may not change the lender's mind. All of this is discussed at length in Chapter 2 in the "Checking Your Credit" section.

If you have too much debt to qualify for a loan, consider paying off some of the debts if you're able. If you're not able but have a good credit history, ask the lender to reconsider.

Appraisal Problems

Most lenders will only give you a loan for a certain percentage of the home's appraised value—for example, 95 percent. If the appraisal is higher than what you're paying, you won't have to worry. If the appraisal is lower, you'll only be able to get a mortgage for the given percentage. In this case, you can try to come up with a larger down payment to cover the difference. Or if you made the sale contingent on an acceptable appraisal and the appraisal is low, you may be able to renegotiate the price.

Sometimes an appraisal will be low because the house needs some type of repair. For example, maybe the home needs to be painted, or it needs a new roof. If this is the case, you can ask the owner to fix the problem or set aside the funds for you to do the repair.

As noted previously, you may be able to appeal the appraisal. Ask your agent for help.

Discrimination Problems

You cannot be turned down for a loan based on race, religion, age, color, national origin, receipt of public assistance funds, gender, or marital status. If you think you've been denied a loan for one of these reasons, you should file a complaint with the U.S. Department of Housing and Urban Development. The address and phone number are listed in Appendix B. You can also visit the website at www.hud.gov.

The Least You Need to Know

- The loan officer takes your loan application and is your primary contact at the lender's office. The loan processor orders the credit check and appraisal and makes sure all the documentation is together. The underwriter decides whether to approve or deny the loan.

- The application process goes like this after you apply for a loan: The lender verifies the information, checks your credit history, orders and checks an appraisal on the property, and then approves or denies the loan.

- You'll most likely be charged a fee for an appraisal. The appraiser will look at the home and property and determine its current market value.

◆ In qualifying you for a loan, the lender will decide whether you can and will pay. The lender will also look at the cash you have now and the collateral you'll have in case you default on the loan.

◆ A loan may not be approved for one of several reasons: insufficient income, a bad credit report, or a low appraisal.

Part 4

Getting the Best Deal

After you find your dream home, you have to begin the negotiation process to buy that dream home. Doing so can be pretty tense. What's a good price to offer? Will the sellers take your offer? Will you have to counteroffer? Your agent can help you with the negotiations. If all goes well, at the end of the process, you'll own a home!

The final step in buying a home is the closing. Part 4, in addition to detailing the offer process, covers the key steps you need to follow to get to that final goal: owning your home. In particular, you need to arrange for insurance, have the home inspected, sign lots and lots of documents (be sure to read the fine print), hand over all your money, and then finally, finally get the keys to your new home.

Chapter 17

Making an Offer on a Home

In This Chapter

♦ Understanding the sales contract

♦ Deciding on a price

♦ Deciding on contingencies and terms

♦ Making a deposit

Making an offer might seem intimidating because there are so many things to think about: agreeing on a price, establishing contingencies, possibly selling your home, moving out, and so on. You might feel like you have to think of everything, and that it all must fall perfectly into place, or else! Well, keep reading: This chapter should put you a little more at ease as to what you can expect when you make an offer on a home.

Writing an Offer

When you have found the home that you want, you make a formal offer on the home usually by filling out a sale or purchase contract (called generically here "offer"). Because real estate laws differ from state to state, the contract's contents and format will vary. This section gives you an overview of what's included in the offer. (Later sections explain the components of an offer in more detail.) This section also includes some tips on making a successful offer.

What the Offer Should Include at the Minimum

Your agent should help you decide what to include in the offer and then help you write the offer. Usually the agent will use a preprinted offer form, which is modified to match what you want to offer. All offers should be submitted in written form and should include the following:

- Names of the buyer(s) and seller(s).

- The address and legal description of the property (lot, block, and square recorded in government records).

- The names of the brokers involved.

- The price, down payment, loan amount, and the amount of the deposit. Deciding on the price to offer is covered in "What Are You Willing to Pay?" later in this chapter. Handling the deposit is covered in the section "Making a Deposit."

- A time limit for the response to the offer, for getting financing and closing on the home, and for moving in.

What Else Can Be Included in the Offer?

In addition to including the price of the home in the offer, you will want to specify the terms of the sale. The following lists common terms and contingencies for consideration:

- What else do you want the seller to provide? For instance, you may ask the seller to help pay for the closing costs or to provide a warranty.

- What else has to happen for the deal to go through (in other words, contingencies)? For example, you will probably want to make the offer contingent upon getting financing and on an inspection and appraisal.

- What are the response time, settlement time, and occupancy time? For example, you may give the seller two days to respond to the offer. You may ask for 60 days to secure financing and then require the seller to be out of the home on the day of the closing. The custom varies depending on the area.

- What else is included with the home, such as appliances, window treatments, or an above-ground hot tub?

◆ What is the required condition of the home at settlement? For example, you may want to request that certain repairs be made. If the seller is a pack rat or there's a lot of clutter, you may request the seller to deliver the home "broom clean." Otherwise, you may be left with the task of hauling all that junk to a dumpster.

Real Deal

Sellers often focus on the price. If you offer the seller's full price, you may be able to get very favorable terms and contingencies.

◆ What other provisions should be considered? For example, the prorating of taxes, club dues, homeowners association fees, and so on.

Tips on Making an Offer

When you are working up an offer, consider that all offers are a combination of price and terms. If you give something on price, you can expect to take something on terms. For instance, you might offer close to the selling price but ask for help on closing costs or other beneficial terms. Or if you see that the roof needs to be replaced, you might want to tell the seller to fix the roof or offer a lower price in exchange for fixing the roof yourself. Any obvious repairs should be addressed in the initial offer.

When you make an offer on a home, everything is negotiable—the price, the terms, the occupancy date, what personal property is included, everything. You can ask for what you want. You may not get it, but you can ask. Unless you are in a very competitive seller's market, don't offer your best price first. Leave room for negotiating.

In the contract, be specific and include everything in writing. You may have a verbal agreement that the washer and dryer stay, but without a written contract, you will have no recourse if suddenly the washer and dryer aren't part of the deal. Being specific is especially important when it comes to personal property, because what *you* consider personal property and what the seller considers personal property may differ. When in doubt, put it in writing.

The more contingencies you include in the offer, the less attractive the offer will be to the seller. That's okay if you're working in a buyer's market. In a seller's market, though, if you really want the home, consider making an offer close to or at the asking price and leave off any contingencies.

Real Deal

Read your offer carefully. Does it include everything? If it is accepted, you cannot go back and say you forgot something. Also, ask your agent to explain anything that you don't fully understand. An offer, once signed, is a legally binding document.

TALK TO TUCKER REALTORS

This is a legally binding contract, if not understood seek legal advice.

A. Listing Broker _____ ( ) By _____ ( )
   (Seller's Agent) (Limited Agent)
B. Selling Broker _____ ( ) By _____ ( )
   (Buyer's Agent) (Limited Agent) (Seller's Subagent) _____

PURCHASE AGREEMENT

1. Date: _____

2. Buyer offers to buy real estate (the "Property") known as _____

3. in _____ Township, _____ County, _____, Indiana

4. _____ Zip Code, which is legally described as: _____

5. _____ in accordance with the terms and conditions set forth below:

6. **A. Purchase Price:** Buyer agrees to pay $_____ for above Property.

7. **B. Improvements and Fixtures:** The above price includes any existing permanent improvements and fixtures attached such as, but not
8. limited to, electrical and/or gas fixtures, heating and central air-conditioning equipment and all attachments thereto, built-in kitchen
9. equipment, sump pump, water softeners/conditioners/filters, gas grills, central vacuum equipment, all window shades/blinds, curtain rods,
10. drapery poles and fixtures, ceiling fans, light fixtures, towel racks and bars, awnings, TV antennas, satellite dishes and controls, storage
11. barns, all landscaping, mailbox, garage door opener with control(s), smoke alarms, fireplace doors and screens, storm/screen doors and
12. windows, AND THE FOLLOWING:

13. _____
14. _____
15. _____

16. **C. Method of Payment:** *(Circle appropriate paragraph number)*

17. **1. CASH:** The entire purchase price shall be paid in cash and no financing is required.

18. **2. NEW MORTGAGE:** Completion of this transaction shall be contingent upon the Buyer's ability to obtain a (Conventional) (FHA) (VA)
19. (Other _____) first mortgage loan
20. for $_____ , payable in not less than _____ years, with an original rate of
21. interest not to exceed _____ % per annum. Buyer shall pay all costs of obtaining financing, except _____
22.

23. **3. OTHER** – See Financing Addendum

24. **D. Time For Obtaining Financing:** Buyer agrees to make application for any financing necessary to complete this transaction, or for
25. approval to assume the unpaid balance of the existing mortgage within _____ days after the acceptance of this Purchase
26. Agreement and to make a diligent effort to obtain financing in cooperation with the Broker and Seller. No more than _____ days
27. after the acceptance of the Purchase Agreement shall be allowed for obtaining favorable commitment(s) or mortgage assumption approval.
28. If a commitment or approval is not obtained within the time specified above, this Agreement shall terminate unless an extension of time for
29. this purpose is mutually agreed to in writing.

30. **E. Closing Date:** Closing date shall be on or before _____ , 19 _____ or within
31. _____ days after _____ , whichever is later.

32. **F. Possession:** The possession of the Property shall be delivered to Buyer (at closing) or (by _____ a.m./p.m.)
33. on _____ . As rent for each day Seller is entitled to possession after closing, Seller shall pay to
34. Buyer at closing $_____ per day. If Seller does not deliver possession by the date required in the first sentence of this
35. paragraph, Seller shall pay Buyer $_____ per day as liquidated damages until possession is delivered and Buyer
36. shall have all other legal and equitable remedies available against the Seller.

37. **G. Lead-Based Paint:** If this housing was built before 1978, Buyer (has) (has not) received a copy of the Lead-Based Paint Certification &
38. Acknowledgment.

39. **H. Inspections:** A Buyer (has) (has not) received a copy of Seller's Disclosure. It is understood by the parties, that any condition or defect
40. affecting the Property disclosed to Buyer in the Seller's Disclosure prior to acceptance of Purchase Agreement shall not be a basis for Buyer
41. cancellation of this Purchase Agreement, unless otherwise agreed to in writing. Inspection(s) required by FHA, VA or lender do not eliminate
42. the need for Buyer to consider additional inspection(s) called for herein.

43. **(#1 or #2 Must Be Circled and Initialed)**

44. _____ 1. Buyer reserves the right to have the property inspected. Inspection(s) may include, but are not limited to such items as heating,
45. cooling, electrical, plumbing, roof, walls, ceilings, floors, foundation, basement, crawl space, well, septic, water analysis, wood
46. destroying insect infestations, radon, lead-based paint or _____ . All inspections shall be at
47. Buyer's expense by qualified inspector(s) or contractor(s), selected by Buyer. All inspections shall be made within _____ days
48. after _____ .
49. Buyer's response shall be delivered within SEVEN days thereafter to Seller and/or Listing Agent. If Buyer does not respond promptly within
50. the Inspection/Response Period or does not make a written objection to any problem revealed in the report within the Inspection/Response
51. Period, the Property shall be deemed to be acceptable. If the Buyer reasonably believes that the Inspection Report reveals a MAJOR
52. DEFECT with the Property and the Seller is unable or unwilling to remedy the defect to the Buyer's reasonable satisfaction before closing or
53. at a time otherwise agreed to by the parties, then this Agreement may be terminated by the Buyer, or such defect may be waived by the
54. Buyer and the transaction shall proceed toward closing. BUYER AGREES THAT ANY PROPERTY DEFECT PREVIOUSLY DISCLOSED
55. BY SELLER, SHALL NOT BE A BASIS FOR TERMINATION OF THIS AGREEMENT, UNLESS OTHERWISE AGREED TO IN WRITING.

56. _____ 2. BUYER HAS BEEN AFFORDED THE OPPORTUNITY TO RESERVE THE RIGHT TO HAVE THE PROPERTY INSPECTED.
57. HOWEVER, BUYER HEREBY WAIVES INSPECTIONS AND RELIES UPON THE CONDITION OF THE PROPERTY BASED
58. UPON BUYER'S OWN EXAMINATION. BUYER RELEASES THE SELLER, BROKER, LISTING AGENT, BUYER AGENT, SUB-
59. AGENT AND/OR LIMITED AGENT FROM ANY AND ALL LIABILITY RELATING TO ANY NON-LATENT OR DISCLOSED
60. LATENT DEFECTS OR DEFICIENCY AFFECTING THE PROPERTY, WHICH WAIVER SHALL SURVIVE THE CLOSING.

61. **I. Real Estate Tax:** BUYER shall pay all real estate property taxes, beginning with the installment due and payable in _____
62. _____ , 19 _____ , and SELLER shall pay all real estate property taxes due prior thereto. In the event real
63. estate taxes are unknown at time of closing, then the last installment of such taxes shall be used as a basis for any credits due Buyer. Buyer
64. and Seller agree that any variance between actual tax liability and the amount credited at closing shall be the Buyer's sole
65. responsibility/property. Buyer agrees, if necessary, to escrow an amount necessary to satisfy the first installment of taxes due after closing.
66. ("Real Estate Taxes" shall include all charges placed on Tax Bill for collection.)

67. **J. Title Evidence:** Prior to closing, Buyer shall be furnished at Seller's expense, a commitment for title insurance in the amount of purchase
68. price. Any encumbrances or defects in title must be removed from said commitment and subsequent title insurance policy issued free and
69. clear of said encumbrances and title defects, with the exception of any mortgage assumed by Buyer. The final policy shall be subject only to
70. taxes; easements and restrictive covenants of record, encumbrances of Buyer; and rights or claims of parties in possession, boundary line
71. disputes, overlaps, encroachments and any other matters not shown by the public records which would be disclosed by an accurate survey
72. or inspection of this Property. Seller agrees to pay the cost of obtaining all documents necessary to perfect title, so that marketable title can
73. be conveyed. The commitment shall be ordered _____ (immediately) (after mortgage approval) (other _____
74. _____).

75. **K. Conveyance:** Conveyance of this Property shall be by General Warranty Deed, or by other insurable conveyance subject to taxes,
76. easements, restrictive covenants and encumbrances of record, unless otherwise agreed to herein.

77. **L. Settlement/Closing Fee:** If the method of payment for this transaction is cash, assumption, or conditional sales contract, the
78. settlement/closing fee shall be paid by _____

79. **M. Survey:** (Buyer at Buyer's expense) or (Seller at Seller's expense) shall obtain a (staked survey) or (mortgage inspection survey) of the
80. Property, which shall be received prior to closing, be reasonably satisfactory to Buyer, show the location of improvements and easements,
81. and show the flood zone designation of the Property.

82. **N. Utilities/Municipal Services:** Seller shall pay for all municipal services and public utility charges through the day of possession.

Side one of a typical purchase agreement.

83. **O. Public Improvement Assessments:** Seller warrants that Seller has no knowledge of any planned improvements which may result in
84. assessments and that no governmental or private agency has served notice requiring repairs, alterations or corrections of any existing
85. conditions. Public or municipal improvements which are not completed as of the date hereof but which will result in a lien or charge shall be
86. paid by Buyer.
87. **P. Risk of Loss:** Seller shall be responsible for risk of loss and/or damage to the improvements on the Property until time of closing when title
88. to or an interest in the Property is transferred to the Buyer.
89. **Q. Maintenance of Property:** Seller agrees that maintaining the condition of the Property, subject to repairs or any inspection is the
90. responsibility of Seller during the period of this Contract and/or until time of possession, whichever is later.
91. **R. Time Is Of The Essence:** Time periods specified in this Agreement shall expire at midnight on the date stated unless the parties agree in
92. writing to a different date and/or time.
93. **S. Earnest Money:** Buyer submits herewith $_____ as earnest money which shall be applied to the purchase price.
94. Earnest money shall be deposited in the listing REALTOR's Escrow Account, immediately upon acceptance of the Purchase Agreement,
95. and held until time of closing the transaction or termination of this Purchase Agreement. Earnest money shall be returned promptly in the
96. event this offer is not accepted. If this offer is accepted and Buyer shall fail or refuse to close the transaction, without legal cause, the
97. earnest money shall be forfeited by Buyer to Seller as liquidated damages, or Seller may pursue any other legal and equitable remedies.
98. The Broker holding any earnest money is absolved from any responsibility to make payment to the Seller or Buyer, unless the parties enter
99. into a Mutual Release or a Court of competent jurisdiction issues an Order for payment.
100. **T. Homeowners Association/Condominium Association:** Documents for a MANDATORY membership association shall be
101. delivered by the Seller to Buyer within _____ days after acceptance of this Agreement. If the Buyer does not make a written response
102. to the documents within _____ days after receipt, the documents shall be deemed acceptable. In the event the Buyer does not accept
103. the provisions in the documents and such provisions cannot be waived, this Agreement may be terminated by the Buyer and the earnest
104. money deposit shall be refunded to Buyer without delay. Any approval of sale required by the Association shall be obtained by the Seller, in
105. writing, within _____ days after Buyer's approval of the documents.
106. **U. Miscellaneous Provisions:** The transaction shall be closed in accordance with the following:
107.   1. Prorations for rent, association dues/assessments, or any other items shall be made and computed through the date of closing.
108.   2. Any tenant deposits shall be transferred to Buyer at closing.
109.   3. Notwithstanding any other provisions of this Agreement, any inspections and charges, which are required to be made and charged to
110.   Buyer or Seller by the lender, FHA, VA, Mortgage Insurer or closing agent, shall be made and charged in accordance with their
111.   prevailing rules or regulations and shall supersede any provisions of this Agreement.
112.   4. The price and terms of financing on a closed sale shall be disseminated to members of the Metropolitan Indianapolis Board of
113.   REALTORS®, to other Brokers upon request, and shall be published in the MIBOR's Multiple Listing Service.
114.   5. The Professional Service fee payable to the Listing Broker is the obligation of Seller.
115.   6. Seller represents and warrants that Seller is not a "Foreign Person" (individual or entity) and therefore is not subject to the Foreign
116.   Investment In Real Property Tax Act.
117.   7. Any amounts payable by one party to the other, or by one party on behalf of the other party, shall not be payable until this transaction is
118.   closed.
119.   8. Buyer hereby discloses to Seller that Buyer is licensed under the Indiana Real Estate Broker and Salesperson Licensing Act and holds
120.   License #_____.
121. **V. Further Conditions:** _____
122. _____
123. _____
124. _____
125. _____
126. _____
127. _____
128. _____
129. **W. Expiration and Approval:** This Purchase Agreement is void if not accepted in writing on or before _____ (AM) (PM)
130.   (Noon) (Midnight) _____, 19 _____.
131. **X. Terms Binding:** All terms and conditions are included herein and no verbal agreements shall be binding.
132. **Y. Acknowledgments:** Buyer and Seller acknowledge that each has received agency disclosure forms, have had their agency options
133. explained, and now confirm the agency relationships previously entered into and confirmed above. They further acknowledge that they
134. understand and accept agency relationships involved in this transaction. By signature below the parties verify that they understand and
135. approve this Purchase Agreement and acknowledge receipt of a signed copy. Broker may refer Buyer or Seller to various vendor/providers
136. including but not limited to lender, title insurers, contractors, inspection/warranty companies. Broker(s) does not guarantee the performance
137. of any service provider. Buyer and Seller are free to select providers other than those referred or recommended by Broker(s).
138. This Agreement may be executed simultaneously or in two or more counterparts, each of which shall be deemed an original, but all of which
      together shall constitute one and the same instrument. Delivery of this document may be accomplished by electronic facsimile reproduction
      (FAX); if FAX delivery is utilized, the original document shall be promptly executed and/or delivered, if requested.

139.
140. BUYER'S SIGNATURE   DATE   BUYER'S SIGNATURE   DATE

141.
142. PRINTED   PRINTED

143.
144. BUYER'S SOCIAL SECURITY # / FEDERAL I.D. #   BUYER'S SOCIAL SECURITY # / FEDERAL I.D. #

145.   **ACCEPTANCE OF PURCHASE AGREEMENT**
146. The above terms and conditions are accepted this _____ day of _____, 19 _____
147. at _____ (AM) (PM) (Noon) (Midnight).

148.
149. SELLER'S SIGNATURE   SELLER'S SIGNATURE

150.
151. PRINTED   PRINTED

152.
153. SELLER'S SOCIAL SECURITY # / FEDERAL I.D. #   SELLER'S SOCIAL SECURITY # / FEDERAL I.D. #

Side two of a typical purchase agreement.

What Are You Willing to Pay?

Remember that when buying a home, you are in a bartering situation. You have to decide how much to pay for the home. Do you offer less than the listing price? If so, how much less? Do you offer the exact listing price, or do you offer more than the listing price? When deciding how much to offer, you need to consider the sales prices of comparable homes as well as the motivation of the seller.

Comparing Other Sales Prices

You probably don't want to pay more for the home than it is worth, but how can you figure out what a particular home is worth? One way is to ask your agent what he or she would consider a fair offer. Your agent has lots of experience in selling homes, so he or she should be able to give you a valid opinion of a fair price, or perhaps justify the price with sales comparisons.

If you are working with a subagent, keep in mind that the agent is actually working for the seller. The agent probably wouldn't (or shouldn't) give you an inaccurate price range, but he or she is motivated to make the sale. If you are working with a buyer's agent, you can rest assured that this agent is working for you only.

Another strategy is to find out the selling price of comparable homes in the area. Ask for statistics of list price vs. sales price. As you look at several homes, you will know what the home is listed for, and you can compare the home you want to purchase to these other listings. But what a home lists for and what it sells for can be quite different. Therefore, you need to ask your agent to investigate the selling prices of comparable homes. If similar homes in the area are selling for $100,000, and the listing price of the home you want is $120,000, you may want to offer less.

Real Deal

Keep in mind that the contract will become a legal document if it is accepted. Consider having an attorney look over the contract before you submit it. Chapter 18 includes a section on what a real estate lawyer can help you with.

Most homes sell for about 6 percent less than the list price, but that's just an average. The actual difference will vary depending on the location, condition, list price, and current market.

Another way to determine the market value of a home is to have an appraisal done before you make an offer. As part of the loan process, the home will be appraised, but this appraisal occurs after the deal has been made. If the home appraises for lower than the offered price, and if you make the offer contingent upon the appraisal, you may be able to negotiate a lower price. See the section entitled "The Offer Is

Contingent On ..." later in this chapter. You may choose to pay to have an appraisal done beforehand. If the sellers sell the home to someone else, though, you will have lost the money you spent.

> ### Real Deal
>
> If you find yourself looking at homes slightly out of your range, you may decide you can—somehow—spend a little more. For example, suppose that you feel you can afford a $150,000 home but find the perfect home for $160,000. You may find a way to come up with a little more money. Perhaps you can sell off some assets. Or perhaps you can consider a different type of financing that will enable you to qualify for a larger loan amount.

How Motivated Is the Seller?

When you are deciding on a fair price, you should also take into consideration the mindset of the sellers. The sellers probably aren't going to come right out and say they are desperate, but certain clues can give away the sellers' thinking. For instance, find out how long the home has been on the market. If the home was just put on the market, the sellers might not be too anxious to take the first offer. If the home has been on the market for several months, the sellers may be more ready to accept an offer.

Find out whether the price has been reduced and, if so, how many times. A home that has been reduced several times may be ripe for an offer. Ask your agent to also tell you when the sellers originally bought the home, what they paid for it, and what their equity is. It can be beneficial to know that the sellers need to sell their home but still want to make a profit, or possibly that they would be willing to carry the loan for you.

A buyer's agent also may be able to ferret out other information from the listing agent. For instance, are the sellers being transferred? Is the couple divorcing? Have they had other offers? Is the home owned by a relocation company? If so, the company will be motivated to sell to get the home off of their inventory book.

> ### Real Deal
>
> Your agent is the best source of information about the seller and the seller's situation. The agent can find out how long the home has been on the market, as well as discover any price reductions. He or she also may know other information related to the seller.

Where are the sellers going? Are they moving to another state? Have they already bought another home? If the sellers have bought a new home, they will be under pressure to sell the current home, so you will know you have an advantage. If they are moving to another state, they may want to quickly sell the home to avoid the hassle of selling the house from their new residence.

Asking the Seller to Pay Part

As this chapter mentions, everything is negotiable. You can ask the seller to do or include anything you want. For example, you may ask the seller to pay for some or all of the allowable closing costs. Suppose that your loan has three points. On a $100,000 home, that's $3,000 you have to come up with at closing. You may ask your seller to pay all or some of the points. You can also ask the seller to pay for other closing costs, such as the inspection, appraisal, title search, document fees, homeowners warranty, and so on.

In addition to monetary requests, you can ask the seller to make changes to the home—contingencies. For instance, you may ask for the seller to have the roof repaired. You may ask the seller to replace the carpeting (or allow for a redecorating fee) or to add central air conditioning. Contingencies are covered in the next section.

The Offer Is Contingent On ...

Suppose that you agree to purchase a home but can't get a loan. Or suppose that you agree to purchase a home but find out in the meantime that the home is riddled with termites. If you didn't include any contingency clauses in your contract, you would be stuck with buying the home anyway. A contingency clause says, "Sure, I'll buy this home, if ...."

The next section covers some common contingencies included in sales agreements.

Getting Financing

If you can't get financing for the home, you will want to be able to bow out of the deal. You will also want to specify exactly what financing is acceptable. For instance, you could get a loan from Eddie the Armbreaker at 20 percent interest, but would you want to?

> **Real Deal**
>
> Remember, if you have been preapproved, you already know just how much you can afford. Getting preapproved also makes your offer more attractive to sellers, because they know that financing should not be a problem. See the "Getting Preapproved for a Loan" section in Chapter 2 for more information.

In your purchase agreement, you should specifically state …

- The amount of time you have to get financing.

- The loan amount.

- The down payment amount.

- The maximum interest rate you will pay.

- The type and term of the loan.

Receiving a Clear Deed and Title

You will want to ensure that you get a clear deed and *title* to the home. The lender will require a title search that will turn up any problems (such as liens). Who pays for this search and what happens if problems pop up should be stated in the contract. Title searches, *deeds*, and insurance are covered in detail in Chapter 19.

Real Estate Terms

The **title** is a legal document proving a person's right to claim entitlement to a property, including the history of the property's ownership. The **deed** is the document conveying the title to a property.

Having the Home Inspected

You may want to make the sale contingent on a professional inspection of the home. (Inspections are covered in Chapter 20.) You will want to specify who pays for the inspection and what happens if a problem is reported as a result of the inspection. For example, just having the sale contingent on an inspection doesn't ensure that the seller has to fix the broken toilet. Is the seller required to fix any problems? All problems? Can you withdraw the offer if the inspection is not acceptable? You will want to work out these terms with your agent.

You may also want to have the home inspected for termites, radon, lead paint, asbestos, or other hazards. Your lender may require some of these tests before approving the loan.

Many states now require a seller disclosure. The sellers have to tell you in writing about any known defects of the home. You may also want to make the offer contingent on the acceptance of the seller disclosure.

Real Deal _____

Keep in mind that the more contingencies you require, the less attractive the offer. Also, it's usually not a good idea to include frivolous contingencies like "I won't buy the home unless the sellers paint it pink."

Having the Home Appraised

Your lender will require an appraisal of the property before the loan is approved. You will probably want to make your offer contingent on an appraisal, and you may want to spell out what to do if the appraisal comes back lower than the selling price. For example, can you renegotiate the price or can you withdraw from the deal?

Other Contingencies to Consider

You may want to include other contingencies as well. For instance, if you own a home, you may want to make the sale contingent upon selling your current home. In order to secure financing, some lenders will make the financing contingent upon the sale of your home.

Sometimes a contingency is countered with an escape clause, or *kickout*. For example, the seller may want to continue to show the home. If the seller receives another offer, you will have the option of removing the contingency or backing out.

Specifying Other Offer Terms

In addition to contingencies, you commonly specify in the purchase agreement the time limits, personal property included with the home, condition of the home, and any prorating of payments. This section discusses these offer elements.

Setting Time Limits

Buying a home is a waiting game. You will want to specify how long you are willing to wait. How long do the sellers have to respond to the offer? You should require a written response within a certain time limit—for instance, 48 hours. If you don't require a response, the seller can sit on your offer, perhaps until a better offer comes along. But remember, you can cancel an offer any time before it is accepted.

Another date you should specify is the closing date. How long until you close on the home—that is, what is the settlement date? In setting this date, you will want to allow enough time for your loan application and approval (usually around 45 to 60 days).

How long until you move in or take occupancy? You will usually want to move in immediately after closing or settlement. It's a good idea to ensure the sellers are out before settlement; otherwise, how are you going to get Mr. and Mrs. McCrocklin, their three kids, two dogs, three fish, and Aunt Hattie out? In some cases, you may make a special arrangement for the sellers to remain in the home after closing and to pay you rent. If this is the case, the exact terms should be spelled out in the contract.

What Personal Property Is Included?

Personal property is defined as anything that can be picked up and moved. Anything that is attached is *real property*. The sellers are entitled to take the personal property but must leave the real property. The law of fixtures determines when personal property becomes real property.

Seems clear enough. That is, until you move into your home and find that the sellers took the wall-to-wall carpeting, curtains, stove, refrigerator, dishwasher, cabinets, and anything else that wasn't nailed down tight.

Real vs. Personal Property

If moveable personal property is permanently attached to a building or land, it is technically a fixture and should be included with the home. This includes, for instance, a chandelier that is attached to the ceiling with bolts. Fixtures encompass existing electrical, lighting, plumbing, and heating fixtures; fireplace inserts and solar systems; air conditioners, water softeners, and built-in appliances; screens, awnings, shutters, window coverings, and attached floor coverings; satellite dishes and related equipment; security and alarm systems; mailboxes; garage door openers, remotes, and keys to all exterior locks; and in-ground landscaping.

If you are selling your home and don't want an item included, it's best to remove it so that there's no question. If you are buying a home and aren't sure, specify the item in your offer.

When there's a dispute, the court uses the following criteria to determine if the property is a fixture (real property):

- ◆ **Method of attachment.** If it is nailed, bolted, glued, wired, built-in, or cemented, it is a fixture. As an example, carpeting that is nailed or glued to the floor is a fixture; area rugs are not. Drapery rods are a fixture, but the drapes themselves are not.

- ◆ **Agreement by parties.** If the buyer includes any personal property as part of the offer, it must stay. If the seller wants to exclude any real property or fixtures, they must specify the items in the contract. If they do not, they must stay.

- **Intent of buyer and seller.** The best thing to do is spell out exactly what you seek in the deal. For example, if you want the refrigerator and washer and dryer, make sure they are listed on your offer as included with the sale. Same thing for other borderline items such as mini-blinds, microwaves, and other items.

- **Adaptability of use.** If an item is specifically adapted to the property (such as built-in speakers), it is a fixture.

- **Relationship of parties.** When the buyer and seller cannot resolve the disagreement and the case goes to litigation, the courts usually favor the buyer over the seller.

To avoid any disagreements, you should explicitly state which items you want the sellers to leave. Do you want all the window treatments? Ceiling fans? What about the pot rack hanging in the kitchen? The chandelier in the dining room? What appliances are included? The washer, dryer, dishwasher, refrigerator, stove? What about any rugs? Mirrors? Stained glass?

Real Deal

The contract may include other provisions, such as confirmation of the type of zoning, an explanation of what happens if the home burns down in the meantime, a statement of the type of sewer and water, a statement of assignability, and so on. Your agent should explain any other provisions included in the contract.

If a certain possession is key to the home layout, you may ask for it to be included. For example, suppose that the kitchen includes a bar and stools for dining at the counter. You may want to ask the sellers to leave the stools; they may not have any need for them in their new home, anyway. Sometimes people will sell all their furniture right along with the home. If you like the furniture, consider it. If you don't want the furniture, just say no.

Specifying the Condition of the Home at Settlement

In the contract, you will want to state in what condition you expect to receive the home. For instance, you may state that the plumbing, heating, mechanical, and electrical systems are in working order at closing. You may want to be sure that the home is left empty and clean.

You should request a walkthrough right before settlement to ensure that the home is in the same condition as when you made the offer. If you want a walkthrough, put it in the offer. If you take one, check for any damage to the property—holes in the wall, broken windows, marks in the flooring, spots on the carpet. Check to be sure the heating, air conditioning, plumbing, and other components are working. See Chapter 21 for information on how to handle problems found at the walkthrough.

If problems were found at the inspection and repairs had to be made, you can request to see the paid receipt from the licensed contractor that made the repairs.

Prorating Tax and Other Payments

The contract should state which items will be prorated and how they will be prorated. For example, the sellers may have already paid taxes on the home for the next three months. Are they entitled to a portion of that money back? Or taxes may be due, and you may want to have the sellers pay a prorated amount for the due taxes. Depending on the type of loan and the situation, different items will be handled differently.

Making a Deposit

Once you have worked out the details of the offer, you then write out a check for a deposit on the home. Because the sellers want to see that you are committed to making the purchase, they will usually require a deposit or earnest money. The amount of the deposit varies but should be specified in the contract. The contract should also state who holds the deposit until closing. (You will want to have a neutral party hold the money—the real estate agent should put the money into escrow. Keep in mind that escrow accounts do not pay interest.)

Finally, be sure to state what happens to the deposit if the deal doesn't go through. If the seller doesn't accept your offer or if the deal falls through because of some fault of the seller, you will want the money returned within a reasonable amount of time.

With the offer penned and the deposit ready, the agent has all he or she needs to present the offer. Turn to the next chapter to see what happens after you make an offer.

The Least You Need to Know

- ◆ After the sales contract is signed by both parties, it is a legally binding contract. Your agent should help you prepare the contract. You may also want to have your attorney look it over.

- ◆ Critical items to cover in the sales agreement include a description of the property, the price, financing terms, response time, settlement date, and any contingencies.

- ◆ You can decide on a fair price to offer by seeing what comparable homes have sold for in the area. Also take into consideration your motivation and the seller's motivation.

- Common contingencies include getting financing and having the home inspected.

- In the sales agreement, spell out any personal property you want included as part of the sale.

Chapter 18

Working the Deal

In This Chapter

- ◆ Understanding the offer process
- ◆ Handling counteroffers
- ◆ Having an offer accepted
- ◆ Withdrawing from an offer
- ◆ Using a real estate attorney

The tennis game begins when you make the first serve. The ball goes to the seller. The seller may decide not to play or may return the offer to you. If he returns the offer, the ball is back in your court. You may decide to quit, or you may return the offer. The ball goes back to the seller. This back-and-forth process of negotiation continues until a deal is made, the seller receives another offer, or someone quits.

Understanding the fine art of negotiating—the topic of this chapter—can help you make a good offer to begin with and then handle any counteroffers.

Understanding the Offer Process

When you decide you want to make an offer on a home, your agent will sit down with you and help you write it. The offer must be written; it cannot be verbal. (Chapter 17 explains the key items included in an offer.) After the offer is written, you sign it and attach your earnest money to show the sellers, "Look. I have some money, and I want your home."

Your agent then conveys the offer to the seller, usually in a face-to-face meeting with the seller's agent. In some cases, the offer may be made over the phone or faxed, and then followed up with a face-to-face meeting. This is one area where your agent can help; he or she can present the offer favorably and start the negotiation process of making the deal.

When you write the offer, you should include a time limit for responding to the offer. During this time, you'll be biting your nails and sitting by the phone, until finally your agent will give you the seller's response: yes, no, or maybe.

The seller may choose to accept the offer, in which case you can skip to the section later in this chapter called "Having an Offer Accepted." You've bought yourself a home.

Real Deal

Buying a home is an emotional process. You may think that only one home will really fit you and your needs, and you may feel devastated if that deal doesn't go through. Keep in mind that there are many, many homes, and you will most likely find another home that you like—maybe even one you like better—if your offer on a particular home is not accepted.

Sometimes the seller chooses not to respond. In this case, no news is not good news. No news means *no*. If the seller rejects the offer and you really want the home, you may want to make another offer. Or you can start looking at other homes of interest.

In many cases, the seller will return the offer with some changes. This is called a *counteroffer*. You can choose to accept the offer and go directly to the section titled "Having an Offer Accepted," or you can choose to counter with your next offer. In this case, see the section "Handling Counteroffers." The back and forth of countering will continue until one side quits or one side accepts the deal.

Using the Best Offer Strategies

When making an offer, find out all you can about the home and the sellers so that you are in the strongest negotiating position. Doing so can help you evaluate your situation and then select an appropriate offer strategy. You may want to use one of the following strategies:

◆ **The lowball offer.** If you are looking for a home in a buyer's market and are not emotionally committed to having the home, you may want to make a lowball offer. A lowball offer is usually way below the asking price. Lowballs may succeed if the seller is desperate. Sometimes the seller will counter, but most times the seller will ignore this type of offer. You definitely don't want to make a lowball offer in a seller's market or if you really, really want the home.

◆ **The anxious offer.** If you feel you must have the home, you may want to make your best offer first. This strategy leaves no room for negotiating but might be necessary in a seller's market in which homes aren't on the market for long. Your agent will probably convey to the sellers that this is your best offer; the sellers may accept, counter, or reject the offer. If the market isn't red hot, you may not want to make your best offer first. Most sellers expect to receive an offer, counter, then receive another offer—that is, they expect to play tennis.

◆ **The bidding war offer.** In a seller's market, you may find yourself bidding with other buyers for the same property. In this case, you lose all your negotiating strength. You have to see the bid, raise it, or fold your cards gracefully and move to the next game.

◆ **The negotiable offer.** In most cases, the best offer is the one that leaves room for negotiating. You should plan what you want to offer first and what you can go up to. If you are working with a buyer's agent, your agent can help you with this strategy. The negotiable offer gives you a start in the point/counterpoint process, described next.

> **CAUTION**
>
> **Buyer Beware**
>
> If you are working with a seller's agent or subagent, keep in mind that this agent is required to pass along all information. If you tell the seller's agent you can go higher, the seller's agent can pass that information along. You can read more about agents in Chapter 4.

Remember that although homebuying is an emotional process, you'd do best to keep your emotions in check. If the seller knows that this is your *dream* home, the seller has the advantage. If, on the other hand, you know the seller has already moved into a new home and is carrying two mortgage payments, you have the advantage. Chapter 17 discusses how to put together an attractive offer.

Handling Counteroffers

It's appropriate that *negotiate* includes the word *go*, because that's what you do—you go back and forth. If the sellers want to consider your offer but want to make some changes, they will return a counteroffer. If you want to make some changes to this counter, you make another counteroffer. And so it goes. You can see an example of a counteroffer in a later section, "Responding to a Counteroffer."

Receiving a Counteroffer

If a seller counters with another offer, that's usually a good sign—at least you know that the seller gave your offer some consideration. Your agent should return the counteroffer and explain the changes. Usually there's a time limit for you to respond to the counteroffer.

Buyer Beware

Don't accept or respond to any verbal counteroffers. If the sellers tell your agent that they want a higher price, have them convey that information in the form of a written offer.

Real Deal

If you are making lots of changes, you may want to use a new offer form. If the sellers see many items crossed off or written in, they may be more aware of the changes. The marked-up form screams, "Here's where I'm trying to get you!" Instead, write up a new offer that looks cleaner. Be sure it says what you want it to say.

Keep in mind that everything is negotiable. The seller may ask for more, may say no to what you asked for, or may ask for something else. For instance, the seller may ask for a higher price. Or the seller may say no to your request to pay closing costs. The seller may agree to the offer but ask for a different closing date or occupancy date. You should look over the counteroffer carefully and be sure you understand the changes.

Items that remain the same are not mentioned again after they have been found satisfactory—only changes are noted on counters. If you're not sure which things are the same and which are different, ask. You may want to restate your understanding in the counter.

In some cases, the counteroffer may be okay with you. You sign the counteroffer, and the deal is made. See the section "Having an Offer Accepted" later in this chapter.

In other cases, you may think the counteroffer is close, but you still want a few changes. In this case, you counter the counteroffer with another counteroffer!

Responding to a Counteroffer

If the seller's counteroffer is close to what you want, but you want to make a few changes, you can offer another counteroffer. Again, your agent will help you draw up the offer. Usually the counteroffers are simply edited versions of the original offer, with changes written in and then initialed by all parties. In some cases, you may want to write a new offer.

In responding to the counteroffer, you should consider what is important to you. Can you come up a little higher on price? Will you give on price in exchange for some help on closing?

An example of a counteroffer.

Buyer Beware _____

When negotiating, be sure you stay within your financial limitations. Don't let the emotions of buying a home sway you into paying more than you can afford.

It's easy to get into a nitpicking situation during countering. You may think that you want the last word. Keep your goal in mind: to buy the home. If you want to change something that is really important, by all means, don't accept the counteroffer. If the reason you want to counter is trivial, consider just accepting the offer. The best type of negotiating is a win-win situation. The sellers should feel as if they got a good price, and the buyers should feel as if they got a good deal on the home they wanted.

If you are close to a deal, the agent may recommend that you "split the difference." For example, if you offer $105,000, and the seller counters with $108,000, you may want to split the difference and offer $106,500. In this case, both sides may feel as if they "won." However, don't do this too soon.

Quitting and Moving On

If the counteroffering has become ridiculous (gone on for too long or fixated on small details), it's time to quit. Sometimes the buyer and seller focus more on the competitiveness of the situation and feel driven to win. The process can get ugly, and usually both the buyer and the seller end up with bad feelings.

Don't let the negotiation process drag you down. Your agent can help keep you focused on the goal (buying the home). Your agent may also be able to get the sellers to focus on their goal (selling the home). If not, you should consider walking away and trying to find another home suited to your needs.

You may also want to quit when it becomes apparent that you and the seller are too far off on terms and price ever to reach an acceptable agreement.

Having an Offer Accepted

The happy part of home hunting occurs when the offer is accepted. This happens when the seller signs and accepts your original offer or any counteroffers, or when you sign and accept the seller's counteroffer. Once both parties have signed, the purchase agreement becomes a legally binding document. You cannot back out now.

When your offer is accepted, you will probably feel two conflicting emotions: happy (you should be glad that you have purchased the home you wanted) and scared (you just made a big commitment, and the process isn't entirely over). You still have to get financing and close on the home. Keep in mind that most people feel nervous after making such a big decision, and the feeling will probably pass.

When you have an offer accepted, make sure that you get a copy of the signed agreement. You may want to have an attorney look over the agreement before you sign it. If your attorney isn't available, you can write "Subject to the approval in form of my attorney." See the section "Do I Need a Real Estate Attorney?" later in this chapter for more information.

You may be asked to increase the amount of money you put down on the home. This money will be held in escrow until you close on the home.

You will also be required to get moving on any contingencies that you need to satisfy. For example, you may have a certain time period (specified in the contract) in which to arrange to have the home inspected. You may also have to apply for a loan within a certain time period. Your agent should remind you what you need to do next.

Withdrawing an Offer

Suppose that you change your mind and decide, *Oops—I don't really want to buy a home.* Can you back out of a deal? In some cases, you can. In other cases, the seller is going to respond with, "Oops—You are getting a home whether you want it or not!"

When can you back out of a deal? You can withdraw from the deal with no legal repercussions in any of the following cases:

- You can withdraw an offer any time before the seller has signed and accepted the offer.

- You can walk away at any time during the offer—counteroffer process. If the seller gives you an offer you don't like, you do not have to respond. You can just quit.

- You can withdraw an offer if any of the contingencies included in the offer are not met. For example, if the offer is contingent on an inspection of the home, and the inspection turns up a major structural

Real Deal _____

If you are feeling anxious about the home, write a list of all the things you like about the home and all the benefits you will receive from owning the home. Start thinking about how you will decorate, who you will have over, and so on. Think about living in the home and enjoying it. Doing so may help ease your mind.

Buyer Beware

An offer is accepted only when all parties have signed the same document. Don't be fooled if the seller or agent says, "The offer is accepted with just a few changes." If the seller made any changes to an offer you presented, it is a rejected offer, and you are not bound to honor the agreement.

flaw, you may be able to withdraw from the offer. (Usually, though, the seller has the opportunity to make the repairs.)

If the offer has been signed by both parties, it is a binding contract. You cannot back out without forfeiting your deposit money. Also, the sellers may be able to sue you for damages if you don't fulfill the contract. On the other hand, the seller can't back out, either. If the seller does, you can sue for damages or try to enforce the contract. You can't really force someone to buy or sell a home unless they want to, though.

Do I Need a Real Estate Attorney?

In addition to the services of an agent, you may want to use a real estate attorney to look over the contract before you sign it. An attorney, for the most part, will not be involved in the price negotiation of the deal but can help ensure that you don't get caught up in a bad deal. The attorney can look over the finer details of the agreement and make sure that you understand them and that they are acceptable.

An attorney can also help with the closing, ensuring that all the necessary steps are completed, and looking over any papers you are required to sign. (You will be signing a lot!)

Your attorney can also help settle any difficulties that arise. For instance, suppose that the deal falls through because of one of the contingencies, but the sellers won't return the deposit. Your attorney can help handle this problem. In addition, the attorney may handle the escrow duties in some states. And, if nothing else, an attorney's presence can provide you with peace of mind.

If you decide to use an attorney, you will want to use one who specializes in real estate law. You can ask friends, relatives, your agent, or others for recommendations. Be sure to inquire about the attorney's fees. You may pay a flat fee or an hourly fee. Also be sure you explain exactly what you want the attorney to help with.

The Least You Need to Know

◆ When you make an offer on a home, the sellers can accept, decline, or counter with their own offer. If you receive a counter, you can then accept, decline, or counter with your next offer. This process continues until a deal is made or someone quits.

◆ When both parties agree to the offer and sign the offer, it becomes a legally binding contract. Once you have a binding contract, you cannot withdraw from the offer without legal consequences.

◆ You can withdraw from the offer before the sellers sign it or at any time during the offer/counteroffer process. If the contingencies you specified in your contract are not met, you may also be able to withdraw your offer.

◆ If you start to quibble about minor things and the process gets ugly, you may consider quitting and moving on to another home. You may also want to quit if it becomes apparent that you and the seller are too far apart on terms or price.

Choosing Insurance

In This Chapter

- ◆ Understanding types of insurance
- ◆ Getting home insurance
- ◆ Getting a title search

When I started to write this chapter, I thought about the things that can happen to a home, and then like most people, I figured that home damage wasn't all that common.

Then I started researching what is covered and what isn't covered in a policy, and I thought about articles in the local paper in the past year or so. Someone's home burned down. Someone drove his car into a person's living room. A plane landed on a home. Hail broke out the windows in a home. Accidents do happen, even though we don't like to think that they will happen to us.

Insurance protects you from many kinds of risks. When you purchase a home, you'll need to purchase a different type of insurance for each of these risks, as covered in this chapter.

Understanding the Types of Insurance

On a home, you probably immediately think of homeowners insurance, but there are actually several types of insurance—two that you'll definitely need and one that may be required by the lender:

♦ **Homeowners insurance** covers your home, your possessions, and people on your property. The lender requires it.

♦ **Mortgage insurance** protects the lender in case you default on the loan. Depending on your financial situation, you may have to pay for this type of premium. This type of insurance is sometimes known as MIP (mortgage insurance premium) or PMI (primary mortgage insurance).

♦ **Title insurance** protects you against any problems with your claim to ownership. The lender requires it.

This chapter covers both homeowners and title insurance. For information on mortgage insurance, see Chapter 12.

Real Deal _____

You may also be required to have flood insurance, depending on whether your house is in a flood plain. Be sure to ask about this when you are looking at homes. It adds to the closing and monthly costs of owning a home.

You can also get other types of insurance—for instance, earthquake insurance—depending on where you live and what types of natural and other disasters are typical.

In some extreme cases, you may not be able to get insurance. Many homeowners who live in the SF Bay Area are unable to obtain earthquake insurance, for instance, and some are unable to obtain fire insurance (after the massive losses insurers took during the Oakland Hills fire in 1991). In this case, ask your agent for recommendations on how to insure your property.

Insuring Your Home

Someone once tried to sell my husband and me life insurance when we were in our twenties. We declined, and the salesperson started telling us, "You could die any day. Even though you're only 26, you could drop dead tomorrow." Then the salesperson started quoting statistics on untimely deaths. Great sales technique, huh?

Most people don't like to think about bad things happening, and rightly so. Still, things happen, and you should be prepared with a good home insurance policy. Your lender will require that you be prepared. Insurance is not optional. All lenders require fire, theft, and liability insurance. But the type of coverage you get and the amount you pay varies.

What Home Insurance Covers

When you purchase insurance on your home, you purchase a homeowners policy that includes two types of protection. With *casualty insurance* (also called *property protection* or *hazard insurance*), you're covered for losses or damages to the home and its contents caused by fire, theft, and certain weather-related hazards. *Personal liability* insurance protects you if you're sued by someone who is injured on your property. For example, if your Aunt Sunny has a few too many and falls off the porch, you're covered. Family members may also be covered if they are away from home.

Your lender will require both types of coverage, but the extent of the coverage is up to you. You can select different types of insurance, as described next.

Real Deal

Insurance costs have sky-rocketed in the past few years. Rates shot up 6 percent in 2002 and are expected to rise an additional 7 percent in 2003. Why? Home repair costs are rising, the industry is still reeling from some of the many disasters in the 1990s (Hurricane Andrew and the earthquake in Northridge, CA), and insurance companies have paid out multi-million dollar claims for mold.

Types of Home Insurance

A homeowners policy includes several kinds of insurance in one package. The most basic policy, HO-1, covers what are known as the 11 common perils. More expensive policies cover these basics plus some:

- Fire or lightning
- Loss of property because of fire or other perils
- Windstorm or hail
- Explosion
- Riots and other civil commotions
- Aircraft

Real Deal

Always insure your home for full replacement value. The current market value is what you can sell your home for today. The replacement value is the cost to replace your home.

- Vehicles

- Smoke

- Vandalism and malicious mischief

- Theft

- Breakage of glass that constitutes a part of the building

The following table lists the various types of coverage. As mentioned, HO-1 is the cheapest and covers the least, HO-2 is more expensive but covers more than HO-1, and so on.

Types of Insurance Coverage

Insurance	Policy	Coverage
HO-1	Basic Policy	Covers fire, windstorm, explosion, smoke, broken glass, and other perils—including theft, vandalism, and liability.
HO-2	Broad Form	Covers the same as HO-1 but adds several items. For instance, this type of policy may protect against damage from burst pipes, exploding furnaces, collapse of building, and falling objects.
HO-3	All-Risk Form	Covers everything not specifically excluded. May cover features that are part of the structure (for example, wall-to-wall carpeting).
HO-4	Renter's Policy	Protects the renter's personal possessions.
HO-5	Comprehensive	Covers everything in HO-3, plus some. Exclusions are specifically listed. This is the most expensive type of insurance.
HO-6	Condo or Co-op	Insurance used for condominiums and cooperatives.

How Much Insurance Do You Need?

When you are deciding how much coverage you need, consider a few things. First, ask your lender how much is required. The lender will require a minimum amount (usually purchase price less land value), but you may want to get additional coverage.

Second, figure out the replacement cost of your home. The amount of insurance you need (and the amount you pay) is based on the cost of replacing the entire structure and a value on personal property. For example, you may have a $125,100 policy for replacement value and personal property covered up to $93,825.

To estimate the replacement costs, figure the square footage of floor space and then multiply this figure by the current construction cost per square foot for similar homes. You can find the construction cost by asking a local builder's association.

Third, consider the amount of insurance needed for your possessions. To cover your possessions, take inventory. You can do this with pen and paper, a video camera, or a computer program. Once you figure a value for your possessions, find an appropriate insurance value.

According to the Insurance Information Institute, 8 out of 10 homeowners carry too little insurance. Be sure you have enough coverage in case something does happen. Also, update your insurance if the market changes, if you have more or fewer possessions, or if you make a major improvement to the home. The following table shows an example of an insurance policy.

A Sample Insurance Policy

Section I	
A-Dwelling	$125,100
Dwelling Extension	$12,510
B-Personal Property	$93,825
C-Loss of Use	Actual Loss

Section II	
L-Personal Liability	$300,000
Damage to Property of Others	$500
M-Medical Payments/per person	$5,000
Replacement Cost	117,200
Inflation Coverage Index	125.1%
Deductibles	$500
Policy Premium	$362

Tips on Home Insurance

Shopping for insurance can be a headache. You should make sure you have enough coverage, that you keep your coverage up-to-date, and that you get the best bargain.

Real Deal _____

You may get a discount from some insurers if you have both home and car insurance with the same company. Also, you may receive a discount if you have a smoke or burglar alarm or a newer home. Finally, some insurers give a discount to those with high credit scores (above 680). Ask your insurer whether you qualify for any discounts!

Don't be tempted to save money and get the least amount of coverage. This is your home! If you want to save money, don't scrimp on the policy. Instead, get a higher deductible. Doing so can lower the cost of the premium. For instance, doubling your deductible from $250 to $500 saves close to 15 percent off your premium. Up the deductible to $1,000 and expect a savings of 25 percent.

It's easy to put off getting insurance until the last minute. Then, because you have to have the policy at closing, you may just call the first company you think of. It's better not to wait until the last minute. Shop around and get quotes from several companies. Rates can vary significantly from area to area and from company to company.

If you make a new purchase, keep your receipts and add the item to your inventory of possessions. Having receipts will help you if you have to file a claim. A standard policy will not cover business assets. If you work from your home, you may need additional coverage.

Check about changing the policy. Can you raise the coverage later? Some policies are tied to the Consumer Price Index and rise accordingly. You may have to pay extra for this feature.

Find out what is not covered. If the pipe in your basement bursts and you have water damage, is it covered? What about earthquakes (usually not covered)? Find out how damages are paid. You want the full replacement cost. If your roof is damaged, you want the insurer to cover the entire payment for a new roof—not a partial fee.

Search the Web for Insurance Information

If you have access to the Internet, you can use it to research insurance companies. Many have their own web page with information on the various types of insurance, including home insurance, they provide. For instance, you can get information on the following:

- **State Farm Insurance, www.statefarm.com.** This site provides articles on insurance-related topics and also helps you find an agent in your area. State Farm insures more than 21 percent of all the nation's homes.

- **The Hartford, www.thehartford.com.** The Hartford provides insurance coverage as well as other financial planning services. From this site, you can review articles, find an agent, find out if you are eligible for any discounts, and download handy software such as home inventory software.

- **Insure.com, www.insure.com.** This site offers quotes for home, auto, life, and other types of insurance from more than 300 different sources. You can also read current articles about the insurance field.

- **MetLife, www.metlife.com.** You may know this insurance company from its use of Snoopy in its ads. Like other sites, you can get information and quotes on home insurance as well as other types of insurance.

This list includes just a few of the available insurance sites. Just about all of the big-name insurance companies have websites with information about their coverage and how to get in touch with their agents. Visit other companies' sites to get a more comprehensive idea of the various insurance companies and policies.

How Insurance Payments Are Made

When you purchase a home, the lender usually requires that you pay for a one-year insurance policy up front. You should ask your lender when the policy has to be delivered. Usually you must do so at or before closing. You'll most likely be asked to bring a paid receipt with the insurance policy. In addition to the prepaid policy, you'll most likely be required to make insurance payments as part of your monthly mortgage payment. The lender sets up an escrow account and collects $\frac{1}{12}$ of the fees each month. When the bill comes due, it is sent to the lender, and the lender pays. You may also have to pay two to three months of insurance at the closing. This money is put into your escrow account and is used to cover any increases in rates.

Comparing Insurance Policies

Use the following list of questions to compare insurance policies:

- **Company information.** Write down the company name, address, phone number, and agent you spoke with.

- **Plan information.** Record the type of plan including the deductible, liability

Buyer Beware

Find out how long the insurance company has been in business. Sure, you may get a great price at FlyByNight Insurance.Com, but you want a company that will be around when you need them.

Real Deal

Ask the sellers to get a copy of their prior insurance claims from the Comprehensive Loss Underwriting Exchange (CLUE) from ChoicePoint (choicetrust.com). As a buyer, you cannot request the data, but the seller can. The cost is reasonable (around $8) and lets you see any prior claims involving the home.

limit, and cost. You may also want to make notes about what is covered and what is not.

- **Additional policy information.** If you need additional information—for instance, if you work out of your home and want to get business insurance for your equipment—include the additional policy information about coverage, cost, and any other details that are pertinent.

- **Discounts.** Inquire about any discounts. For instance, many companies provide a break on insurance if you have both home and auto insurance with the company.

- **Claim handling.** An insurance company is only as good as its claim handling. Investigate this *before* you need to file a claim. How are claims handled? Do you get and submit estimates? Or does an adjuster visit your home? What is the typical turnaround time for a claim?

- **Rate adjustments.** Find out how often rates are increased. If you file a claim, will your insurance go up? Can you increase your home insurance?

Getting Title Insurance

Another type of insurance that is required on all homes is title insurance. This type of insurance is purchased at the closing and ensures clear and trouble-free ownership. Trouble-free ownership doesn't guarantee that the plumbing is not going to go haywire or the roof isn't going to cave in. It does insure against any losses you might incur if the seller's long-lost Uncle Bob shows up with a solid claim to ownership of the home.

The Title Search

The lender does two things to guard against claims. First, it does a title search, which the seller usually pays for. Second, it requires title insurance.

In a title search, someone searches all the records and traces the history of ownership for the home. The searcher starts with the current seller and works backward from owner to owner until the very beginning (when the land was originally granted or sold). This person usually looks manually through many, many public records: deaths, divorces, court judgments, liens, taxes, wills, deeds, tax assessor's information, surveyor's information, and more.

A title search uncovers not only the chain of owners, but also whether there are any unpaid taxes on the property, easements, or encroachments. An *easement* is a permanent right to use another's property. For example, the phone company may have an easement to put up phone lines or poles. The same goes for other utility companies. You may also have an easement if you share a driveway.

The title search also uncovers any *encroachments*. This search ensures that nothing of yours is actually on your neighbor's property, and that nothing of the neighbor's is on your property.

If during the title search, a cloud appears on the horizon, it has to be cleared up. The person with the claim can release the debt lien or sign a *quit claim deed*. A quit claim deed releases any right to the property. Or if there is a record-keeping error, it can be corrected.

Bet You Didn't Know

Someone in the title business must have been a frustrated meteorologist; that would explain all the weather terms. You want a *clear* title. If it's not clear, it has a *cloud* on it, which indicates a problem with the title. For example, any claims made against a property by a person or any tax assessment for payment of a debt could cloud up a title.

What Title Insurance Protects

The title search is intended to uncover any problems, but it is not guaranteed. That's why the lender requires title insurance. There are two types of policies. A lender's policy is required by the lender—it protects the lender against any losses if any parties challenge your ownership. (You can think of this type of policy as "cover our butts first.") You can also purchase an owner's policy, which protects you from loss if anyone challenges the title search.

The cost of title insurance will vary depending on the area. You make a single payment up front that is good for the entire time you own the home. Usually the cost of the title search and title insurance are shared by you and the seller. Here, sellers pay the bulk of the cost and you pay a fixed amount. Still, you may want to shop around for title insurance. The prices can vary.

Some locations don't require title insurance but use another form of guarantee for the title, such as a title abstract. If you have any questions about a title abstract, ask your agent.

The Least You Need to Know

◆ Your lender will require a certain amount of homeowners insurance. Don't get the minimum amount. Instead, get enough to cover the replacement value of the home, plus your possessions.

◆ If you want to save money on your homeowners policy, don't scrimp on the coverage. Instead, get a higher deductible, shop around among insurers, and ask about any discounts.

◆ At or before the closing, you'll have to show a one-year, paid homeowners policy. Your lender will also collect insurance money each month to put in an escrow account.

◆ Title insurance backs up the title search and protects the lender against losses if a claim arises. If you have both a lender's and owner's policy, you're protected against claims as well. The fees for the title search and title insurance are usually shared between the buyer and seller.

Chapter 20

Having the Home Inspected

In This Chapter

- ◆ Understanding seller disclosure
- ◆ Scheduling an inspection
- ◆ Knowing what the inspector checks and doesn't check
- ◆ Reading the inspection report
- ◆ Handling any problems

Fear buying a home, moving in, and then finding out the home has termites? Or finding out the roof is ready to cave in? Or turning on the shower only to see black goo ooze out? You probably don't want to relive *The Money Pit.* And while you should look carefully at the home before you make an offer, it is imperative that you have a professional inspector look through the home.

Seller Disclosure: It's the Law

The seller must disclose any known defects in the property that might affect the value of the home. Depending on the law in your area, the seller may be required to complete a seller disclosure form. Even if the law does not require this form, you can ask the seller to complete it. Basically, the form asks the seller to disclose any problems with the roof, pests, structure, basement, attic, heating and cooling, electrical system, toxic substances, and other matters. A new federal rule also requires the seller to disclose any known lead paint within a home. For a discussion of seller disclosure laws and a sample seller disclosure form, see Chapter 21.

Usually the seller will say that the current price takes into consideration the problems listed on the seller disclosure. Or the seller may provide a certain amount of money to take care of needed repairs.

Even with a seller disclosure, you should still have a professional inspection done.

Why Get an Inspection?

When you are adding up all the costs associated with buying a home, you may want to skimp on some fees. For example, you may want to ask your Uncle Charlie to take a look at the home. Even though he sells mattresses now, he once built homes and knows a little about home construction.

Not a good idea.

You should hire a professional inspector and make your offer contingent upon a satisfactory inspection. An inspection can help you identify problems before you purchase a home. If there are problems, the inspection can help you negotiate an adjustment in purchase price or get sellers to pay for needed repairs. If the problems are big, the inspection report may enable you to withdraw your offer. If there aren't problems, the inspection will make you feel more secure in your decision to purchase the home.

Scheduling an Inspection

If you have made the offer contingent on an inspection, you usually have a certain time period in which to schedule the inspection. You'll want to do so early on so that you have time to review the findings and make any changes, if necessary.

Real Deal

Ask to see a sample inspection report. By looking over the report, you can tell what the inspector normally checks for and how thoroughly the home will be inspected.

You can find a good inspector by asking friends and relatives for referrals, asking your agent, or looking in the Yellow Pages. You can also contact the American Society of Home Inspectors (ASHI) for a referral. Inspectors affiliated with ASHI have completed a minimum number of home inspections, testing, and training. The address of ASHI is listed in Appendix B.

You can also try finding home inspection companies on the Internet. You can expect to find sample reports, fee information, and articles on home maintenance and other topics. Check out the American Society of Home Inspectors at www.ashi.com.

When you are shopping around for an inspector, ask about the inspector's training and background. Use the following checklist of questions to rate and evaluate home inspectors:

◆ **How long has the inspector been in the business?** Most home inspectors serve an apprenticeship of 500 to 1,000 inspections. Ask approximately how many homes the inspector has viewed and inspected.

◆ **What certification does the inspector have?** Does he or she belong to a professional association—American Society of Home Inspectors (ASHI), National Association of Home Inspectors (NAH), or similar state organizations. These associations set strict standards and require ongoing education. Watch out for inspectors that *say* they adhere to the standards but are not members of any association.

◆ **What is the cost?** You can expect to pay from $200 to $400. You may also have to pay additional fees if you want certain tests done, such as a water test, radon test, or termite certification. Keep in mind that your home is probably the single most expensive thing you will ever buy. Don't scrimp on inspection fees, but don't get bilked either.

◆ **Does the inspector offer errors and omission insurance (E&O)?** This type of insurance covers undiscovered defects such as a faulty electrical system. Good inspectors carry E&O insurance.

◆ **Ask for a sample report.** Doing so can help you evaluate the thoroughness of the inspection as well as how clearly the problems in the report are presented.

Real Deal

If the home uses city or town water, you don't need to worry about water quality, because the water supply companies are required to conduct testing. If, on the other hand, the home has well water, you may consider doing a water test.

What the Inspector Checks

An inspector does *not* determine the value of the home; that's an appraiser's job. Instead, an inspector evaluates the condition of the property. The inspector visually checks the home and then completes a report.

It's a good idea to accompany the inspector during the inspection. In fact, the inspector will encourage you to do so. If you go along for the inspection, you are in a better position to understand the report. You can also ask questions, and you can see how extensively the inspector looks at the home. He should crawl down in the crawlspace, get up on the roof, poke around in the insulation, turn on all the faucets, and more. Expect to spend about two hours doing a home inspection.

Buyer Beware

Be sure to schedule the inspection during the day. An evening inspection may be more convenient for you and your schedule, but you'll want to be sure the inspector takes a good look during the daylight hours. If it is dark or dusk, the inspector may not be able to do as thorough an inspection of the outside of the home. Also make sure the weather conditions permit a thorough inspection. For example, if the roof is covered in snow, the inspector may not be able to inspect it for problems.

What the Inspector Should Check

At a minimum, the inspector should visually examine the following:

- **Foundation.** Carefully check for cracks and any separation in the foundation.

- **Doors and windows.** Make sure all the windows and doors open and close properly.

- **Roofing, chimney, gutters, vents, and fans.** Determine whether the gutters drain properly and are in good condition, and whether the roof system needs to be replaced or repaired.

- **Plumbing.** Check to see how well the sinks drain, how strong the water pressure is, whether there are any signs of leaks, and that the water heater is in good condition.

- **Electrical system.** Check the wiring connection to fuses or circuit breakers and groundings. Also check whether there is proper and safe wiring at outlets and switches.

- **Heating and cooling systems.** Check the condition and operation of the furnace and note any apparent unsafe conditions. If you buy a home in the winter, the inspector will make a note that the air conditioning was not checked.

- **Ceilings, walls, and floors.** Note any cracks, moisture problems, or significantly uneven floors or walls.

◆ **Insulation and ventilation.** Note whether the home has adequate insulation and proper ventilation.

◆ **Septic tanks, wells, or sewer lines.** Usually, you get a separate report on septic and well water because the water must be tested for bacteria.

◆ **Exterior (decks, doors, windows).** Check for signs of rot and determine whether the home needs to be repainted.

◆ **Property.** Check the drainage of the yard, garage, fences, paved areas, and other outside facilities.

◆ **Basement and attic.** Check to see if the basement is wet, and if the basement or attic shows signs of current or past water damage. Is there mold on the walls or attic framing, for instance?

CAUTION

Buyer Beware

If you are purchasing a new home, it doesn't mean that you should skip the inspection. You may want to have an inspection done to check the construction of the home, the installation of appliances, and other items. Some inspectors will work with you the entire time your home is being built, or you might only want to hire him or her to perform the final walkthrough.

The lender will usually require a termite inspection that the inspector may do and may charge an additional fee for. Usually the seller pays for the termite inspection on VA loans, while the buyer pays for termite inspections when applying for conventional loans.

In addition to the routine inspection, you can ask for other tests to be performed. Some states *require* these tests. For example, you may want to test for radon, lead paint, asbestos, hazardous waste, and other environmental concerns. You may be charged extra for these tests.

CAUTION

Buyer Beware

According to the Environmental Protection Agency, about 1 in 15 homes has unacceptably high radon levels. And you may not realize that indoor radon gas is the second leading cause of lung cancer in the country.

Therefore, include this test in your inspection or purchase a kit from a home improvement store and check for yourself. If the level is higher than 4, you are at risk. You can get more information on this topic as well as find a qualified radon service technician at www.epa.gov/aw/radon.

What the Inspector Doesn't Check

The inspector does not check the cosmetic features of the home, such as the carpeting and wall coverings. Also keep in mind that the inspector does not warrant the home against any problems. He is just reporting on existing problems at that moment. Finally, most inspectors are generalists. If they uncover a problem, they may recommend a specialist. For instance, if the electricity is troublesome, the inspector may recommend having an electrician take a look.

Real Deal

You can search online for an ASHI-affiliated inspector in your area by visiting the ASHI website at www.ashi.com/fi.cfm. Simply type in your zip code, click the Find an Inspector button, and a list of inspectors will display with their contact information.

What the Inspector Shouldn't Do

During the inspection, the inspector shouldn't tell you what the home is worth. Also, the inspector shouldn't give you advice on whether you should buy the home. Finally, the inspector shouldn't offer to make repairs on the home and shouldn't refer you to someone to make the repairs.

Reading the Inspection Report

After the inspector has flipped on all the light switches, crawled around in the attic, climbed up on the roof, and checked how well all the sinks drain, he will write up an inspection report (see the following page of a sample inspection report). This report will include general information about the property as well as information about when the inspection took place—for instance, the weather conditions.

Why include the weather conditions? If an inspector inspects during the middle of winter, he or she may not be able to check the air conditioning. In this case, the inspector may make a note to do so later. Also, the inspector may not be able to check all components because of inclement weather. In some cases, the inspector may make a return trip to fully inspect the home. There is usually a charge for the return trip.

The report will then cover each element of the home, broken down into categories. The categories and format of the report will vary. An ASHI inspector, for instance, will generally have reporting areas for the basement; crawlspace; slab; central heating, cooling, electrical, and plumbing systems; interior structure; attic; doors and windows; garage; exterior structure; grounds; and appliances. Usually the report includes a description of each system. For example, for an electrical system, the inspector may note the system amps and volts. The inspector may note whether the system is satisfactory or not applicable, or he or she may note a problem.

SECURITY HOME INSPECTIONS, INC. - PROPERTY ADDRESS _____ 7

VI. INTERIOR ELECTRICAL SYSTEM

A. SYSTEM ___100___ AMPS ___240___ VOLTS GENERAL CONDITION: ___Satisfactory at time of inspection___

NO. OF CIRCUITS ___18___

NOTES: _____

B. COMPONENTS

1. MAIN SERVICE PANEL	breakers	CONDITION:	Satisfactory at time of inspection
2. SUBPANEL(S)	breakers	CONDITION:	Satisfactory at time of inspection
3. MAIN SERVICE WIRE	aluminum	CONDITION:	Satisfactory at time of inspection
4. VISIBLE BRANCH WIRE	copper	CONDITION:	Satisfactory at time of inspection
5. SWITCHES & RECEPTACLES		CONDITION:	SEE NOTES #1 & #2
6. LIGHT FIXTURES		CONDITION:	SEE NOTES #3 & #4
7. DOOR BELL		CONDITION:	NOT APPLICABLE
8. SMOKE DETECTOR(S)		CONDITION:	SEE NOTE #5

NOTES: _____

1. Receptacle on south wall of kitchen is wired with reverse polarity.
2. G.F.I. receptacle in master bath is wired with reverse polarity. Also, receptacle does not function as a G.F.I. Repairs are needed.
3. Light fixtures in master bath are not installed.
4. Globe is missing from ceiling light in south bedroom.
5. A working smoke detector should be installed on each level.

A sample page from an inspection report.

Handling Any Inspection Problems

If the inspection report turns up any problems, which it most likely will, you'll need to decide whether the problem must be fixed prior to closing or after you move in. This section helps you decide how dire a problem is, as well as your recourse for handling any problems.

Big Problems vs. Little Problems

Some problems are small, such as a leaky faucet or rooms that require painting. You should note these problems when you are viewing the home and make any adjustments to your offer accordingly. For instance, if the washer and dryer or other appliances are outdated (and included in the sale), you may request a monetary amount for new appliances. Or you may make a lower offer, asking the owner to consider that you will need to purchase new appliances.

Some problems are in the medium range and include items that are almost but not quite a problem … yet. For instance, perhaps the roof is satisfactory but will need to be replaced soon. Or perhaps some of the windows are cracked or don't have screens. Maybe the exterior is on the borderline of needing a paint job. Depending on the market and your offer, you may have to accept these things (seller's market), or you may again ask for some concessions (in a buyer's market).

Finally, you have the uh-oh problems—problems that you should consider dealing with and might merit withdrawing the offer. These include problems with the main components of the home: foundation problems (buckling or uneven), plumbing and water problems (unsafe drinking water), and major electrical problems.

Ways to Handle Problems

After you evaluate the severity of the problem, you can decide how to handle it. If the problem is minor, you may choose to ignore it. For instance, you probably aren't going to have a big fit if one window screen is missing or if the porch light doesn't work.

If the problem is significant, you'll want to make a response to the inspection (see the figure that follows for an example of how this is done). In this response, you may ask the seller to renegotiate the price. For example, if you have to pay $6,000 for a new roof, you may ask the seller to lower the price by $6,000 or some percentage of $6,000.

Instead of lowering the price, you may ask the seller to make certain repairs or to set aside money to have repairs done. For example, you may ask the seller to fix the roof or to set aside the $6,000 to have this work done after the closing.

If the problem is of such magnitude that you are reconsidering the purchase, you may be able to withdraw the offer. Usually you must give the sellers a chance to make the repairs, though.

Generally, you ask sellers to make repairs to items that affect habitability. The seller has the option of making the repairs or allowing you to withdraw your offer. In some areas, purchase agreements specify an amount of money up to which the seller agrees to make repairs. After that, it is the buyer's option.

If you have found that the seller or agent has grossly misrepresented the home, you should withdraw the offer.

```
                        INSPECTION AMENDMENT
                          (Mark applicable box below)
                    ☐ WAIVER OF INSPECTION(S)
                    ☒ RESPONSE TO INSPECTION REPORT(S)

1   Purchaser (has) (has not) received an Inspection Report from  The Inspection Co
2   on the property known as  869 Ashwood Ct
3   in  Pike  Township,  Marion  County,  Naples,  Indiana,
4   which is legally known as  Lot 131, Crooked Creek Heights
5   and agrees to: (circle applicable box)
6   [1]  Waive Inspection(s) and rely upon the condition of the property based upon his own examination.
7   [2]  Accept the property in the condition reported in said Inspection Report(s).
8   [☒]  Accept the property provided Seller corrects the following condition(s) on or before ___6___ (AM) (PM) (Noon) (Midnight)
9        7/31 , 19 00 , or within  3  days after loan approval , whichever is later,
10  and the Purchaser shall have the right to inspect and accept Seller's repairs (prior to closing) (within  2  days after
11  notice of completed repairs.          );
12
13  ①Seller shall put electrical system in good working order to
14  meet code - work to be done by licensed electrician.
15  ②Broken floor of master bathroom shower to be replaced.
16  ③Missing shingles on roof to be replaced
17
18
19  The Seller shall respond to this (Waiver Of Inspection) (Response To Inspection Report) on or before ___6___ (AM) (PM)
20  (Noon) (Midnight) 7/18/00 , 19 ___
21  After compliance with selected item above, the Purchaser hereby releases the Seller, Brokers, REALTORS, named in said Purchase Agreement
22  dated  7/10/00  from any and all liability relating to any defect, except for latent defect(s)
23  affecting said real estate, which shall survive the closing of the transaction
24  This Agreement may be executed simultaneously or in two or more counterparts, each of which shall be deemed an original, but all of
25  which together shall constitute one and the same instrument.

26  X Michael True              7/13/00   X Terry True              7/13/00
27  PURCHASER SIGNATURE           DATE     PURCHASE SIGNATURE          DATE

28  Seller responds as follows: (circle applicable box)
29  [☒]  Seller agrees to correct condition(s) contained in Item 3 above
30  [2]  Seller is unable or unwilling to make the corrections requested by Purchaser.
31  [3]  Seller agrees to correct the following condition(s) at Seller's expense (prior to closing the transaction)
32  (within _____ days after _____ ), whichever is later
33  work to be completed no later than 7/28/00
34
35
36
37
38  If item #3 is selected, the Purchaser shall respond on or before _____ (AM) (PM) (Noon) (Midnight) _____ , 19 ___
39  This Agreement may be executed simultaneously or in two or more counterparts, each of which shall be deemed an original, but all of which
40  together shall constitute one and the same instrument. Delivery of this document may be accomplished by electronic facsimile reproduction
41  (FAX); if (FAX) delivery is utilized, the original document shall be promptly executed and/or delivered, if requested.

42  X Richard Wright            7/16/00   Sandra Wright            7/16/00
43  SELLER SIGNATURE              DATE     SELLER SIGNATURE            DATE

44  ACCEPTED BY PURCHASER:

45
46  PURCHASER SIGNATURE          DATE     PURCHASER SIGNATURE          DATE

    Ⓡ        Approved by and restricted to use by members of the Metropolitan Indianapolis Board Of REALTORS.
  REALTOR®   This is a legally binding contract, if not understood seek legal advice   | MIBOR 1992   (Form No. 230-01/92)      ⌂
                                                                                                    EQUAL HOUSING
                                                                                                    OPPORTUNITY
                                                                      5-92/P-212A
```

A response to an inspection report.

The Least You Need to Know

◆ The seller must disclose any known defects in the home. In some states, the seller is required to complete a seller disclosure form.

◆ When you make a sales offer, be sure to include a contingency for an inspection. You should be sure that you state in the offer that the inspection must meet your satisfaction.

◆ To find an inspector, ask your agent or friends and relatives for a referral. You can also contact the American Society of Home Inspectors (ASHI).

◆ The inspector should check the foundation, doors, windows, roof, chimney, gutters, plumbing, electrical system, heating and cooling, ceilings, walls, floors, insulation, ventilation, septic tanks, wells, sewer lines, exterior of the home, and property.

◆ After the inspection, the inspector will give you a written inspection report. Usually the seller receives a copy of this report as well. If the inspection uncovers a problem(s), you can choose to ignore the problem, ask the seller to renegotiate the price, ask the seller to fix the problem, or in extreme cases, withdraw your offer.

Chapter 21

Handling the Closing: Buyer's Perspective

In This Chapter

◆ Understanding what you must do before the closing

◆ Preparing for the closing costs

◆ Going to the closing

◆ Handling problems

◆ Closing and moving in

Finally! The big day has arrived. The last step in buying a home is the closing. At the closing, you'll sign document after document after document, turn over all your money, then get the much-anticipated keys to your new home. This chapter tells you what to expect at closing.

What Has to Happen Before the Closing

Getting to the closing is a kind of race. You have to pass over several hurdles before you cross the finish line. Here are the hurdles you can expect to jump.

Real Deal _____

Don't wait until the last minute to get insurance. Once the closing is approaching, you may be so excited that you'll sign up with the first insurance company available. It makes more sense to shop around and get several quotes so that you get the best deal.

First, you must obtain financing. This topic is the subject of Part 3. Unless you are paying cash for the home, you have to have the backing from your lender. Backing comes in the form of a commitment letter from the lender. Once you receive this commitment letter, you have the money to buy the home. You've jumped hurdle one.

Second, the lender will require that you have a homeowners insurance policy on the home. Before the closing, you'll need to arrange for insurance. Usually you must show a one-year paid policy. Insurance is covered in Chapter 19.

Third, there may be other requirements that you or the seller must meet before the closing. For instance, if you are getting an FHA loan, the lender may require certain repairs to be made before the loan is closed. Or if your home lies in a flood plain, you may be required to get flood insurance. Any other requirements of the lender will be spelled out in the commitment letter.

The final two things that must be done—deciding how to hold the title and having the final walkthrough—are described here.

Who Owns the Home?

As part of the closing, you'll be asked how you want to "hold the title." An appropriate response is not "In my hands." Holding the title refers to the ownership. Do you own the home alone? Do you own it with a partner? How is the property shared? You spell out the ownership by selecting how to hold the title. Here are the most common ways:

- **Sole ownership.** You are the only owner. If you are buying the home alone, you'll probably select this.

- **Tenancy by the entirety.** Available for married couples only. With this type of ownership, both owners have to agree before the home can be sold or refinanced. If one spouse dies, the other automatically gets the home without going through probate (the legal process of settling a will).

- **Joint tenancy.** Used when two or more people purchase a home. The owners agree that during their lifetimes, any of the owners can sell their interest to whomever they want without any type of approval from the others. When one owner dies, the surviving owner automatically gets the deceased's share.

♦ **Tenancy in common.** The property is owned jointly. If one owner dies, his or her share goes to his or her heirs.

The Final Walkthrough

As part of the contract, you may stipulate that you want a final walkthrough. Final walkthroughs are a good idea to ensure that the property is in the same condition it was in when you made the offer on the home. You may want to make sure that all the systems are in working order and that no damage has been done to the home.

As part of the purchase agreement, the seller agrees to turn the property over in the same condition as it was during the inspection process. If the home has been inspected and you have removed the inspection contingency, then you have agreed you are satisfied with the property. A final walkthrough is just to be sure that there have been no major changes since that time. If there have been, the transaction can be opened up for renegotiation.

If you want a final walkthrough, be sure to say so in the contract. You should schedule the walkthrough before the closing. Give yourself enough time to settle any problems that pop up. For instance, if you schedule the walkthrough the morning of the closing and find problems, you won't have any time to resolve them.

During the final walkthrough, check the major systems (electrical, plumbing, and so on) and check the appearance of the home.

Next, check the personal property in the home. Is property that is supposed to be there really there? For example, if you asked the sellers to leave the washer and dryer as part of the deal, are the washer and dryer still there? Are the curtains and floor coverings still there? Is property that is supposed to be gone truly gone? For example, if the sellers had an old refrigerator in the basement that you wanted them to take with them, did they take it? Or did they leave it for you to haul out? Any disputes about personal property should be taken care of before you close.

Finally, make sure the sellers are out of the home (or ready to be out). When you take possession of a home depends on local customs. In many places, the seller must be out before closing. In some places, the seller must move out a

Buyer Beware

If the seller is supposed to be out before closing and is not out when you go through the final walkthrough, you may have a problem. Packing up and moving an entire home full of possessions isn't an afternoon's task. If you are going through the home and the sellers show no signs of budging, you are looking at trouble. You should insist the sellers are out before you close.

week after closing. Also, in some special cases, the seller may have arranged to remain in the home and pay you rent after closing.

If the home is in the shape you expect and the sellers and all their worldly goods are moved out, you are ready to close.

What You Pay at Closing

Closing on a home can be exciting, because at the end of the proceedings, you'll have the keys to your new home. You'll also have an empty pocketbook or wallet, because at the closing, you'll be expected to have the money for your down payment and all the closing costs.

Don't Forget the Down Payment

At the closing, you'll need to pay the balance of the down payment on the home. The down payment amount will vary, depending on the purchase price and the amount you are putting down. If you are buying a $100,000 home and putting 10 percent down, you must have $10,000 for the down payment. Keep in mind that your earnest money will be applied toward the down payment in most cases. So if you gave the sellers $1,000 in earnest money, you'll need to come up with the remaining $9,000 for the down payment.

Keep in mind that you cannot pay with a personal check. Plan to get a cashier's check from your bank.

Bet You Didn't Know

Ask your accountant to confirm the number of points you can deduct on your tax return (it varies depending on where you live). This is important because sometimes it is more convenient to have the lender "pay the loan origination fee for you" and instead, charge you a point. This way, you can deduct the point instead of pay an origination fee that you cannot deduct.

Closing Costs

In addition to the down payment, you'll have to pay closing costs. When you apply for the loan, the lender is required by law to give you a Truth-in-Lending estimate of your closing costs. The lender will base this estimate on local practice as well as your sales agreement with the seller.

Closing costs that are not paid at the time of closing are listed as POC, or paid outside of closing. Application fees, the cost of obtaining a credit report, and homeowners insurance fall under this type of fee.

The following sections list the fees you can expect to pay at closing. Keep in mind that some closing costs may be paid by the seller, and some will be paid *before* closing. For example, you probably paid a loan application fee, which is considered a closing cost. This fee, however, is paid at the time of application.

Also, FHA loans and VA loans have different restrictions on what the buyers and sellers are allowed to pay.

Paid as Part of the Loan

The following are items payable in connection with the loan:

- **Points.** Depending on the loan package you selected, you may have to pay points. One point is equal to 1 percent of the loan amount. Points are usually tax-deductible in the year paid. In some cases, the seller may agree to pay points.

- **Loan origination fee.** A loan origination fee is similar to a point; it is usually 1 percent of the loan amount. Loan origination fees are not tax-deductible. In some agreements, the seller may pay this fee.

- **Assumption fee.** If you are assuming a mortgage, you may have to pay an assumption fee.

- **Application fee.** When you apply for the loan, you may be charged an application fee. This fee may run up to $350 and is paid at the time of application.

- **Credit report.** At the time of application, you may be asked to pay the fee for checking your credit history. This fee can run from $40 to $60 and is paid outside of closing (POC). Sometimes this fee is included as part of the application fee.

- **Appraisal fee.** Paid at application, this fee runs from $225 to $300.

- **Home inspection.** To have the home inspected, you'll most likely hire a professional inspector. This fee can run from $225 to $275 and is usually paid before closing (at the time of the inspection). The lender will require a pest inspection. You or the seller may have to pay this fee.

- **Processing fees.** The lender may charge you various fees for processing the loan. These fees may include a mail or delivery fee, a document preparation fee, an underwriting fee, and other fees. You can expect to pay from $100 to $400 when all these fees are totaled.

Paid in Advance

The following are items required by the lender to be paid in advance:

- **Prepaid interest.** Depending on when you close on your home, you may have to prepay the interest for the month you move in. For example, if you close on August 15, you have to prepay interest for the remaining days in August (August 16 through 31, or 16 days). The payment for September would be due October 1 and would pay for September 1 through 30. In essence, you skip a payment for September.

- **Mortgage insurance.** If your loan requires mortgage insurance, you'll be required to pay the necessary amount at the time of closing. Mortgage insurance is covered in Chapter 12.

- **Insurance.** You'll be expected to have a one-year prepaid policy on your home. You usually pay this POC and show the receipt. Chapter 19 covers home insurance.

Prepayments (Reserves) Held by the Lender

To make sure you have the money to pay for insurance and taxes, the lender collects a partial payment each month (and at closing). These are held in escrow until the bill comes due. The following are reserves on deposit with the lender:

- **Insurance.** At the time of closing, you'll need to pay a few months' worth of insurance payments for the escrow account. See the section "Keeping a Reserve in an Escrow Account," later in this chapter.

- **Mortgage insurance.** You may have to pay a few months' worth of mortgage insurance if it is required by your lender.

- **Property taxes.** You may have to set aside money for the tax escrow. You may also have to pay for a tax service contract.

Title Charges

As mentioned in Chapter 19, you need to make sure the title is clear. And yes, you have to pay for various title charges, including:

- **Settlement fee.** A fee may be charged for the services of the settlement company. This fee can run from $150 to $400.

- **Attorney.** If you have hired an attorney, you'll be responsible for the attorney's fees. Also, sometimes the lender charges you an attorney's fee for its attorney.

- **Title search and insurance.** The lender will require a title search and title insurance. Expect to be charged $170 to $400. Which party pays which fees varies depending on where you live.

Government Recording and Transfer Charges

Next, you can't forget the government's cut. The following are government recording and transfer charges:

- **Recording fees.** You may be charged a fee for recording the deed and the mortgage. This fee can run from $25 to $75.

- **Transfer charges.** Depending on the location, some local and state governments charge transfer taxes. You may have to pay county, city, and/or state taxes.

Still More Settlement Charges

In addition to the fees already mentioned, you may have to pay the following settlement charges:

- **Survey.** The lender requires an unstaked survey (more informal) to see that there are no encroachments on your property.

- **Condo and co-op fees.** You may be charged a move-in fee or association transfer fees.

- **Taxes.** You may owe money for tax prorations, or the seller may pay you money on the proration, depending on how taxes are paid. For example, if the sellers have prepaid taxes for six months but lived in the home for only three months, they may ask for the fee to be prorated and for you to pay the three month's worth for the time you'll be living in the home. Any prorations should be spelled out in the contract.

Keeping a Reserve in an Escrow Account

Your lender wants to make sure that you pay your property taxes and insurance. To be sure you have the money to do so, the lender will usually require you to prepay your insurance a year in advance. For taxes and insurance, the lender will take the total bill and divide it by 12 to get a monthly amount due for each. Then the lender will usually collect a few months of fees for taxes and insurance. (The number of months will vary, depending on when you close.) This money is put aside in an escrow account.

Real Deal

If you have 20 percent or more down on a conventional loan, the escrow account may be negotiable. Ask your lender. Some lenders charge a fee to waive the escrow account. You may be able to negotiate your way out of this.

Buyer Beware

Keep in mind that even if you get a fixed-rate mortgage, your payments can still go up. How? Taxes or insurance fees can be raised. If you don't have enough money in escrow to cover the new payment, you'll have to pay back any amount not covered, plus pay an increased amount, so that when the next tax bill comes due, there will be enough.

Each month when you make a payment, you pay principal and interest, plus $1/12$ of your bill for taxes and insurance. The tax and insurance money is put into your escrow account. When the tax bill or insurance bill comes due, the lender pays it using the money in your escrow account.

Some buyers prefer to have the lender take care of the tax and insurance bills. But keep in mind that your money sits in the escrow account and doesn't earn interest.

And the Total Comes to ...

Before the actual closing, the lender will tell your agent (who in turn will tell you) the precise amount of money you must bring to the closing. You have the right to review the settlement charges one business day before the closing. You often will not get much lead time with the "final" figures, but refusing to close only hurts the buyers and sellers. The settlement statement (shown in the next section) explains exactly who pays which fees.

You'll need to bring a cashier's check or certified check for the balance of the down payment and closing costs. It's a good idea to have the check made out to yourself. You can then endorse the check at the closing.

What Happens at the Closing

You can think of a closing as an invitation to a big event. Here are the juicy details:

♦ **Event.** Depending on the location, closing can be referred to as *closing*, *settlement day*, or whatever. This is the big day—the final step in buying a home.

◆ **Guests.** Depending on local customs, different people may attend the closing. *You* definitely must attend. In addition, you may expect the sellers, sellers' agent, your agent, lender, attorneys, and a closing agent, depending on the circumstances.

◆ **When.** After you receive your commitment letter for your loan or notice of your approval (which may be a phone call), you can set the date for the closing.

◆ **Where.** Again, the location for closing depends on local practice. The closing may be held at the title company, attorney's office, escrow company, lending institution, or county courthouse.

◆ **Occasion.** And finally, the reason for the closing: to sign papers and exchange money.

Real Deal _____

If you have locked in your rate, you should be sure to close before your lock expires. Don't let the lender or sellers drag out the closing, especially if rates have gone up. If rates have gone down, you may want to delay. Also, if your commitment expires on the last day of the month, don't wait until the last day to close.

What You Should Bring to the Closing

When you are preparing to attend the closing, you should expect to bring a cashier's check, as described in the section "And the Total Comes to …," earlier in this chapter. You'll also need to bring a homeowners insurance policy and a one-year prepaid receipt as well as any other documentation required by the lender.

If you want, you can have your attorney attend with you. Your attorney can review and advise you on the documents you'll sign.

Buyer Beware _____

There generally isn't time to read the documents entirely at closing. If you want to read them, ask to have them prepared and ready for you a day in advance. This is what attorneys do.

Signed, Sealed, Delivered

One of the main purposes of the closing is to review and sign all the appropriate documents. You should carefully look over each document you are asked to sign before signing. If you notice any discrepancies, you should bring them to the attention of your agent, the lender, and the closing agent. You should also get a copy of every document.

Buyer Beware _____

If the lender is selling your mortgage, the lender should give you a name and phone number to call if you have trouble with your loan. If you have problems and the lender isn't involved anymore, you'll want to know whom to contact.

During the closing, you can expect to review the following documents:

- **Truth-in-Lending statement.** The lender is required by law to give you a copy of this document within three days of your loan application. This document will tell you the true APR, terms of the loan, finance charge, amount financed, and total payments required. Sometimes at application the lender will give you an estimate. If the APR is different from the estimate given, the lender will give you another form at closing listing the true APR. Note: This is your promise to pay and the terms of your payment. The document includes the terms of the loan, date on which your payments must be made, location to send payments, penalties assessed, and other loan information.

Real Deal

Put all these papers in a safe place and keep them together. When you sell the home, you will want to have the information available for your review.

Real Deal

With all the paperwork, you may wish that the promise of a "paperless" office were a reality. Note that the Mortgage Industry Standards Maintenance Organization released in 2002 a set of paperless data structures required for applying and serving a loan. We may soon see a "paperless" mortgage or at least progress in that direction.

- **Mortgage, or deed of trust.** This document is the lien against your home held by the lender. This lien gives the lender claim to your property if you default. The document restates the information in the mortgage note.

- **Affidavits.** Certain affidavits may be required by state law, the lender, or the secondary market agency. For instance, you may have to sign an affidavit stating that you'll use the property as your primary residence.

- **Deed.** The seller turns over property by means of a warranty deed. Sellers attest that they have not taken any new loans on the property. The deed should be properly signed and notarized. The transfer of the deed will be recorded at the registry of deeds or clerk's office.

- **IRS forms.** You'll be asked to sign any forms required by the IRS for the sale or purchase of a home.

- **Disclosure statements.** If the lender plans to sell your loan to the secondary market, the lender must disclose this information. In this case, you may be asked to sign a disclosure statement acknowledging that you received this information.

- **Compliance agreement.** This document says you'll agree to re-sign documents if any error is made.

◆ **Sanity documents.** You'll also be asked to sign other documents that state you have not been declared mentally incompetent, you are still employed at the same place, you are over 18 years old, and so on.

A. SETTLEMENT STATEMENT	U.S. DEPARTMENT OF HOUSING AND URBAN DEVELOPMENT		

ENTERPRISE TITLE
8440 Woodfield Crossing, #100
Indianapolis, IN 46240

OMB No. 2502-0265

B. TYPE OF LOAN

1. ☐ FHA 2. ☐ FmHA 3. ☒ CONV. UNINS.	6. File Number:	7. Loan Number:	8. Mortgage Insurance Case Number:
4. ☐ VA 5. ☐ CONV. INS.			

C. NOTE: This form is furnished to give you a statement of actual settlement costs. Amounts paid to and by the settlement agent are shown. Items marked "(p.o.c)" were paid outside the closing; they are shown here for informational purposes and are not included in the totals.

D. NAME AND ADDRESS OF BORROWER:	E. NAME AND ADDRESS OF SELLER/TAX I.D.No.:	F. NAME AND ADDRESS OF LENDER:

G. PROPERTY LOCATION:	H. SETTLEMENT AGENT: Enterprise Title Services of Indiana Inc.	
	PLACE OF SETTLEMENT: 8440 Woodfield Crossing, #100 Indianapolis, IN 46240	I. SETTLEMENT DATE: 07/18/00

J. SUMMARY OF BORROWER'S TRANSACTION		K. SUMMARY OF SELLER'S TRANSACTION	
100. GROSS AMOUNT DUE FROM BORROWER:		400. GROSS AMOUNT DUE TO SELLER:	
101. Contract Sales Price	124,900.00	401. Contract Sales Price	124,900.00
102. Personal property		402. Personal property	
103. Settlement charges to borrower (line 1400)	1,462.78	403.	
104.		404.	
105.		405.	
Adjustments for items paid by seller in advance		Adjustments for items paid by seller in advance	
106. City/town taxes to		406. City/town taxes to	
107. County taxes to		407. County taxes to	
108. Assessments to		408. Assessments to	
109.		409.	
110.		410.	
111.		411.	
112.		412.	
120. GROSS AMOUNT DUE FROM BORROWER	126,362.78	420. GROSS AMOUNT DUE TO SELLER	124,900.00
200. AMOUNTS PAID BY OR IN BEHALF OF BORROWER:		500. REDUCTIONS IN AMOUNT DUE TO SELLER:	
201. Deposit or earnest money	1,000.00	501. Excess deposit (see instructions)	
202. Principal amount of new loan(s)	91,900.00	502. Settlement charges to seller (line 1400)	9,339.00
203. Existing loan(s) taken subject to		503. Existing loan(s) taken subject to	
204. CUSTOMER DEPOSIT	1,319.00	504. Payoff of first mortgage loan 1st IND	80,209.43
205.		505. Payoff of second mortgage loan	
206.		506.	
207.		507.	
208.		508.	
209.		509.	
Adjustments for items unpaid by seller		Adjustments for items unpaid by seller	
210. City/town taxes to		510. City/town taxes to	
211. County taxes to		511. County taxes to	
212. Assessments to		512. Assessments to	
213.		513.	
214. NOVEMBER 1994 TAXES	630.65	514. NOVEMBER 1994 TAXES	630.65
215.		515.	
216.		516.	
217.		517.	
218.		518.	
219.		519.	
220. TOTAL PAID BY/FOR BORROWER	94,849.65	520. TOTAL REDUCTION AMOUNT DUE SELLER	90,179.08
300. CASH AT SETTLEMENT FROM/TO BORROWER		600. CASH AT SETTLEMENT TO/FROM SELLER	
301. Gross amount due from borrower (line 120)	126,362.78	601. Gross amount due to seller (line 420)	124,900.00
302. Less amounts paid by/for borrower (line 220)	94,849.65	602. Less reductions in amount due seller (line 520)	90,179.08
303. CASH (☒ FROM) (☐ TO) BORROWER	31,513.13	603. CASH (☒ TO) (☐ FROM) SELLER	34,720.92

Previous edition is obsolete.

HUD-1 (8-87)
RESPA, HB 4305.2

The front side of the HUD-1 statement.

-2-

L. SETTLEMENT CHARGES

	PAID FROM BORROWER'S FUNDS AT SETTLEMENT	PAID FROM SELLER'S FUNDS AT SETTLEMENT
700. TOTAL SALES/BROKER'S COMMISSION		
based on price $ 124,900.00 @ 7.00 %= 8,743.00		
Division of Commission (line 700) as follows:		
701. $ 4,371.50 to		
702. $ 4,371.50 to		
703. Commission paid at Settlement		8,743.00
704.		
800. ITEMS PAYABLE IN CONNECTION WITH LOAN		
801. Loan Origination Fee %		
802. Loan Discount %		
803. Appraisal Fee to	275.00	
804. Credit Report to	108.00	
805. Lenders Inspection Fee		
806. Mortgage Insurance Application Fee to		
807. Assumption Fee		
808. PROCESSING FEE	125.00	
809. TAX/INS. VERIFICATIO	90.00	
810.		
811. MORTGAGE BROKERAGE FEE 1838.00		
900. ITEMS REQUIRED BY LENDER TO BE PAID IN ADVANCE		
901. Interest from 07/18/00 to 08/01/00 @$ 20.771918 /day	290.78	
902. Mortgage Insurance Premium for months to		
903. Hazard Insurance Premium for 1 years to STANDARD MUTUAL $321.00		
904. Flood Insurance Premium for years to		
905.		
1000. RESERVES DEPOSITED WITH LENDER		
1001. Hazard Insurance months @$ per month		
1002. Mortgage Insurance months @$ per month		
1003. City property taxes months @$ per month		
1004. County property taxes months @$ per month		
1005. Annual assessments months @$ per month		
1006. Flood insurance months @$ per month		
1007. months @$ per month		
1008. months @$ per month		
1100. TITLE CHARGES		
1101. Settlement or closing fee to ENTERPRISE TITLE	240.00	
1102. Abstract or title search to		
1103. Title examination to		
1104. Title insurance binder to		
1105. Document preparation to		
1106. Notary fees to		
1107. Attorney's fees to MICHAEL J. CURRY		35.00
(includes above items numbers:)		
1108. Title insurance to ENTERPRISE TITLE	95.00	550.00
(includes above items numbers:)		
1109. Lender's coverage $ 124,900.00 95.00		
1110. Owner's coverage $ 91,900.00 550.00		
1111. EXPRESS/PO ENTERPRISE TITLE		11.00
1112.		
1113.		
1200. GOVERNMENT RECORDING AND TRANSFER CHARGES		
1201. Recording fees: Deed $ 7.00 Mortgage $ 16.00 :Releases $	23.00	
1202. City/county tax stamps: Deed $:Mortgage $		
1203. State tax/stamps: Deed $:Mortgage $		
1204. DISCLOSURE FEE MARION COUNTY AUDITOR	5.00	
1205. MORTGAGE EXEMPTION MARION COUNTY AUDITOR	1.00	
1300. ADDITIONAL SETTLEMENT CHARGES		
1301. Survey to HAHN & ASSOCIATES	110.00	
1302. Pest inspection to		
1303.		
1304. SETTLEMENT TO NBDMC	100.00	
1305.		
1400. TOTAL SETTLEMENT CHARGES(enter on lines 103,Sect J and 502,Sect K)	1,462.78	9,339.00

I have carefully reviewed the HUD-1 Settlement Statement and to the best of my knowledge and belief it is a true and accurate statement of all receipts and disbursements made on my account or by me in this transaction. I further certify that I have received a copy of the HUD-1 Settlement Statement.

Marion E. Ayers   Marion L. Bugh

Borrowers Elizabeth Ayers Lathrop   Sellers Martha O. Bugh

The HUD-1 Settlement Statement which I have prepared is a true and accurate account of this transaction. I have caused or will cause the funds to be disbursed in accordance with this statement.

Settlement Agent Sarah Gregory   07/18/00
                                                    Date

Warning: It is a crime to knowingly make false statements to the United States on this or any similar form. Penalties upon conviction can include a fine and imprisonment. For details see: Title 18 U.S. Code Section 1001 and Section 1010.

The reverse side of the HUD-1 statement.

Exchanging Money

In addition to signing documents, you'll exchange money. You'll pay the amount you owe, and the sellers will receive the amount they are due. The agent will receive a commission, and the loan company will receive its money.

To sort out who pays what and who gets what, you'll receive the RESPA HUD-1 statement (see the preceding figure), which breaks down the costs involved.

Statement Side 1: The Totals

The front side of the HUD-1 statement lists the buyer's name and address, seller's name and address, lender's name and address, property location, settlement agent, place, and date.

The form is then split into two columns. The first column lists the money due from you (the buyer)—the sales price and the closing costs. Then the monies you have already paid and the monies being paid by someone else (for instance, the seller) are listed. Your credits are subtracted from the amount due to get the total due at closing.

The second column summarizes the seller's transactions and lists the sales price due to the seller as well as any reductions. For instance, your earnest money will be listed as a reduction as well as any closing costs paid for by the seller. The total amount due to the seller is listed at the bottom.

Statement Side 2: The Closing Costs

The second side of the HUD-1 statement breaks down the closing costs. The first column lists the appropriate costs. Then there are two columns—one for you and one for the seller. If the fee is in your column, you owe the money. If the fee is in the sellers' column, they owe the money. If the fee isn't due, it isn't listed, and if the fee was paid before closing, you'll see POC noted. Remember that POC stands for "paid outside of closing."

The total closing costs for you and the seller are listed at the bottom of the form.

The Passing of the Keys

After all the documents have been signed and all the money exchanged, you are finally the proud owner of the home. The seller should give you all keys to the home, and you are ready to take possession. Congratulations!

Buyer Beware

For the sake of security, consider having all the locks in your new home changed by a locksmith. You may also change the codes for any security system and reprogram the garage door opener.

Be sure to get any mailbox keys or garage door openers. The seller may forget these items, but you'll wonder how *you* could have when you need to pick up your mail or park your car.

Finally, the owner should leave instruction manuals and applicable warranties for all appliances. If you schedule a walkthrough, check for these items at that time.

Handling Problems

The closing is a hectic time for all involved. The seller is getting ready to move. The lender has to organize all the appropriate paperwork for the loan package. The settlement company has to be sure the event is orchestrated perfectly. You have to gather your money. Problems, both minor and major, can occur. This section describes some problems you might encounter.

Walkthrough Problems

If you have a final walkthrough and find a problem, you'll need to decide how to handle it. If the problem is a minor one, you may decide to ignore it. If the problem is major, your course of action will depend on whether or not it was disclosed at the time of the sale. If the seller told you that the basement leaks, and you walk through and see water, you don't have much recourse. If the seller didn't tell you the basement leaks, and it is flooded, you should call your agent and seek to have the problem fixed. You may have legal recourse.

Money Problems

With all the number crunching, you may find that sometimes the numbers don't add up. For example, you may owe more than you originally thought. The lender should have prepared you for the total closing costs at the time of application; you should have received a written estimate. If that estimate is wildly incorrect, you can complain, but you may have to pay anyway. Remember that when you applied for the loan, you agreed to pay certain charges.

There shouldn't be any disputes about what the seller is required to pay, because this information should be spelled out in the sales contract. If there are disputes, your agent may handle them, or you may need to have your attorney get involved.

Loan Problems

For the closing to take place, you need the loan package—the documents that spell out the terms of the loan. Without these documents, you cannot close on the home.

If the documents are late, the lender may be able to send them by courier or overnight express. Or you may have to postpone the closing a day or two.

If there is disagreement about documents, you need to clear up any inaccuracies before the closing. For example, if the loan documents say you are paying 8.75 percent interest, but you had agreed to pay 8.5 percent interest and can prove that, the error must be corrected.

CAUTION **Buyer Beware**

You don't close on a home very often, so the charges may seem confusing. Your agent is much more familiar with this part of the transaction. Be sure that your agent goes over the final charges in advance and agrees with them.

Title Problems

Remember that the title is your evidence that you own the home. To be sure the seller has the right to grant that title freely, a title search has been conducted and you have been required to take out title insurance. If a title problem pops up before the closing, it must be cleared up before you close.

Moving In!

At the end of the entire homebuying process, you may find yourself exhausted. So much has to be done before you get your dream home. So many problems, big and small, can make the entire process tense. Your satisfaction will come when you can finally move in. The dream of owning a home is then yours!

Pre- and Post-Move Tips

Here are a few tips about getting ready for the move:

- **Don't take everything with you.** Have a garage sale or give items away to charity. Moving is a great time to get rid of possessions you don't need or don't use.

- **Start saving newspapers and boxes as soon as you know that you'll be moving.** You can use them when you pack your stuff.

◆ **If possible, do your redecorating before you move in.** Painting or wallpapering a room that is full of furniture is more difficult than painting or wallpapering an empty room.

◆ **Put the utilities in your name.** You should contact the phone company, gas company, electric company, water company, garbage collection company, recycling company, and any other utilities or services to put them in your name. Your seller should be able to provide you with the name, number, and billing date for utilities. Likewise, discontinue the utilities at your old residence. Arrange for a change of service around three to five days before you take possession. Doing so ensures that the service won't be disconnected and that you won't be charged a reconnection fee.

◆ **Fill out a change-of-address card.** Be sure to let the post office know your new address and to send address-change postcards to friends, family, businesses, magazines, and so on.

◆ **Meet the neighbors.** As you move in, your neighbors are probably going to see the moving trucks and be curious. Now is a great time to say hello and to get to know your new neighbors.

◆ **Start a home file.** In this file, keep all the documents pertaining to the purchase of your home. You should keep copies of the purchase agreement, disclosure documents, inspection reports, title report, the recorded deed that transferred the title from the seller to you, insurance, and work-related invoices and permits. You can deduct the interest paid on the home as well as property taxes, so you'll want to keep a record for tax purposes. (In some cases, you can deduct moving expenses.) Also, these forms come in handy if there are any disputes. And finally, you can use these forms as a reference when you sell this home.

◆ **Continue your home file.** It's a good idea to keep a record of home improvements and other home-related receipts. Doing so will help you when/if you sell the home.

Hiring a Professional Mover

Rather than do all the packing and loading yourself, you may want to hire a professional moving company. Perhaps your company pays for this service, or you may want to pay the money to save yourself the time, stress, and effort for a move.

If you plan to use a moving service, keep these tips in mind:

- **Ask for recommendations.** Like other services, someone that has had a good experience (or bad one) can help you find (or avoid) a mover. Also, check the Better Business Bureau (www.bbb.org) for complaints against any companies in consideration.

- **Shop around.** Get at least two to four different *written* quotes from movers.

- **Inquire about the various services and look for ways to save money.** For instance, perhaps you will pack the house yourself and just use the mover to haul the boxes. Or perhaps you want the whole job done by the mover. What you decide depends on you and your budget as well as what services the mover offers.

- **Schedule the move 30 to 45 days *before* the move.** You'll have a hard time lining up a mover at the last minute. Also, the end of the month is the busiest time for movers. If you plan to close then, secure a reservation so that you aren't stuck.

The Least You Need to Know

- Before the closing, you need to have received loan approval, paid for a one-year insurance policy, and taken care of any other requirements spelled out in the commitment letter.

- If you want, you can do a final walkthrough of the home to make sure it is in the same condition as when you made the offer. If you want a final walkthrough, be sure to put it in the contract.

- At the closing, you must pay the remaining amount of the down payment (the down payment minus your earnest money). You should also be prepared to pay closing costs. Before closing, the lender will call and tell you the exact amount you need to bring.

- The HUD-1 statement lists all the closing costs as well as which party is responsible for paying them.

- The closing is scheduled after you receive your loan commitment. It may be held at a title company, attorney's office, county courthouse, escrow company, or someplace else, depending on local custom.

- At the closing, you can expect to sign the mortgage note, the mortgage, affidavits, disclosures, and any other forms required by the lender.

Part 5

Selling Your Home

Rare is the case that a person buys one home and never moves. Nowadays, most people stay in their homes an average of five to seven years. That means that just when you finish all your remodeling projects and your home is exactly the way you want it, it's time to move. You are back on the homebuying merry-go-round, but this time around you get to experience both buying *and selling*.

You'll have a new appreciation for all that's involved in selling a house, and because you've already been through the buying process, you'll be more prepared and better equipped for your next home purchase.

Part 5 concentrates on all the steps involved in selling your home, including selling with an agent or selling it yourself. Get out your toolkit and cleaning supplies, and let's get to work.

Deciding to Sell Your Home

In This Chapter

- ◆ Understanding why you want to sell
- ◆ Timing the sale
- ◆ Understanding the costs involved in selling your home
- ◆ Knowing what to expect

Those of you reading this section have probably already endured the joys of being a homebuyer and a homeowner; now you're preparing for the delights available only to the homeseller. Dozens of muddy-footed strangers trudging through your home criticizing your wallpaper, your bathrooms, your wedding portrait. Weeks spent cleaning, polishing, repairing, till the home looks so good you may wonder why you're moving.

Why *are* you moving, anyway? Are you tired of standing in line outside the one bathroom, waiting for your turn to shower and shave every morning? Tired of hearing your teenage daughter complain about having to share a bedroom with her four-year-old sister? Or maybe you love your current residence but are being transferred to a new city and must move.

No matter what the reason, you have decided to sell your home. Unfortunately, you can't just stick a For Sale sign in the yard and hope for the best. Selling a home takes a lot of preparation. This chapter helps with the initial decision: Do you really want to sell?

Why Do You Want to Sell?

Before you decide to put that For Sale sign up and move on, you should take a careful look at why you want to move. It's easy to put your home on the market for the wrong reason. To avoid making a mistake, ask yourself why you want to sell.

If you have to move because of your job, you may not have to look into your motivation much further than that simple reason. If you are moving simply because you want a new home, that may not be a good enough reason. You might be better off considering other options. For instance, suppose that you have school-age children and like the school district and the location of the home, but the home is simply too small. Rather than pull up stakes and move, you may consider adding on.

This section helps you check your motives for moving by answering the question "Why do you want a new home?"

Tallying Your Likes, Dislikes, Wishes, and Wants

Before you decide to pack up and move to a new home, you want to be sure you aren't packing up your troubles and moving them with you. Maybe it's really your furniture that you hate. Maybe you love the home but just need a few changes. It's a good idea to analyze what you like and dislike about your home.

Real Deal

You can use your list of likes and dislikes when you are shopping for a new home. Defining your dream home is covered in Chapter 7.

What do you dislike about the home? If you're frustrated with your home, you can probably easily make a list of what you dislike. For example, suppose that it's July 1, 104°F outside, and you don't have central air conditioning. You may hate the home because it's hot. Or suppose that you have a galley kitchen and have no place to store your pots, pans, dishes, and so on.

After you make a list of what you don't like, look over your list and note whether you can change any of the dislikes into likes. For example, if you could change the home, what would be different? Would you have more bedrooms? Central air? A bigger yard?

Some changes aren't possible. If you hate the location of the home, you simply cannot change that. If changes are possible (for instance, you can always add central air), consider the cost.

Next, make a list of what you like about the home. Perhaps it has a nice view or you like the neighborhood. Maybe the home has built-in cabinets that you enjoy. Perhaps you like more than you think.

Once you have a good idea of what you like and dislike, you can take a better look at why you want to move. As mentioned, if you love the location but simply need more room, you may want to add on a room rather than move. Or maybe you just need some redecorating or new furniture.

Real Deal

Have you ever dreamed of moving to Charleston? Or Montana? If so, you can calculate the cost of living life in your "dream" city by trying the cost-of-living calculator at the Homebuyer's Fair website at www.homefair.com. You can compare the cost of living in two different cities using this tool.

On the other hand, if the home can't be redone to suit your needs, you'll know you really do want to move. You'll also have a better understanding of what to look for in your next home so you get that added benefit when tallying up your likes and dislikes.

What Do You Hope to Gain by Selling?

In addition to reviewing the home's pluses and minuses, ask yourself what you hope to gain by moving. You may answer "a bigger home, more money, and fewer commitments." Knowing what you hope to gain can help you plan your strategy.

Ask yourself how realistic your goals are. For example, suppose that it is currently a hot market for selling homes and you want to sell now so that you can make a profit. Making money is the primary reason you are selling. In this case, you'll want to keep in mind that you are still going to need someplace to live. If you sell in a seller's market, you'll most likely also have to buy in a seller's market. Will you really gain anything? Also, you'll want to consider the time, energy, and money involved in selling. Is the gain worth the pain? The section "What Costs Are Involved in Selling a Home?" later in this chapter discusses the costs involved in selling a home.

As another example, suppose that you have a large home, your children are grown and have moved out, and you are retiring. You want to sell your home and buy a condominium so that you do not have the maintenance and expensive upkeep of a large home. You want to sell your home to another family that will enjoy the pleasures of your home. Your motivation here is a release from current commitments.

If you can verbalize your reasons, you can better plan when to sell and what is important when you do sell.

Are You Ready to Sell?

The best time to sell is when you are ready to sell. Many things can affect your readiness to sell.

One factor is your job. If you are being transferred, you may want to put your home on the market right away. If you have just been promoted and received a pay increase, you may be able to move up to a more expensive home. If you are retiring, you may be ready to sell the family home and retire to a home more suited to your needs.

Another thing that can affect readiness is your family situation. If you live in a two-bedroom home and are about to have your second child, you may be ready to move to a bigger home. If you are divorcing, you may want to sell the home. If you are taking in an elderly parent, you may be ready to look for a more accommodating home. If your last child has just moved out, you may not need your big four-bedroom home and may be ready for a smaller home.

The economy is another factor that can determine how ready you are to move. For example, if interest rates are sky high, you may have to stay in your current home, regardless of whether it meets your needs. If interest rates are low, you may want to take advantage of the situation and trade up to a more expensive home as an alternative to refinancing.

Another good time to make a move up is in a buyer's market. You may have to sell your present home at a lower price, but you'll be in a stronger position to buy a more expensive home.

Only you can determine how ready you are to move. And when you are ready to move, you are ready to sell.

Timing the Sale of Your Home: Sell First vs. Buy First

Timing the sale of your home with the purchase of a new home can be tricky. Should you buy first and then sell? Or should you buy and sell at the same time? Or should you sell and then buy? Each of these methods has its strengths and weaknesses. Review this section to consider the various timing schemes.

Buy First, Sell Later

If you find your next home first and then purchase it, you know you have somewhere to live. You don't have to worry about being forced to find a home after you sell yours. Also, your home may show better when it is empty (after you have moved out). Suppose that you have several young children whose toys are stacked about or suppose that you have a huge fossil and rock collection cluttering your home. If you have moved out, buyers can more readily imagine themselves in your home.

On the other hand, this strategy is risky. You don't want to end up with two homes and two mortgage payments, which could happen. Also, you will have to pay the down payment and closing costs on your new home from your own resources rather than from the proceeds from the home of your sale.

To avoid doubling up on the mortgages, you can make the purchase of your new home contingent on the sale of your existing home. Keep in mind that sellers don't usually like offers with this contingency. They don't know anything about your home. What if it is a dump and you never get rid of it? They may not want to tie up their property while yours is on the market. They may reject your offer.

Real Deal

You can use the Internet to research the current interest rates. You can find several sites with mortgage interest rates information, such as www. bankrate.com.

Buyer Beware

Making an offer on a home with the contingency of your home selling puts pressure on you to sell. You may accept an offer that you wouldn't have if you weren't under the gun.

The sellers may also limit your contingency. For example, they may continue to keep their home on the market. If they get another offer, you have the right to remove your contingency (and buy the home) or withdraw your offer.

Sell First, Buy Later

Many sellers choose to sell their home first. Doing so puts them in a strong bargaining position. First, they don't have to include a contingency for selling their home. Second, they know how much money they have made (or lost) from the sale of their first home.

The danger in this strategy is that you'll end up with nowhere to live. If your new buyers want in and you haven't found a home, you may end up living in an apartment or with relatives for a while.

Real Deal

If you have not yet found a home, consider asking the buyers whether you can rent from them until you find a house.

Buy and Sell Together

Most people put their home on the market and begin looking for a new home at the same time. This strategy could work out perfectly; you could close on your current home one day and your new home the next day. But it's not always possible to coordinate this dream timing. You may have a gap. Perhaps your home is sold, but you haven't found a home. In this case, you'll feel the pressure as you look for and make offers on homes. If you find your house and haven't sold yours, you'll have the same issues described in the preceding section, "Buy First, Sell Later."

Bottom line: It's best to have a contingency plan for all possible outcomes.

What Costs Are Involved in Selling a Home?

When you sell something, you usually focus on what you get. You have something to offer, and a buyer gives you something for that item. You may forget that you have to give something to get something. That is, selling a home is an involved process, and many costs are involved in selling.

Here are some of the costs involved in selling your home:

- **Repair expenses.** As you get your home ready, you may find that certain repairs need to be made. You can do the repairs yourself, or you can hire someone to complete them. Deciding which repairs to make is the topic of Chapter 25. Even if you think the home is in perfect condition, the buyer is most likely going to have your home professionally inspected. If the inspection report turns up problems, you may have to pay for repairs or lower the sales price.

- **Sales commission.** If you list your home with an agent, you pay for the agent's commission, usually 6 percent of the sales price. If you sell the home yourself, you don't pay the commission. Selling your home yourself is covered in Chapter 23.

- **Closing costs that you must pay.** The seller customarily pays some closing costs.

- **Closing costs that you offer to pay.** As part of the negotiating process, you may offer to pay additional closing costs for the buyer. Deciding what you want to offer is covered in Chapter 26.

- **Moving expenses.** Unless you have one duffel bag of stuff, moving your entire home is going to cost some money—even if you do it yourself. You may have to hire a moving company or rent a moving truck.

♦ **Costs for buying a new home.** If you are buying a new home after selling your current one, don't forget to plan for the costs involved in buying a home. Chapter 3 gives you a preview of the costs you can expect to pay.

What to Expect When You Sell Your Home

The remaining chapters in Part 5 discuss all the aspects of selling a home. This section gives you a preview of what to expect.

Step 1: Getting the Home Ready

When you decide to sell your home, you need to get it ready to sell. You need to decide what repairs to make and what information to collect.

As you get your home ready, expect to "un-decorate." This advice is usually surprising to first-time sellers. "What? Put away all my family portraits? But that's what makes the home look like a home! Paint all the walls white? Where's the character in that?"

The buyer wants to start with a blank canvas (like an artist). It gives the feeling that everything is new, even if someone else has previously lived in the home. See Chapter 25 for more help with this.

Step 2: Deciding Whether to Use an Agent

Deciding whether to use an agent or sell your home yourself is an important decision. You may be tempted to stick a For Sale sign in the front yard and BAM!—you save 6 percent commission. But are you prepared for the negotiating and haggling that must be done? And remember, most buyers will expect you to share your savings with them.

But what if it's a strong seller's market? If you notice a lot of For Sale signs going up and down quickly, chances are you can make out just fine without an agent. Chapter 23 covers all the ins and outs of selling the home yourself. Even if you decide to do so, also read Chapter 24. This chapter covers all the tasks an agent can help with.

You may also decide to use a service to help you promote and sell your home, at a reduced commission. You can find out more about this option in both Chapters 23 and 24.

Step 3: Pricing and Marketing the Home

Setting the price for your home can be tricky. The price will depend on the current market, what your home has to offer, and how quickly you want to sell. Your agent can help you come up with the listing price you want to start with. Chapter 26 covers these tasks.

If you don't plan to use an agent, you'll have to do some research on home prices yourself. See Chapter 23 for how-to advice.

In addition to pricing, you should work on marketing the home—getting buyers to notice your home over all the other homes for sale in the area.

Also, expect to be interrupted with showing appointments (usually just as you sit down to dinner!). And don't be upset with any criticism of your home. While you may love the red velvet wallpaper in the bathroom, others may not. Don't let the criticism weigh you down. While one person may hate the wallpaper, another one may come along who loves it as much as you do.

Step 4: Negotiating Offers

If you are lucky, you'll have several offers on your home and you can pretty much dictate the terms. In most cases, though, you'll have to negotiate the terms. Negotiating means a little give and a little take; your agent can help you negotiate offers. Chapter 27 covers the strategies for handling offers.

If you plan to sell your home yourself, you'll have to handle the negotiations. Again, see Chapter 23 for advice on handling offers.

Step 5: Closing on the Home

Once you accept an offer and the buyer has done his job (getting financing, for example), you are ready to close on the home—take your money and hand over the keys. Chapter 28 covers all the details of closing.

Step 6: Buying a New Home

Unless you are moving to an apartment, closing on the home is not the end of the process. Usually you'll buy a new home. In this case, it's back to square one, Chapter 1, to learn all you ever wanted to know about buying a home.

The Least You Need to Know

♦ Ask yourself what you like and dislike about your home. If you love the location but just need more room, you may want to add on rather than sell.

♦ Ask yourself what your motivation is for selling the home. What do you hope to gain? A better home? Money? Less commitment? Knowing what you hope to gain can help you plan your selling strategy.

♦ Timing the sale can be tricky. Your family situation, your job, the economy, and other factors affect your readiness to sell. These factors affect whether you buy first and then sell, or sell and then buy.

♦ Keep in mind the various costs you incur when selling, including repair expenses, sales commission if you use an agent, closing costs, moving costs, and costs for purchasing a new home.

♦ The sales process involves these steps: getting the home ready, hiring an agent or deciding to sell the home yourself, pricing and marketing the home, handling purchase offers, and closing on the home.

23

Selling Your Home Yourself

In This Chapter

- ◆ Pricing your home for the market
- ◆ Marketing and showing your home
- ◆ Negotiating with the buyers
- ◆ Handling the closing on the home
- ◆ Knowing what to do if the house doesn't sell
- ◆ Using the services of others to help with certain aspects of the process

Approximately one in six home sales closes without the work of an agent. Are you one of the six that can sell practically anything? Do you know a lot about your home and neighborhood? Do you understand the real estate market—financing, negotiating, and closing? If so, you may want to forego signing an agent and sell your home yourself. Why should you consider going it alone? To save money. Agents typically charge a 6 percent commission. On a $100,000 home, that comes to $6,000!

Selling a home by yourself isn't easy, but you can do it. You should be prepared for all the various aspects, and this chapter gives you a solid background for what you will need to do.

FSBO: What to Expect

When you sell your home on your own, you need to handle the following things:

- **Pricing the home.** You will need to research the selling prices for comparable homes. In addition, you should have a good understanding of the current market. Is it a buyer's market? A seller's market?

- **Marketing your home.** In addition, you will need to prepare the fact sheets or information flyers with all the pertinent information. You also will need to arrange for yard signs, advertisements, and open houses.

Real Estate Terms

FSBO is the acronym for For Sale By Owner and is pronounced "fizz-bo."

- **Handling financing.** You may also need to help the buyer arrange for financing. At the very least, you need to be sure that the prospective buyer is financially qualified to make an offer on your home.

- **Negotiating offers.** Without an agent as the go-between, you are literally faced with handling the offers you receive on your home and dealing with the buyer or buyer's agent directly.

- **Arranging the closing.** The seller is usually the one that schedules and makes arrangements for the closing. This will also be your responsibility as a FSBO.

Basically, you need to be a "mini" real estate agent. Are you up for the task? If so, read on!

Pricing Your Home

The single most important aspect of the sale of a home is the price. Setting the price is critical to a successful home sale. If you set the price too high, buyers may avoid your property. When a property sits and sits, it becomes a target for lowball bids. On the other hand, you don't want to price the home too low. You want to get the best deal possible! The best way to set the price of your home is to investigate sales of similar homes in your area. This topic is covered in Chapter 26.

Comparable homes are of the same style (brick, frame, bungalow, two-story), have the same number of bedrooms and bathrooms, have the same types of rooms (dining room, rec room, living room), and are located in the same area. You can find the list price for homes by reading the local paper or by calling agents. You may want to attend open houses of similar homes to see how yours compares.

If you do not want to do the research yourself, you may want to hire the services of an agent to do the research for you. You may also consider having your home appraised.

Figuring Your Net Proceeds

To prepare for negotiation, you will want to figure your net proceeds from the sale of your home. Chapter 26 explains how to calculate this total. You will want to include the costs you incur for the sale of your home (advertising fees, attorney costs, and so on). You will also want to investigate which closing costs may pertain to your sale—which costs you expect to pay and how much they are.

Real Deal _____

Be sure you have reasonable expectations when you price your home and plan for your net proceeds. Many FSBOs expect to pocket the entire commission savings. Savvy buyers may want to share in the savings. So don't overestimate your proceeds.

Defining Acceptable Financial Terms

In addition to the list price for the home, you should decide on the amount of down payment you (and the lender) will require. You will also want to determine the amount of earnest money you expect to accompany an offer. Again, use the customary practices in your area as the basis. A buyer won't want to come up with a larger down payment just because you say so.

Marketing Your Home—Doing It Yourself

After you decide on the price for the home, the next step is to get the attention of potential buyers. No matter how wonderful your home is, it isn't going to sell unless buyers know it is available. This section discusses some strategies for getting your home noticed.

Putting a Sign in Your Yard

One of the first steps in marketing your home is to put up a sign. A sign alerts neighbors that you are selling your home (and agents, so watch out!). It also tells others driving through the neighborhood that your home is for sale.

You can purchase a sign at a local hardware store. It should clearly say "For Sale by Owner" and include space for you to write in your phone number. (Be sure to use a big black marker so that your number is clearly visible.) When you put the sign in your yard, make sure it can easily be seen from both directions.

In addition to a yard sign, you may want to put other signs around the neighborhood, including one on the main road into your neighborhood.

Buyer Beware _____

Before you put up your sign, check any city laws or neighborhood ordinances pertaining to signs in your area. You may be limited in the size or type of sign you can put up.

Be prepared for two things once the sign goes up. First, agents will flock to you. Second, people will stop by, ring the doorbell, and want to see your home. You can handle stop-bys by giving the potential buyers a tour, if it is convenient for you. Or you can give them an information sheet about your home (described later in this chapter) and schedule an appointment for a showing. As for agents, see the section "Other Key Players Who Can Help You Sell Your Home."

Taking Out an Ad

In addition to signs, you will most likely want to advertise your home in the local paper and perhaps other publications. Usually, most city papers have a large section devoted to real estate in the Sunday edition. You may choose to take out an ad for this edition.

You don't have to take out a full-page ad to advertise your home. A small ad works perfectly well. Most buyers in the home market read all the small ads, so you don't have to worry about size. You *should* worry about making your small ad stand out, and you can do this by making sure your ad is to the point, descriptive, and inviting.

A good ad should include the following:

◆ Price

◆ Your phone number

◆ Number of bedrooms and baths

◆ Style of home and condition of property

In the ad, emphasize the benefits of your home. What is its best feature? What do you like best about the home? What will buyers like best? After reading the ad, the buyer should want to visit your home.

Notice that you don't have to put the address in. You can give the area. Or you can schedule appointments and give the address when interested buyers call. You should include your address if you hold an open house, though. Otherwise, how will potential buyers find your home?

Marketing Your Home Online

In addition to print advertisements, you may consider listing your home for sale on the Internet. To find sites that list homes, try searching for real estate listing sites.

When you visit the site, see how many homes are listed. Is it enough to attract the attention of browsers? Would you use this service to find a home? Also find out if any fees are involved for the listing. Many sites list the homes for free (the more homes, the better the site). Some may charge a fee for the listing or for other services. Be sure you know about any fees before you submit your listing. To list your home, you usually complete a form detailing the information about your home.

Preparing Fact Sheets

When buyers visit your home, you will want them to remember it after they leave. You will also want to anticipate questions the buyers may have and provide that information in printed form. To do so, create a fact sheet that you can hand out during open houses and showings.

You can study the Multiple Listing System (MLS) used by agents for ideas of what to include. (See Chapter 8 for additional information.) Also visit other open houses and collect fact sheets from homes. Here is some information you may want to include on your fact sheet:

◆ Address of your home

◆ List price

◆ Best features of your home

◆ Number of bedrooms and bathrooms (probably the first thing a buyer wants to know)

◆ A description of other rooms in the home (living room, family room, dining room, great room, office, and so on)

◆ Information about the age, construction (adobe, siding, block, brick, frame, stone, stucco, wood), style (bungalow, Cape Cod, Colonial, contemporary, Dutch Colonial, ranch, Spanish, split-level, traditional, Tudor), and condition (move-in, needs work, as-is)

◆ Information about the size of the home—number of stories; total square footage; lot size; and dimensions of living room, dining room, bedrooms, den, and other rooms

- Any special features—fireplace, patio, pool, and so on

- Description of the garage (if you have one)

- Types and age of major systems (heating, cooling, electrical, plumbing, water heater) and a record of utility costs

- A list of appliances included with the home

- Information about the neighborhood—for example, school district and annual taxes

- Information about the current mortgage

To make the fact sheet more appealing, you may want to include a photo of your home. You can also include a drawing of the layout or survey. You may also attach your seller disclosure form. In most states, seller disclosures are required. (See Chapter 25 for additional information.)

Showing Your Home

If you have done a good job marketing your home, you will have plenty of visitors. Expect, especially at first, to have a lot of snoopers (curious neighbors, agents, other potential FSBOs comparing properties) and hopefully some potential buyers. This section explains what else you need to do when showing your home.

Handling Sales Calls

Because you do not have an agent to schedule appointments, you will have to do so yourself. You should be prepared to handle phone calls and stop-bys.

For phone calls, you may want to write up a script to follow so that you are sure to tell the potential buyer everything you think is important. For instance, you will want to give the buyer directions to your home, a description of the home, and the list price.

You may want to ask the buyers a few questions also. For instance, you can ask how the caller heard about the home to gauge the effectiveness of your marketing strategy. You will probably also want to ask for the caller's name and phone number. You can write these down in your visitor log so that you know who has called and visited.

You may then want to set up an appointment to show the home if you think the buyer may indeed be interested. You can set up a time that is convenient for both you and the buyer.

In some cases, you may have buyers that just stop by and knock on the door. How you handle this interruption is up to you. If it is convenient, you may want to arrange for a showing right then and there. If it isn't convenient (if your four-year-old has just finger-painted himself, your spouse has decided to dismantle the dishwasher at that moment, and you are in the middle of giving your mother a home perm), you may want to give the buyers a fact sheet and schedule an appointment for a more convenient time.

Showing Your Home

When potential buyers visit your home, have them sign some sort of visitor register and list their names and addresses. Doing so will provide you with a record of who visited your home. You can keep your phone calls in the same or in a separate ledger. This type of information is good to keep track of if you want to review where people have come from to view your home, which might help your advertising efforts.

You may want to point out a few things of interest and then let the buyers wander through the home. Or you may want to accompany the buyers on the tour. When you tag along, though, the buyers may feel stifled. Be sure to put away any valuables, especially if you let the visitors tour the home alone.

During the tour, be prepared for questions about the area, your home, and financing. As part of the preparation process, you should get to know the area and your home. You should also look into financing options. If you don't know the answer, say so. Don't lie and don't exaggerate.

Real Deal

Be flexible. One of the benefits of having an agent is that you don't have to be available for showings during the day. If you are selling alone and you work away from the home, you may be able to schedule all your showings during the evenings, but be flexible. You may have to arrange for weekday showings as well.

Holding Open Houses

In addition to scheduled showings, you may want to hold an open house or two. Open houses are traditionally held on Sunday afternoons.

If you plan an open house, be sure to advertise it in the paper. Also make sure you have enough fact sheets on hand for the visitors. Finally, you may want to put up some additional signs in the neighborhood directing visitors to your home. As with regular showings, have the visitors sign in.

Handling Buyer Financing

One of the benefits of using an agent is that the agent can prequalify a buyer and help a buyer obtain financing. Without an agent, you are going to have to do this yourself.

First, you will want to prequalify any buyers who are serious about making an offer. Just because Pam and Steve seem like a nice couple doesn't mean they have the money to buy your home. You won't want to spend hours and hours of time working with one buyer only to find out that the buyer can't afford your home.

Real Deal

Be willing to work with a buyer's agent. The agent can help with key tasks including financing. See "Other Key Players Who Can Help You Sell Your Home" later in this chapter.

To prequalify a buyer, you may want to purchase a buyer qualification form from an office supply company. Or you may want to draw up your own form with your attorney's help. You will want to know the buyer's income, job situation, current debt, and other information. Chapter 2 includes information on prequalifying and explains the ratios most lenders use. You can use this information to qualify a buyer yourself. Be sure that you are comfortable asking for this type of information. Money is a touchy subject. If a buyer gets angry when you ask for financial information, be sure to explain why you need it. After you do so, the buyer should understand.

Real Deal

You may want to consider putting together an information sheet that lists the names of various lenders, maximum loan amounts, points charged, and other fees. You can include this information along with your fact sheet.

You will want to help the buyer obtain financing once you have accepted an offer. An offer without financial backing isn't going to do you any good. To do this, you should be familiar with the different types of financing available. You can find this information in Part 3 of this book. You can also talk to local lenders.

Another source for home financing information is the Internet. You can visit some of the mortgage sites not only to get information about mortgage rates, but also to review prequalification information. Homebuyer's Fair (www.homefair.com), for instance, has a Mortgage Qualification Calculator. Many sites have this type of feature. Check Appendix B for a list of useful websites.

Negotiating an Offer

When you have an agent, all offers are delivered to the agent. The agent serves as a go-between, discussing the offer with the buyers and their agent and then relaying that information to you.

Without an agent, you will have to negotiate face to face with the buyers and possibly with the buyers' agent. Put on your poker face and leave your thin skin at home. This section will help you get ready.

Be Prepared

Face-to-face negotiating is tough. You have to be prepared for any negative comments made about your home. If you take the comments personally, the offer process is going to be extremely stressful. If you understand that the comments are probably just part of the buyer's strategy to get more favorable terms, you can be prepared to handle any objections.

You may want to role-play with your spouse or a friend. Have that person say all the bad things about your home—even if they aren't true. "Well, the roof needs to be repaired. The kitchen tile is the worst. And who picked the wallpaper in the living room? It's hideous!" You can then counter with "The roof was replaced last year. The list price takes into consideration the kitchen tile, and if you don't like the wallpaper, you can select something that you do like."

Draw Up Offers

If your buyers are working with an agent, the agent may help them draw up an offer. If not, they may have an attorney do the work. Or the buyers may come to you with their own purchase agreement. In this case, you don't need to worry about writing up an offer.

If, on the other hand, the buyers don't have anyone to help with an offer and need help, you can offer to do so. You may want to buy some contract forms from an office supply store and have them available. If the standard contract isn't to your liking, you can ask your attorney to draw up a contract.

Real Deal

You can help prepare yourself by figuring out the bottom line for different scenarios. Knowing what price and terms you will accept can help you when you have to evaluate offers.

Review Offers

When a buyer has an offer, you should schedule an appointment—it can be at your home if you like. When you receive an offer, thank the buyers and ask for time to review it. Usually a sales contract stipulates a time for a response (24 to 48 hours is typical).

During that response time, you can look over the offer. What price are the buyers offering? What terms? How does this compare to what you expected? Reviewing offers and making counteroffers are covered in Chapter 27.

The offer/counteroffer process can continue until someone withdraws an offer or until both parties agree to the same offer. When you have both signed the same agreement, you have successfully sold your home!

Closing on the Home

The final stage of selling your home is the closing. At the closing, you and the buyer exchange money and keys. To handle the closing, you should probably hire the services of an escrow company. (See "Using an Escrow Company" later in this chapter.) The escrow agent will prepare a *settlement sheet* and will need from you the original purchase contract to get started.

Using the contract as a blueprint, the escrow agent draws up the instructions for you and the buyers. (Chapter 28 describes the function of the escrow agent.) You should be prepared to carry out all the instructions the agent gives you and to provide any information the escrow agent needs (deed, title report, mortgage, mortgage note, property tax statements, survey, and so on).

Real Estate Terms

When escrow agents prepare for a closing, they complete a **settlement sheet**. This is the collection of information necessary to prepare escrow instructions; it includes the property description, parties involved, escrow information, sales price, your loan information, and the buyers' loan information.

Note that the escrow agent will not reveal information about escrow to other parties and will not revise the instructions without authorization from you and the buyers.

Before the closing, the escrow agent will let you and the buyers know the closing costs that must be paid and by whom. He or she will also calculate any prorations. At the closing, the escrow agent will ensure that all the proper documents have been prepared and are signed. Additionally, he or she will arrange for your original loan(s) to be paid off and for the new deed to be recorded. After the deed has been recorded, the escrow company will release to you your hard-earned check for any proceeds on the sale of your home.

Other Key Players Who Can Help You Sell Your Home

Now that you have a good idea of what selling a home involves, you may consider doing it all or parts of it. For instance, you may decide to price and market the house, but have an attorney deal with financing and contracts.

In addition, you need to consider how to handle agents. Perhaps you want to use an agent to do a market comparison for your home to help in pricing and marketing the home. You should also be prepared to deal with agents that the buyers are working with.

This section covers some of the real estate experts you may tap for some of the key tasks in selling your home.

Working with Agents

Once you put a For Sale sign in your yard, be prepared for a procession of real estate agents asking you to list your home with them. You may see more agents than buyers at first!

The agents may promise you quick sales, tell you horror stories of "The for sale by owner that never sold," and give you their best sales pitch. You should be firm with the agents—tell them you have made up your mind to sell the home yourself.

Buyer Beware

You will want to understand up front the charges that you will incur, including outside fees. The attorney will most likely charge by the hour. You should draw up a contract that lists the hourly fee and spells out what services you want the attorney to help with. The agent may want a commission or a flat fee. Know what you are willing to accept beforehand.

In some cases, you may want to consider using some services from an agent. For instance, you may hire an agent to research comparable home sales and give advice on your list price. In this case, you may want to offer a set fee or an hourly fee for the service. You may also let the agents do market reports for you. Some will do so for free in the hopes that you will eventually list your home with them. Be sure to be up front with the agent. That is, let the agent know that you want to try to sell the home yourself.

Also, you may want to consider an open listing. This type of listing usually pays a lower commission (3 percent) to the agent who brings you a buyer. You can sign open listings with more than one agent. Many FSBOs advertise this type of arrangement by saying "Brokers welcome at 3 percent." Keep in mind that many agents won't be interested in this type of agreement.

Buyer Beware

Feel free to listen to any agents who give a sales pitch, but don't let agents intimidate you. If they go too far, consider calling their home office and telling the broker about the situation.

In addition, you should be willing to negotiate with the buyer's agent. A buyer that is represented by an agent has too many benefits to simply cast them off. Usually, the buyers are prequalified and are serious about buying a home. It is in your best interest to consider working with the buyers' agent and negotiating a fair commission. It's better to pay 3 percent to an agent and sell your home than it is to exclude this type of arrangement and wait for an unrepresented buyer. Remember: In the most successful negotiations, both sides feel as if they won.

Hiring an Attorney

Even if you don't hire anyone else, you will definitely want to hire the services of an attorney. An attorney can advise you on the disclosure laws in your state, draw up or look over any contracts, and make sure your interests are protected. The attorney can ensure that you do everything properly and legally—for instance, that you don't unwittingly discriminate against any buyers.

When looking for an attorney, ask for recommendations from friends, relatives, agents, and co-workers. Keep in mind that you will want to hire an attorney who specializes in real estate. You don't want to use your sister the divorce attorney to handle the transaction.

Using a Homeselling Service

You can also find services that will help you sell your home (such as HomeYeah. com). These companies help you market your house, but let you handle all the other stuff such as home tours, negotiating the deal, and so on. This type of company typically charges half the commission of an agent (typically around 3 percent).

Using an Escrow Company

In addition to an attorney, another consultant you will most likely want to use is an escrow holder. An escrow holder works for an escrow company that serves as a neutral third party in real estate transactions. The escrow holder is the maestro of the transaction. You can expect the escrow holder to prepare, obtain, and record documents; handle the mechanics of property transfer; calculate any prorations; and receive and disburse money.

You may want to ask your attorney or any real estate agents you know for recommendations on escrow companies. Make sure you know the charges you will incur for using a particular escrow company. Also be sure you know exactly what duties the escrow agent will perform. For example, an escrow agent cannot offer advice and cannot negotiate with you and the buyer.

What to Do If Your Home Doesn't Sell

If you have had your home on the market for a while and have not sold it, take a second look. Why hasn't the home sold? Chapter 27 lists some reasons why a home may not sell, including the price, the market, the terms, and the condition of the home. Review these items and try to pinpoint the problem.

You may also consider using an agent, especially if it turns out that exposure (getting buyers to the home) is the main problem. An agent might increase the number of visitors and thus potential buyers.

Finally, if the market is so slow or interest rates are so high that you are not getting any acceptable offers, consider offering some financing incentives (perhaps paying loan points). If you are able to, you may want to take your home off the market for a while and wait until the market improves.

The Least You Need to Know

- Be sure you understand what is involved in selling your home yourself.

- The most important aspect of selling a home is setting the price. To come up with a price, compare similar homes in the area. You may want to hire an agent to help you with pricing.

- To get your home noticed, put a for sale by owner sign in your yard and advertise in the local daily paper and neighborhood weeklies.

- Create a fact sheet about your home to hand out to potential buyers when they visit your home.

- Negotiating face to face with a buyer can be tough. Be prepared to deal with criticism and objections, and know your bottom line.

- You may want to hire consultants—for example, a real estate attorney, agent, or escrow company—to help with some of the steps.

◆ The final step in selling a home is the closing. You should hire the services of an escrow company to prepare the instructions for the closing, to ensure that all documents are prepared and properly signed, and to hold all the money and distribute it when the deal is complete.

Chapter 24

Selling Your Home with an Agent

In This Chapter

◆ Deciding whether to use an agent

◆ Selecting an agent

◆ Understanding listing agreements

Remember all that you went through when you purchased a home? You have to go through that again, on the other side of the net, when you sell your home. Selling a home isn't as easy as placing an ad and then taking calls. You have to set the price, market the home, qualify buyers, and more. To help you handle all the details of selling, you may want to hire an agent. This chapter helps you decide whether to use an agent and tells you how to select a good agent.

If you decide to sell the home yourself, see Chapter 23, which covers FSBOs (for sale by owner).

Should You Use an Agent or Sell Alone?

Why go without an agent? To save money. Many sellers don't want to pay the 6 percent commission on the home. On a $100,000 home, you can save $6,000 if you sell the home yourself.

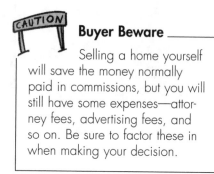

Buyer Beware

Selling a home yourself will save the money normally paid in commissions, but you will still have some expenses—attorney fees, advertising fees, and so on. Be sure to factor these in when making your decision.

But that money is hard-earned. You have to be prepared mentally and psychologically for selling a home yourself. A lot of work and time are involved. First consider what an agent can do for you. Then consider what it takes for you to sell your home yourself. After reviewing this information, you should be able to make your decision.

As you know from buying a home, there are a lot of *i*'s to dot and *t*'s to cross in the home-selling process. An agent has the experience both as a salesperson and as a real estate expert to help you through this.

Here are some of the things an agent can do for you:

- **Help you set the listing price.** You'll want the most money you can get from your home, but a home that is priced too high is just going to sit there. And you won't like it one little bit. Starting with a good price is the first step for a successful sale. The agent can help determine the asking price by looking at comparable homes in the area.

- **Make suggestions on repairs and renovations.** An agent knows what buyers look for when they tour a home. Does a deck really add value? Or do most buyers ignore it? An agent can turn an objective eye on your home and tell you what problems stick out and what changes you should consider making.

- **Screen potential buyers.** Do you want to open your home to every Curious Carole and Nosey Ned? Or do you want to spend that time showing the home to buyers who are *really* interested? An agent can help screen buyers. Are the buyers serious? Is this home appropriate for them? Also, if you sell the home yourself, you have to be available to show it, and you have no buffer between you and the buyer. Think about how you will react when potential buyers start opening your closets, laughing at your carpeting, and complaining about the small garage. An agent is an objective go-between. He or she can still solicit feedback from the buyers, but it won't hurt his or her feelings if the buyers say the wallpaper is tacky.

- **Help qualify buyers.** You want buyers who are really looking for a home, and you also want buyers who can *afford* your home. Many home buyers don't know what they can afford. You don't want to waste time showing your home to any-one with two nickels. Instead, an agent can financially prequalify the buyers to be sure they can afford your home.

♦ **Market the home.** An agent will add your home information to the *Multiple Listing Service (MLS)*, a computerized collection of all listed homes. Other agents use this service to find matches to their buyers. For example, a couple may be looking for a home just like yours. If your home is listed and an agent searches the listing, your home will come up as a match. This service helps bring buyers to your home. Instead of one agent, you have all the agents using the MLS representing your home. In addition to the MLS, the agent will have other strategies for marketing your home—open houses, ads, flyers, and so on. Some of the more motivated buyers are moving from out of town with only a weekend to look for a home. These buyers are usually working with an agent.

♦ **Handle negotiations.** There's a lot of back and forth when a deal is being negotiated. A good agent should be an adept negotiator and can keep the deal alive. Often buyers feel uncomfortable dealing directly with the seller. They think you'll be offended when they offer less than the list price, so rather than offer, they will walk away. An agent, on the other hand, is a mediator. The buyers won't have any qualms about telling the agent what's wrong with the home and what price *they* think the home is worth. Your agent has the resources to show the buyer the true market value of your home.

♦ **Oversee the closing process.** Once an offer is accepted, there's still more work to be done—paperwork that has to be completed, inspections that have to be responded to, and more. An agent can help you manage the final hurdles up to and including the closing. The agent can also help spot any red flags and resolve any glitches that pop up.

Finding an Agent

A good way to find an agent is to ask friends and neighbors. Who sold their home? How long was it on the market? Did they get the asking price? Did the sellers think they could get more, or did they think they got a good deal? Most sellers will remember bad experiences vividly; by asking around, you'll find out who *not* to use, and with luck, you'll also find out who *to* use.

You can also check your local paper for advertisements or visit a local broker's office. As another resource, you can use the Internet to locate an agent. Many real estate companies have web pages with agent information, and some agents even have their own web page. Look for web addresses of your local real estate companies on their signs. For instance, FC Tucker, an Indiana company, advertises their website (www.talktotucker.com) on all their For Sale signs. Or try searching for a particular company. As a third strategy, you can find links to agent information on some of the general real estate sites.

Quizzing the Agent

Once you have a few agents in mind, you may want to call and talk to each one on the phone or set up a meeting. You can use the following checklist to interview and evaluate the agent(s):

♦ How long have you been a real estate agent? Preferably you want someone with three or more years of experience. But don't rule out newcomers who may bring enthusiasm to the sale.

♦ Do you work full- or part-time? Some agents work their way into the field by starting part-time. To sell your home, you want someone that is readily available, not just working during the "off" hours.

♦ What broker do you work for? What qualities make this brokerage unique? Many agents work for a broker such as Prudential or ReMax. Having a major firm behind the agent may help attract buyers because they most likely recognize the broker's name. Ask also questions about the broker's reputation. How does the broker rate compare to other local brokers? What qualities make that broker most suited to being your agent?

♦ How many homes have you listed in the last six months? How many have you sold? These are cold hard facts that indicate just how active the agent is. If he or she hasn't listed a house, let alone sold a house in six months, look elsewhere.

♦ What marketing will you do for my home? At the minimum, the agent should have access to the Multiple Listing Service (MLS). Look for an agent that doesn't rely on just this listing though. Ask about advertisements in the paper, open houses, information sheets, and other marketing materials.

Real Deal

Ask for the addresses of the properties an agent has listed and sold. Then drive by and take a look at the houses. What kind of houses does the agent work with? Are there any special features worth noting?

♦ What commission do you charge? Most agents charge a 6 percent commission, which they split with the buyer's agent. (You can learn more about brokers, fees, and other agent details in Chapter 4.) Make sure your rate is the standard and customary rate in your area.

- Do you specialize in a particular area? Some agents may specialize in a special market or area of town. If your home is unique in this way, you may weigh the decision based on an agent's specialties.

- What will you do to facilitate the sale of the home? Remember the list of what an agent can do (help qualify buyers, do a market comparison, and so on). The agent should respond with a solid plan of action.

- What lenders do you work with? The agent should have a good understanding of the home finance market and should have contacts in that area.

- Do you have a list of references? You may want to talk with others who have worked with this agent to get a first-hand account of the agent's work ethic and abilities.

Evaluating the Agent's Listing Presentation

A potential agent should also complete a detailed listing presentation. This presentation should include …

- Information about the agent.

- Information about the housing market, such as how many homes are for sale in your area.

- Information about your home. For example, the agent may make suggestions on what repairs should be made.

- A list of what the agent will do to sell your home. For example, how will the agent advertise the home and what additional information will he or she create, such as flyers or information sheets?

- All recent comparable sales (both sold and pending sales) in your area, including detailed listings of the home information—number of stories, number of bedrooms, number of baths, other rooms, other amenities (fireplace, basement, special features), the list date, list price, sales date, and sales price of the homes. May also include the MLS listings and pictures of the comparable homes.

Real Deal

You may be tempted to solicit several market analyses and then just go with the one that gives you the highest price, but this isn't the best strategy. What if you can't get that price? Also, most agents should be within the same price range, because they are working with the same data. Instead, pick an agent who knows the area, has good experience, and presents the best marketing plan.

Using the information from this MLS report, the agent should then make a recommendation on an asking price for your home. The agent may give you a range. For example, he or she may give you a price for a 30-day sale, a 60-day sale, and a 90-day sale.

The agent should also provide a Net Proceeds Statement that shows you different scenarios for the different asking prices. This sheet should list the commission and closing costs you should expect to pay and give you a rough estimate of your net at closing. The following table shows you a sample Net Proceeds Statement from a marketing report. Finally, the agent should give you an explanation of various listings.

Net Proceeds Statement

Property Date Prepared by	55 N. Main Street 8/14/2003 Agent Lewis		
Sales Price	**$115,000**	**$112,500**	**$110,000**
1st mortgage payoff	$85,000	$85,000	$85,000
2nd mortgage payoff			
Brokerage fee	$8,050	$7,875	$7,700
Title Insurance	$400	$400	$400
Mortgage Discount Points			
Origination Fee			
Deed and Affidavit	$50	$50	$50
Document Preparation			
Taxes	$249	$249	$249
Buyer's Closing Costs			
Closing Fee			
Assessments			
Inspections			
Termite Inspection			
Underwriting Fee			
Tax Service Fee			
Repairs			
Other			
Costs of Selling	$8,749	$8,574	$8,399
Net at Closing	**$21,251**	**$18,926**	**$16,601**

Signing a Listing Contract

Once you agree to use an agent, he or she will most likely ask you to sign a listing contract, which gives the agent the right to list the home. This section teaches you about the different types of contracts and what a contract should include. See the following sample, "Listing Contract (Exclusive Right to Sell)," for an example of one of the most common types of contracts.

Types of Contracts

The contract basically spells out who gets the commission. You can expect to see these common contract types:

- **Exclusive right to sell.** Your agent will most likely push this type of contract, because he or she will get the commission no matter who sells the property. If your brother Joe buys the home, your agent still gets the commission.

- **Exclusive agency.** You don't pay the commission if you find your own buyer without help from the agent. For example, if it turns out that your co-worker is looking for a home just like yours, and you arrange for the co-worker to buy the property, you don't pay the commission. This type of agreement may be a good idea if you know of someone who is interested in buying.

- **Open.** You pay the commission to any agent who finds you a buyer. It's a free-for-all, and as such, many agents won't spend a lot of time working on selling your home. This type of agreement is useful for sellers who want to do the selling but want agents to bring buyers to the home. For example, you may see ads that say, "Brokers welcome at 2 percent." This means the seller will pay the agent 2 percent for bringing a buyer.

 Buyer Beware

Ask to see the MLS listing to be sure your home has been entered. A friend of mine found out that her home—which had been on the market for a few months—was never entered in the MLS. While this glitch is rare, you might want to have your agent show you the listing to be sure.

GRAVES
REALTORS®

LISTING CONTRACT
(Exclusive Right to Sell)

1. In consideration of services to be performed by   A. H. M. GRAVES COMPANY, INC.
2. (Broker/Company, hereinafter referred to as "REALTOR") for _John & Irma Seller_,
3. (SELLER), Seller hereby appoints REALTOR as Seller's agent with irrevocable and exclusive right to sell the property known
4. as _8169 Ashwood Ct Indple, In_ Zip Code _46268_
5. for the price and upon the terms and conditions herein, or otherwise acceptable to Seller.
6. **LEGAL DESCRIPTION:** The property is legally described as _Lot 131 Crooked Creek Height_
7. in _Pike_ Township, _Marion_ County, _Indpls._ Indiana.
8. **FAIR HOUSING:** This property shall be offered, shown, and made available to all persons without regard to race, color, religion,
9. sex, handicap, familial status or national origin.
10. **TERM:** This contract begins on _June, 30, 2000_ and expires at midnight
11. on _December 31, 2000_ unless extended in writing by all parties hereto. Provided, however, that if the
12. Seller and a Buyer sign a Purchase Agreement, Option to Purchase Real Estate, or the closing of the sale of the property will not
13. take place until after the term of this contract, then this contract shall automatically be extended to coincide with the closing date.
14. **PRICE:** The property will be offered at a price of $ _109,900_
15. **ACCEPTABLE FINANCING:** Said property may be sold for cash or any of the following methods indicated below:
16. __X__ Conventional Mortgage
17. __X__ Insured Conventional Mortgage
18. _____ Assumption of Existing Mortgage Balance
19. _____ Conditional Sales Contract
20. _____ FHA
21. _____ VA
22. _____ Other _____
23. Seller agrees to pay costs associated with financing not to exceed _0 –_
24. **PROPERTY OFFERED FOR SALE:** The above sale price includes the property and all improvements and fixtures
25. permanently installed and affixed thereto, except _N/A_
26.
27. **SELLER DISCLOSURE OF PROPERTY CONDITION:** Seller represents to the best of Seller's knowledge and belief, the
28. property is structurally and mechanically sound and all equipment to be included in the sale is in good operating condition. Seller
29. agrees that maintaining the condition of the property and related equipment is Seller's responsibility during the period of this
30. contract and/or until Buyer's time of possession, whichever is later.
31. **PROPERTY DEFECTS:** Seller discloses the following known defects: _none known_
32.
33. **INDEMNITY:** If a dispute arises at any time concerning the condition of the property, the structures, improvements permanently
34. installed and affixed thereto, property defects, or health hazards, Seller agrees to indemnify and hold harmless the REALTOR®,
35. cooperating Broker, and/or Metropolitan Indianapolis Board of REALTORS®, Inc. (MIBOR) and MIBOR Service Corporation
36. (MSC) from and against any liabilities, judgments, damages, expenses, costs and/or reasonable attorney fees which they may
37. incur as a result of any such dispute.
38. **REALTOR' SERVICES:**
39. 1. REALTOR' warrants that REALTOR' holds a valid Indiana real estate license.
40. 2. REALTOR' will make an earnest and continued effort to sell the property in accordance with the terms and conditions of this
41. contract.
42. 3. REALTOR' is a member of MIBOR and the Multiple Listing Service (MLS).
43. 4. REALTOR' will enter detailed information, a photo of the property, if available, and types of financing acceptable to Seller
44. into the MLS computer system and all available MLS publications.
45. 5. Print-outs of this listing will be readily available to members of MLS by computer and will be provided to other REALTORS'
46. and Brokers upon request.
47. 6. REALTOR' has given Seller a written estimate of selling expenses.
48. 7. REALTOR' will cooperate with all other REALTORS' and Brokers in an effort to procure a Buyer for the property.
49. 8. REALTOR' may advertise the property and place a "For Sale" sign upon the premises. REALTOR' may provide a lockbox
50. for the keys to the property in order to facilitate showings. REALTOR' will follow Seller's instructions for making
51. appointments for the property to be shown.
52. 9. REALTOR' will promptly present all Purchase Agreements received on the property for Seller's consideration. After a
53. Purchase Agreement has been accepted by Seller, REALTOR' will continue to present any offers received until the
54. transaction is closed.
55. 10. REALTOR' may place a "SOLD" or a "SALE PENDING" rider upon the sign after a Purchase Agreement has been
56. accepted, and will remove all signs after the transaction has been closed.
57. 11. REALTOR' will assist the Buyer in obtaining financing, if requested.
58. 12. REALTOR' will make arrangements for closing time and place in cooperation with all parties.
59. **PROFESSIONAL SERVICE FEE:** The Professional Service Fee charged by the listing REALTOR' for services rendered, with
60. respect to any listing, is solely a matter of negotiation between REALTOR' and Seller and is not fixed, controlled, suggested,
61. recommended or maintained by MIBOR, the MLS or any person not a party to the contract.
62. Seller agrees to pay REALTOR' a fee of _seven per cent of sales price._ which shall be
63. paid upon the occurrence of any of the following events:
64. 1. At the time of closing the sale, when title to or an interest in the property is transferred to a Buyer; or
65. 2. At the time of default by Seller if, at that time, Seller and Buyer have entered into a fully executed, written Purchase
66. Agreement; or
67. 3. At the time REALTOR' procures a written offer to purchase from a Buyer who is ready, willing and able to purchase the
68. property according to the terms herein, but the Seller refuses to accept the offer; or
69. 4. At the time Seller sells the property to a Buyer procured in whole or in part by the efforts of REALTOR', a cooperating
70. Broker or the Seller during the term of this contract, if such sale occurs within 120 days after this contract terminates;
71. however, this paragraph #4 shall not apply if this contract terminates and the property is listed exclusively with another
72. licensed Broker.
73. 5. At the time of closing a sale on an Option to Purchase and/or Lease Option entered into during the term of this contract,
74. even though the closing takes place after the expiration of this contract.
75. **AGENCY DISCLOSURE:** Seller acknowledges that REALTOR' has advised the Seller that the property may be sold with the
76. assistance of a cooperating Broker, operating in either of the following capacities, and that the REALTOR'S' policy is to
77. compensate such Broker as indicated by a check on the appropriate corresponding line:

1-00/L-100

A sample listing contract, page 1.

78. __X__ Sub-Agents
79. Sub-Agents are licensees who procure buyers, but who agree to act as an agent of the listing REALTOR', are compensated
80. by the listing REALTOR', and who represent the interest of the Seller.
81. __X__ Buyer-Agents
82. Buyer-Agents are licensees who represent the interest of the buyer, even if compensated by the listing REALTOR'. (NOTE:
83. Listing REALTOR' will always cooperate with Buyer-Agents compensated by the Buyer, even if this line is not checked.)

84. **POTENTIAL DUAL AGENCY:** Dual Agency exists when both Buyer and Seller are represented by the same person or
85. company in a transaction. When one of REALTOR'S' agents, acting as a Buyer-Agent, wishes to show the property, Seller will
86. be notified that there is a potential for dual agency. Only after full disclosure, and Seller's written consent for REALTOR' to act as
87. a dual agent in this instance, will a Purchase Agreement be written or negotiations begun.

88. **SELLER AUTHORIZATION AND COOPERATION:** Seller agrees to provide REALTOR' with the required information
89. necessary for entry into the MLS. The Seller will cooperate with REALTOR' by permitting the property to be shown at reasonable
90. times and authorizes REALTOR' to place "For Sale" and other signs on the property.
91. 1. Seller hereby authorizes REALTOR' to conduct or allow cooperating Brokers to conduct key-entry showings of the
92. property.
93. 2. Seller will provide REALTOR' with key(s) necessary to open the primary door of the property.
94. 3. Seller authorizes REALTOR' to have duplicate keys made for use in case of an emergency.
95. 4. Seller agrees not to rent or lease the property during the term of this contract without written notification to REALTOR'.
96. 5. Seller agrees that REALTOR' may appoint or work with sub-agents and Buyer-Agents, to assist in performing
97. REALTOR'S' duties according to the terms of this contract.
98. 6. Seller authorizes REALTOR' to disseminate price and terms of financing on a closed sale to members of MIBOR, to
99. other Brokers upon request, and this information shall be published in the MIBOR MLS.
100. 7. Seller authorizes its lending institution to divulge all mortgage information to REALTOR' and to provide copies of the
101. note and mortgage, if requested. Seller's lending institution is _first federal S + L Indpls_ and the
102. mortgage loan number is _0036754_ . If Seller's mortgage is subject to a pre-payment penalty, Seller agrees
103. to give timely written notice to Seller's lender that the mortgage is to be pre-paid from the sale proceeds of the real
104. estate. It is acknowledged that Seller's failure to give said notice may result in a pre-payment penalty.

105. **LOCKBOX AUTHORIZATION/USE:** To facilitate showings of real estate, a lockbox installation (is __X__) (is not _____)
106. authorized, subject to the following acknowledgments/conditions:
107. 1. Seller will provide keys.
108. 2. Seller will safeguard valuables.
109. 3. Seller acknowledges REALTOR' is not an insurer of Seller's real estate and personal property and waives claims
110. against REALTOR' and REALTOR'S' authorized agents for loss and/or damage to such property pursuant to showing
111. the property. Seller further agrees to indemnify and hold harmless REALTOR' and all authorized agents from claims by
112. third parties from loss and/or damage pursuant to showing the property.
113. 4. Seller instructs REALTOR' to make reasonable efforts to notify Seller of showing requests. If Seller cannot be contacted
114. to schedule a showing, Seller (wants __X__) (does not want _____) REALTOR' to use the lockbox for access to the
115. property.
116. 5. Where a tenant/leasee occupies the Property, it is Seller's full responsibility to obtain tenant/leasee consent to allow the
117. use of a lockbox.

118. **EARNEST MONEY:** Earnest money, tendered with an accepted Purchase Agreement, shall be deposited immediately in listing
119. REALTOR'S' Escrow Account until the sale is closed. In the event the sale is not closed, the earnest money shall be disbursed
120. based on either the mutual agreement of the Seller and Buyer or upon court order. In the event that the Seller is to receive any
121. portion of the earnest money, Seller agrees that REALTOR' shall be entitled to retain any or all of Seller's portion of the earnest
122. money in payment of advertising and/or other expenses. In no event shall the amount retained exceed the amount of the
123. professional service fee had the transaction been closed.

124. **ADDITIONAL PROVISIONS:**
125. 1. Seller understands the terms of this contract, and has received a copy hereof.
126. 2. Seller acknowledges receipt of an estimate of selling expenses.
127. 3. Seller represents that Seller has the capacity to convey the property by a general Warranty Deed or by _____ .
128. 4. Seller represents and warrants that Seller is not a "Foreign Person" (individual or entity) and therefore is not subject to
129. the Foreign Investment in Real Estate Property Tax Act.
130. 5. The parties to this contract agree that this contract contains the entire agreement of the parties and cannot be changed
131. except by their written consent.
132. 6. The parties to this contract agree that this contract is binding upon the parties hereto, their heirs, administrators,
133. executors, successors and assigns.
134. 7. The parties to this contract agree that if it becomes necessary for the REALTOR' to retain an attorney or initiate any
135. legal proceedings in order to secure compliance with this contract, then, in addition to all other sums to which the
136. REALTOR' may be entitled to recover, the REALTOR' shall also be entitled to recover court costs and reasonable
137. attorney fees.
138. 8. The parties to this contract further agree that this contract may be executed simultaneously or in two or more
139. counterparts, each of which shall be deemed an original, but all of which together constitute one and the same
140. instrument. Delivery of this document may be accomplished by electronic facsimile reproduction (FAX). If FAX delivery
141. is utilized, the original document shall be promptly executed and/or delivered, if requested.

142. **FURTHER CONDITIONS:** _____
143. _____
144. _____
145. _____

146. _Excellent Agent_
147. SALESPERSON/AGENT   INDIANA LICENSE #   _John Seller_
                                                                SELLER   DATE
148. A. H. M. GRAVES COMPANY, INC.   C081297143   _304-12-3434_
149. REALTOR'/BROKER OR COMPANY NAME   INDIANA LICENSE #   SOCIAL SECURITY #/FED. I.D. #
150. _The Best Manager_   _Anna Seller_
151. ACCEPTED BY: NAME AND TITLE   SELLER   DATE
152. _6/3/00_   _304-34-5656_
153. DATE   SOCIAL SECURITY #/FED. I.D. #
154.   _8169 Ashwood Ct Indpls In. 46768_
155.   MAILING ADDRESS   ZIP CODE

R REALTOR'

Approved by and restricted to use by members of the Metropolitan Indianapolis Board Of REALTORS®.
This is a legally binding contract. If not understood seek legal advice. ©MIBOR 1994 (Form No. 250-01/94)

EQUAL HOUSING OPPORTUNITY

A sample listing contract, page 2.

What the Listing Contract Should Include

Your listing agreement should state the following:

- **Length of the contract.** Contracts usually range from 90 to 180 days, and you can extend them if you want. Be sure you don't sign a contract that is automatically extended. Also, a shorter contract may be better, because at the end of that time period, you can re-evaluate. Why isn't the home selling? Do you need a different agent?

- **How long the agent is protected after the agreement expires.** If an agent has a buyer but the contract has expired, the agent is going to want the commission anyway. Usually the agent is protected for 30 to 60 days after the expiration for any buyers the agent brought to the home.

- **The commission rate.** The commission is based on the sales price; 6 percent is common, but the commission rate is negotiable.

- **A statement of the condition of the property.** Are you selling the property as-is? Or are you making repairs? If so, what will you repair? What will you change?

- **A marketing plan.** The agreement should spell out how the agent plans to market the home. Where will the agent advertise the home? Will the agent hold open houses? If so, how often? What else will the agent do? Will he or she create flyers? Signs? How soon will the home be entered in the MLS listing?

- **A statement of the price and terms for the sale of the home.** For example, the agreement should include the list price, the amount of deposit you require, and the terms of the sale you are willing to accept. Also, the agreement should list what is included in the sale—appliances, draperies, and so on.

- **Permissions.** The agreement should grant explicit permission for the agent to do certain things, such as use a lockbox, put a sign in the yard, and so on.

Getting Out of a Listing

If you are unhappy with an agent, you can't just fire him. You have a signed agreement, remember? If you're not satisfied with the agent's performance, start by asking yourself what you are dissatisfied with. Are you unhappy because you haven't sold the home in the first month? Or are you unhappy because the home has been on the market for one month, but there's still no sign in the yard, and you haven't had a single showing? Are you unhappy because you don't like the feedback you're getting from the agent? Remember, don't shoot the messenger!

You'll be anxious to sell, but you have to keep your expectations reasonable. If they aren't, you need to be more patient. If you have reasonable expectations that are unfulfilled, you should voice your concerns to the agent. Tell the agent what you expect to be done and then give him or her a second chance.

Look at your listing contract. Does it provide any conditions for terminating the contract? That's why a solid listing contract specifying all of the details covered in the preceding section is key. You should know beforehand what the agent will do. If the agent doesn't live up to these commitments, you then have a legitimate complaint.

> **CAUTION**
>
> **Buyer Beware**
>
> You can't just take the home off the market for any reason. If you have a legitimate reason (for example, a death in the family), the agent will most likely be understanding. If you don't have a legitimate reason (for example, you want to take the home off the market because you found a seller yourself), the agent isn't likely to be as accommodating.

If you are still unsatisfied, ask for your listing back. The agent doesn't *have* to give the listing back but may. If the agent doesn't, you may want to complain to the agent's broker, to the real estate board, and to the Better Business Bureau. If you become a nuisance, the agent may change his or her mind.

It's best to ask the agent up front in which situations you can take the home off the market.

The Least You Need to Know

- ◆ Your first decision should be whether you want to use an agent. An agent can help you set your list price, suggest which repairs to make, screen buyers, market the home, and negotiate the deal.

- ◆ When selecting an agent ask about his or her background, experience, number of listings, and number of homes sold.

- ◆ Your agent should prepare a marketing report for your home that includes information about comparable homes for sale or that have sold in your area. In addition, this report should include a recommendation on a list price for your home, a net proceeds sheet, and a marketing plan.

- ◆ Your agent will require you to sign a listing agreement that gives him or her permission to list and sell your home. This agreement should include the length of the contract, the commission charged, the marketing plan for the home, the list price of your home, and a description of what terms you'll accept.

25

Getting the Home Ready for Sale

In This Chapter

- ◆ Doing repairs
- ◆ Cleaning up
- ◆ Uncluttering the home
- ◆ Collecting pertinent information
- ◆ Understanding seller disclosure

Once you've decided to put your home on the market, you have to get it ready. If your home is in perfect condition, getting it ready may only involve straightening up. If your home is like most, though, you may need to do some repairs. Got a leaky faucet? Better fix it. Roof need repair? You can have it repaired or take the repairs into consideration when you price the home.

In addition to cleaning and repairing, you should start to collect the information you'll need to sell the home. Buyers will want to know about maintenance and upkeep. For example, what does the electric bill run a month? When was the furnace last checked? This chapter helps you prepare for the sale of your home.

Doing Home Repairs

There are several types of do-it-yourselfers. There's the ideal Mr. and Ms. Fixit, who love to work on the home, do a perfect job, and finish all the work they start. On the other end of the scale, there's the handyman who's not handy at all and doesn't even attempt repair work. He hires someone to do the repairs. If either of these descriptions fits you or your spouse, you're lucky—for the most part, you won't have problems with the repairs.

A dangerous type of do-it-yourselfer is the one who can do the work but gets bored or preoccupied halfway through the job and starts something new. (That would be my husband.) Another dangerous type *thinks* he or she can do repairs, attempts to do the work, and then has to hire someone to clean up. You usually pay twice as much money for a muddled job. If you or your spouse is a danger to your home, you may have problems.

Real Deal

If you want to be super-prepared, you can hire a professional home inspector. This will allow you to make any major adjustments before the buyer's inspector shows up.

This section helps you decide what repairs to make when you are about to sell your home.

Inspecting the Home Yourself

To start, you should do a thorough inspection of your home. Look through each and every room as if you were a buyer. What problems do you see? What sticks out? If you were a buyer, what would you notice? Take a clipboard and note any problems. You may be tempted to leave off some problems. For example, you may think that the buyer won't notice the missing tile in the bathroom. But if you noticed it, the buyer will notice it. Put the problem on your list.

Real Deal

If you have to repaint or repaper, select a neutral color. White and off-white are good choices. They may not do much to set off your tiger-striped couch, zebra chairs, and beaded doorways, but not everyone will have your tastes. It's better to stick with something neutral.

Once you have a list of the problems, you can decide what to fix yourself, what you need to hire someone to fix, and what you can let go. Here are some areas to check:

◆ **Check all your floors.** Do you have any missing tiles? Are the baseboards in good shape? Do they need to be cleaned? Does the floor creak anywhere? Is the vinyl curling at the seams on the kitchen floor? Check the stairs for loose handrails.

◆ **Check all the walls and ceilings.** Are the paint and wallpaper in good shape? Do any holes or cracks need to be fixed? Do rooms need to be repainted? Is wallpaper peeling in spots? Do your children have posters on the walls?

◆ **Check all the doors and windows.** Do they open smoothly? Do they shut completely? Any doorknobs missing? Any loose hinges? Are the windows caulked? Any broken or cracked panes? You could combine checking and cleaning in one process and wash the windows as you check. Clean windows make a good impression. Repair any broken doors or windows.

◆ **Inspect the bathrooms.** Are the tiles clean and caulked? Any missing tiles? Do the faucets leak? You should replace damaged tiles in the kitchen and bath and fix any leaking faucets. Does the toilet flush properly? What about the walls? Does the bathroom need to be painted or wallpapered? Check the water pressure. Make sure the water drains properly. Check under the sink for leaks.

◆ **Take a close look at your kitchen.** Do all the appliances work? Is the floor clean and free of missing tiles or curling vinyl? What about the cabinets? Paint or wallpaper? What about the sink? Does it drain okay? Any leaks?

Real Deal _____

A quick coat of paint on painted cabinets will make the entire kitchen brighter. Also, new knobs on the cabinets go a long way to update a kitchen.

◆ **Examine your basement or attic.** Clean out stored stuff (see "Eliminating Clutter," later in this chapter). In the basement, check pipes for leaks and check for any sign of dampness.

Real Deal _____

Open your windows and let the natural light shine in. You want the appearance of a light, spacious home. Be sure you take down any suncatchers or other decals, and wash those windows!

◆ **Make sure the electrical system is in good shape.** Do you have any outlets that don't work? Any broken switches? Replace any burnt-out light bulbs in your home so that it is bright and cheery. Use newer, brighter bulbs for maximum impact. When showing your home, turn on all the lights.

- **Check the heating and cooling systems.** Make any necessary repairs. Replace dirty air filters. You may want to have the heating and cooling systems professionally serviced.

- **Check the roof, gutters, exterior walls, driveway, garage, and yard.** Does the roof need repairs? If so, make them. Does the outside need to be painted? Is the yard in good shape? Check for overgrown bushes and for tree limbs touching the roof or gutters. Repair any missing siding. Patch any cracks in the driveway. Weed! Make sure the garage is neat and tidy and that the garage door opener (if you have one) works.

- **Inspect your appliances** (those you plan to include with the sale). Do they work? Are they clean and well-maintained? Clean the oven. Scrub off all the leftover soap from on top of the washer or dryer.

After you do your inspection tour, you may become depressed. You may see problems you never noticed before. Don't fret. Break down the list into repairs that are essentially cleaning tasks, repairs that you can do, repairs that you need to hire someone to do, and repairs you are going to ignore.

You'll uncover some problems on your inspection tour that are simply cleaning tasks. No one likes to scrub the bathroom floor until it shines, but maybe that's all it needs. Mark all the cleaning tasks and save them for later. Cleaning is covered in the next section. This section focuses on repairs.

Getting a Professional Inspection

In addition to your own walkthrough, you may want to have a professional inspection done. (You can find information about what an inspector does, where to find one, and how much it costs in Chapter 20.) Why get your own inspection when the buyers are going to have the home inspected—and pay for that inspection themselves? To be prepared.

If the inspection is going to turn up problems, you may want to know which problems. Then you are better prepared for the negotiations. Know and acknowledge the problems first so that you don't lose any negotiating power. Plus, inspections often turn up little problems that are easy to fix. Buyers can get overwhelmed with all the stuff found in an inspection. "What? There's a crack in one of the windows!" You can sometimes fix the little stuff.

Deciding What Repairs to Make

As you review the repairs on your list, first decide which ones really need to be made. If you notice, for instance, that the roof needs to be repaired, you can choose to have it repaired and pay for the new roof. Or you may note that the roof needs to be repaired and then price the home accordingly. For example, if you do not have the money to have the roof repaired, you may want to use the second strategy—lower your selling price. In this case, you'll want to get estimates for the repair so that you can adjust the price accordingly. You should submit this estimate with your disclosure statement.

Be sure that your buyer knows that you have adjusted your price accordingly to take into account the roof problems. Or don't adjust the price, but be prepared to negotiate in consideration for the roof problems. Some buyers won't be bothered by problems if they can get the home for a good price. Also, the buyers will know that you are being up front about the problem if you acknowledge it right away instead of later when the problem turns up during inspection.

Do It Yourself or Hire Someone?

Once you decide the repair has to be made, the next decision is whether you are going to do it yourself or whether you need to hire someone. Some repairs are easy enough. For instance, most people can paint. Other repairs require a professional. If you need to rewire outlets, unless you are an electrician, you'll probably want to hire someone.

Be realistic when deciding what you can and cannot do. You may want to save money by doing the repairs yourself, but if you don't have the time or talent, hire someone. You'll save money in the long run.

Also, keep in mind that most people overestimate the costs for minor repairs; they may not be as bad as you think.

Real Deal

If you hire a contractor for repairs or remodeling, look for one who has experience, is insured, and has good references. Get *written* estimates of the work, and it's in your best interest to get a couple of estimates to compare. Don't pay more than 10 percent down when you sign the contract and pay with a check or money order, not cash.

Should You Remodel?

When you think about the repairs in your home, don't get carried away with remodeling. It's hard to recoup money on extensive remodeling and renovations. You may think that adding a deck will add a huge value to your home, but that's unlikely. (Kitchen remodeling is one thing that does add a great value.) It's better to leave the extensive remodeling to the buyer.

Real Deal

The most cost-effective improvements you could make are to the kitchen or bathroom. For instance, if you convert a one-bathroom home into a one-and-a-half bathroom home, you'll expand your market of possible buyers. In a recent report, major kitchen and bathroom improvements paid back at least 70 percent of their investment in the Midwest. You can find other remodeling information at www.remodeling.hw.net.

Also, you won't enjoy any of the benefits of the remodeling. You may have always dreamed of a greenhouse, so you add one in order to make the home more appealing. You won't ever get to enjoy the greenhouse, and the potential buyers might not share your enthusiasm for gardening.

It's also a mistake to think that you can make even more money by fixing up the home. There's probably a top price for a home with your home's type of amenities. You may get this top price, but you'll most likely not get more.

Real Deal

Hire professional cleaners to do the initial, thorough scrub-down. This will ensure that the home is in tip-top condition. If a home looks well-kept and clean, buyers are more apt to think it also has been well maintained.

You may want to consider making changes if you have eccentric decor. Most buyers are not very imaginative. They cannot look past the decor of the home. If they hate the red velvet wallpaper, they may ignore the home without realizing they can easily redo the wallpaper. If you have any out-of-the-ordinary decorating touches, you may want to make them more subdued.

Cleaning Up the Home

Does anyone really like to clean? Does anyone get up and think that they can't wait to tackle the grime in the oven today? I don't know anyone who actually enjoys cleaning, but there must be some people out there who do.

Cleaning is hard work, but it does give you a sense of satisfaction. When that oven sparkles, so do you. Cleaning your home in preparation for selling it is an ongoing process. First, you need to do a deep clean. Then you need to keep the home picked up so that when a potential buyer wants to stop by, you don't have to run around sweeping and dusting and mopping. This section covers the deep clean.

First Impressions Count—Clean Up the Outside

Start with the outside. Stand back on the curb and take a look at your home. What do you notice? Are the hedges neat? Is the lawn overgrown? What is the first impression of the home?

The first impression of the home makes a big impact on the buyers. (A University of Florida study found that homes with well-manicured lawns sold an average of 15 days faster. Curb appeal affects not only the speed of the sale, but also the sale price.) Even if the inside is their dream home, buyers are going to remember driving up and seeing fallen shutters and overgrown shrubs. They're going to remember trudging through the knee-high grass to get to the door—if they even get that far. Therefore, you should make the home look as inviting as possible from the outside.

Trim the hedges. Mow the lawn. Weed the walk. Plant flowers. Get rid of dead trees. Shovel the walk in the winter, rake the yard in the fall. Sweep the sidewalk. Clean up the street curb. Take down holiday lights (especially if it's no longer a holiday!). Fix the fence. Remove any visible junk piles. Put away bikes, lawn equipment, and other yard stuff.

Check the outside lights. Make sure they work and have new bulbs. Check that the path to the home is free of clutter and inviting.

Also repair any problems (such as a damaged roof) that you uncovered during your home inspection. Be sure to repaint ceilings damaged by a leaky roof.

Real Deal _____

You don't always have to spend a lot of money or time to make a big impact on the appearance of your home. Little things go a long way. Consider painting the front door, and cleaning the carpet in high traffic areas. Mulch your flower beds. Patch nail holes in the walls.

Real Deal _____

Flowers really make the outside of the home look inviting. If you're selling during the spring, plant flowers to make the yard look colorful and pleasant. You can plant them in the yard or in flowerboxes. Put down mulch. A pretty wreath on the door and a welcome mat are also nice touches.

Clean the Inside

Next put away your hedge trimmers and lawnmower and get your mop, broom, bucket, and other supplies. It's time to start on the inside. Start with one room, and clean it so that it passes the white-glove mother-in-law test. Don't just do your normal once-over with the feather duster; *really* clean. Scrub the cabinets, wash the baseboards, remove all the stuff from the shelves and dust them, and clean the walls. Don't forget the corners!

Shampoo the carpets or have them professionally cleaned. Wash the drapes. Clean the walls, floors, and ceilings. Every room should sparkle when you finish with it. Then move on to the next room, and the next room, and the next room.

Eliminating Clutter

When buyers walk into your home, you don't want them to be taken with your collection of Amish cross-stitch samplers. Yes, the samplers are beautiful, but the buyers aren't there to admire your possessions. Hopefully, they are there to buy the *home*.

What you want the buyers to think about when they tour the home is where they will put their furniture. You want the buyers to mentally move in. To do so, you need to do two things. First, you need to get rid of any clutter. Second, you need to depersonalize the home. The home shouldn't look "lived in."

Put Everything Away!

The kitchen is the worst clutter culprit. You may have all your appliances on the counter, baskets of stuff on the table, little Mikey's artwork on the refrigerator, cookbooks on the shelves, coupons on the windowsills. Get rid of all of it! Yep, put everything away. All surfaces should be clean and clear, including the kitchen desk, if you have one. Clutter makes the buyer think the home is too small and doesn't have enough storage. Reducing the clutter will make the home look cleaner and more spacious—more room for those buyers to move in their artwork, cookbooks, and appliances.

You should unclutter each and every room in the home. You may be blind to clutter, so have someone follow you to point out the clutter—for example, your agent or your mother-in-law. Also, unclutter places where clutter breeds—the basement, the attic, and closets.

Buyer Beware _____

Be sure to put your valuables someplace safe. Most of the time, the agent will escort any potential buyers through your home, but you won't want to leave money or jewelry out in the open.

You can't unclutter by shoving everything in a drawer or cabinet, because buyers like to peak in the drawers and cabinets. Therefore, for clutter you want to keep (old books, photo albums, baby clothes), pack it away neatly. If necessary, store it in a commercial storage area or a friend's home. You're going to have to pack anyway once you sell your home, so now's a good time to start.

You may also want to get rid of furniture, especially if you have a lot. Consider rearranging the furniture so that the areas are roomier. You want the home to look spacious.

Uncluttering the home and making it neat also makes the buyer think, "I'll bet they take really good care of this home. Look how all the tools are hung on that pegboard." A clean, uncluttered home gives the impression that the home and all its underpinnings are well cared for.

Undecorating the Home

Okay, you've gotten rid of the clutter. Almost. Now you need to be brutal. You need to declutter even more—get rid of things you may not think of as clutter. Remember that you want the buyer to focus on the home, not on the cute way you've decorated it. It may pain you to do so, but you should depersonalize the home as much as possible.

Put away your family photos; you want the buyers to imagine *their* family pictures on the mantel. Put away knickknacks and other collectibles. Remember, you aren't striving for a home that looks lived in, but one that looks *ready* to be lived in.

Collecting Home Information

The buyer will be interested not only in how the home looks, but also in the maintenance and upkeep of the home. Collect the following information for your potential buyers:

- **Property tax statements.** Know how much you pay for property tax as well as *when* you pay and *how* you pay. Buyers need to know the tax amount to figure it into their monthly payment. Knowing when you pay is important for prorating any prepaid amount. For example, if you have prepaid for the next six months and then sell the home, you may ask for a partial refund for the amount you have prepaid.

- **Utility bills.** The buyer will want to know approximately what it costs to heat the home, how much the electric bill runs, and what you pay for water and sewage. Collect a few months of utility bills and have this information available.

- **Warranties.** If you are leaving your appliances, collect all warranties for them. For example, if you have a new stove, the buyer will need the warranty information. You'll also want any warranties on repairs done on the home—for instance, if you redid the roof.

♦ **Maintenance information.** It's a good idea to keep a record of the maintenance you have done on the home. A record indicates to the buyers that you have kept track of the maintenance. For example, they may want to know when you had the heating system serviced, the chimney cleaned, and so on.

It's a good idea also to round up all keys to the house and mailbox as well as garage door openers.

Understanding Seller Disclosure

In the past, the rule of buying was *caveat emptor*—"let the buyer beware." If you bought a home and there were problems, you were stuck. Recently, the rule has changed to more of a *caveat venditor*—"let the seller beware."

Since 1984, most states have passed laws requiring the seller to tell the buyer about substantial defects that the seller knows about. Real estate agents back the laws because if there are problems, agents don't want the finger pointed at them. If it clearly points at the seller, the real estate agent is free and clear.

Do You Have to Disclose?

Whether you have to disclose depends on where you live. Most states require disclosure. In some states, legislation is pending or in review regarding disclosure. Check with your agent about seller disclosure laws in your state. In some cases, the buyer or real estate agent may ask you to disclose, even if the laws don't require it.

Buyer Beware

If a potential buyer or agent asks a direct question, you must answer truthfully or be subject to a lawsuit.

If disclosure is required, you should do so before the buyer makes an offer. You may want to include a disclosure form in your information sheets about your home.

What Must You Disclose?

Basically, you must disclose any physical defects that would change the buyer's assessment of the property value. Most states use a seller disclosure form, which covers the areas a seller must respond to. See the following Seller's Residential Real Estate Sales Disclosure form for an example.

This disclosure form covers water in the basement, mechanical systems, appliances, water supply, sewer system, roof, wood floors, structures, and other systems. In addition to these areas, you may also be required to disclose any environmental hazards—radon, lead, asbestos, urea-formaldehyde insulation, and so on.

Some states require that you disclose any potential problems in the area—for example, zoning changes or upcoming assessments.

New federal rules also require that you disclose any known presence of lead paint in the home. You can get more information on lead paint by calling the National Lead Information Center at 1-800-LEAD-FYI.

What about *stigmatized* properties? If the home is believed to be haunted, do you have to tell the buyer? If someone has been murdered on the property, do you have to tell the buyer? The answer depends on the state. Check with your agent or local state officials to find out what you are required to disclose.

Completing a Seller Disclosure Form

When you are completing a disclosure form, remember that you are not providing a warranty for the home. You are not saying the water heater won't break; you are saying it works now and you don't know of any problem. Also, you don't necessarily have to fix any problems; you just have to let the buyer know about any defects that could affect the home's value.

If there is a problem, be precise in describing it. For example, if the basement floods, how much does it flood and how often? If you don't know about a feature, say so. It's better to say "unknown" than to lie or guess about a feature.

If you want to be fully prepared for all problems, have the home inspected. An inspector can more easily spot problems. Also, an inspector puts another person in the blame circle. You can point your finger at the inspector if a problem turns up later on the home.

If you have any questions about what you have to disclose, you may want to consult an attorney.

SELLER'S RESIDENTIAL REAL ESTATE SALES DISCLOSURE
State Form 46234 (R/1293)

Date *(month, day, year)*

Seller states that the information contained in this Disclosure is correct to the best of Seller's CURRENT ACTUAL KNOWLEDGE as of the above date. The prospective buyer and the owner may wish to obtain professional advice or inspections of the property and provide for appropriate provisions in a contract between them concerning any advice, inspections, defects, or warranties obtained on the property. The representations in this form are the representations of the owner and are not the representations of the agent, if any. This information is for disclosure only and is not intended to be a part of any contract between the buyer and the owner. Indiana law (IC 24-4.6-2) generally requires sellers of 1-4 unit residential property to complete this form regarding the known physical condition of the property. An owner must complete and sign the disclosure form and submit the form to a prospective buyer before an offer is accepted for the sale of the real estate.

Property address *(number and street, city, state, ZIP code)*

8169 Ashwood Court Indianapolis, In. 46268

1. The following are in the conditions indicated:

A. APPLIANCES	None/Not Included	Defective	Not Defective	Do Not Know
Built-In Vacuum System	X			
Clothes Dryer	X			
Clothes Washer	X			
Dishwasher			X	
Disposal			X	
Freezer	X			
Gas Grill	X			
Hood			X	
Microwave Oven			X	
Oven			X	
Range			X	
Refrigerator	X			
Room Air Conditioner(s)	X			
Trash Compactor	X			
TV Antenna / Dish	X			

C. WATER & SEWER SYSTEM	None/Not Included	Defective	Not Defective	Do Not Know
Cistern	X			
Septic Field / Bed	X			
Hot Tub	X			
Plumbing			X	
Aerator System	X			
Sump Pump	X			
Irrigation Systems	X			
Water Heater / Electric			X	NEW '9.
Water Heater / Gas	X			
Water Heater / Solar	X			
Water Purifier	X			
Water Softener	X			
Well	X			
Other Sewer System *(Explain)*			CITY	

	Yes	No	Do Not Know
Are the improvements connected to a public water system?	X		
Are the improvements connected to a public sewer system?	X		
Are the improvements connected to a private / community water system?		X	
Are the improvements connected to a private / community sewer system?		X	

B. ELECTRICAL SYSTEM	None/Not Included	Defective	Not Defective	Do Not Know
Air Purifier	X			
Burglar Alarm	X			
Ceiling Fan(s)			X	
Garage Door Opener / Controls			X	
Inside Telephone Wiring and Blocks / Jacks			X	
Intercom	X			
Light Fixtures			X	
Sauna	X			
Smoke / Fire Alarm(s)			X	
Switches and Outlets			X	
Vent Fan(s)			X	
60 / 100 / (200) Amp Service (Circle one)			X	

D. HEATING & COOLING SYSTEM	None/Not Included	Defective	Not Defective	Do Not Know
Attic Fan	X			
Central Air Conditioning			X	
Hot Water Heat	X			
Furnace Heat / Gas	X			
Furnace Heat / Electric Ht Pump			X	
Solar House-Heating	X			
Woodburning Stove	X			
Fireplace	X			
Fireplace Insert	X			
Air Cleaner	X			
Humidifier	X			
Propane Tank	X			

NOTE: "Defect" means a condition that would have a significant adverse effect on the value of the property that would significantly impair the health or safety of future occupants of the property, or that if not repaired, removed or replaced would significantly shorten or adversely affect the expected normal life of the premises.

6-00/L-137

Sample disclosure form, page 1.

2. ROOF	YES	NO	DO NOT KNOW
Age. If known: ORIGINAL Years.	X		
Does the roof leak?		X	
Is there present damage to the roof?		X	
Is there more than one roof on the house?		X	
If so how many? _____ roofs.			

3. HAZARDOUS CONDITIONS	YES	NO	DO NOT KNOW
Are there any existing hazardous conditions on the property, such as methane gas, lead paint, radon gas in house or well, radioactive material, landfill, mineshaft, expansive soil, toxic materials, asbestos insulation or PCB's?		X	

4. OTHER DISCLOSURES	YES	NO	DO NOT KNOW
Do improvements have aluminum wiring?			X
Are there any foundation problems with the improvements?		X	
Are there any encroachments?		X	
Are there any violations of zoning, building codes or restrictive covenants?		X	
Is the present use a non-conforming use? Explain:		X	
Have you received any notices by any governmental or quasi-governmental agencies affecting this property?		X	
Are there any structural problems with the buildings?		X	
Have any substantial additions or alterations been made without a required building permit?		X	
Are there moisture and/or water problems in the basement or crawl space area?		X	
Is there any damage due to wind, flood, termites or rodents?		X	
Are the furnace / woodstove / chimney / flue all in working order?	X		
Is the property in a flood plain?		X	
Do you currently pay flood insurance?		X	
Does the property contain underground storage tank(s)?		X	
Is the seller a licensed real estate salesperson or broker?		X	
Is there any threatened or existing litigation regarding the property?		X	
Is the property subject to covenants, conditions and / or restrictions of a homeowner's association?		X	
Is the property located within one (1) nautical mile of an airport?		X	

E. ADDITIONAL COMMENTS AND / OR EXPLANATIONS: *(Use additional pages if necessary.)*

The information contained in this Disclosure has been furnished by the Seller, who certifies to the truth thereof, based on the Seller's CURRENT ACTUAL KNOWLEDGE. A disclosure form is not a warranty by the owner or the owner's agent, if any, and the disclosure form may not be used as a substitute for any inspections or warranties that the prospective buyer or owner may later obtain. At or before settlement, the owner is required to disclose any material change in the physical condition of the property or certify to the purchaser at settlement that the condition of the property is substantially the same as it was when the disclosure form was provided. Seller and Purchaser hereby acknowledge receipt of this Disclosure by signing below:

Signature of Seller	Date	Signature of Buyer	Date
Irma Seller			
Signature of Seller	Date	Signature of Buyer	Date
John Seller			

Sample disclosure form, page 2.

The Least You Need to Know

◆ Thoroughly examine every room and all major systems of your home, and note any problems. Check for any sale-killing problems, such as water in the basement, bad wiring, a damaged roof, or heating problems.

◆ If you are planning extensive remodeling, keep in mind that it's hard to recoup that money.

◆ Clean up the outside and the inside of your home. You want a clean, clutter-free home that looks bright and spacious.

◆ To prepare for the sale of your home, collect information on taxes, utilities, warranties, and maintenance.

◆ You may have to complete a seller disclosure form. You are required by law to tell the buyer of any known defects that would affect the value of your home.

Chapter 26

Pricing and Marketing the Home

In This Chapter

- ◆ Setting the listing price
- ◆ Deciding which terms to offer
- ◆ Figuring your net profit or loss
- ◆ Showing the buyer your home

Every year, there are approximately four million homes on the market. How many will sell? And how quickly will they sell? The answers to these questions depend on a lot of factors—the most important being the price. This chapter first covers how to set the listing price for your home and then the marketing techniques for getting buyers to your home.

Setting the Listing Price

It's easy to make a mistake when thinking about the price to ask for your home. As a seller, you want to get the highest price you can, but you also want to avoid the many pitfalls:

◆ **Pitfall 1.** Pricing the home as high as you can and worrying about lowering the price later. Mistake! When an agent and potential buyers see your overpriced home, they will most likely move on. By the time you wise up and set a more reasonable price, your home will have been on the market for a while. In this case, the property just sits, and the price is lowered and lowered and lowered until it finally sells. Buyers may think there is something wrong with the home, since it has been on the market for so long.

◆ **Pitfall 2.** Coming up with a reasonable price and setting the listing price there. Again, mistake. Most buyers *expect* to pay less than the asking price, except in very hot markets. You should leave room for negotiation.

◆ **Pitfall 3.** Determining the profit you need and setting the price accordingly. Another mistake. Of course, you should consider what you hope to gain from the sale. Doing so will enable you to plan for the next home you purchase. But you can only get for your home what someone is willing to pay. What you need and what you expect should not really factor into pricing the home.

Setting the price is a tricky balancing act. This chapter gives you some advice on setting the right price.

Studying Comparable Homes for Sale

The best way to find out what a home like yours is worth is to look at what similar homes have sold for in your area. It's key to compare like homes to like homes. The first determining factor is the area. You can't compare a home in one neighborhood to a similar home in a neighborhood across town. Remember: location, location, location.

Real Deal

Figure the percentage spread of the listing price and selling price to gain an understanding of the market. For instance, homes selling for 95 percent of the list price means the market is hot, 80 to 90 percent means the market is weak. The difference, or spread, may vary depending on the area.

The second determining factor is what the home has to offer—how many bedrooms, how many baths, how many other rooms (dining room, living room, family room), amenities (fireplace, hardwood floors, and so on). You may find some homes very similar to yours and some that are close.

Your agent's marketing report should contain a survey of homes that have recently sold or are currently on the market (called a comparable market analysis or CMA). The following table compares a seller's home to four comparable homes (or *comps*) in the area that have recently sold, and to four comparable homes in the area that are still on the market. Features compared in the analysis are number of stories; number of bedrooms; number of bathrooms; whether the home has a dining room (DR), front room (FR), fireplace (FP), air conditioning (A/C), basement (BSMT); the age of the home; and any of the following special features:

HF = Hardwood floors	NC = New carpet
NR = New roof	WD = Wood deck
NF = New furnace	PO = Porch
HO = Home office	PA = Patio

The table also shows the list date and price for the properties still listed, and the sales date and price for the properties sold.

Comparative Market Analysis

Address	Stories	Bdrm	Bath	DR	FR	FP	A/C	BSMT	AGE	Features
Your Property										
57 S. Riley	2	3	2	X	X	X	X	X	50	HF
Properties Sold										
55 S. Main	2	3	2	X	X	X	X	X	50	NR
79 N. Central	2	3	1.5	X	X	No	X	X	55	NF
77 S. New	1	3	2	X	X	X	X	No	40	HO
89 N. Greene	2	3	2	X	No	X	X	X	35	NC
Properties Now on Market										
89 N. Meridian	2	3	2	X	X	X	X	X	39	WD
45 N. Market	2	3	2	X	X	X	X	No	40	PO
64 W. 55th	1	3	1.5	X	X	X	X	No	40	PA
80 E. 55th	2	3	2.5	X	X	No	X	X	35	HF

Address	List Date	List Price	Sales Date	Sales Price
Properties Sold				
55 S. Main	Jul-03	$115,000	Aug-03	$110,400
79 N. Central	May-03	$112,000	Jul-03	$108,640
77 S. New	May-03	$113,000	Jul-03	$109,610
89 N. Greene	Jun-03	$116,000	Aug-03	$109,040

Comparative Market Analysis (continued)

Address	List Date	List Price	Sales Date	Sales Price
Properties Now on Market				
89 N. Meridian	Jul-03	$116,000		
45 N. Market	Aug-03	$115,000		
64 W. 55th	Aug-03	$113,000		
80 E. 55th	Sep-03	$112,000		

The report may also include listings that did not sell (called expired listings). Most commonly an expired listing did not sell because the price was too high.

Your agent is key in selecting the comparable homes. Ideally, you want an agent that has seen and is familiar with these comparable properties. The agent shouldn't rely just on data he or she has pulled together; firsthand knowledge of the house can make the difference.

Once you know what similar homes have sold for, you can compare your home and come up with a reasonable price. For instance, if one home has a little more to offer than your home, you may want to price your home a little under what that one sold for. Others will have less to offer, and you can price your home a little over what they sold for. This method helps price your home based on market data—what people are willing to pay.

Real Deal _____

When discussing the value of a home, you may hear the term "fair market value." This is the price that your home sells for on the market today, the price a buyer is willing to pay. Fair market value doesn't take into consideration how much you originally paid for the house or how much you need to make on the sale. It is what it is: the price you can get in the current market.

Looking at the list prices for homes that are currently on the market can be helpful, but keep in mind that these homes have not sold. The sales price could be significantly lower than the list price.

Getting an Appraisal

If you cannot come up with a listing price by looking at comparables, you may want to get an appraiser to help in setting the price. You can hire an independent appraiser for around $250 to $300 to provide you with a professional opinion on the market value of the home. The appraiser will study similar homes, look at your home, and come up with a value. You may especially want to get an appraisal if you and your agent are not in agreement on what the home is worth.

Getting the appraisal beforehand can help in another way. When a buyer applies for a loan, the lender is going to require an independent appraisal. If your home appraises for more than the asking price, the lender will not have any trouble approving the loan. If your home appraises for less, the lender may not give the buyer the loan for the entire amount. You may have to renegotiate the offer. It helps to find out what the home is worth *before* you start taking offers.

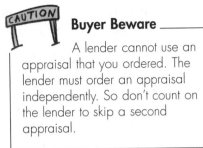

Buyer Beware

A lender cannot use an appraisal that you ordered. The lender must order an appraisal independently. So don't count on the lender to skip a second appraisal.

Make sure your appraiser knows that you are using the appraisal to come up with a selling price. Appraisers, hired by lenders, often simply make sure the house value is within the loan/selling price and don't go beyond that in appraising the value. Your appraiser should do a detailed check of your home, measuring rooms, inquiring about the heating, air conditioning, and other systems.

How the Market Affects Price

In a hot market, homes are in demand, and there are more buyers than sellers. What this means for you is that a buyer may be willing to overlook a few maintenance items, you may be able to get top price for your home, and your home may sell more quickly.

In a medium market, there are both a lot of buyers and a lot of sellers. In this market, you can expect to wait one to three months to sell your home, and the price and terms will be midrange. Because there are a lot of homes on the market, a buyer may use the condition of the home to make a decision. For example, if the buyer sees two similar homes, one in good condition and the other needing work, the buyer is likely to select the home in good condition.

In a cool market, there are a lot of sellers but not a lot of buyers. You are going to have to work on adding incentives to entice the few buyers out there.

Deciding What Else to Offer

In addition to deciding the listing price, consider what else you want to offer the buyer. If you are selling in a hot market, you may not have to offer incentives. If you are selling in a slow market, on the other hand, you may want to entice buyers by offering them something extra.

For example, you may agree to pay some of the closing costs. You may pay one point for the buyer or agree to pay other closing fees. If the home needs repairs, you may offer the seller a repair allowance to have the repairs done rather than do the repairs yourself. Or you may want to offer a redecorating allowance. For instance, you might offer $1,000 for new carpeting. Or you may want to purchase a home warranty (around $300 a year), which protects the major systems and appliances in the home. This warranty may make an older home more attractive to the buyer.

If you find a prospective buyer, but the buyer cannot get financing, you may want to help with financing. For example, you may want to buy down the mortgage rate or take back a mortgage. Creative financing choices such as these are covered in Chapter 15.

You should have a good idea of what you want to offer the buyer so that you are prepared for the costs involved in selling.

Figuring Your Net Proceeds

When you sell your home, you'll most likely be buying another home. Therefore, you need to plan financially for what you can afford on your new home. This may depend on your proceeds from the sale of your existing home.

For this reason, you should consider several scenarios to determine your net profit (or loss). Again, your agent should give you a Net Proceeds Statement as part of the market research (see the following Net Proceeds Statement table—it is the same as in Chapter 24, so it should look familiar.)

Consider different selling prices. Doing so may help you come up with the least amount you are willing to accept. Consider any repairs you must make. If you need a new roof, be sure to account for the expense. Know beforehand what other incentives you want to offer the buyer. For example, if you plan to offer help with the closing costs, be sure to include these costs in your net proceeds estimate.

Know the closing costs you'll be responsible for. The seller traditionally pays for some closing costs. For example, the seller usually pays for some part of the title search and/or insurance. You should get an estimate of the fees from your agent.

Taking a look at the financial aspect of the sale will help you evaluate the offers you receive. It gives you a game plan for negotiating.

Net Proceeds Statement

Property	55 N. Main Street		
Date	8/14/2003		
Prepared by	Agent Lewis		
Sales Price	**$115,000**	**$112,500**	**$110,000**
1st mortgage payoff	$85,000	$85,000	$85,000
2nd mortgage payoff	_____	_____	_____
Brokerage fee	$8,050	$7,875	$7,700
Title insurance	$400	$400	$400
Mortgage discount points	_____	_____	_____
Origination fee	_____	_____	_____
Deed and affidavit	$50	$50	$50
Document preparation	_____	_____	_____
Taxes	$249	$249	$249
Buyer's closing costs	_____	_____	_____
Closing fee	_____	_____	_____
Assessments	_____	_____	_____
Inspections	_____	_____	_____
Termite inspection	_____	_____	_____
Underwriting fee	_____	_____	_____
Tax Service fee	_____	_____	_____
Repairs	_____	_____	_____
Other	_____	_____	_____
Costs of selling	$8,749	$8,574	$8,399
Net at closing	**$21,251**	**$18,926**	**$16,601**

Marketing Your Home

If you sign with a listing agent, the agent should have provided a detailed marketing plan. Make sure this plan includes all of your ideas. If there's something additional you would like done, ask. If you are selling your home yourself, you are responsible for the marketing. In both cases, you can expect these general marketing plans:

◆ **Detailed home listing.** Your agent or you should prepare a detailed information sheet about the home, including the number and size of rooms, location and directions to the home, mortgage and tax information, description of the home and property, information about amenities, listing agent, and a picture. Some agents may use the plain old MLS listing (see Chapter 8); however, you may prefer to jazz up the presentation. You may also want to include other information such as tax rate, utility payments, and seller disclosure.

◆ **Advertisements.** You or your agent should also arrange for advertising the house. You may choose just to advertise when you have an open house. Or you may run an advertisement throughout the sale process. Ask your agent (preferably before you hire him or her) which advertisements are routinely done and which may cost extra. Some areas have local real estate TV shows that highlight houses for sale. Some areas publish big books listing homes for sale. Ask your agent about these additional advertising opportunities.

◆ **Online listings.** More and more homes are being listed on the Internet. Again, ask your agent whether this is standard or extra. Check out the broker's site to see the number and quality of homes listed. You may also want to go all out and provide a virtual tour of the home via the Internet. As another option, some brokers include a tour that you can listen to on a radio station or by calling a phone number.

◆ **Yard signage.** You need a sign in the yard that either you purchase (if you are a FSBO) or your agent provides. The number to call should be easy to spot. You may also include a box with information sheets so that passers-by can pick up a sheet.

◆ **Open houses.** You will also most likely schedule open houses. The next section "Showing Your Home" covers this aspect of marketing.

Showing Your Home

As part of the agent's services, he or she will arrange for showings. Or another agent may pull your listing from the MLS and arrange for a showing. This section covers the preparation for the showing—preparing the home and preparing yourself.

Scheduling a Showing

If you had to rush to unlock your house each time someone wanted to show it, you would quickly tire of running back and forth and back and forth. Usually the agent makes arrangements to make the home more convenient to show. For instance, the agent may put a lockbox on your front door with the keys inside. If another agent wants to visit the home, that agent calls your agent, who calls back to verify that the agent is really an agent and not some thief looking for a quick way into the home. Then your agent will tell the other agent the combination to the lockbox so that he or she can show the home.

If you don't use a lockbox, the agent will use another security measure for showing your home, but the idea is the same. Only agents can show the home.

Plan on having showings at the most inconvenient times. Just when you are sitting down to dinner. Just when you climb in the bath. You can always say no when your agent calls with a showing, but what if that person was *the* person to buy your home?

You can stay during the showing, but your presence may make the buyer uncomfortable, and you want the buyer to feel as comfortable as possible. For this reason, you'll probably spend a lot of time driving aimlessly around your neighborhood or sitting at some fast food restaurant for an hour or so.

Real Deal

While it may be inconvenient, it's usually best to try not to say no or to reschedule a showing. You want your home to be accessible, and if you refuse to make your home available, the buyer may just decide your home isn't worth the effort.

Also, if you have a dog, you may have to arrange for the dog to be locked up during the day for showings or take him with you during showings in the evenings.

Getting the Home Ready for a Showing

When you get the call for a showing, you need to get the home ready as quickly as possible. This is another hassle of having your home on the market; you have to keep it clean and tidy all the time.

Also, try to set the mood for the showing. For example, if it is winter, you may want to have a fire in the fireplace. You may want to simmer some potpourri so that the home smells nice. Bake some fresh bread or a pie. If the showing is during the day, open the windows and let the sunshine in. Turn on all the lights. You want the home to look bright and cheerful, not drab and dreary. Finally, put on some soft music.

Dealing with Criticism

After the potential buyers take a look through your home, their agent will most likely ask them what they thought about the home. Then their agent will call your agent and relay the news. "Loved the fireplace. Hated the small bathroom."

Be prepared to hear criticism. It's going to hurt, especially after you went to so much trouble, but you want to see the home through the buyers' eyes. If you have three buyers who say the carpeting in the living room is pathetic, you can do something about it.

Keep in mind that the buyers are going to critique the home, and they are going to nit-pick. You probably do too when you look at a home for sale. Don't take offense. Use the criticism as a basis for evaluating your home from the eyes of potential buyers.

Holding an Open House

In addition to showings, your agent may schedule open houses, traditionally on Sundays. You can think of an open house as one long showing with more browsers than buyers.

If you are thinking an open house is a surefire way to sell your home and you'll have rooms and rooms full of buyers, think again. A 1991 survey of the National Association of Realtors found that just 3 percent of homeowners found their homes through an open house. Most people who stop by don't even know the price of the home, so they may not even be qualified to buy the home. Sometimes an agent finds a buyer through an open house, but more often the agent finds new clients through an open house. Does that mean that you shouldn't have open houses? No.

Real Deal

Most real estate agents suggest holding an open house within one or two weeks after listing the home for sale. Avoid scheduling the open house on a holiday or if there is a conflict with a local event. For instance, in Indianapolis, the weekend of the Indianapolis 500 would not be a good weekend for an open house.

Open houses, even if they attract mostly lookers, do call attention to the home. The agent will advertise the open house in the paper and put up signs. If potential buyers are looking through the paper or driving by, they may notice your home.

Also, sometimes buyers feel more comfortable visiting an open house. They can scout the house pressure-free and if they are interested, schedule a more formal showing.

Your agent can also use an open house to gauge the interest in the house, pinpoint any weak areas, and evaluate the asking price. Also, even the lookers can be beneficial. Maybe they aren't in the market for a home, but they may know of someone who is. Word of mouth can't hurt. The more people who see your home, the better.

The Least You Need to Know

- The best way to figure your listing price is to study data on comparable sales in your area. Check the listing price and sales price of these homes. Also, see when they were listed and when they were sold to find out how long they were on the market.

- After you decide on your listing price, also think about the terms that you want to offer to the buyer. For example, will you help with loan discount points? You should have a good idea of what you'll pay for the buyer as well as what you'll be required to pay at closing.

- When you know the price and terms, you can come up with different scenarios that would work for you. Having a target bottom line will help you evaluate any offers you receive.

- Your agent will most likely market the home by entering the home information into the Multiple Listing Service, creating advertisements and flyers, arranging for showings, and holding open houses.

Chapter 27

Dealing with Purchase Offers

In This Chapter

- ◆ Dealing with other agents
- ◆ Evaluating an offer
- ◆ Making a counteroffer
- ◆ Accepting an offer
- ◆ Re-evaluating if you don't get any offers
- ◆ Helping buyers with financing

All the cleaning, repairing, decision-making, marketing, and so on that you've done has been with the explicit goal in mind of getting an offer on your home. All that work for one simple piece of paper that says "Yes! I want to buy your home." What should you expect when you receive an offer? How can you decide whether you should accept an offer? What happens if you don't get any offers? This chapter covers these questions and more.

Dealing with Other Agents

When you sign an agreement with an agent, the agent agrees to do his or her best to sell your home at the price you decided on. The agent is entirely responsible to you and has only your interests in mind. Remember that getting the best price is in the agent's best interests as well. The higher the price, the more the agent stands to earn on commission.

Real Deal

You should ask what type of agent the buyers have when you receive an offer. Depending on the type of agent, you can expect to receive different information from the agent.

The buyers will also most likely have an agent who represents them. In recent years, many buyers have elected to use a buyer's agent—an agent who represents the buyer and no one else. This agent is not required to pass along any confidential information and has only the buyers' interests in mind.

If the buyers don't use a buyer's agent but a subagent instead, that agent actually works for you. (Chapter 4 describes the types of agents in more detail.)

Although the subagent is helping the buyers, you are paying the bill, and therefore, the agent owes his or her loyalty to you. A subagent should pass along all information regarding offers. If buyers offer $100,000 but tell the agent they are willing to go to $105,000, the agent should let you know.

Evaluating an Offer

Before you even think about evaluating an offer, you should spend some time thinking about what you want from the sale of your home. You should have in mind several scenarios of both price and terms, as described in Chapter 26. What is the lowest price you find acceptable? Which terms are okay? Which terms are not okay? You should discuss the price and terms with your agent so that he or she knows what is acceptable and what isn't.

Knowing your bottom line can help you evaluate any offers you receive. You can compare the offers to your different scenarios to see how they match up.

When potential buyers want to make an offer, they will sit down with their agent and draw up a sales, or purchase, agreement. Usually the buyer's agent will contact your agent and convey the offer—generally in person, but sometimes on the phone. The buyer's agent will then give your agent the offer. You should accept only written offers accompanied by a check for earnest money. (See Chapter 17 for a sample purchase agreement.)

The buyers will most likely give you a time for responding to the offer (usually one or two days). During that time, you and your agent can evaluate the offer, as described next.

What an Offer Should Include

You can expect an offer to include the following:

- Address and legal description of the property (lot, block, and square recorded in government records).

- Names of the brokers involved.

- Price, down payment, loan amount, type of loan, and amount of deposit.

- A time limit for the response to the offer, for getting financing and closing on the home, and for moving in.

- Certain conditions, or *contingencies*, that must be met.

- Other provisions, such as what personal property is included; whether certain payments are prorated; how assumptions, damages, and other special circumstances are handled; and so on.

What Price and at What Terms?

The first thing you are going to want to know is *how much?* How much did the buyers offer? Unless you are in a really hot market, the buyers are most likely going to offer less than your asking price. Before you tear up the offer, though, look at how much less. Is the price close enough? Also, look at the terms of the contract. If the buyers offered less, did they give more on the terms?

Next, look at the money you have in hand—the deposit. How much of a deposit did the buyers put down? Is it sufficient? Does the deposit show that the buyers are serious about purchasing the home?

Also look at the down payment the buyers are offering. Is it sufficient? Does it show you that they have the funds to purchase the home? Ask your agent if the buyers are well qualified.

Checking the Contingencies

Look through any contingencies the buyers have included in the contract. A contingency makes the sale conditional on something else. For instance, the buyers will most likely make the sale contingent on being able to get financing.

As you look through the contingencies, ask yourself whether they are acceptable. Are they reasonable? For example, a financing contingency is pretty common and pretty reasonable.

Look also at the limits of the contingencies and note how they are removed. For instance, yes, the buyers have to have financing, but if they don't specify how long they have to get financing or specify outrageous terms, the contingency may not be acceptable.

Commonly, the sale is contingent on the buyers getting financing. You should be sure the buyers specify a time frame in which to apply for the loan. Also, you will want to know whether the buyers are likely to qualify for a loan—their agent or yours should prequalify them. Remember that you can prequalify informally and get a ballpark figure. Be sure you know whether the buyers are truly *preapproved*. Buyers who are preapproved have submitted all the financial paperwork and details and are assured of getting the loan. You don't have to worry about formally preapproved buyers having trouble with the financing. Also, you should make sure you know when the buyers obtain financing, as well as what happens if they don't get financing.

The sale is often contingent on a satisfactory inspection. The buyers usually want a thorough inspection of your home. If you did your job in preparing the home, you should know where the problems are. Make sure that the buyers have a certain time frame in which to have the home inspected, that you get a copy of the report, and that they use an independent inspector.

The sale may also be contingent on the buyers selling their home. This contingency should give you serious pause. Do you really want to tie up your home sale with the sale of an unknown home? If you agree to this contingency, you may want to ask your agent to evaluate the buyers' current home at the price listed. Is it listed now? Is it priced reasonably? Is it in good condition? Is it likely to sell? You may also want to include some protection for yourself in case the home doesn't sell. For example, you may want to keep the home on the market and give the buyers the right of first refusal. If you get another offer during that time, the first buyers can remove the contingency and buy the home, or they can withdraw their offer, and you can accept the new offer.

Checking the Time Limits

The contract should specify certain time limits. For example, you want the buyers to commit to applying for a loan and having the home inspected within a certain time frame.

Real Deal

In a seller's market, you may be bombarded with multiple offers. Lucky you! In this case, you should consider each offer carefully and pick the one that most closely matches your needs. You want to look closely at the price offered, the type of financing the buyers have, and when they want to move in. For instance, suppose that you have not purchased your new home. You may want to choose the offer from the newlyweds since they might be able to delay moving in. Or suppose that you have an offer from a preapproved buyer vs. someone that hasn't started the financial qualification process. Obviously, the preapproved offer should be given more consideration.

Your agent should help you evaluate the offers. It's best to only have one counteroffer out at a time. Also, don't make the mistake of sitting on a good offer just to see if you can get something better.

In addition, the buyers will want you to respond to the offer by a certain time and to be out of the home within a certain time. The buyers may specify a settlement date (when you close) and an occupancy date (when they move in). Be sure these dates are acceptable. For instance, will you be able to move out by the date specified?

Real Deal

If you can't move out by the date specified and the buyers aren't in a hurry to move in, you may be able to make arrangements for a rental agreement. You sell the home to the buyers but then rent from them for a few months until you can move out. Some buyers will agree to this arrangement. This option may also help you time the sale of your current home and the purchase of your new home.

Making a Counteroffer

After evaluating an offer, you have three options. You can say, "Yes! We'll take it." In this case, see the next section, "Accepting an Offer."

Real Deal

Don't be too hasty in rejecting offers—especially if your home has not been on the market long. You may think, *Wow! I already have an offer. I won't take this one; I'll just wait until a better one comes along.* That better offer may not come along. Consider each offer carefully. You don't want to end up five months later wishing that you would have taken or at least countered that first offer.

You can say, "No! Forget it." In this case, you may want to reconsider. Sometimes buyers like to dangle the worm a little bit to see if you will bite. Even if the offer isn't close to what you want, you may want to consider returning the offer with some changes.

This brings up your third option. When you consider the offer but want to make some modifications, you make a *counteroffer*. Making a counteroffer is like saying, "Not this, but how about this?" You may want to up the price or change the terms. Whatever changes you make, your agent will help you complete the counteroffer. You may make changes directly on the original offer or submit a new offer. Refer to the sample counteroffer in Chapter 18 to see what a counteroffer looks like.

Be sure to spell out all the changes you want to make. If you neglect to mention something, the buyers will assume you found it acceptable. If you are unsure, write in your conditions again.

Your agent will relay any counteroffers back to the buyers' agent, who will relay the offer to the buyers. The buyers can accept the offer or counter again.

Real Deal

If you are close on the deal, you may not want to push it. Consider taking the deal and being satisfied. Any time you make a counteroffer, you give the potential buyers the opportunity to walk away. The better the offer is, the more you risk losing that offer when you make a counteroffer.

Accepting an Offer

You have an accepted offer when both parties sign the same agreement. That is, when you accept the buyers' original offer or a counteroffer made by them. Or when the buyers accept your counteroffer.

Congratulations! You've sold your home. You should get a copy of the accepted offer and prepare for the final step—the closing. This topic is discussed in Chapter 28.

What to Do If You Don't Get Any Offers

You are sitting in your home patiently waiting and waiting and waiting. What if you don't get any nibbles? What if your home has been on the market, but not one person has made an offer? When you aren't getting any offers, you should evaluate the situation to find out where the problem lies. Ask yourself the following questions:

◆ **Have you given yourself enough time?** If you don't have an offer in the first week, it's not time to give up. Selling a home takes time—it can take several months or more, depending on the current market. You should ask yourself whether you are being overly anxious, whether you have given it enough time, and perhaps whether another problem exists.

◆ **Has the home gotten enough exposure?** That is, are people coming to see it? Have you had a lot of showings? How many? How many calls? How many open houses? Were the open houses well attended? Buyers can't buy the home unless they know it is for sale. If you haven't had buyers looking, you can't expect to have buyers buying. If this is the problem, you may want to discuss with your agent what else can be done. Has the agent done enough advertising? Held enough open houses? If you are selling your home yourself, you may want to re-evaluate your marketing plan. If you haven't had much luck, you may consider listing the home with an agent.

◆ **What is the current market like?** Is it hot, warm, lukewarm, cool, cold, frosty? Real estate professionals like to use a lot of hot/cold and hard/soft terms to describe the market. For a seller, hot is good, cold is bad. Many things can determine the current market. For example, what are the interest rates? If the rates are sky high, buyers may be unable to afford a home. If you are selling in a cool or cold market, you may want to wait for better market conditions. If you can't wait, you may want to offer additional incentives for the buyer, such as help with financing.

Real Deal

To get a good idea of the market, read the real estate section of your paper and also visit some websites devoted to real estate. These sources can provide you with a good overview of current market conditions. Also, note general economy factors such as the unemployment rate, stock market prices, and other financial indicators.

◆ **What is your neighborhood like?** Remember, location is the most important factor in determining the desirability of a home. If you live in a war zone, you may have a hard time selling your home. There's not much you can do about a bad neighborhood. You can try to improve the neighborhood, which is most likely not going to happen overnight. Or you can lower the price.

◆ **What is the condition of the home?** Go back to Chapter 25 and look through your assessment of the condition of the home. Does the home have curb appeal (look good from the street)? What problems do you see? Ask the opinions of others. For instance, you should be getting feedback from the showings. Why weren't the buyers interested? You may also want to get a professional opinion from an inspector. If the condition of your home is the problem, you may want to make improvements or lower the price.

◆ **Is the price too high?** If you have had a few offers, what price was offered? If you are getting offers, but at a much lower price, you may need to lower the

price. Also get feedback from your showings. What did potential buyers say about the price? What does your agent think about the price? If you are having serious concerns about the price, you may want to have an appraisal done.

♦ **What terms are you offering (or not offering)?** Is what you are offering reasonable? Do you need to add incentives to help the buyers? Is there a particular problem with this property that you need to address?

Should You Help with Financing?

When sellers can't sell their homes, many are tempted to consider seller financing. You as a seller might decide to help the buyer in a number of ways. You might buy down the mortgage or take back a second mortgage (basically, you loan the buyers the money). Alternative financing is covered in Chapter 15.

Before you agree to help with financing, consider the buyers' motivation. Why can't the buyers get a traditional loan? Do they have bad credit? Won't their income qualify for a loan? Don't they have the money for a down payment? There are usually good reasons why a lender won't lend to a buyer. Are you willing to do what a lender won't do?

In some cases, you may decide to help the buyer. For example, if interest rates are really high, it may be more difficult than usual to qualify for a loan. Or perhaps you want to sell to a couple that just graduated from college. They have good income potential but just don't have any money for a down payment now.

If you decide to help the buyers, you need to take several precautions. Lending money is risky. You should first check out the buyers. Do a thorough credit report. Get an explanation of any problems. If the buyers have a history of missed payments, are you sure you want to count on them to pay you back, even if they do seem really nice?

Make sure the buyers are committed to the property. For example, if you take out a second mortgage on the home for the buyers, you may want to insist on a big down payment. It's also a good idea to keep the loan at a short term. Make sure you are not giving your money away. Insist on a fair interest rate.

Finally, consider the worst-case scenario. What if the buyers skip town to Tupelo, Mississippi, with four months' worth of overdue payments? Can you get your missing payments? How do you foreclose on a property? What is the cost of foreclosure?

The Least You Need to Know

- ◆ Your agent represents your interests. The buyers will also most likely be working with an agent. If the buyers use a buyer's agent, the agent represents only the interest of the buyers. If the buyers use a subagent, that agent actually works for you and should pass along all information about the price and terms that the buyers are willing to accept.

- ◆ When you receive an offer, you most often jump at the price offered. Before doing so, make sure you look over any contingencies or terms included in the contract carefully. Make sure that any contingencies are reasonable, acceptable, and limited.

- ◆ You do not have to accept a buyer's first offer. You may want to counter with your own offer. Countering continues until one party walks away or until the deal is signed by both parties. Be careful not to haggle over frivolous terms.

- ◆ If you aren't getting any offers on your home, evaluate whether you have given it enough time and whether the home has had enough exposure. Take a look at the market conditions, the condition of your home, the price, and the terms to see whether you can pinpoint the problem.

- ◆ In a tough market, you may want to offer the buyer help with financing. Be careful! Seller financing is risky. Be sure to get a thorough credit check on the buyers and have your attorney review or draft an agreement. Get at least the going market rate for interest and try to keep the term of the loan short. Know the consequences of the worst-case scenario.

Handling the Closing: Seller's Perspective

In This Chapter

◆ Knowing what to expect at closing

◆ Realizing what you have to do before closing

◆ Handling problems that come up

◆ Understanding the tax implications of selling your home

◆ Moving out of your home

After months and months of waiting to sell your home, you may get an acceptable offer and then want to know, "Where's my money?" Money is handled at the closing. At this time, you hand over the deed and keys to your property, and the buyers hand over the check.

This doesn't usually occur the day after the offer; it requires some preparation time for both you and the buyers. This chapter explains how to get ready for closing, what happens at closing, and what happens after closing.

Knowing What to Expect at Closing

If you own a home, you most likely attended the closing. To refresh your memory, this section gives you a brief overview of the closing process.

The term *closing* refers to the final step in the process of selling or buying a home. At this point, documents are signed and money is exchanged. You may hear closing referred to as *settlement*. It doesn't matter what it's called—the function is the same.

Usually the closing is attended by the buyers and their entourage (agent, attorney, lender) and you and your entourage (agent, attorney, psychic advisor, whoever). A closing agent orchestrates the event.

The closing may be held at the title company, attorney's office, escrow company, lending institution, or county courthouse, depending on local custom. And finally, the closing is scheduled after the buyers obtain financing, have a loan commitment, and have met all other obligations. Your agent should let you know the precise time and place for the closing. If you sold your home yourself, you'll already know the time and location.

Both the buyer and seller have certain tasks to accomplish, covered in the next section.

Most of the preclosing work falls to the buyers. The buyers usually have to obtain financing, get insurance, and meet any other requirements of the lender. The buyers will also schedule a home inspection sometime before closing. (Chapter 21 gives you an overview of the closing from the buyer's point of view.)

Real Deal _____

If you are buying *and* selling a home, expect to attend two closings. In the best scenarios, you close on the home you sold first and then close on the home you purchased.

Buyer Beware _____

As the seller, you should make sure the buyers are moving along with their to-do list. For example, you don't want to find out 60 days after the offer that they haven't applied for a loan. If there are problems, you will want to know about them as soon as possible—especially problems that can make the deal fall through. You and your agent should keep yourselves informed about the buyers' progress.

What You Have to Do

In addition to checking up on the buyers, you will have some responsibilities to meet. This section explains what you will have to do before closing.

Handling Termites and Other Critters

You may need to have a termite inspection done on the home. A termite inspection is usually the responsibility of the seller for FHA and VA loans. Lenders won't approve a loan until the inspection is done, so you will need to schedule the inspection. At the closing, you should bring the inspection report. If you have termites, you will have to have the home treated.

Checking the Chain of Ownership

You will need to have a title search done on the home. A title search traces the ownership of the property from you to the previous owner to the previous owner to the previous owner and so on. You will be required to pay for this search.

The purpose of the title search is to uncover any claims to your property. For example, if your great-great-grandpappy and great-great-uncle Elmer once owned the property jointly, but your grandpappy took over the property when Uncle Elmer was at war, Uncle Elmer and clan may have a claim to the property.

Handling title problems is covered in the section "Handling Problems with Closing" later in this chapter.

Buyer Beware _____

If you don't pay your bills, someone may be able to put a lien, or claim, against your property. Even a lien for a small amount is enough to prevent your home from being sold.

Bet You Didn't Know

A title search and title insurance protects buyers from any secret or hidden deals that pertain to the property such as forgeries or a married person selling the home as if he or she were single.

Handling the transfer of land ownership is older than our country and is based on an English system. Originally, if you purchased a property, you received an abstract, basically a list of everyone (heirs, birthright, and so on) who had an interest in the property, all the way back to the treaty with the Indians. Title insurance prevents someone with a previous interest in claiming the property.

Collecting Documents

At the closing, you should expect to bring a copy of the sales contract, with documentation showing that any contingencies have been removed and any conditions have been met. For example, if a termite inspection is required, you have to show the original termite inspection report. The title company usually asks for this when the title work is ordered, so you may not have to bring it again.

Bring receipts of paid utilities and taxes. The buyers won't want to pay your water bill for the past month. You may be required to show documentation of paid utilities. You should also bring in receipts as proof that repairs required by the buyers were made.

Also bring any information on your current loan. You should know the mortgage balance and the date to which you have paid. The money you receive from the buyers isn't going directly into your pocket. You will most likely be paying off the loan on the home. The escrow officer will ensure the payment of your current loan. The title company will order the payoff as of the date of closing.

Hiring a Closing Orchestrator

What if you closed on the home but forgot to pay off your existing loan? What if you sold the home, but the deed wasn't transferred to the buyers' name? What if the buyers assumed the mortgage, but no one recorded the transaction? You'd be in hot water, that's what. To make sure everything is done, and done in the proper order, you set up an escrow account and let the escrow agent or attorney do the orchestrating.

An escrow agent (also called a *closing agent*) is a third party who handles the title to the property, collects the buyers' money, and concludes the sale. Your agent will probably recommend an escrow company. You may use the buyers' escrow company, or you can select an escrow company yourself.

The escrow agent or company starts by collecting the sales agreement. This agreement is the blueprint for the proceedings. The escrow agent will use the agreement to prepare a list of instructions for you and the buyers, basically assigning you your homework. The buyers should know what they have to do, and you should know what you have to do.

Real Deal

Comparison shop for escrow companies, and compare the fees charged. Also, the agent's franchise may own an escrow company. You don't have to use the agent's company, and if the agent is affiliated with a company, he or she must disclose that.

At the closing, the escrow agent collects all the necessary documents and prepares the documents for signatures. If you have to sign a million pieces of paper, glare at the escrow agent. He's the paper pusher in the deal.

The escrow agent is also the money handler. He will calculate all figures and tell you who pays what—the total deposit amount, the down payment, the closing costs. The escrow agent will collect the money due from the sale and then hold the money in a trust account until the sale is final (usually when the deed is recorded, which is also done by the escrow agent).

Finally, the escrow agent will *disburse* (a fancy word for *hand out*) the money. The escrow agent should take care of paying off your current loan and then pay you your remaining *equity* (what's left over after your loan is paid off).

Handling Problems with Closing

Most problems will crop up *before* closing and will have to be dealt with before you can close. Think about hurdles popping up throughout a race course. The number of hurdles you have to jump will depend on your situation. Here are some common hurdles:

- **Holdups in the loan process.** If the lender doesn't approve the loan, the buyers cannot buy the home. For this reason, you will want progress reports on the loan application. If a problem occurs, you will want to know how serious it is. Is the process just delayed? Is the process held up by something you must do? Or have the buyers been denied?

- **Problems with the appraisal.** Before approving the loan, the lender will require an independent appraisal. Usually a lender will approve a loan for a certain percentage of the appraised value—for instance, 80 percent. If your appraisal comes in a lot lower than the selling price, you may have problems. Either the buyers are going to have to come up with more money, or you are going to have to lower the price. If the buyers made the sale contingent on an appraisal, they hold the upper hand.

- **Problems with the inspection.** If the inspection report turns up problems, and if the buyers have a contingency in the contract for a successful inspection, you have to mediate the problems. The buyers may ask you to make certain repairs or to renegotiate the price. Your agent can help you deal with any problems with the inspection. You can refuse to make the repairs and kill the deal, but you should realize that you are most likely going to be asked to make the same repair with the next buyers' offer.

Real Deal _____

When you are considering offers, remember that buyers who have been formally preapproved already have a commitment for a loan within a certain range. With this type of buyer, you won't have as many financial snags.

Real Deal

Sometimes you can appeal the appraisal. Your agent can help you research the market and document why your home is worth a certain amount. Ask your agent for help.

◆ **Repairs required for loan approval.** Even if the buyers say it's okay to skip some repairs, the lender may require certain repairs. FHA and VA loans, for example, require the appraisal to reflect the property value subject to certain minimum requirements. You have to make the repairs, or FHA or VA won't underwrite the loan.

◆ **Problems with the title.** If the title search turns up problems, you have to clear them up before the closing. You can pay off a lien if you have a bad debt, or you can get the person with the claim to sign a release. If the claim is in error, you must have it corrected.

The details of the agreement are spelled out in the contract, so you shouldn't hear any surprises at closing. If you do, you can refer to the agreements. If disputes do pop up, they usually pertain to the deposit, condition of property, or definition of personal property. Check the contract. If you can't come to an agreement, you may want to agree to mediation. A third party hears both sides and then makes a ruling. Some contracts will spell out how disputes are to be handled.

What Happens at Closing

At the closing, the buyers sign their loan agreements, and you sign over the deed. You also go over the final reckoning of closing costs. The closing costs you are expected to pay will vary depending on the local custom, the lender, and what you have agreed to in the sales agreement. For instance, in most areas, the seller traditionally pays for the title search and possibly part of the title insurance. The lender will charge different fees for processing the loan. Usually the buyers pay loan fees, but if you agreed to pay for part of the fees in the sales agreement, you may pay some of the buyers' closing costs.

Fees You Can Expect to Pay at Closing

Here are some of the fees you, as the seller, may be expected to pay:

◆ **Commission.** You are responsible for the commission fee charged by your agent. This fee should be agreed upon as part of the listing agreement. A common fee is 6 percent of the selling price.

- **Points.** A *point* is a fee associated with the loan and is 1 percent of the loan amount. For example, if the loan amount is $100,000, one point totals $1,000. You may have, as part of the sales agreement, agreed to pay points for the buyer. A similar fee is the loan origination fee, charged by the lender to process the loan. Again, if you agreed to it, you'll have to pay this fee.

- **Processing fees.** The lender will charge various fees for processing the loan. These fees may include a mail or delivery fee, a document preparation fee, an underwriting fee, and other fees. Which fees end up in your column depends on your agreement.

- **Title search and insurance.** You may be charged a fee to perform a title search. Depending on how the title is secured, you may also be charged other examination and binder fees. You may also pay all or part of the title insurance.

- **Attorney.** If you have hired an attorney, you will be responsible for the attorney's fees.

- **Taxes.** You may owe money for tax *prorations*.

- **Express mail.** To pay off your loan, you may use an express mail service. You pay interest daily, so you can save money if you get the payment there as quickly as possible.

Real Deal _____

You should get the figures and check them before closing. Your agent is experienced with the closing details, but you should check over the figures to ensure that they are correct.

Real Estate Terms _____

A **proration** is a division of bill or payment. For example, suppose that you pay your taxes in arrears (you pay backward). In the six-month tax period, you will live in the home three of those months, so you should have to pay for those months. To come up with how much you have to pay, the escrow agent takes the total payment, divides it by six (the number of months) and then multiplies it by the number of months you are responsible for (three). Proration varies by area.

The HUD-1 Statement—My Column or Yours?

At the closing, you will receive the HUD-1 statement, which on the front side lists the names and addresses of those involved (buyer, seller, lender, settlement agent).

A. SETTLEMENT STATEMENT	U.S. DEPARTMENT OF HOUSING AND URBAN DEVELOPMENT

ENTERPRISE TITLE
8440 Woodfield Crossing, #100
Indianapolis, IN 46240

OMB No. 2502-0265

B. TYPE OF LOAN

1. ☐ FHA	2. ☐ FmHA	3. ☒ CONV.UNINS.	6. File Number:	7. Loan Number:	8. Mortgage Insurance Case Number:
4. ☐ VA	5. ☐ CONV.INS.				

C. NOTE: This form is furnished to give you a statement of actual settlement costs. Amounts paid to and by the settlement agent are shown. Items marked "(p.o.c)" were paid outside the closing; they are shown here for informational purposes and are not included in the totals.

D. NAME AND ADDRESS OF BORROWER:	E. NAME AND ADDRESS OF SELLER/TAX I.D.No.:	F. NAME AND ADDRESS OF LENDER:

G. PROPERTY LOCATION:	H. SETTLEMENT AGENT:
	Enterprise Title Services of Indiana Inc.

	PLACE OF SETTLEMENT:	I. SETTLEMENT DATE:
	8440 Woodfield Crossing, #100 Indianapolis, IN 46240	07/18/00

J. SUMMARY OF BORROWER'S TRANSACTION		K. SUMMARY OF SELLER'S TRANSACTION	
100. GROSS AMOUNT DUE FROM BORROWER:		**400. GROSS AMOUNT DUE TO SELLER:**	
101. Contract Sales Price	124,900.00	401. Contract Sales Price	124,900.00
102. Personal property		402. Personal property	
103. Settlement charges to borrower (line 1400)	1,462.78	403.	
104.		404.	
105.		405.	
Adjustments for items paid by seller in advance		Adjustments for items paid by seller in advance	
106. City/town taxes to		406. City/town taxes to	
107. County taxes to		407. County taxes to	
108. Assessments to		408. Assessments to	
109.		409.	
110.		410.	
111.		411.	
112.		412.	
120. GROSS AMOUNT DUE FROM BORROWER	126,362.78	**420. GROSS AMOUNT DUE TO SELLER**	124,900.00
200. AMOUNTS PAID BY OR IN BEHALF OF BORROWER:		**500. REDUCTIONS IN AMOUNT DUE TO SELLER:**	
201. Deposit or earnest money	1,000.00	501. Excess deposit (see instructions)	
202. Principal amount of new loan(s)	91,900.00	502. Settlement charges to seller (line 1400)	9,339.00
203. Existing loan(s) taken subject to		503. Existing loan(s) taken subject to	
204. CUSTOMER DEPOSIT	1,319.00	504. Payoff of first mortgage loan 1st IND	80,209.43
205.		505. Payoff of second mortgage loan	
206.		506.	
207.		507.	
208.		508.	
209.		509.	
Adjustments for items unpaid by seller		Adjustments for items unpaid by seller	
210. City/town taxes to		510. City/town taxes to	
211. County taxes to		511. County taxes to	
212. Assessments to		512. Assessments to	
213.		513.	
214. NOVEMBER 1994 TAXES	630.65	514. NOVEMBER 1994 TAXES	630.65
215.		515.	
216.		516.	
217.		517.	
218.		518.	
219.		519.	
220. TOTAL PAID BY/FOR BORROWER	94,849.65	**520. TOTAL REDUCTION AMOUNT DUE SELLER**	90,179.08
300. CASH AT SETTLEMENT FROM/TO BORROWER		**600. CASH AT SETTLEMENT TO/FROM SELLER**	
301. Gross amount due from borrower (line 120)	126,362.78	601. Gross amount due to seller (line 420)	124,900.00
302. Less amounts paid by/for borrower (line 220)	94,849.65	602. Less reductions in amount due seller (line 520)	90,179.08
303. CASH (☒ FROM) (☐ TO) BORROWER	31,513.13	**603. CASH (☒ TO) (☐ FROM) SELLER**	34,720.92

Previous edition is obsolete.

HUD-1 (8-87)
RESPA, HB 4305.2

The front side of the HUD-1 statement.

-2-

L. SETTLEMENT CHARGES		PAID FROM BORROWER'S FUNDS AT SETTLEMENT	PAID FROM SELLER'S FUNDS AT SETTLEMENT
700. TOTAL SALES/BROKER'S COMMISSION			
based on price $ 124,900.00 @ 7.00 %= 8,743.00			
Division of Commission (line 700) as follows:			
701. $ 4,371.50 to			
702. $ 4,371.50 to			8,743.00
703. Commission paid at Settlement			
704.			
800. ITEMS PAYABLE IN CONNECTION WITH LOAN			
801. Loan Origination Fee %			
802. Loan Discount %			
803. Appraisal Fee to		275.00	
804. Credit Report to		108.00	
805. Lenders Inspection Fee			
806. Mortgage Insurance Application Fee to			
807. Assumption Fee			
808. PROCESSING FEE		125.00	
809. TAX/INS. VERIFICATIO		90.00	
810.			
811. MORTGAGE BROKERAGE FEE 1838.00			
900. ITEMS REQUIRED BY LENDER TO BE PAID IN ADVANCE			
901. Interest from 07/18/00 to 08/01/00 @$ 20.771918 /day		290.78	
902. Mortgage Insurance Premium for months to			
903. Hazard Insurance Premium for 1 years to STANDARD MUTUAL $321.00			
904. Flood Insurance Premium for years to			
905.			
1000. RESERVES DEPOSITED WITH LENDER			
1001. Hazard Insurance months @$ per month			
1002. Mortgage Insurance months @$ per month			
1003. City property taxes months @$ per month			
1004. County property taxes months @$ per month			
1005. Annual assessments months @$ per month			
1006. Flood insurance months @$ per month			
1007. months @$ per month			
1008. months @$ per month			
1100. TITLE CHARGES			
1101. Settlement or closing fee to ENTERPRISE TITLE		240.00	
1102. Abstract or title search to			
1103. Title examination to			
1104. Title insurance binder to			
1105. Document preparation to			
1106. Notary fees to			
1107. Attorney's fees to MICHAEL J. CURRY			35.00
(includes above items numbers:)			
1108. Title insurance to ENTERPRISE TITLE		95.00	550.00
(includes above items numbers:)			
1109. Lender's coverage $ 124,900.00 95.00			
1110. Owner's coverage $ 91,900.00 550.00			
1111. EXPRESS/PO ENTERPRISE TITLE			11.00
1112.			
1113.			
1200. GOVERNMENT RECORDING AND TRANSFER CHARGES			
1201. Recording fees: Deed $ 7.00 Mortgage $ 16.00 Releases $		23.00	
1202. City/county tax stamps: Deed $:Mortgage $			
1203. State tax/stamps: Deed $:Mortgage $			
1204. DISCLOSURE FEE MARION COUNTY AUDITOR		5.00	
1205. MORTGAGE EXEMPTION MARION COUNTY AUDITOR		1.00	
1300. ADDITIONAL SETTLEMENT CHARGES			
1301. Survey to HAHN & ASSOCIATES		110.00	
1302. Pest inspection to			
1303.			
1304. SETTLEMENT TO NBDMC		100.00	
1305.			
1400. TOTAL SETTLEMENT CHARGES (enter on lines 103,Sect J and 502, Sect K)		1,462.78	9,339.00

I have carefully reviewed the HUD-1 Settlement Statement and to the best of my knowledge and belief it is a true and accurate statement of all receipts and disbursements made on my account or by me in this transaction. I further certify that I have received a copy of the HUD-1 Settlement Statement.

_____   _____
Marion E. Ayers   Marion L. Bugh

Borrowers Elizabeth Ayers Lathrop   Sellers Martha O. Bugh

The HUD-1 Settlement Statement which I have prepared is a true and accurate account of this transaction. I have caused or will cause the funds to be disbursed in accordance with this statement.

07/18/00
_____
Settlement Agent Sarah Gregory   Date

Warning: It is a crime to knowingly make false statements to the United States on this or any similar form. Penalties upon conviction can include a fine and imprisonment. For details see: Title 18 U.S. Code Section 1001 and Section 1010.

The reverse side of the HUD-1 statement.

Buyer Beware

If you note any discrepancies, don't sign the document. Signing means that you agree with the document. It is difficult to get agreements changed after you sign. You may want to bring your attorney to review the documents.

The left side shows the amount due from the borrower or buyer. This amount is calculated by taking the sales price, adding the closing costs, and subtracting the earnest money and any other credits, such as taxes.

The right side of the form tallies up what money is due to you. This total is calculated by taking the sales price and subtracting the closing costs you owe.

The back side of the form details the closing costs. In the first section, you see a description of the closing costs with two columns. If you are responsible for the fee, the fee appears in your column. On the other hand, if the buyers are responsible, the fee goes into their column. The bottom of the form totals the closing costs for the buyers and you. You may see the abbreviation *POC* on the settlement statement. POC stands for *paid outside of closing*. That means that the fee was charged, but it was paid before the closing.

Sign on the Dotted Line

You will be required to sign several documents at the closing. Before you sign, make sure the information is correct. Is the commission correct? Is the proration correct? Title insurance and escrow charges correct?

You will also sign the deed transmitting the property to the buyers. Then you turn over all your housekeys, mailbox keys, and garage door openers to the buyers. After the deed is delivered, you will receive the check for your proceeds.

Tax Implications for Home Sales

The IRS likes to know when you make money, because when you do, it wants part of it. Fortunately, the tax laws are a little more lenient for homeowners. You'll want to check the most recent laws for the amount of profit that you can receive tax-free on the sale of your principal residence. There are no age restrictions, and you do not have to roll over the proceeds of a home sale into a new home of equal or greater value to avoid paying a tax.

Real Deal

For the most current information about the tax implications of selling your home, visit the IRS website at www.irs.gov.

Keep in mind that tax laws change every year. When you sell your home, be sure to check with your accountant or attorney to make sure you understand the current requirements.

Reporting the Sale of Your Home

In the year that you sell, you are required to report the sale using one of those easy-to-understand IRS forms. You must fill in the basis (your home's value for tax purposes) of your home, sales price of the home you sold, and sales price of the home you purchased. The next section explains how to calculate your basis.

You should keep track of the costs you paid at closing on both the home you are selling and the home you are buying. You should also keep records of any improvements you made to your existing home. This total affects your basis. It's a good idea to use an accountant for any year in which you buy or sell a home.

Figuring the Tax Basis

Figuring the tax basis is a four-step process:

1. Find the adjusted basis on the home you are selling using the following equation:

   Purchase Price + Costs associated with Purchase + Cost of Improvements = Adjusted Basis

   Not all closing costs can be included. For example, you may not be able to include tax prorations, insurance, and some points.

2. Calculate the adjusted sale price of the home you are buying using the following equation:

   Sale Price – Costs associated with Sale = Adjusted Sale Price

3. Determine the gain on the sale using this formula:

   Adjusted Sale Price (from step 2) – Adjusted Basis (from step 1) = Gain

4. Calculate the adjusted basis on your next home—that is, how much you are rolling over:

   Purchase Price – Costs associated with Purchase – Deferred Gain (from step 3) = Adjusted Basis for New Home

Notice that the rollover decreases the tax basis. That has nothing to do with what your home is *worth*. You want a lower tax basis, because that means you owe less in taxes. The following table illustrates how to use the preceding steps to figure your tax basis.

Calculating Your Tax Basis

Step	Amount	Description
1	$80,000	Price you paid for current home
	+ $5,000	Costs associated with purchase
	+ $7,000	Improvements
	= $92,000	Adjusted basis
2	$120,000	Sales price for current home
	− $10,000	Costs associated with sale
	= $110,000	Adjusted sales price
3	$110,000	Adjusted sales price
	− $92,000	Adjusted basis
	= $18,000	Gain
4	$180,000	Purchase price of new home
	− $6,000	Costs associated with purchase
	− $18,000	Deferred gain
	= $156,000	Adjusted basis of new home

Moving Out!

When it's time to move out, you may have mixed emotions. You've sold your home, possibly made a profit, and may be moving on to another home. This makes you happy. On the other hand, you may really have enjoyed your old home and have many good memories wrapped up in it. Just keep in mind that you will make new memories in your next home.

Real Deal

Use the opportunity of packing to get rid of items you no longer need. Don't take everything with you. You may want to have a garage sale or donate items to charity. Packing or unpacking is also a good time to take inventory of your possessions.

To prepare to move, contact the utility companies. Ask for a final reading so that you know what you owe for the bills. Also, have the buyers call at the same time to have the utilities transferred to their name. Buyers sometimes must make a cash deposit.

Fill out change-of-address cards, and make any other arrangements for the move. For instance, you may hire a moving company. (Chapter 21 provides some advice on moving.)

Welcome the new buyers. The sellers of our first home left a bottle of wine with a nice note in the refrigerator. This was a pleasant surprise and made my husband and me really feel welcome in the home.

Start a home file. In this file, keep all the documents pertaining to the sale of your home. You will need this information when you file your tax returns.

The Least You Need to Know

- The buyers and their agent attend the closing. The buyers' attorney and lender may also attend. On your side, you and your agent will attend, as well as your attorney, if you want. The closing agent is the neutral third party who handles the proceedings.

- The closing may be held at a title company, lending institution, escrow office, attorney's office, or someplace else, depending on local custom. Your agent will let you know the time and place of the closing.

- Buyers have certain responsibilities to meet before closing, including securing a loan, getting insurance, and having the home inspected. You also have certain things to arrange: a termite inspection, title search, and the preparation of certain documents (deed, utility bills, loan payoff).

- Problems with the loan, appraisal, title, or inspection must be handled before the closing.

- The HUD-1 statement lists all closing costs as well as who pays them. What you have to pay depends on local custom, charges incurred, and your sales agreement.

Glossary

80-10-10 loan   A combination of an 80 percent loan-to-value first mortgage, a 10 percent down payment, and a 10 percent home equity loan. It can also be a combination of 80-15-5. This method eliminates the need for private mortgage insurance. For expensive homes, it can eliminate the need for a jumbo mortgage by reducing the first mortgage to a conventional mortgage.

acre   An area of land equal to 43,560 square feet.

adjustable-rate mortgage (ARM)   A type of mortgage in which the interest rate is keyed to a certain economic index and is adjusted as the index rises and falls. If you have this type of mortgage, your monthly payment could go up or down, depending on the prevailing rates.

agent   A person authorized to work on another's behalf—for instance, a person authorized to sell or buy a house on your behalf.

amortization   The process of paying off a loan balance. As you make payments, a certain amount is applied to the principal and a certain amount to the interest. The *schedule* or *table of amortization* shows the declining balance as you make payments.

annual percentage rate (APR)   The true rate of interest for a loan. This rate includes the cost of any points paid, mortgage insurance, and other fees.

appraisal   An estimate of the value of a certain property by a qualified, independent individual.

appraised value   An opinion of a property's fair market value, based on an appraiser's inspection and analysis of the property.

appreciation   Changes in market conditions, or improvements to the property that increase the value of the property.

assessed value   The public tax assessor value of a property as determined for the purpose of taxation (usually lower than your appraised value).

association fee   *See* homeowners association (HOA).

assumable mortgage   A type of purchase in which the buyer assumes the responsibility of making payments on the seller's home.

back-end ratio   A borrower's other debts, such as auto loans and credit cards, figured into the debt-to-income ratio.

balloon mortgage   A type of mortgage in which the loan amount is amortized over the full length of the loan (usually thirty years), but the loan actually comes due after a few years (usually five or seven). The first payments go mostly toward interest. The balance of the loan is due in one final installment called the balloon payment.

basic policy   A homeowners insurance policy that covers certain perils such as fire and water damage. Also called HO-1.

basis points   Relates to changes in the interest rate for your home. If an interest rate changes 50 basis points, for example, it has moved ½ of 1 percent.

broker   An agent who is authorized to open and run his or her own agency. All real estate offices have one principal broker.

buydown   A type of financing in which a developer or seller arranges for the buyer to get a loan at a rate below the current market rate. The developer or seller pays interest costs in order to lower the interest rate, but usually raises the price of the house to recoup this loss.

buyer's agent   An agent hired by buyers to help them find and negotiate the purchase of a home. This agent works for the best interests of the buyers, not the sellers.

cap   A limit on an adjustable-rate mortgage. Depending on the ARM, the loan may have a cap on how much the interest rate can increase, for instance.

CCRs   *See* covenants and restrictions.

closing   The process of finalizing all the dealings associated with the sale and purchase of a home. Also called the *settlement*.

closing costs   Expenses incurred by buyers and sellers in transferring ownership of a property.

commission   The fee an agent earns for the sale of a home—usually a percentage of the selling price.

commitment letter   A formal offer of a loan by a lender. The letter states the terms under which the lender has agreed to the loan.

comparable market analysis   A report created by your agent that surveys homes that have recently sold or are on the market. The report includes "comps" or comparable homes.

comparables or "comps"   Recently sold properties that are similar in size, location, and amenities to the home for sale. These properties help an appraiser determine the fair market value of a property.

comprehensive insurance   The most expensive type of homeowners insurance; covers the most potential damages.

condominium   A form of home ownership in which the owner owns the airspace within the walls but doesn't own the actual walls, ceilings, or floors of the home. The owner may also own a percentage of the common areas, such as the swimming pool.

contingency   A provision included in a sales contract stating that certain events must occur or certain conditions must be met before the contract is valid.

conventional mortgage   A type of mortgage made by banks and other lending institutions that is not insured by the *Federal Housing Administration* (*FHA*), *Farmers Home Administration* (*FmHA*), or *Veterans' Administration* (*VA*).

convertible ARM   An *adjustable-rate mortgage* (*ARM*) that can be converted to a fixed-rate mortgage under certain conditions.

cooperative (co-op)   A form of home ownership in which you own shares in a corporation. In return for the purchase of shares, you are allowed to live in a unit in the co-op building.

counteroffer   An offer made by one party that makes changes to the original or latest offer of the other party. A counteroffer can be made by the seller or the buyer.

covenants and restrictions   Rules and regulations in effect for a community that control what types of changes and additions you can make to your home or condo. Also referred to as CCRs (community covenants and restrictions).

credit report   A report of all your debt information compiled by an independent agency. The credit report shows all outstanding debt as well as a record of payment on outstanding debts.

debt-to-income ratio   The percentage of a person's monthly earnings used to pay off all debt obligations. Lenders consider two ratios, constructed in slightly different ways: the *front-end-ratio* and the *back-end ratio*. Lenders usually take both ratios into account and set an acceptable ratio, which might be expressed as 33/39. Some lenders, and some lending qualifying agencies such as FHA, take only the back-end ratio into account.

deed   The legal document that conveys the title to a property.

default   To fail to make payments on a loan.

depreciation   A decline in the value of property because of poor location, dilapidation, or other factors; the opposite of *appreciation*.

developer   A company or person that markets, builds, and sells new homes.

discount points   A type of point (1 percent of a loan) paid by the borrower to reduce the interest rate.

down payment   The money you pay up front for the purchase of a home.

earnest money   A deposit you make when you make an offer on a house.

easement   A right given by the landowner to use the property. For example, you may have easements on your property for phone lines, utility poles, and so on.

equity   The financial interest or cash value of your home, minus the current loan balance(s). If you are selling the home, this would also be minus any costs incurred in selling the home.

escrow   A trust account created by a neutral third party to hold money for the seller or buyer. When you put down a deposit on a house, for example, you should put that money into an escrow account. When the sale is complete, the money can be released from this account to the seller. You also should set up an escrow account for your taxes and insurance. Your monthly mortgage payment includes payment for $\frac{1}{12}$ of your taxes and insurance. This money is kept in an escrow account. When the bill comes due, your mortgage company uses the escrow money to pay it.

Fannie Mae   Name used for the Federal National Mortgage Association, which is a government-chartered, nonbank, financial services company and the nation's largest source of financing for home mortgages.

FHA (Federal Housing Authority) mortgage   The government guarantees Federal Housing Authority loans. You can put down a smaller down payment on an FHA loan, but you will also be required to pay mortgage insurance.

FICO score   A number between 300 and 800 (above 600 being good) that creditors use to rate your credit.

fixed-rate mortgage   A type of mortgage in which the interest rate is fixed for the life of the loan.

fizz-bo   *See* FSBO.

flood insurance   Insurance that compensates for physical property damage resulting from rising water. This insurance is required for properties located in federally designated flood areas.

foreclosure   The legal process by which a mortgage property is seized and sold because of default.

Freddie Mac   Name for Federal Home Loan Mortgage Corp., which is a financial corporation chartered by the federal government to buy pools of mortgages from lenders and sell securities backed by these mortgages.

front-end ratio   The ratio of the borrower's monthly housing expenses—including principal, interest, property taxes, and insurance (PITI)—compared to the borrower's gross, pretax monthly income.

FSBO   "For sale by owner"; pronounced *fizz-bo*. A home offered for sale without the use of an agent.

gated community   A community of homes where you must pass through a security gate in order to enter the community.

gift letter   If an individual gives you money for a down payment as a gift, that person must write you a gift letter so that it can be included in your loan documentation.

Ginnie Mae   Name for the *Government National Mortgage Association* (*GNMA*), which is a government-owned corporation within the U.S. Department of *Housing and Urban Development* (*HUD*).

Good Faith Estimate   A lender must give a prospective homebuyer a written estimate of closing costs within three days of submitting a mortgage loan application. It is a good idea to request this estimate before choosing a lender so that you can compare lenders' fees.

gross income   The amount of income you earn before paying your expenses.

hazard insurance   Insurance coverage that compensates for physical damage to a property from natural disasters such as fire or other hazards. Depending on where a piece of property is located, lenders may also require flood insurance or policies covering windstorms (hurricanes) or earthquakes.

home warranty   A guarantee for certain features of a new home—for instance, the materials and workmanship, the main components of the house, and so on.

homeowners association (HOA)   A nonprofit association that manages the common areas of a condominium or *planned unit development* (*PUD*). Unit owners pay a fee to the association in order to maintain areas such as a pool or playground that are owned jointly.

homeowners insurance   An insurance policy that combines personal liability insurance and hazard insurance coverage for a residence and its contents.

housing ratio   The ratio of your housing payment (principal, interest, taxes, and insurance) to your monthly gross income. Lenders use this ratio to qualify you for a loan. Sometimes this ratio is called the *front-end ratio*. A common housing ratio is 28 percent.

index   An economic indicator used to set the rate for adjustable-rate mortgages.

inspection   A close and thorough examination of a house and property. A licensed individual usually does the inspection.

interest rate   The percentage the lender charges you for borrowing money.

investment property   A property you purchase with the intention of using it as rental income or for investment purposes rather than to live in.

joint tenancy   An equal, undivided ownership in a property by two or more individuals.

jumbo mortgages   Mortgages larger than the limits set by Fannie Mae and Freddie Mac ($252,700 for the year 2000; $379,050 in Alaska and Hawaii). A jumbo mortgage carries a higher interest rate than a conventional mortgage. *See also* 80-10-10 loan.

lease purchase mortgage   A financing option that allows potential homebuyers to lease a property with the option to buy. Often constructed so the monthly rent payment covers the owner's first mortgage payment, plus an additional amount as a savings deposit to accumulate cash for a down payment. Sellers may agree to a lease purchase option if the housing market is saturated and they are having difficulty selling the property.

lien   A claim against a property.

lifetime rate cap   In an adjustable-rate mortgage (ARM), this cap limits the amount the interest rate can increase or decrease over the life of the loan.

loan origination fee   A fee charged by the lender—usually 1 percent of the loan amount.

lock in   To guarantee a certain interest rate for a certain period of time.

loan-to-value (LTV) ratio   Used by lenders to state how much you have financed. If you put down 20 percent on a purchase, you finance 80 percent and have an 80 percent LTV.

maintenance fee   A fee charged by condominium associations, co-ops, or other homeowners associations for the upkeep of the property.

mortgage   A legal document that pledges your property as security (like collateral) for a loan.

mortgage banker   A company that originates mortgages and sells them to a secondary market.

mortgage broker   An intermediary who ensures a loan between a borrower and lender. The broker takes the loan and packages it for the lender.

mortgage insurance premium (MIP)   A policy that insures the lender against loss if the homeowner defaults on a mortgage. Depending on the loan, the insurance can be issued by a government agency such as the FHA or a private company. The MIP is part of the monthly mortgage payment. *See also* private mortgage insurance (PMI).

mortgagee   The lender.

mortgagor   The borrower.

Multiple Listing Service (MLS)   A computerized listing of the homes for sale in an area listed with a Realtor. Agents are granted access to the MLS and can use it to find a house in a particular price range or area.

negative amortization   A type of loan situation that occurs when the monthly payments do not cover the principal or interest. Instead of declining, the balance on the loan actually increases.

net income   The amount of income you earn after you pay your expenses.

origination fee   A fee paid to a lender for processing a loan application.

overall debt ratio   The ratio of your overall debt (housing payments plus any other long-term debt) to your monthly gross income. Lenders use this ratio—sometimes called the *back-end ratio*—to see whether you qualify for a loan. Common overall debt ratios are 33 or 36 percent.

PITI   Principal, interest, taxes, and insurance—the total monthly payment you make on a house.

point   One point is equal to 1 percent of a loan amount. Lenders charge points in exchange for lowering the interest rate.

preapproved   Meeting with a lender and providing all the necessary financial details to get preapproved for a loan. When you are preapproved, you have a definite commitment from a lender. Compare this to *prequalify*.

prequalify   Meeting or talking with a lender informally, providing the lender with your financial information, and having the lender qualify you for a loan for a certain amount. When you are prequalified, the lender gives you an estimate but does not formally commit to giving you a loan. Compare this to *preapproved*.

principal   The amount of money borrowed and still owed on a loan not including the interest.

private mortgage insurance (PMI)   Insurance that protects mortgage lenders against default on loans by providing a way for mortgage companies to recoup the costs of foreclosure. PMI is usually required if the down payment is less than 20 percent of the sale price. Homebuyers pay for the coverage in monthly installments. PMI is usually terminated when the homebuyer has built up 20 percent equity in the property.

proprietary lease   A lease used for co-ops that gives the share owners the right to live in a particular unit.

proration   The division of certain fees. If the sellers have paid for taxes six months in advance, for example, they may want a portion of that payment back for the months you are living in the house.

qualifying ratio   The percentages a lender compares to see whether you qualify for a loan. *See* overall debt ratio and housing ratio.

quit claim deed   A formal document that denies a claim to certain property often used to clear problems with a title or as part of a divorce settlement.

rate lock   A commitment issued by a lender to a homebuyer or to the mortgage broker guaranteeing a specific interest rate for a specified amount of time.

Realtor   An agent or agency that belongs to the local or state board of Realtors and is affiliated with the *National Association of Realtors* (*NAR*).

refinance   To obtain a new loan in order to pay off the existing mortgage or to gain access to the existing equity in the home.

Real Estate Settlement Procedures Act (RESPA)   This act requires the lender to disclose certain information about a loan, including the estimated closing costs and APR.

sales contract   The contract you draw up when you want to make an offer on a home. Sometimes called the *purchase agreement*.

second mortgage   A type of mortgage on property that has a lien already on the first mortgage. This mortgage is usually on the remaining equity (sometimes over that amount) in the home.

seller disclosure   A form required by most states; the seller uses this form to disclose any known defects of the home.

seller takeback   A type of financing in which the seller arranges for the financing on a property.

settlement sheet   The collection of information necessary to prepare escrow instructions, including the property description, parties involved, escrow information, sale price, your loan information, and the buyers' loan information.

subagent   An agent who works with you to purchase a house but is paid by the seller. Compare with *buyer's agent.*

subdivision   A piece of land divided into several plots on which homes are built.

subprime mortgage   A mortgage granted to a borrower who is considered *subprime*—that is, a person with a less-than-perfect credit report. Subprime borrowers have missed payments on a debt or have been late with payments. Lenders charge a higher interest rate to compensate for potential losses from customers who may run into trouble or default.

survey   An examination of a property's boundaries to determine the quantity of land, location of improvements, and other information. Usually, the surveyor creates a map or drawing of the legal boundaries of the property.

term   The length of a loan.

title   The right of property ownership.

title insurance   Insurance that protects the lender and buyer against any losses incurred from disputes over the title of a property.

title search   The process of reviewing court records and other records to ensure that there are no liens or claims against the property you are buying.

tract home   A type of new home that is standardized to minimize the cost of materials and labor. Also called "production homes."

Treasury index   An index used to determine interest-rate changes for certain adjustable-rate mortgages (ARMs). This index is based on the results of auctions the U.S. Treasury holds for its Treasury bills and securities or is derived from the U.S. Treasury's daily yield curve, which is based on the closing market bid yields on actively traded Treasury securities in the over-the-counter market.

underwriting   The process of evaluating a loan to determine whether the loan is a good risk.

VA loan   A type of loan available to veterans and guaranteed by the Department of Veterans' Affairs.

wraparound mortgage   A new mortgage that includes the remaining balance on an old mortgage, plus a new amount.

zoning   Laws that establish how a property can be used and what codes must be followed when erecting new buildings.

Resources

Phone Numbers and Addresses

Organization	Resource
American Society of Appraisers 555 Herndon Parkway Suite 125 Herndon, VA 20170 1-800-272-8258 703-478-2228 703-742-8171 (fax) www.appraisers.org	Gives you a referral for an appraisal. The association requires two years of experience, and member appraisers must pass exams in their specialty.
American Society of Home Inspectors 932 Lee Street Suite 101 Des Plaines, IL 60016-6546 1-800-743-2744	Provides a list of ASHI-certified inspectors.
Capital Pacific Mortgage 4625 S. Lakeshore Drive Tempe, AZ 85282 480-820-1169 mtglend@concentric.net	Provides answers to your mortgage questions.

continues

Phone Numbers and Addresses (continued)

Organization	Resource
Comprehensive Loss Underwriting Exchange 527-2600 choicetrust.com	Provides a report on (866) prior insurance claims of a home.
Equifax P.O. Box 740241 Atlanta, GA 30374 1-800-997-2493 www.equifax.com	Provides a copy of your credit report, for a fee.
Experian P.O. Box 2350 Chatsworth, CA 91313 1-800-392-1122 www.experian.com	Provides a copy of your credit report, for a fee.
Fannie Mae Customer Education 3900 Wisconsin Avenue, NW Washington, D.C. 20016 1-800-732-6643 www.fanniemae.com	Provides free consumer information on buying a home.
Federal Housing Administration Washington, D.C. 20410 www.hud.gov/fha	Provides information about FHA programs.
Freddie Mac Information www.freddiemac.com	Numerous office locations and numbers are available online for direct contact. In addition, you can send feedback via e-mail with comments and questions.
Ginnie Mae Contact Information Government National Mortgage Association 451 Seventh Street, SW Washington, D.C. 20410-9000 www.ginniemae.gov	Numerous phone numbers are available online for direct contact. In addition, you can send feedback via e-mail with comments and questions.
HSH Associates 1200 Route 23 Butler, NJ 07405 1-800-873-2837 www.hsh.com	Provides a mortgage kit and other mortgage information for homebuyers.

Organization	Resource
National Association of Housing Cooperatives 1401 New York Avenue, NW Suite 1100 Washington, D.C. 20005-2160 202-737-0797 www.coophousing.com	Provides and promotes housing co-ops.
National Cooperative Bank 1401 Eye Street, NW, Suite 700 Washington, D.C. 20005 1-800-955-9622 202-336-7700 www.ncb.com	Provides loans and other financial services for co-ops.
Rural Housing Service U.S. Department of Agriculture Washington, D.C. 20250 www.rurdev.usda.gov/rhs/index.html	Provides information about loans.
Trans Union P.O. Box 2000 Chester, PA 19022 1-800-888-4213 www.transunion.com/consumer	Provides a copy of your credit report, for a fee.
U.S. Department of Housing and Urban Development Customer Service Center PO Box 23699 Washington, D.C. 2020026 1-800-697-6967 www.hud.gov	Publishes a free book on fair housing (your rights). Also provides information about FHA loans and MMI/MIP cancellation.
Veterans' Administration 810 Vermont Avenue, NW Washington, D.C. 20420 www.homeloans.va.gov	Provides information on VA loans.

Online Resources

Organization	Resource
American Builders Network www.americanbuilders.com	Helps you find a new home and lists information on HUD-approved warranty companies.
Appraisal Institute www.appraisalinstitute.com	Provides information on appraisals.
Bankrate www.bankrate.com	Lists companies that specialize in risky creditors.
Co-Op home page www.cooperative.org/housing.cfm	Provides information on co-op housing.
Cyberhomes www.cyberhomes.com	Lists homes for sale.
FSBO.com www.fsbo.com	Lists homes for sale by owner.
The Hartford www.thehartford.com	Provides information on home insurance and other financial planning topics.
Homebuilder www.homebuilder.com	Lists communities and new homebuilders, depending on where you are looking to purchase a new home.
Homebuyer's Fair www.homefair.com/home	Publishes information on buying a home. Offers many helpful "exhibits," including a salary calculator, moving calculator, and relocation wizard.
HomeGain www.homegain.com	Lists homes for sale.
Insure.com www.insure.com	Offers quotes for home, auto, life, and other insurance types from more than 300 different sources.
The International Real Estate Directory www.ired.com	Promotes itself as "The single source for independent real estate information on the web."
Keystroke Financial Network www.keystrokenet.com	Provides information on financing a home.
LendingTree www.lendingtree.com	Provides quotes from several loan sources.

Organization	Resource
Mortgage Market Information Services www.interest.com	Provides information on mortgage rates.
National Association of Realtors (NAR) www.realtor.com	Provides home listings as well as information about buying and selling homes.
NewHome Search newhomesearch.com	Helps locate new homes for sale.
Prudential www.prudential.com	Provides information on financing.
Select Lenders www.selectlenders.com	Provide loan quotes from various lenders.
State Farm Insurance www.statefarm.com	Publishes information on insurance, including home owners insurance.

Loan Payment Tables

You can use the following table to find the principal and interest payment on a given loan amount. First, find the amount financed (along the left column), and then find the appropriate interest rate (along the top of the page).

Keep in mind that your mortgage payment will include principal and interest along with taxes and insurance. Your actual monthly payment will be higher. This table just figures the principal and interest amount.

Amount Financed	Interest Rate							
	5.75%	6.0%	6.25%	6.5%	6.75%	7.0%	7.25%	7.5%
$ 40,000	233	240	246	253	259	266	273	280
$ 45,000	263	270	277	284	292	299	307	315
$ 50,000	292	300	308	316	324	333	341	350
$ 55,000	321	330	339	348	357	366	375	385
$ 60,000	350	360	369	379	389	399	409	420
$ 65,000	379	390	400	411	422	432	443	454
$ 70,000	409	420	431	442	454	466	478	489
$ 75,000	438	450	462	474	486	499	512	524
$ 80,000	467	480	493	506	519	532	546	559
$ 85,000	496	510	523	537	551	566	580	594
$ 90,000	525	540	554	569	584	599	614	629
$ 95,000	554	570	585	600	616	632	648	664
$ 100,000	584	600	616	632	649	665	682	699
$ 105,000	613	630	647	664	681	699	716	734
$ 110,000	642	660	677	695	713	732	750	769
$ 115,000	671	689	708	727	746	765	785	804
$ 120,000	700	719	739	758	778	798	819	839
$ 125,000	729	749	770	790	811	832	853	874
$ 130,000	759	779	800	822	843	865	887	909
$ 135,000	788	809	831	853	876	898	921	944
$ 140,000	817	839	862	885	908	931	955	979
$ 145,000	846	869	893	916	940	965	989	1,014
$ 150,000	875	899	924	948	973	998	1,023	1,049
$ 155,000	905	929	954	980	1,005	1,031	1,057	1,084
$ 160,000	934	959	985	1,011	1,038	1,064	1,091	1,119
$ 165,000	963	989	1,016	1,043	1,070	1,098	1,126	1,154
$ 170,000	992	1,019	1,047	1,075	1,103	1,131	1,160	1,189
$ 175,000	1,021	1,049	1,078	1,106	1,135	1,164	1,194	1,224
$ 180,000	1,050	1,079	1,108	1,138	1,167	1,198	1,228	1,259
$ 185,000	1,080	1,109	1,139	1,169	1,200	1,231	1,262	1,294
$ 190,000	1,109	1,139	1,170	1,201	1,232	1,264	1,296	1,329
$ 195,000	1,138	1,169	1,201	1,233	1,265	1,297	1,330	1,363
$ 200,000	1,167	1,199	1,231	1,264	1,297	1,331	1,364	1,398
$ 205,000	1,196	1,229	1,262	1,296	1,330	1,364	1,398	1,433
$ 210,000	1,226	1,259	1,293	1,327	1,362	1,397	1,433	1,468
$ 215,000	1,255	1,289	1,324	1,359	1,394	1,430	1,467	1,503
$ 220,000	1,284	1,319	1,355	1,391	1,427	1,464	1,501	1,538
$ 225,000	1,313	1,349	1,385	1,422	1,459	1,497	1,535	1,573
$ 230,000	1,342	1,379	1,416	1,454	1,492	1,530	1,569	1,608
$ 235,000	1,371	1,409	1,447	1,485	1,524	1,563	1,603	1,643
$ 240,000	1,401	1,439	1,478	1,517	1,557	1,597	1,637	1,678
$ 245,000	1,430	1,469	1,509	1,549	1,589	1,630	1,671	1,713
$ 250,000	1,459	1,499	1,539	1,580	1,621	1,663	1,705	1,748
$ 255,000	1,488	1,529	1,570	1,612	1,654	1,697	1,740	1,783
$ 260,000	1,517	1,559	1,601	1,643	1,686	1,730	1,774	1,818
$ 265,000	1,546	1,589	1,632	1,675	1,719	1,763	1,808	1,853
$ 270,000	1,576	1,619	1,662	1,707	1,751	1,796	1,842	1,888

Amount Financed	Interest Rate							
	7.75%	8.0%	8.25%	8.5%	8.75%	9.0%	9.25%	9.5%
$ 40,000	287	294	301	308	315	322	329	336
$ 45,000	322	330	338	346	354	362	370	378
$ 50,000	358	367	376	384	393	402	411	420
$ 55,000	394	404	413	423	433	443	452	462
$ 60,000	430	440	451	461	472	483	494	505
$ 65,000	466	477	488	500	511	523	535	547
$ 70,000	501	514	526	538	551	563	576	589
$ 75,000	537	550	563	577	590	603	617	631
$ 80,000	573	587	601	615	629	644	658	673
$ 85,000	609	624	639	654	669	684	699	715
$ 90,000	645	660	676	692	708	724	740	757
$ 95,000	681	697	714	730	747	764	782	799
$ 100,000	716	734	751	769	787	805	823	841
$ 105,000	752	770	789	807	826	845	864	883
$ 110,000	788	807	826	846	865	885	905	925
$ 115,000	824	844	864	884	905	925	946	967
$ 120,000	860	881	902	923	944	966	987	1,009
$ 125,000	896	917	939	961	983	1,006	1,028	1,051
$ 130,000	931	954	977	1,000	1,023	1,046	1,069	1,093
$ 135,000	967	991	1,014	1,038	1,062	1,086	1,111	1,135
$ 140,000	1,003	1,027	1,052	1,076	1,101	1,126	1,152	1,177
$ 145,000	1,039	1,064	1,089	1,115	1,141	1,167	1,193	1,219
$ 150,000	1,075	1,101	1,127	1,153	1,180	1,207	1,234	1,261
$ 155,000	1,110	1,137	1,164	1,192	1,219	1,247	1,275	1,303
$ 160,000	1,146	1,174	1,202	1,230	1,259	1,287	1,316	1,345
$ 165,000	1,182	1,211	1,240	1,269	1,298	1,328	1,357	1,387
$ 170,000	1,218	1,247	1,277	1,307	1,337	1,368	1,399	1,429
$ 175,000	1,254	1,284	1,315	1,346	1,377	1,408	1,440	1,471
$ 180,000	1,290	1,321	1,352	1,384	1,416	1,448	1,481	1,514
$ 185,000	1,325	1,357	1,390	1,422	1,455	1,489	1,522	1,556
$ 190,000	1,361	1,394	1,427	1,461	1,495	1,529	1,563	1,598
$ 195,000	1,397	1,431	1,465	1,499	1,534	1,569	1,604	1,640
$ 200,000	1,433	1,468	1,503	1,538	1,573	1,609	1,645	1,682
$ 205,000	1,469	1,504	1,540	1,576	1,613	1,649	1,686	1,724
$ 210,000	1,504	1,541	1,578	1,615	1,652	1,690	1,728	1,766
$ 215,000	1,540	1,578	1,615	1,653	1,691	1,730	1,769	1,808
$ 220,000	1,576	1,614	1,653	1,692	1,731	1,770	1,810	1,850
$ 225,000	1,612	1,651	1,690	1,730	1,770	1,810	1,851	1,892
$ 230,000	1,648	1,688	1,728	1,769	1,809	1,851	1,892	1,934
$ 235,000	1,684	1,724	1,765	1,807	1,849	1,891	1,933	1,976
$ 240,000	1,719	1,761	1,803	1,845	1,888	1,931	1,974	2,018
$ 245,000	1,755	1,798	1,841	1,884	1,927	1,971	2,016	2,060
$ 250,000	1,791	1,834	1,878	1,922	1,967	2,012	2,057	2,102
$ 255,000	1,827	1,871	1,916	1,961	2,006	2,052	2,098	2,144
$ 260,000	1,863	1,908	1,953	1,999	2,045	2,092	2,139	2,186
$ 265,000	1,898	1,944	1,991	2,038	2,085	2,132	2,180	2,228
$ 270,000	1,934	1,981	2,028	2,076	2,124	2,172	2,221	2,270

Amount Financed	Interest Rate							
	9.75%	10.0%	10.25%	10.5%	10.75%	11.0%	11.25%	11.5%
$ 40,000	344	351	358	366	373	381	389	396
$ 45,000	387	395	403	412	420	429	437	446
$ 50,000	430	439	448	457	467	476	486	495
$ 55,000	473	483	493	503	513	524	534	545
$ 60,000	515	527	538	549	560	571	583	594
$ 65,000	558	570	582	595	607	619	631	644
$ 70,000	601	614	627	640	653	667	680	693
$ 75,000	644	658	672	686	700	714	728	743
$ 80,000	687	702	717	732	747	762	777	792
$ 85,000	730	746	762	778	793	809	826	842
$ 90,000	773	790	806	823	840	857	874	891
$ 95,000	816	834	851	869	887	905	923	941
$ 100,000	859	878	896	915	933	952	971	990
$ 105,000	902	921	941	960	980	1,000	1,020	1,040
$ 110,000	945	965	986	1,006	1,027	1,048	1,068	1,089
$ 115,000	988	1,009	1,031	1,052	1,074	1,095	1,117	1,139
$ 120,000	1,031	1,053	1,075	1,098	1,120	1,143	1,166	1,188
$ 125,000	1,074	1,097	1,120	1,143	1,167	1,190	1,214	1,238
$ 130,000	1,117	1,141	1,165	1,189	1,214	1,238	1,263	1,287
$ 135,000	1,160	1,185	1,210	1,235	1,260	1,286	1,311	1,337
$ 140,000	1,203	1,229	1,255	1,281	1,307	1,333	1,360	1,386
$ 145,000	1,246	1,272	1,299	1,326	1,354	1,381	1,408	1,436
$ 150,000	1,289	1,316	1,344	1,372	1,400	1,428	1,457	1,485
$ 155,000	1,332	1,360	1,389	1,418	1,447	1,476	1,505	1,535
$ 160,000	1,375	1,404	1,434	1,464	1,494	1,524	1,554	1,584
$ 165,000	1,418	1,448	1,479	1,509	1,540	1,571	1,603	1,634
$ 170,000	1,461	1,492	1,523	1,555	1,587	1,619	1,651	1,683
$ 175,000	1,504	1,536	1,568	1,601	1,634	1,667	1,700	1,733
$ 180,000	1,546	1,580	1,613	1,647	1,680	1,714	1,748	1,783
$ 185,000	1,589	1,624	1,658	1,692	1,727	1,762	1,797	1,832
$ 190,000	1,632	1,667	1,703	1,738	1,774	1,809	1,845	1,882
$ 195,000	1,675	1,711	1,747	1,784	1,820	1,857	1,894	1,931
$ 200,000	1,718	1,755	1,792	1,829	1,867	1,905	1,943	1,981
$ 205,000	1,761	1,799	1,837	1,875	1,914	1,952	1,991	2,030
$ 210,000	1,804	1,843	1,882	1,921	1,960	2,000	2,040	2,080
$ 215,000	1,847	1,887	1,927	1,967	2,007	2,047	2,088	2,129
$ 220,000	1,890	1,931	1,971	2,012	2,054	2,095	2,137	2,179
$ 225,000	1,933	1,975	2,016	2,058	2,100	2,143	2,185	2,228
$ 230,000	1,976	2,018	2,061	2,104	2,147	2,190	2,234	2,278
$ 235,000	2,019	2,062	2,106	2,150	2,194	2,238	2,282	2,327
$ 240,000	2,062	2,106	2,151	2,195	2,240	2,286	2,331	2,377
$ 245,000	2,105	2,150	2,195	2,241	2,287	2,333	2,380	2,426
$ 250,000	2,148	2,194	2,240	2,287	2,334	2,381	2,428	2,476
$ 255,000	2,191	2,238	2,285	2,333	2,380	2,428	2,477	2,525
$ 260,000	2,234	2,282	2,330	2,378	2,427	2,476	2,525	2,575
$ 265,000	2,277	2,326	2,375	2,424	2,474	2,524	2,574	2,624
$ 270,000	2,320	2,369	2,419	2,470	2,520	2,571	2,622	2,674

Amount Financed	Interest Rate							
	11.75%	12.0%	12.25%	12.5%	12.75%	13.0%	13.25%	13.5%
$ 40,000	404	411	419	427	435	442	450	458
$ 45,000	454	463	472	480	489	498	507	515
$ 50,000	505	514	524	534	543	553	563	573
$ 55,000	555	566	576	587	598	608	619	630
$ 60,000	606	617	629	640	652	664	675	687
$ 65,000	656	669	681	694	706	719	732	745
$ 70,000	707	720	734	747	761	774	788	802
$ 75,000	757	771	786	800	815	830	844	859
$ 80,000	808	823	838	854	869	885	901	916
$ 85,000	858	874	891	907	924	940	957	974
$ 90,000	908	926	943	961	978	996	1,013	1,031
$ 95,000	959	977	996	1,014	1,032	1,051	1,069	1,088
$ 100,000	1,009	1,029	1,048	1,067	1,087	1,106	1,126	1,145
$ 105,000	1,060	1,080	1,100	1,121	1,141	1,162	1,182	1,203
$ 110,000	1,110	1,131	1,153	1,174	1,195	1,217	1,238	1,260
$ 115,000	1,161	1,183	1,205	1,227	1,250	1,272	1,295	1,317
$ 120,000	1,211	1,234	1,257	1,281	1,304	1,327	1,351	1,374
$ 125,000	1,262	1,286	1,310	1,334	1,358	1,383	1,407	1,432
$ 130,000	1,312	1,337	1,362	1,387	1,413	1,438	1,464	1,489
$ 135,000	1,363	1,389	1,415	1,441	1,467	1,493	1,520	1,546
$ 140,000	1,413	1,440	1,467	1,494	1,521	1,549	1,576	1,604
$ 145,000	1,464	1,491	1,519	1,548	1,576	1,604	1,632	1,661
$ 150,000	1,514	1,543	1,572	1,601	1,630	1,659	1,689	1,718
$ 155,000	1,565	1,594	1,624	1,654	1,684	1,715	1,745	1,775
$ 160,000	1,615	1,646	1,677	1,708	1,739	1,770	1,801	1,833
$ 165,000	1,666	1,697	1,729	1,761	1,793	1,825	1,858	1,890
$ 170,000	1,716	1,749	1,781	1,814	1,847	1,881	1,914	1,947
$ 175,000	1,766	1,800	1,834	1,868	1,902	1,936	1,970	2,004
$ 180,000	1,817	1,852	1,886	1,921	1,956	1,991	2,026	2,062
$ 185,000	1,867	1,903	1,939	1,974	2,010	2,046	2,083	2,119
$ 190,000	1,918	1,954	1,991	2,028	2,065	2,102	2,139	2,176
$ 195,000	1,968	2,006	2,043	2,081	2,119	2,157	2,195	2,234
$ 200,000	2,019	2,057	2,096	2,135	2,173	2,212	2,252	2,291
$ 205,000	2,069	2,109	2,148	2,188	2,228	2,268	2,308	2,348
$ 210,000	2,120	2,160	2,201	2,241	2,282	2,323	2,364	2,405
$ 215,000	2,170	2,212	2,253	2,295	2,336	2,378	2,420	2,463
$ 220,000	2,221	2,263	2,305	2,348	2,391	2,434	2,477	2,520
$ 225,000	2,271	2,314	2,358	2,401	2,445	2,489	2,533	2,577
$ 230,000	2,322	2,366	2,410	2,455	2,499	2,544	2,589	2,634
$ 235,000	2,372	2,417	2,463	2,508	2,554	2,600	2,646	2,692
$ 240,000	2,423	2,469	2,515	2,561	2,608	2,655	2,702	2,749
$ 245,000	2,473	2,520	2,567	2,615	2,662	2,710	2,758	2,806
$ 250,000	2,524	2,572	2,620	2,668	2,717	2,765	2,814	2,864
$ 255,000	2,574	2,623	2,672	2,722	2,771	2,821	2,871	2,921
$ 260,000	2,624	2,674	2,725	2,775	2,825	2,876	2,927	2,978
$ 265,000	2,675	2,726	2,777	2,828	2,880	2,931	2,983	3,035
$ 270,000	2,725	2,777	2,829	2,882	2,934	2,987	3,040	3,093

Amount Financed	Interest Rate							
	13.75%	14.0%	14.25%	14.5%	14.75%	15.0%	15.25%	15.50%
$ 40,000	466	474	482	490	498	506	514	522
$ 45,000	524	533	542	551	560	569	578	587
$ 50,000	583	592	602	612	622	632	642	652
$ 55,000	641	652	663	674	684	695	706	717
$ 60,000	699	711	723	735	747	759	771	783
$ 65,000	757	770	783	796	809	822	835	848
$ 70,000	816	829	843	857	871	885	899	913
$ 75,000	874	889	904	918	933	948	963	978
$ 80,000	932	948	964	980	996	1,012	1,028	1,044
$ 85,000	990	1,007	1,024	1,041	1,058	1,075	1,092	1,109
$ 90,000	1,049	1,066	1,084	1,102	1,120	1,138	1,156	1,174
$ 95,000	1,107	1,126	1,144	1,163	1,182	1,201	1,220	1,239
$ 100,000	1,165	1,185	1,205	1,225	1,244	1,264	1,284	1,305
$ 105,000	1,223	1,244	1,265	1,286	1,307	1,328	1,349	1,370
$ 110,000	1,282	1,303	1,325	1,347	1,369	1,391	1,413	1,435
$ 115,000	1,340	1,363	1,385	1,408	1,431	1,454	1,477	1,500
$ 120,000	1,398	1,422	1,446	1,469	1,493	1,517	1,541	1,565
$ 125,000	1,456	1,481	1,506	1,531	1,556	1,581	1,606	1,631
$ 130,000	1,515	1,540	1,566	1,592	1,618	1,644	1,670	1,696
$ 135,000	1,573	1,600	1,626	1,653	1,680	1,707	1,734	1,761
$ 140,000	1,631	1,659	1,687	1,714	1,742	1,770	1,798	1,826
$ 145,000	1,689	1,718	1,747	1,776	1,804	1,833	1,862	1,892
$ 150,000	1,748	1,777	1,807	1,837	1,867	1,897	1,927	1,957
$ 155,000	1,806	1,837	1,867	1,898	1,929	1,960	1,991	2,022
$ 160,000	1,864	1,896	1,927	1,959	1,991	2,023	2,055	2,087
$ 165,000	1,922	1,955	1,988	2,021	2,053	2,086	2,119	2,152
$ 170,000	1,981	2,014	2,048	2,082	2,116	2,150	2,184	2,218
$ 175,000	2,039	2,074	2,108	2,143	2,178	2,213	2,248	2,283
$ 180,000	2,097	2,133	2,168	2,204	2,240	2,276	2,312	2,348
$ 185,000	2,155	2,192	2,229	2,265	2,302	2,339	2,376	2,413
$ 190,000	2,214	2,251	2,289	2,327	2,365	2,402	2,440	2,479
$ 195,000	2,272	2,310	2,349	2,388	2,427	2,466	2,505	2,544
$ 200,000	2,330	2,370	2,409	2,449	2,489	2,529	2,569	2,609
$ 205,000	2,388	2,429	2,470	2,510	2,551	2,592	2,633	2,674
$ 210,000	2,447	2,488	2,530	2,572	2,613	2,655	2,697	2,739
$ 215,000	2,505	2,547	2,590	2,633	2,676	2,719	2,762	2,805
$ 220,000	2,563	2,607	2,650	2,694	2,738	2,782	2,826	2,870
$ 225,000	2,622	2,666	2,711	2,755	2,800	2,845	2,890	2,935
$ 230,000	2,680	2,725	2,771	2,816	2,862	2,908	2,954	3,000
$ 235,000	2,738	2,784	2,831	2,878	2,925	2,971	3,018	3,066
$ 240,000	2,796	2,844	2,891	2,939	2,987	3,035	3,083	3,131
$ 245,000	2,855	2,903	2,951	3,000	3,049	3,098	3,147	3,196
$ 250,000	2,913	2,962	3,012	3,061	3,111	3,161	3,211	3,261
$ 255,000	2,971	3,021	3,072	3,123	3,173	3,224	3,275	3,327
$ 260,000	3,029	3,081	3,132	3,184	3,236	3,288	3,340	3,392
$ 265,000	3,088	3,140	3,192	3,245	3,298	3,351	3,404	3,457
$ 270,000	3,146	3,199	3,253	3,306	3,360	3,414	3,468	3,522

Index

SYMBOLS

11 common perils, homeowners insurance coverage, 243-244
15-year fixed-rate mortgages, 170-171
30-year fixed-rate mortgages, 170-171
5/25 two-step mortgages, 189-191
7/23 two-step mortgages, 189-191
80-10-10 loans, 187-188
80-15-5 loans, 187-188

A

accepting an offer (seller), 236-237, 348
adjustable-rate mortgage loans. *See* ARMs
adjustment interval, ARMs (adjustable-rate mortgage loans), 179
advance payments, closing, 266
advantages
    ARMs (adjustable-rate mortgage loans), 176
    condominium ownership, 119
    existing homes, 83-84
    fixed-rate mortgages, 168
    new homes, 130
    owning a home, 4-5
advertisements, FSBO homes, 294
affidavits, 270

affordability, buying a home, 15
    calculating how much you can borrow, 18-19
    calculating income and expenses, 16-18
    self-employment, 17
agents, 10, 43-45
    buyer's agents, 46-48
    closing the deal, 52-53
    dealing with other agents when selling, 343-344
    deciding whether to use an agent for selling, 287
    discount brokers, 50
    finding new homes, 134
    firing an agent, 56
    helping you find a house, 51-52
    listing agents versus selling agents, 44
    locating, 53-56
    navigating the financial steps, 50-51
    new-home agents, 45
    seller's agents, 49
    selling your home with an agent, 301-302, 306-307
        evaluating listing presentation, 309-310
        finding an agent, 307
        listing contracts, 311-314
        quizzing the agent, 308-309
American Society of Home Inspectors. *See* ASHI
amortization, 155
    negative amortization, ARMs (adjustable-rate mortgage loans), 180

annual percentage rate. *See* APR
anxious offers, 233
application fees, 37
applying for a mortgage, 197-209
    denial of loan, 211-213
    disclosing financial status, 202-204
    ensuring a smooth process, 211
    estimating closing costs, 208-209
    estimating interest rates, 209
    loan originators/officers, 198
    loan processors, 198
    locking in interest rates, 207
    mortgage brokers, 198
    process the lender goes through, 198-202
        applicant's capacity to repay debt, 201
        appraisal of the home, 200-201
        approval or denial of loan, 201
        capital, 201
        collateral, 201
        credit history, 201
        examination of credit report, 199
        taking the loan application, 199
        verification of information, 199
    underwriters, 198
appraisal of home
    as contingency of sale, 226
    fees, closing costs, 37

approval of loan, mortgage application, 201
APR (annual percentage rate), 155
ARMs (adjustable-rate mortgage loans), 175-183
    adjustment interval, 179
    advantages, 176
    disadvantages, 176-177
    indexes, 178
    margin, 178
    negative amortization, 180
    rate caps, 179
    selecting an ARM, 180-182
    teaser rate, 177-178
    worst-case scenario, 182-183
asbestos inspection, 255
ASHI (American Society of Home Inspectors), 252
association
    condominiums, 120-121
    fees, 6
assumable loans, 159, 186-187
attics, 86-87
attorneys
    closing fees, 40
    hiring when selling your own home, 302
auctions, finding a home, 101-102

B

back-end ratio. *See* overall debt ratio
bad credit, 30
BAGI (Builders Association of Greater Indianapolis), 139
balloon mortgages, 187
basements, 86-87
basic lending, 154
bedrooms, 85
best time to buy a home, 95-96
    buyer's market versus seller's market, 96-97
    seasonal sales, 97-98

bidding war offers, 233
biweekly 30-year fixed-rate mortgages, 170-171
board members, condominiums, 120-121
bond-backed mortgages, 192
borrowing money
    calculating how much you can borrow, 18-19
    subprime borrowers, 28
brokers, 44
    discount brokers, 50
    franchised brokers, 45
    mortgage brokers, 10, 198
builders and developers
    as loan source, 60
    new homes, 137-139
    warranty, 147
Builders Association of Greater Indianapolis. *See* BAGI
building a new home, 129-131
    advantages, 130
    custom homes, 132-133
    disadvantages, 130-131
    finding a new home, 133
        agent assistance, 134
        subdivisions, 134-137
    getting a good deal, 145-146
    home plans, 139-140
    lots, 140-141
    mortgage holdbacks, 146
    potential problems, 147-148
    sales contracts, terms of the contract, 141
    selecting a builder, 137-139
    semi-custom homes, 131-132
    tract homes, 131-132
    upgrades, 142-144
    warranties, 146-147
building equity, 5
buy downs, 188
buyer financing, FSBO homes, 298
buyer's agents, 46-48
buyer's market versus seller's market, 96-97

buying a home, 81, 117-118
    affordability, 15
        calculating how much you can borrow, 18-19
        calculating income and expenses, 16-18
        self-employment, 17
    agents, 43-45
        agent-comfort test, 54-56
        buyer's agents, 46-48
        closing the deal, 52-53
        discount brokers, 50
        finding an agent, 53-54
        firing an agent, 56
        helping you find a house, 51-52
        listing agents versus selling agents, 44
        navigating the financial steps, 50-51
        new-home agents, 45
        seller's agents, 49
    best time to buy, 95-96
        buyer's market versus seller's market, 96-97
        seasonal sales, 97-98
    brokers, 44
        discount brokers, 50
        franchised brokers, 45
        mortgage brokers, 10, 198
    closing (buyer's perspective)
        before closing requirements, 261-262
        details of the closing, 268-269
        escrow account reserves, 267-268
        exchanging money, 273
        final walkthrough, 263
        government recording and transfer charges, 267
        handling problems, 274-275
        how to hold the title, 262-263

HUD-1 statement, 273
moving in, 275-277
passing of the keys, 273-274
payments, 264-266
prepayments held by the lender, 266
settlement charges, 267
signing documents, 269-272
title charges, 266-267
totaling closing costs, 268
what you should bring to the closing, 269
co-ops, 118, 123
financing a co-op, 124
selecting a co-op, 123-124
condominiums, 118
advantages, 119
association/board, 120-121
disadvantages, 119-120
luxury condos, 123
making an offer, 122-123
rental restrictions, 122
selecting a community, 121-122
simplified living condos, 123
credit history, 24
bad credit, 30
FICO score, 27-28
obtaining a credit report, 25-29
risky creditors, 28
strengthening your credit, 29-30
deciding where you want to live, 71
available recreational facilities, 75-76
community traffic pattern, 75
employment considerations, 72-73
family needs, 73

general tax considerations, 74-75
how long you plan to stay, 72
medical facility locales, 75
new home communities, 78-79
personal neighborhood assessment, 77-78
school districts, 73-74
sources of community information, 76-77
defining ideal house style, 82-83
dream house wish list, 91-93
existing homes, 105-114
comparing home to list of needs, 107-111
comparison checklist, 115
evaluating the neighborhood, 113-114
maintenance, 111-113
touring homes, 106-107
versus new homes, 83-84
expectations, 11-12
exterior features, 88
amenities, 90-91
direction home faces, 89
heating and cooling systems, 89
landscaping, 90
facts, 8-10
financing, 153
applying for a mortgage, 197-213
basic lending, 154
deciding on the type of financing, 162-164
home loan lending, 154-162, 168-195
finding a home, 98
auctions and foreclosures, 101-102
driving through neighborhoods, 98
Internet, 102-103

local papers, 98-100
MLS listings, 100-101
word of mouth, 101
fixer-uppers, 127
FSBO homes, 56-57
home inspections, 251
expectations, 253-256
handling problems, 257-259
reading the inspection report, 256
reasons to get an inspection, 252
scheduling an inspection, 252-253
seller disclosure, 251-252
indoor features, 84
attics, 86-87
basements, 86-87
bedrooms, 85
closets, 87
family/living/great rooms, 86
garage space, 87-88
home office space, 86
kitchens, 85
insurance, 242
earthquake insurance, 242
flood insurance, 242
homeowners insurance, 242-248
mortgage insurance, 242
title insurance, 242, 248-249
keeping an open mind, 81-82
lender ratios, 19-22
housing expense ratio, 19-22
overall debt ratio, 19-20
making an offer, 217-238
anxious offers, 233
bidding war offers, 233
contingency considerations, 224-226
counteroffers, 233-236

deciding what you are willing to pay, 222-224
deposit, 229
having an offer accepted, 236-237
lowball offers, 233
minimum considerations, 218
negotiable offers, 232-233
real estate attorneys, 238
terms of the sale, 218-219, 226-229
withdrawing, 237-238
new homes, 129-131
advantages, 130
custom homes, 132-133
disadvantages, 130-131
finding a new home, 133-137
getting a good deal, 145-146
home plans, 139-140
lots, 140-141
mortgage holdbacks, 146
potential problems, 147-148
sales contracts, 141
selecting a builder, 137-139
semi-custom homes, 131-132
tract homes, 131-132
upgrades, 142-144
warranties, 146-147
patio homes, 118
prequalifying for a loan, 22
advantages and disadvantages, 23-24
requirements, 23
Realtors, 45
relocating, 125-126
taxes and insurance, 21
townhouses, 118
up-front costs
closing costs, 36-41
down payments, 33-36

vacation homes, 126
zero lot line homes, 118

C

calculating
borrow amount, 18-19
income, gross income versus net income, 16-18
maximum mortgage payment, 20-22
monthly expenses, 16-18
online calculators, 65
canceling mortgage insurance, 161-162
capacity, applicant's capacity to repay debt, 201
capital, current financial standing, 201
casualty insurance versus personal liability insurance, 243
CCRs (community covenants and restrictions), 135
chain of ownership, selling your home, 355
ChoicePoint, CLUE (Comprehensive Loss Underwriting Exchange), 248
city water versus well water, 90
cleaning your home, preparing for selling, 322
eliminating clutter, 324-325
exterior features, 323
interior features, 323-324
undecorating your home, 325
clear deed and title, receipt as contingency of sale, 225
clear titles, 249
closets, 87
closing
buyer's perspective
before closing requirements, 261-262
details of the closing, 268-269

escrow account reserves, 267-268
exchanging money, 273
final walkthrough, 263
government recording and transfer charges, 267
handling problems, 274-275
how to hold the title, 262-263
HUD-1 statement, 273
moving in, 275-277
passing of the keys, 273-274
payments, 264-266
prepayments held by the lender, 266
settlement charges, 267
signing documents, 269-272
title charges, 266-267
totaling closing costs, 268
what you should bring to the closing, 269
costs, 36-41
attorney fees, 40
closing, 264
escrow account money, 38-39
escrow fees, 40
estimating, 208-209
flood certification fee, 40
inspector fees, 40
lender fees, 36-38
mortgage insurance, 39
recording fees, 40
selling your home, 286, 358-359
totaling, 41
seller's perspective
checking chain of ownership, 355
collecting documents, 355
costs, 358-359
FSBO homes, 300

handling problems, 357-358

hiring a closing orchestrator, 356-357

HUD-1 statement, 359-362

signing documents, 362

termite inspections, 355

CLUE (Comprehensive Loss Underwriting Exchange), 248

co-ops (cooperatives), 118-124

financing a co-op, 124

selecting a co-op, 123-124

co-signers (loans), 192

collateral, 201

commercial banks, as loan source, 60

community covenants and restrictions. *See* CCRs

community information, deciding where you want to live, 75-77

The Complete Idiot's Guide to Real Estate Investing, Second Edition, 127

compliance agreement, 270

Comprehensive Loss Underwriting Exchange. *See* CLUE

condition of the home at settlement, as term of sale, 228-229

condominiums, 118-123

advantages, 119

association/board, 120-121

disadvantages, 119-120

luxury condos, 123

making an offer, 122-123

rental restrictions, 122

selecting a community, 121-122

simplified living condos, 123

conforming loans versus nonconforming loans, 160

Consumer Credit Counseling Services, 29

consumer credit reports

contents, 26-27

correcting mistakes, 28-29

obtaining, 25-26

contingencies of sale

evaluating offers when selling, 345-347

making an offer, 224-226

appraisal of home, 226

getting financing, 224

inspection of home, 225

receiving clear deed and title, 225

conventional loans, 158

cooling systems, 89

cooperatives. *See* co-ops

costs, selling your home, 286

closing costs, 286

moving expenses, 286

repair expenses, 286

sales commission, 286

counteroffers, 233-348

quitting and moving on, 236

responding to, 234-236

credit bureaus, 25

credit

check fees, closing costs, 37

history, 24

bad credit, 30

FICO score, 27-28

obtaining a credit report, 25-29

risky creditors, 28

strengthening your credit, 29-30

reports

contents, 26-27

correcting mistakes, 28-29

obtaining, 25-26

unions, as loan source, 60

custom homes, 132-133

Cyberhomes, 103

D

deciding to sell your home, 282-283

buying a new home, 288

closing, 288

costs involved, 286

deciding whether to use an agent, 287

getting home ready, 287

negotiating offers, 288

pricing and marketing, 288

readiness to sell, 284

timing the sale, 284-286

what you hope to gain, 283

deciding where you want to live, 71-79

available recreational facilities, 75-76

community traffic pattern, 75

employment considerations, 72-73

family needs, 73

general tax considerations, 74-75

how long you plan to stay, 72

medical facility locales, 75

new home communities, 78-79

personal neighborhood assessment, 77-78

school districts, 73-74

sources of community information, 76-77

deed, 270

receipt as contingency of sale, 225

deed of trust, 270

denial of loan, mortgage application, 201, 211-213

appraisal problems, 213

credit problems, 212-213

discrimination problems, 213

income problems, 212

Department of Housing and Urban Development. *See* HUD
deposit on the home, 229
disadvantages
    ARMs (adjustable-rate mortgage loans), 176-177
    condominium ownership, 119-120
    existing homes, 84
    fixed-rate mortgages, 168-169
    home ownership, 6-8
    new homes, 130-131
disbursement of money, escrow agent, 357
disclosure statements, 270
discount brokers, 50
discount points, 155
discrimination, applying for a mortgage, 213
documents
    closing, 269-272
    preparation fees, closing costs, 37
down payments, 33
    affordability, deciding on the type of financing, 163
    closing, 264
    earnest money, 35-36
    percentage you pay, 34
    strategies for getting money, 35
    where to get down payment, 34
dual agencies, 46

E

E&O insurance (errors and omission insurance), 253
earnest money, 35-36
earthquake insurance, 38, 242
easements, 135, 249

economic index, ARMs (adjustable-rate mortgage loans), 178
employment considerations, deciding where you want to live, 72-73
encroachments, 249
Equifax, 25
equity, 4
    building, 5
    sweat equity, 35
errors and omission insurance. *See* E&O insurance
escape clause, making an offer, 226
escrow
    accounts
        closing fees, 38-39
        reserves, closing, 267-268
    companies, FSBO homes, 302-303
    fees, closing fees, 40
    officers, 11
estimating
    closing costs, 208-209
    interest rates, 209
evaluating home inspectors, 253
exchanging money at closing, 273
exclusive agency listing contract, 311
exclusive right to sell listing contract, 311
existing homes, 105
    advantages, 83-84
    comparing home to list of needs, 107-111
    comparison checklist, 115
    disadvantages, 84
    evaluating the neighborhood, 113-114
    maintenance, 111-113
    touring homes, 106-107
    versus new homes, 83
expenses, calculating, 16-18

Experian, 25
exterior of the home, 88
    amenities, 90-91
    cleaning house for selling, 323
    direction home faces, 89
    heating and cooling systems, 89
    landscaping, 90
    structure of existing homes, 111

F

fact sheets, FSBO homes, 295-296
Fannie Mae (Federal National Mortgage Association), 61 83
Federal Home Loan Mortgage Corporation. *See* Freddie Mac
Federal Housing Administration. *See* FHA
Federal Housing Finance Board's National Average Contract Mortgage Rate, 178
Federal National Mortgage Association. *See* Fannie Mae
FHA (Federal Housing Administration Federal Housing Administration), 35, 60
    assumable loans, 159
    qualified assumptions, 159
FICO credit score, 27-28
final walkthrough, closing, 263
financing, 153
    applying for a mortgage, 197-213
        denial of loan, 211-213
        disclosing financial status, 202-204
        ensuring a smooth process, 211
        estimating closing costs, 208-209

estimating interest rates, 209

loan originators/officers, 198

loan processors, 198

locking in interest rates, 207

mortgage brokers, 198

process the lender goes through, 198-202

underwriters, 198

basic lending, 154

buyer financing, FSBO homes, 298

calculating how much you can borrow, 18-19

co-ops (cooperatives), 124

credit history, 24-30

    bad credit, 30

    FICO score, 27-28

    obtaining a credit report, 25-29

    risky creditors, 28

    strengthening your credit, 29-30

deciding on the type of financing, 162-164

    down payment affordability, 163

    how long you will live in the house, 164

    monthly payment affordability, 163-164

home loan lending

    80-10-10 loans, 187-188

    80-15-5 loans, 187-188

    adjustable-rate mortgage loans, 158, 175-183

    assumable loans, 186-187

    balloon mortgages, 187

    buydowns, 188

    co-signers, 192

    conforming loans versus nonconforming loans, 160

    conventional loans, 158

    fixed-rate mortgage loans, 157-158, 168-173

    government-backed loans, 159-160, 186

    graduated payment plans, 192

    interest rates, 154-155

    layaway payments, 189

    lease with option to buy, 191

    mortgage insurance, 160-162

    municipal mortgages, 192

    paying loan points, 155-156

    private loans, 192

    refinancing, 193-195

    Rural Housing Service, 191

    seller carrybacks, 188-189

    shared-equity mortgages, 192

    subprime mortgages, 192-193

    terms of loan, 156

    two-step mortgages, 189-191

lender ratios, 19-20

    housing expense ratio, 19-22

    overall debt ratio, 19-20

prequalifying for a loan, 22-24

    advantages and disadvantages, 23-24

    requirements, 23

selling your home, helping buyer with financing, 350

taxes and insurance, 21

up-front costs

    closing costs, 36-41

    down payments, 33-36

firing an agent, 56

first payment, closing costs, 37

fixed-rate mortgage loans, 157-158, 168-170

    advantages, 168

    disadvantages, 168-169

    interest rates, 169-170

    points, 169-170

fixer-uppers, 99, 127

fixtures (real property), 227

floating interest rates, 65

flood certification fee, closing fees, 40

flood insurance, 38, 242

floor plans, new homes, 139-140

"for sale by owner" homes. *See* FSBO homes

foreclosures, 6, 101-102

franchised brokers, 45

Freddie Mac (Federal Home Loan Mortgage Corporation), 61

front-end ratio. *See* housing expense ratio

FSBO ("for sale by owner") homes, 56-57, 292-303

    buyer financing, 298

    buying a home, 56-57

    closing, 300

    escrow companies, 302-303

    expectations, 292

    hiring an attorney, 302

    homeselling services, 302

    marketing your home, 293

        advertising, 294

        online, 295

        yard signs, 293-294

    negotiating offers, 298-299

        drawing up offers, 299

        reviewing offers, 299-300

    preparing fact sheets, 295-296

    pricing your home, 292

        defining acceptable financial terms, 293

        figuring net proceeds, 293

showing your home, 296-297
  open house, 297
  sales calls, 296-297
  when the home does not sell, 303
  working with agents, 301-302

G

garage space, 87-88
Ginnie Mae (Government National Mortgage Association), 61
Good Faith Estimate, 208-209
government agencies, as loan source, 60-61
Government National Mortgage Association. *See* Ginnie Mae
government recording charges, closing, 267
government-backed loans, 159-160
  VA loans, 186
graduated payment plans, 192
great room, 86
gross income versus net income, 16

H

handling problems at closing, 274-275
  loan problems, 275
  money problems, 274
  title problems, 275
  walkthroughs, 274
handyman specials, 99
Hartford, 247
hazard insurance. *See* casualty insurance
hazardous waste inspection, 255
heating systems, 89

historic homes, 91
HO-1 (homeowners insurance coverage), 243-244
holding the title options, 262-263
home inspections, 251-259
  expectations, 253-256
  handling problems, 257-259
  reading the inspection report, 256
  reasons to get an inspection, 252
  scheduling an inspection, 252-253
  seller disclosure, 251-252
  selling your home, 320-321
home loan lending, 154-157
  80-10-10 loans, 187-188
  80-15-5 loans, 187-188
  adjustable-rate mortgage loans, 158, 175-182
    adjustment interval, 179
    advantages, 176
    disadvantages, 176-177
    indexes, 178
    margin, 178
    negative amortization, 180
    rate caps, 179
    selecting an ARM, 180-182
    teaser rate, 177-178
    worst-case scenario, 182-183
  assumable loans, 186-187
  balloon mortgages, 187
  buydowns, 188
  co-signers, 192
  conforming loans versus nonconforming loans, 160
  conventional loans, 158
  deciding on the type of financing, 162-164
    down payment affordability, 163
    how long you will live in the house, 164

monthly payment affordability, 163-164
  fixed-rate mortgage loans, 157-158
    advantages, 168
    disadvantages, 168-169
    interest rates, 169-170
    points, 169-170
    prepaying, 171-173
    terms, 170-171
  government-backed loans, 159-160
    VA loans, 186
  graduated payment plans, 192
  interest rates, 154-155
  layaway payments, 189
  lease with option to buy, 191
  mortgage insurance, 160-162
  municipal mortgages, 192
  paying loan points, 155-156
  private loans, 192
  refinancing, 193-195
    money savings, 194-195
    shopping for loans, 195
  Rural Housing Service, 191
  seller carrybacks, 188-189
  shared-equity mortgages, 192
  subprime mortgages, 192-193
  terms of loan, 156
  two-step mortgages, 189-191
home ventilation and air conditioning. *See* HVAC
Homebuilder, 103
HomeFair, 125
HomeGain, 103
homeowners association fees, 6
homeowners insurance, 242-248
  casualty insurance versus personal liability insurance, 243
  common perils, 243-244

comparing policies, 247-248

how much insurance is necessary, 244-245

how payments are made, 247

researching insurance companies, 246-247

homeowners warranty. *See* HOW

HomeSeekers, 103

HomeYeah.com, 302

Housing and Urban Development Department. *See* HUD

housing expense ratio, 19

calculating maximum mortgage payment, 21-22

HOW (homeowners warranty), new homes, 147

HUD (Department of Housing and Urban Development), 63

HUD-1 statement, 271-273

seller's perspective, 359-362

HVAC (home ventilation and air conditioning), 87

I

implied warranty, new homes, 146

incentives, selling your home, 335-336

income, calculating, 16-18

indexes, ARMs (adjustable-rate mortgage loans), 178

initial rate, ARMs (adjustable-rate mortgage loans), 177-178

inquiries, credit reports, 26

inspection of the home, 251-259

as contingency of sale, 225

expectations, 253-256

handling problems, 257-259

reading the inspection report, 256

reasons to get an inspection, 252

scheduling an inspection, 252-253

seller disclosure, 251-252

selling your home, 320-321

inspector fees, closing fees, 40

installment credit, 28

insurance, 242

earthquake, 38, 242

flood, 38, 242

homeowners insurance, 21, 242-248

casualty insurance versus personal liability insurance, 243

common perils, 243-244

comparing policies, 247-248

how much insurance is necessary, 244-245

how payments are made, 247

researching insurance companies, 246-247

mortgage, 29, 160-162, 242

title insurance, 242, 248-249

title searches, 248-249

trouble-free ownership, 248

types of policies, 249

Insurance Information Institute, 245

Insure.com, 247

interest payments, closing costs, 37

interest rates, 9, 154-155

estimating, 209

fixed-rate mortgages, 169-170

floating, 65

locking in, 65, 207

interior of the home, 84

attics, 86-87

basements, 86-87

bedrooms, 85

cleaning house for selling, 323-324

closets, 87

family/living/great rooms, 86

garage space, 87-88

home office space, 86

kitchens, 85

structure and maintenance of existing homes, 113

International Real Estate Directory. *See* IRED

Internet

advertising FSBO homes, 295

finding a home, 102-103

locating lenders, 64-65

online calculators, 65

researching insurance companies, 246-247

IRED (International Real Estate Directory), 103

IRS forms, 270

J-K

joint tenancy (title), 262

jumbo loans, 62

kickout (contingency), making an offer, 226

kitchens, 85

L

landscaping, 90

Law of Expanding Possessions, 9

layaway payments, 189

lead paint inspection, 255

lease with option to buy, 191

lender fees, 36-38

appraisal fees, 37

credit check fees, 37

document preparation fees, 37

first payment, 37
interest payments, 37
loan application fees, 37
loan origination fees, 37
points, 36
lender's policy, title insurance,
249
lenders (mortgage lenders), 10
applying for a mortgage,
197-213
denial of loan, 211-213
disclosing financial status,
202-204
ensuring a smooth
process, 211
estimating closing costs,
208-209
estimating interest rates,
209
loan originators/officers,
198
loan processors, 198
locking in interest rates,
207
mortgage brokers, 198
process the lender goes
through, 198-202
underwriters, 198
basic lending, 154
builders and developers, 60
commercial banks, 60
credit unions, 60
government agencies, 60-61
Fannie Mae, 61
Freddie Mac, 61
Ginnie Mae, 61
home loan lending, 154-193
80-10-10 loans, 187-188
80-15-5 loans, 187-188
adjustable-rate mortgage
loans, 158, 175-183
assumable loans, 186-187
balloon mortgages, 187
buydowns, 188
co-signers, 192

conforming loans versus
nonconforming loans,
160
conventional loans, 158
deciding on the type of
financing, 162-164
fixed-rate mortgage
loans, 157-158, 168-173
government-backed
loans, 159-160, 186
graduated payment plans,
192
interest rates, 154-155
layaway payments, 189
lease with option to buy,
191
mortgage insurance,
160-162
municipal mortgages, 192
paying loan points,
155-156
private loans, 192
refinancing, 193-195
Rural Housing Service,
191
seller carrybacks,
188-189
shared-equity mortgages,
192
subprime mortgages,
192-193
terms of loan, 156
two-step mortgages,
189-191
jumbo loans, 62
locating a lender, 62-65
agent assistance, 63
Internet, 64-65
mortgage advertisement
reviews, 63-64
mortgage bankers, 60
mortgage brokers, 60
portfolio loans, 61
questions to ask, 65-66

ratios, 19-20
housing expense ratio,
19-22
overall debt ratio, 19-20
S&Ls, 60
secondary loan markets, 61
LendingTree, 65
liens, 102
lifetime caps, ARMs, 179
listing agents versus selling
agents, 44
listing contracts (agents),
309-314
contents, 314
getting out of a listing, 314
selling your home, 311
exclusive agency, 311
exclusive right to sell,
311
open, 311
listing price, selling your home,
331-335
getting an appraisal,
334-335
market trends, 335
studying comparable homes,
332-334
loan officers, 11
loan-to value. *See* LTV
loans
applying for a mortgage,
197-213
denial of loan, 211-213
disclosing financial status,
202-204
ensuring a smooth
process, 211
estimating closing costs,
208-209
estimating interest rates,
209
loan originators/officers,
198
loan processors, 198
locking in interest rates,
207

mortgage brokers, 198
process the lender goes through, 198-202
underwriters, 198
credit history, 24-30
bad credit, 30
FICO score, 27-28
obtaining a credit report, 25-29
risky creditors, 28
strengthening your credit, 29-30
home loan lending, 154-193
80-10-10 loans, 187-188
80-15-5 loans, 187-188
adjustable-rate mortgage loans, 158, 175-183
assumable loans, 186-187
balloon mortgages, 187
buydowns, 188
co-signers, 192
conforming loans versus nonconforming loans, 160
conventional loans, 158
deciding on the type of financing, 162-164
fixed-rate mortgage loans, 157-158, 168-173
government-backed loans, 159-160, 186
graduated payment plans, 192
interest rates, 154-155
layaway payments, 189
lease with option to buy, 191
mortgage insurance, 160-162
municipal mortgages, 192
paying loan points, 155-156
private loans, 192
refinancing, 193-195
Rural Housing Service, 191

seller carrybacks, 188-189
shared-equity mortgages, 192
subprime mortgages, 192-193
terms of loan, 156
two-step mortgages, 189-191
loan application fees, 37
loan origination fees, 37
mortgage lenders, 59-66
builders and developers, 60
commercial banks, 60
credit unions, 60
government agencies, 60-61
jumbo loans, 62
locating a lender, 62-65
mortgage bankers, 60
mortgage brokers, 60
portfolio loans, 61
questions to ask, 65-66
S&Ls, 60
secondary loan markets, 61
prequalifying, 22-24
locating
agents, 53-56
agent-comfort test, 54-56
selling your home, 307
homes, 98-103
auctions and foreclosures, 101-102
driving through neighborhoods, 98
Internet, 102-103
local papers, 98-100
MLS listings, 100-101
word of mouth, 101
mortgage lenders, 62-65
agent assistance, 63
Internet, 64-65
mortgage advertisement reviews, 63-64

new homes, 133-137
agent assistance, 134
subdivisions, 134-137
locking in interest rates, 65, 207
lots, new homes, 140-141
lowball offers, 233
LTV (loan-to value), 34
luxury condominiums, 123

M

maintenance, 6
existing homes, 111-113
home systems, 111-112
structure, 111
making an offer, 217-238
anxious offers, 233
bidding war offers, 233
condominiums, 122-123
contingency considerations, 224-226
appraisal of home, 226
getting financing, 224
inspection of home, 225
receiving clear deed and title, 225
counteroffers, 233-236
quitting and moving on, 236
responding to, 234-236
deciding what you are willing to pay, 222-224
asking the seller to pay part, 224
comparing other sales prices, 222-223
motivation of the seller, 223
deposit, 229
having an offer accepted, 236-237
lowball offers, 233
minimum considerations, 218
negotiations, 232-233

real estate attorneys, 238
terms of the sale, 218-219, 226-229
    condition of the home at settlement, 228-229
    personal property included, 227-228
    prorating tax and other payments, 229
    setting time limits, 226
withdrawing, 237-238
margin, ARMs (adjustable-rate mortgage loans), 178
market trends, setting listing price, 335
market value appreciation, 162
marketing your home, 337-338
    FSBO homes, 288, 293-295
    advertising, 294
    online, 295
    yard signs, 293-294
maximum mortgage payment, calculating, 20-22
MetLife, 247
MIP (mortgage insurance premium), 39, 159
MLS (Multiple Listing System), 45
    locating homes, 100-101
MMI (mutual mortgage insurance), 160
monthly payments, affordability, 163-164
mortgage insurance premium. *See* MIP
Mortgage Market Information Services, 64
mortgages
    80-10-10 loans, 187-188
    80-15-5 loans, 187-188
    adjustable-rate mortgage loans, 158, 175-183
    adjustment interval, 179
    advantages, 176
    disadvantages, 176-177
    indexes, 178

margin, 178
    negative amortization, 180
    rate caps, 179
    selecting an ARM, 180-182
    teaser rate, 177-178
    worst-case scenario, 182-183
applying for, 197-213
    denial of loan, 211-213
    disclosing financial status, 202-204
    ensuring a smooth process, 211
    estimating closing costs, 208-209
    estimating interest rates, 209
    loan originators/officers, 198
    loan processors, 198
    locking in interest rates, 207
    mortgage brokers, 198
    process the lender goes through, 198-202
    underwriters, 198
assumable loans, 186-187
balloon mortgages, 187
brokers, 10
buydowns, 188
calculating maximum mortgage payment, 20-22
co-signers, 192
conforming loans versus nonconforming loans, 160
conventional loans, 158
fixed-rate mortgage loans, 157-158
    advantages, 168
    disadvantages, 168-169
    interest rates, 169-170
    points, 169-170
    prepaying, 171-173
    terms, 170-171

government-backed loans, 159-160
    VA loans, 186
graduated payment plans, 192
holdbacks, new homes, 146
insurance, 39, 160-162, 242
layaway payments, 189
lease with option to buy, 191
lenders, 59-66
    builders and developers, 60
    commercial banks, 60
    credit unions, 60
    government agencies, 60-61
    jumbo loans, 62
    locating a lender, 62-65
    mortgage bankers, 60
    mortgage brokers, 60
    portfolio loans, 61
    questions to ask, 65-66
    S&Ls, 60
    secondary loan markets, 61
municipal mortgages, 192
private loans, 192
refinancing, 193-195
    money savings, 194-195
    shopping for loans, 195
Rural Housing Service, 191
seller carrybacks, 188-189
shared-equity mortgages, 192
subprime mortgages, 192-193
two-step mortgages, 189-191
motivated sellers, 99, 223
    readiness to sell, 284
    what you hope to gain, 283
move-in condition, 100
moving expenses
    professional movers, 275-277
    selling your home, 286

Multiple Listing System. *See* MLS
municipal mortgages, 192
mutual mortgage insurance. *See* MMI

N

NAR (National Association of Realtors), 45, 102
National Association of Realtors. *See* NAR
negative amortization, ARMs (adjustable-rate mortgage loans), 180
negotiating offers, 232-233
    FSBO homes, 298-299
        drawing up offers, 299
        reviewing offers, 299-300
    selling your home, 288
neighborhoods
    deciding where you want to live, 77-78
    existing homes, 113-114
net income versus gross income, 16
net proceeds
    FSBO homes, 293
    selling your home, 336-337
new homes, 129-131
    advantages, 130
    agents, 45
    consultants, 10
    custom homes, 132-133
    disadvantages, 130-131
    finding a new home, 133-137
        agent assistance, 134
        subdivisions, 134-137
    getting a good deal, 145-146
    home plans, 139-140
    lots, 140-141
    mortgage holdbacks, 146
    potential problems, 147-148
    sales contracts, 141
    selecting a builder, 137-139

semi-custom homes, 131-132
tract homes, 131-132
upgrades, 142-144
versus existing homes, 83
warranties, 146-147
nonconforming loans versus conforming loans, 160

O

obtaining a credit report, 25-29
    contents, 26-27
    correcting mistakes, 28-29
offers
    evaluating when selling your home, 344-348
        accepting an offer, 348
        contingencies, 345-347
        counteroffers, 347-348
        price and terms, 345
        time limits, 346-347
    strategies, 233
    when you have no offers, 348-350
officers (loan officers), 198
one-way ARMs, 182
online
    advertising, FSBO homes, 295
    calculators, 65
    home listings, 102-103
open houses, 53
    selling your home, 340-341
    showing your home, 297
open listing contract, 311
origination fees, 37, 60
originators (loan originators), 198
overall debt ratio, 19-20
owner's policy, title insurance, 249

P

paid outside of closing. *See* POC
passing of the keys (closing), 273-274
patio homes, 118
payment caps, ARMs (adjustable-rate mortgage loans), 179
payments, closing, 264-266
    advance payments, 266
    closing costs, 264
    down payment, 264
    part of the loan payments, 265
periodic caps, ARMs, 179
personal liability insurance versus casualty insurance, 243
personal property included, as term of sale, 227-228
planned unit developments. *See* PUDs
PMI (private mortgage insurance), 39
PMMs (purchase money mortgages), 188-189
POC (paid outside of closing), 264
points, 36, 155-156
    fixed-rate mortgages, 169-170
policy comparisons, homeowners insurance, 247-248
portfolio loans, 61
preapproval for a loan, 24
prepaying mortgage, fixed-rate mortgages, 171-173
prequalifying for a loan, 22-24
pricing your home, 288, 331-335
    FSBO homes, 292
        defining acceptable financial terms, 293
        figuring net proceeds, 293

getting an appraisal, 334-335
market trends, 335
studying comparable homes, 332-334
principal (loans), 156
principal brokers, 44
franchised brokers, 45
private loans, 192
private mortgage insurance. *See* PMI
process (mortgage loan process), 199-201
applicant's capacity to repay debt, 201
appraisal of the home, 200-201
approval or denial of loan, 201
capital, 201
collateral, 201
credit history, 201
examination of credit report, 199
taking the loan application, 199
verification of information, 199
processors (loan processors), 198
professional movers, 276-277
property protection insurance. *See* casualty insurance
proprietary lease, 123
prorating tax, as term of sale, 229, 359
PUDs (planned unit developments), 135
purchase money mortgages. *See* PMMs
purchasing a home. *See* buying a home

Q-R

qualified assumptions, 159, 186
qualifying ratios, 19-20
Quality Assurance Builder Standards, 139
questions to ask lenders, 65-66
quit claim deeds, 249

radon inspection, 255
rate caps, ARMs (adjustable-rate mortgage loans), 179
rating home inspectors, 253
ratios (lender ratios), calculating maximum mortgage payment, 19-22
housing expense ratio, 19
overall debt ratio, 19
readiness to sell, 284
reading the inspection report, 256
real estate attorneys, 238
Real Estate Settlement Procedures Act. *See* RESPA
real property versus personal property, 227-228
realtors, 10, 45
recording fees, closing fees, 40, 267
redecorating cycle, 10
refinancing loans, 193-195
Registrar of Contractors, 132
relocating, 125-126
Relocation Crime Lab, 74
remodeling, selling your home, 322
rental restrictions, condominiums, 122
repairs, selling your home, 286, 318-322
deciding what repairs to make, 321
hiring versus doing repairs alone, 321
inspecting your own home, 318-320
professional home inspections, 320-321
remodeling, 322
replacement costs, homeowners insurance, 245
reporting sale of your home, tax implications for home sales, 363
Reserve Officers' Training Corps. *See* ROTC members
reserve payments held by the lender, closing, 266
RESPA (Real Estate Settlement Procedures Act), 208
responding to counteroffers, 234-236
reviewing offers, FSBO homes, 299-300
revolving credit, 28
risky creditors, 28
ROTC members (Reserve Officers' Training Corps), VA loans, 186
Rural Housing Service, 191

S

S&Ls (savings and loans), 60
sales
associates, 10, 44
listing agents versus selling agents, 44
commission, selling your home, 286
contracts
condominiums, 122
new homes, terms of the contract, 141
prices, comparing prices when making an offer, 222-223
sanity documents, 271
savings and loans. *See* S&Ls
scheduling
inspections, 252-253
showing your home, 339

school districts, deciding where you want to live, 73-74
Seasonal Energy Efficiency Ratio. *See* SEER
seasonal sales, 97-98
secondary loan markets, 61
SEER (Seasonal Energy Efficiency Ratio), 89
Select Lenders, 65
self-employment, affordability of buying a home, 17
selling a home
    accepting an offer, 348
    agents, 44, 49, 306-314
        evaluating listing presentation, 309-310
        finding an agent, 307
        listing contracts, 311-314
        quizzing the agent, 308-309
    carrybacks, 188-189
    cleaning up the house, 322-325
        eliminating clutter, 324-325
        exterior features, 323
        interior features, 323-324
        undecorating your home, 325
    closing, 288, 354-362
        checking chain of ownership, 355
        collecting documents, 355
        costs, 358-359
        handling problems, 357-358
        hiring a closing orchestrator, 356-357
        HUD-1 statement, 359-362
        signing documents, 362
        termite inspections, 355
    collecting home information, 325-326
    costs involved, 286

closing costs, 286
moving expenses, 286
repair expenses, 286
sales commission, 286
counteroffers, 347-348
dealing with other agents, 343-344
deciding whether to use an agent, 287
disclosure, 326-327
    forms, 327
    home inspections, 251-252
    required disclosures, 326-327
evaluating offers, 344-347
    contingencies, 345, 347
    price and terms, 345
    time limits, 346-347
expectations, 12
figuring net proceeds, 336-337
FSBO homes, 292-303
    buyer financing, 298
    closing, 300
    escrow companies, 302-303
    expectations, 292
    hiring an attorney, 302
    homeselling services, 302
    marketing your home, 293-295
    negotiating offers, 298-300
    preparing fact sheets, 295-296
    pricing your home, 292-293
    showing your home, 296-297
    when the home does not sell, 303
    working with agents, 301-302

getting home ready, 287
helping buyer with financing, 350
marketing your home, 337-338
motives for selling, 282-284
    readiness to sell, 284
    what you hope to gain, 283
moving out, 364-365
negotiating offers, 288
no offers, 348-350
offering incentives, 335-336
pricing and marketing, 288, 331-335
    getting an appraisal, 334-335
    market trends, 335
    studying comparable homes, 332-334
repairs, 318-322
    deciding what repairs to make, 321
    hiring versus doing repairs alone, 321
    inspecting your own home, 318-320
    professional home inspections, 320-321
    remodeling, 322
seller disclosure, 326-327
    forms, 327
    required disclosures, 326-327
seller's market versus buyer's market, 96-97
showing your home, 338-341
    dealing with criticism, 340
    open houses, 340-341
    preparing home, 339
    scheduling, 339
takebacks, 188-189

tax implications for home sales, 362-364
  figuring tax basis, 363-364
  reporting sale of your home, 363
  timing the sale
    buying and selling together, 286
    buying first, selling later, 284-285
    selling first versus buying first, 284
    selling first, buying later, 285
semi-custom homes, 131-132
setting listing price, 331-332
  getting an appraisal, 334-335
  market trends, 335
  studying comparable homes, 332-334
settlement costs. *See* closing, costs
settlement day. *See* closing
shared-equity mortgages, 192
showing your home, 338-341
  dealing with criticism, 340
  FSBO homes, 296-297
    open houses, 297
    sales calls, 296-297
  open houses, 340-341
  preparing home, 339
  scheduling, 339
signing documents
  closing, 269-272
  seller's perspective, 362
simplified living condominiums, 123
sole ownership (title), 262
spec homes, 135
State Board of Realtors, 45
State Farm Insurance, 246
strategies, offer strategies, 233
strengthening your credit, 29-30

structure of existing homes, 111
subprime borrowers, 28
subprime mortgages, 192-193
sweat equity, 35

T

taxes
  buying a home, 21
  proration, 359
  tax implications for home sales, 363-364
    figuring tax basis, 363-364
    reporting sale of your home, 363
teaser rate, ARMs (adjustable-rate mortgage loans), 177-178
tenancy by the entirety (title), 262
tenancy in common (title), 263
termite inspections, 255
  selling your home, 355
terms
  loans, 156
    fixed-rate mortgages, 170-171
  sales contract
    evaluating offers when selling, 345
    new homes, 141
    writing an offer, 218-219, 226-229
This Old House, 91
time limits
  as term of sale, 226
  evaluating offers when selling, 346-347
timeshare units, 126
timing the sale of your home
  buying and selling together, 286
  buying first, selling later, 284-285

selling first versus buying first, 284
selling first, buying later, 285
title
  charges, closing, 266-267
  how to hold the title, 262-263
  insurance, 242
    title searches, 248-249
    trouble-free ownership, 248
    types of policies, 249
  receipt as contingency of sale, 225
totaling closing costs, 41, 268
touring existing homes, 106-115
  comparing home to list of needs, 107-111
  comparison checklist, 115
  evaluating the neighborhood, 113-114
  maintenance, 111-113
townhouses, 118
tract homes, 131-132
Trans Union, 25
transfer charges, closing, 267
trouble-free ownership, title insurance, 248
Truth-in-Lending statement, 209, 270
two-step mortgages, 189-191

U

undecorating your home, cleaning house for selling, 325
underwriters (loans), 60, 198
up-front costs of buying a home
  closing costs, 36-41
    attorney fees, 40
    escrow account money, 38-39

escrow fees, 40
flood certification fee, 40
inspector fees, 40
lender fees, 36-38
mortgage insurance, 39
recording fees, 40
totaling, 41
down payments, 33-36
earnest money, 35-36
percentage you pay, 34
strategies for getting
money, 35
where to get down pay-
ment, 34
upgrades, new homes, 142-144
utility bills, 6

V-W

VA (Veterans' Administration),
60
loans, 159, 186
vacation homes, 126
Veterans' Administration. *See*
VA

walkthroughs
final closing walkthrough,
263
handling problems, 274
warranties, new homes,
146-147
websites
credit bureaus, 25
Cyberhomes, 103
Fannie Mae, 61
finding a home, 102-103
Freddie Mac, 61
Ginnie Mae, 61
Homebuilder, 103
HomeFair, 125
HomeGain, 103
HomeSeekers, 103
HomeYeah.com, 302
insurance companies,
246-247

IRED (International Real
Estate Directory), 103
LendingTree, 65
Mortgage Market
Information Services, 64
NAR (National Association
of Realtors), 102
Relocation Crime Lab, 74
Select Lenders, 65
Yahoo! Real Estate, 103
well water versus city water, 90
withdrawing an offer, 237-238
writing an offer, 217-226,
233-236
anxious offers, 233
bidding war offers, 233
contingency considerations,
224-226
appraisal of home, 226
getting financing, 224
inspection of home, 225
receiving clear deed and
title, 225
counteroffers, 233-234
quitting and moving on,
236
responding to, 234-236
deciding what you are willing to pay, 222
asking the seller to pay
part, 224
comparing other sales
prices, 222-223
motivation of the seller,
223
deposit, 229
having an offer accepted,
236-237
lowball offers, 233
minimum considerations,
218
negotiable offers, 232-233
real estate attorneys, 238
terms of the sale, 218-219,
226-229
condition of the home at
settlement, 228-229

personal property
included, 227-228
prorating tax and other
payments, 229
setting time limits, 226
withdrawing, 237-238

X-Y-Z

Yahoo! Real Estate, 103
yard signs, FSBO homes,
293-294

zero lot line homes, 118

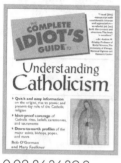

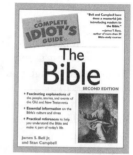

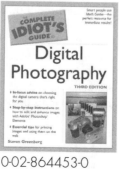